Beginning classical social theory

T0286455

Manchester University Press

Beginnings
Series editors: Peter Barry and John McLeod
Former series editor: Helen Carr

'**Beginnings**' is a series of books designed to give practical help to students beginning to tackle recent developments in English, Literary Studies and Cultural Studies. The books in the series

- demonstrate and encourage a questioning engagement with the new;
- give essential information about the context and history of each topic covered;
- show how to develop a practice which is up-to-date and informed by theory.

Each book focuses uncompromisingly upon the needs of its readers, who have the right to expect lucidity and clarity to be the distinctive feature of a book which includes the word 'beginning' in its title.

Each aims to lay a firm foundation of well understood initial principles as a basis for further study and is committed to explaining new aspects of the discipline without over-simplification, but in a manner appropriate to the needs of beginners.

Each book, finally, aims to be both an introduction and a contribution to the topic area it discusses.

Also in the series

Beginning theory (4th edition)
Peter Barry

Beginning film studies
Andrew Dix

Beginning realism
Steven Earnshaw

Beginning ethnic American literatures
Helena Grice, Candida Hepworth,
Maria Lauret and Martin Padget

Beginning Shakespeare
Lisa Hopkins

Beginning postcolonialism (2nd edition)
John McLeod

Beginning modernism
Jeff Wallace

Beginning postmodernism (2nd edition)
Tim Woods

Beginning classical social theory

Marcel Stoetzler

Manchester University Press

The right of Marcel Stoetzler to be identified as the author of this work has been
asserted by him in accordance with the Copyright, Designs and Patents Act 1988.

Published by Manchester University Press
Altrincham Street, Manchester M1 7JA

www.manchesteruniversitypress.co.uk

British Library Cataloguing-in-Publication Data
A catalogue record for this book is available from the British Library

Library of Congress Cataloging-in-Publication Data applied for

ISBN   9781 7 8499 145 6 paperback

First published 2017

The publisher has no responsibility for the persistence or accuracy of URLs for
any external or third-party internet websites referred to in this book, and does
not guarantee that any content on such websites is, or will remain, accurate or
appropriate.

Typeset in Monotype Ehrhardt by
Servis Filmsetting Ltd, Stockport, Cheshire
Printed in Great Britain by
Bell and Bain Ltd, Glasgow

Contents

Acknowledgements

I am extremely grateful to Christian Klesse, Hae-Yung Song, Susan Jacobs, Howard Davis and, in particular, Stefan Machura for comments on the manuscript. All remaining flaws and errors are mine. I also thank all the students on my SocTheory modules at Bangor for keeping me busy thinking about how to teach. I am also grateful to the School of Social Sciences, Bangor, for financing the production of the index, to Andrew Kirk for his excellent work on the manuscript and to Martin Hargreaves for indexing.

Preface

Beginning Classical Social Theory introduces you to thirteen key texts of social theory, beginning with a text from 1824 by Auguste Comte – who was one of the first to use the word 'sociology' – and ending with one from 1965 by Theodor W. Adorno.

This is not a textbook in the usual sense – a comprehensive, well-balanced and conclusive summary of whatever it is most important to know about all the main theorists. There are quite a few such books, and I list the ones that I find to be the best in the last chapter. *Beginning Classical Social Theory* does both less and more than your regular textbook.

Less, because I would not want to claim that all the 'important' theorists are represented, and the book will not address everything that is important about the ones who are covered. In fact, you are introduced to only one text by each author, not any author's life work as a whole. *More*, because you are invited to take a *very close look* at these thirteen texts. I have selected texts

- that make interesting and important but wildly differing arguments,
- that give you an idea of how their authors think and write, and
- that, taken together, create an overview of some of the key themes of classical social theory.

Nothing more than that – although this should be enough to expect from a small book like this in terms of content covered. But then, there is something else.

My hope is that this book will help you to get under the skin of these classic texts, and that it will inspire you first of all to read the texts in question – after you read this book, or perhaps even in parallel with it – and then other texts by these and other authors. I want this book not only, and not even primarily, to be a source of information and knowledge, but to be a tool for you: a tool for learning *how to read theory*. There is a technique to reading theory, and knowing this technique is more important than knowing theories. This is not rocket science: the technique consists simply of systematically, as completely as possible, excerpting *everything* the text says, and also any immediate thoughts I have about it – as in brainstorming – including anything noteworthy about *how* the text operates. This includes highlighting words that point to the logical structure of the text, such as 'but', 'however', 'therefore', 'nevertheless', 'on the contrary'. The point is to avoid quick judgements: not to shoot from the hip. As I can better show than explain this method, this book is a bit like an invitation to watch me doing my homework. Other people will have different ways of working, and you will find your own, but here you will find basically a protocol of what I do when I study.

I hope I have written this book in the spirit of 'what I am doing here you can do too': this is the attitude signalled by the philosopher and sociologist Theodor W. Adorno to his audiences, as described by one of his students (Detlev Claussen, in the German news magazine *Der Spiegel*, 2003). I have always found the grand, definite, complete student textbook that speaks from an all-knowing perspective to be a rather authoritarian form of text. By contrast, an assemblage of fragmentary, incomplete but detailed analyses that only in the mind of an active reader can form some kind of coherent picture is educational in the strict sense of the term. You are this active reader.

Studying theory means dealing with texts, and therefore requires you to know how to work with texts. Texts have a materiality of their own – their structure, patterns of argument, rhetorical strategies of persuading a reader. After all, the Latin word *textum* means 'something that has been woven together', a fabric. To understand the textile structure of the text, you need to take it apart, look at the threads and put it back together again. Luckily you do not need to do this all the time: once you have done it a number of times with texts that are sufficiently typical, you can X-ray through the surface of many related texts in the same way that a carpet dealer can tell the value of a carpet from a distance.

Beginners in any discipline, such as undergraduate students, should study some selected things very closely, and get a rough idea of everything else. At least when it comes to social theory, most of our universities are, by and large, better at the second than at the first. The fact that learning is speeding up like everything else is one of the major absurdities of the contemporary world: as society now produces all its bare necessities in much less time than ever before, we should really have much *more* time for studying and other fun things. The opposite is the case. Speed-learning packs ever more information into relatively fewer hours, and thus relies more on general overviews, drowning out the detailed 'theory-practice' – the practice of chewing over concepts, like chewing dry bread that slowly turns sweet – which might just lead to independent thinking. There is too much that needs to be covered in a hectic schedule by students who often also need to earn their living and must demonstrate their earnest striving for 'employability'. The modern university is correspondingly becoming a less good place for the kind of immersive studying from which theoretical thinking can emerge. That's why you need this book.

Some well-meaning commentators argue that learning how to grasp conceptually and theoretically the nature of modern society is also a real bonus for getting an edge in a competitive 'labour market'. Others suspect – less optimistically – that the better you understand modern society, the more difficult you will find it to 'function' in it smoothly. (Health and safety warning: many of the giants of social theory suffered mental breakdowns, including Auguste Comte, John Stuart Mill, Eleanor Marx, Max Weber, Charlotte Perkins Gilman ... which may be not entirely coincidental.) Be that as it may: getting the best available education, including that simple but difficult thing, learning how to read, is equally useful for your glittering graduate career as it is for finding happiness without one.

In the age of the internet, what we lack more than ever is not information but the techniques for engaging with arguments, and that is what studying theory is chiefly about. In order to get the full benefit of the study of theory, one needs to have done a lot of chewing of concepts. Only putting in the hours of theory-practice allows one to really 'own', as opposed to only 'knowing about', concepts: this is the difference between being able to actually *think* with a concept, and being able to pass an exam by saying all the right things *about* it.

The first step in methodical studying must be to learn how to take in what a text actually says – beyond what fits on a PowerPoint slide:

- How does the text work?
- How does the argument move forward?
- What are the contradictions in the text?
- How can I explain these contradictions and make them work for my own argument?

If you study at Oxford or Cambridge, you probably won't need this book as you will undergo the relevant coaching in your weekly one-to-one tutorials. If you study at any other university, including the University of Your Bedroom, this book will help you to learn how to read and produce theory.

Overview of contents

1 Introduction: If it is not mysterious, it is not social theory

The introduction examines the concept and the function of theory. I argue that social theory is 'good theory', i.e. worth your while, only if it adds something to the perception of the social world that cannot be perceived otherwise: theory in this sense must be somewhat mysterious (and mystifying). If it is not, it is just the banal, wordy, laborious and often pompous restatement of the obvious.

2 The well-planned reorganization of society: Auguste Comte

Auguste Comte was the main promoter of the concepts of 'sociology' and 'positivism'. This chapter examines his early programmatic text 'Plan of the Scientific Work Necessary for the Reorganization of Society' (1822–24) which sets out what the new science of sociology was to be all about: the safeguarding of the changes brought about by the French Revolution, but also the safeguarding of (modern, still precarious) society from the perceived danger of more revolutions to come.

3 If you can't beat democracy, join it: Alexis de Tocqueville
This chapter looks at sections from Alexis de Tocqueville's *Democracy in America* (1835–40). Tocqueville uses 'democracy' as a social rather than a narrowly political concept, i.e. a concept that points to a general tendency underlying the development of modern society. Tocqueville regrets the decline of aristocratic society and its values, but thinks it is irreversible. Instead, he finds in the USA some of the mechanisms – including religion and 'individualism properly understood' – that can turn democracy into a good thing, after all.

4 Pariahs of the world, unite! Flora Tristan
This chapter examines a chapter from one of the founding texts of feminist socialism, *The Workers' Union* (1843) by Flora Tristan. She made the case that workers have to constitute themselves as a class in the form of an internationalist organization, and that equality of women had to be one of its priorities.

5 Capitalist modernity is the real savagery: Karl Marx
In the first volume of *Capital* (1867), Karl Marx sarcastically turns the concept of 'fetishism', a concept with which defenders of bourgeois capitalist modernity including Hegel, Comte and Tyler classified (and denigrated) non-European civilizations, against modern civilization itself. In his description of the 'commodity-fetish' as the basic structure of the form and dynamic of modern society, Marx unfolds what all subsequent sociology would address as the complex play of structure and agency.

6 The conflict of community and society: Ferdinand Tönnies
This chapter examines an essay by Ferdinand Tönnies that serves as the 'Introductory Article' to the English edition of his famous *Community and Association* (originally 1887; more often rendered *Community and Society*). Tönnies proposes to examine societies under the perspective of how their members will and want things, and distinguishes between 'natural' and 'deliberate will', from which he derives his two ideal types of *society-as-community* and *society-as-society* (or association). Tönnies is on the one hand nostalgic about a lost world of (village-type) communal life, while on the

other hand he describes modern society merely as a temporary form of appearance of what still remains its essence – community life.

7 There is some Thing out there: Emile Durkheim

This chapter examines sections from Emile Durkheim's *The Rules of Sociological Method* (1895). Durkheim argues here that it is the purpose of science to disturb established ideas. One such idea is that things (in society as elsewhere) exist for the purpose of fulfilling the function that they happen to be fulfilling. Against this he hammers home the need to distinguish between the *cause* of something and the *function* it has assumed (or has been subsumed to). Most of all, Durkheim's insistence that society is not something that merely happens in our minds but is actually something *thing-ly*, out there, for real, acknowledges the fact of alienation that others like Marx also reflect on.

8 The double-consciousness: W. E. B. Du Bois

William Edward Burghardt Du Bois, one of the pioneers of sociology in the USA, formulated in his *The Souls of Black Folk* (1903) a powerful argument on identity in modern society. He describes post-emancipation Afro-Americans as 'born with a veil', as they are only indirectly able to gain consciousness of themselves, namely through the eyes of the others who despise them; at the same time, though, the resulting 'double-consciousness' of being both *of* and *not of* this society can be turned into an advantage: the broken, indirect and precarious vision may see more, and more deeply. Du Bois talks about more than cognition and epistemology, however: both the African and the American strive to be 'co-workers' in the 'kingdom of culture'. Overcoming 'the color-line' is indispensable to the creation of a better, modern, human and humane civilization.

9 From good to bad capitalism and back: Max Weber

In his famous double-essay *The Protestant Ethic and the Spirit of Capitalism* (1904–05) Max Weber translated a generally felt discontent with modern capitalist civilization into a theme for the (then still emergent) discipline of sociology. Like many of his contemporaries, Weber both affirmed and critiqued modern, liberal, capitalist society, celebrating capitalism's dynamism and creative energy (which propelled Western civilization to its well-deserved world-dominating position) while deploring its tendency to become an 'iron casing' through which it fetters and destroys itself. Weber felt that promoting what he perceived as the original, Puritan capitalist spirit against corrupt, 'utilitarian', hedonistic capitalism might help to slow down, or even reverse, the decay of Western civilization.

10 Strangers who are from here: Georg Simmel
The 'Excursus on the Stranger' is one of the most influential sections of Georg Simmel's *Sociology* (1908) and is examined in this chapter. Simmel describes through 'the stranger' a person who has come from elsewhere but stays, and is thereby close and remote at the same time, detached and attached: the stranger belongs and has a function but could probably leave any moment if she or he chose to. The notion brings to mind the diatribe by Geriatrix (in *Asterix and Caesar's Gift* [1974]) who holds against presumed immigrants from Lutetia that *'these strangers ... are not from here'*: there is a sense (or a hope?) in which strangers become acceptable once they are 'from here', somehow.

11 Love, marriage and patriarchy: Marianne Weber
This chapter looks at an essay published in 1912, 'Authority and Autonomy in Marriage' by Marianne Weber, a key representative of liberal feminism. Weber explores the contradictory character of marriage as both diminishing individual autonomy and making a meaningful, ethically autonomous life possible for the individual. She is particularly interested in the idea that the spiritual deepening of monogamy has disciplined men.

12 Critical versus traditional theory: Max Horkheimer
Max Horkheimer's essay 'Critical and Traditional Theory' (1937) is the most explicitly programmatic statement of the Critical Theory of the 'Frankfurt School'. It addresses the interrelations between the mode of organizing social research and the nature of the social reality that is being researched. He rejects what both empiricism and rationalism share, namely a conceptual separation of facts and theories. For both, empiricism and rationalism, facts are to be collected like books in a library, and theories are like the catalogue that

organizes them. Horkheimer's critique affects our understanding of what 'facts' are and what 'theories' are. Critical Theory is presented as neither 'deeply rooted' in any existing reality, nor detached from societal interests, but instead committed to the 'obstinacy of fantasy' (or imagination) that must also be in conflict with the views prevailing among the oppressed.

13 What is a woman, and who is asking anyway? Simone de Beauvoir

Although society maintains that 'woman is always woman', it also complains that 'woman is losing her ways'. Apparently not every female human being is a woman – the latter requires possession of a mysterious something called 'femininity'. In *The Second Sex* (1949), one of the emblematic texts of the feminist tradition, Simone de Beauvoir argues that 'civilization as a whole' produces 'woman'. However, to *be* this or that means to *have become*, and thus not necessarily to remain, this or that. One must actively become what society has set out in advance, and thereby one may also change it (sometimes more, sometimes less).

14 Society as mediation: Theodor W. Adorno

This final chapter looks at a short but densely argued article by Theodor W. Adorno that was first published in 1965 as a handbook entry titled 'Society'. Adorno agrees with Durkheim that society is a bit like a thing – 'thing-like' – but emphasizes that it is also very different from actual things as it cannot be experienced immediately: society is essentially 'mediation', namely a specific form of relationships between people, between people and things, and between people treating each other as things. Not only 'society', though, but also individuals are *mediated* – structured, ruled, determined – by institutions and cannot exist otherwise. Institutions, in turn, cannot exist without that which they mediate – *us*. We made this world, and therefore we can re-make it, too. The problem is that we made it in such a way that it has become quasi-independent, namely thing-like, and this in particular makes it so difficult for us to change it. A tricky situation …

1

Introduction: If it is not mysterious, it is not social theory

As long as there is any life in society, as well as suffering, trouble and unease, there will also be the desire for methodical, sustained, critical inquiry into its nature, dynamics, contradictions and – as yet – unfulfilled possibilities: *social theory*. Social theory takes many forms. In the academic context, it mediates between social science and societal practice: social theory is the self-reflection of social-scientific practice on its societal backgrounds, functions, aims and purposes. Social theory asks *why, how and what for?* It is only through theory that research can become practical: reflection on the *why, how and what for* turns a heap of data and observations into a purposeful practice, a kind of doing that has a relation and a relevance to society. Perhaps one can go even further: without at least a vague idea of the *why, how and what for*, no heap of data and observations would ever have been assembled in the first place. This is the importance of theory in the academic context.

All this applies similarly, however, if 'social science' is understood in its most fundamental, generic sense: 'methodical, sustained, critical inquiry' (i.e., *science*) into that most familiar but at the same time most alien thing, *society*. Such inquiry does not exclusively take place at universities. It is conceivable even that it might increasingly migrate elsewhere, upwards to specialized institutions of 'higher learning' or 'think tanks', and downwards to self-organized discussion circles formed by those who really feel the need. In the university, social theory has nowadays a strangely ambiguous standing: it is considered to be 'difficult' and carries quite a bit of prestige for that, but at the same time it is looked at with some suspicion.

Theorists are seen as hard-working scholars only about as much as chess players are seen as hard-working sportspeople: not quite, really. No sweat there, like in an honest game of rugby or a good old feast of data-crunching. The hard-working contemporary university tends to think of a more than cursory acquaintance with the big, theoretical questions as a luxury that should not distract from the steady production of 'deliverables': concrete, quantifiable 'outputs'. Asking conceptual questions is still fine, though, as long as it results in downloads and citations.

On reflection, however, not even the busiest practitioner of applied social science would want to deny that discussing questions of *why, how and what for* makes datasets and deliverables more acute and relevant. Furthermore, it increases what many now think is the main purpose of university study, the students' expected 'employability'. Many employers assert that they want their workforce to be good at critical and conceptual thinking – on the assumption and under the condition, however, that 'thinking outside the box' serves profitability. It is good to hear this, but at least some of the 'employers' might have second thoughts on this matter: in an economic order that is shaped by a hierarchical division of labour, *some* jobs do indeed require a critical and experimental imagination, and a capitalist society that fails to nurture it will be savaged by the competition. Only an inquisitive mind invents new technologies and products. At the same time, however, a majority of jobs continue to result in the 'torpor of [the] mind' that the division of labour produces in the worker, as described by the Enlightenment philosopher Adam Smith in *The Wealth of Nations* in 1776: for most people, to be 'employable' means being able to do as you are told. You must be disciplined rather than critical and imaginative, however boring and stultifying the job may be. Critical thinking can therefore lead to *un*-employability as well, because reflection on societal purposes may increase one's unwillingness to be 'employed' by another person or agency for purposes that are not necessarily one's own. And where is the employer who invites the employees to have an open-ended discussion of the purposes of the company?

The pragmatic and very sensible counter-argument is, of course, that even the most beautifully autonomous and critical individual needs to eat, and that 'employability' is therefore a good thing to have, as long as society makes eating conditional on 'being employed'. The hint is in the passive voice: I am *being employed*, rather than employing my own faculties to some purpose that I have willed to commit to. There's the rub: the survival of the *autonomous* individual ('autonomous' meaning self-directed, self-governing) is based on his or her acceptance of the *heteronomous* order ('heteronomous' meaning other-directed). The conflicting claims of autonomy and heteronomy are mediated only through the concept of 'society' – which happens to be just what this book is chiefly about. I have dwelt on the issue of 'employability' for a bit because it illustrates – I hope – how a social-theoretical perspective can turn an apparently straightforward, benign phenomenon into something not quite so benign and surely a lot less straightforward. Therefore – BUY THIS BOOK!

To sum up: this book is for students who are lucky enough to be required within their university studies to immerse themselves in some theory, or those who want in their own time to compensate for not being required to do so, or anyone else who simply feels an appetite for open-ended and unpredictable reflection on society – social theory.

Those with little time for introductions to introductions may want to skip to the first chapter proper, as I have made my principal point. On the following pages I will explore what these two words, 'social' and 'theory', mean. This is probably the most abstract and difficult part of the entire book and can be read just as well at the end – as you wish. You must be warned that I take pride in making existing questions *more complicated* and *more numerous* rather than simply answering them. In social theory, to have many questions – more than many answers – counts as a form of wealth. At least in this sense, I hope you will find this book enriching.

Society and the social

Social theory is the theory of society. But what is society?

– *Society is a social relation.*

But what is a social relation, and to what kind of social relation does the concept of 'society' refer?

– *Well, the search for an answer to that question is in fact one of the things that social theory is about.*

Geologists have it easy: they study rocks, and they start their research with a pretty clear idea of what a rock is. They will make this idea more complex in the course of their research, but they do not need to ask themselves all the time, *now, what actually is a rock?*

It is different for social theorists. The question 'what is society' is one of the things that never stop occupying the minds of those practising social theory. That's why our strange discipline never really comes to a conclusion on anything … and quite proudly so: that is exactly the beauty of it. With its object, it also reinvents itself all the time. 'The social' and 'society' cannot be defined, and this is an important part of what defines them. I will keep my thoughts on how to define 'society' by not defining it rather short for now because this entire book is really dedicated to exploring a range of different answers to this question.

Society is a mystery, but of young age. Although social theorists are in no agreement on what exactly it is, we can say with reasonable certainty that society came into existence some three to four hundred years ago, as part of a package of related conundrums called 'modernity'. When we talk about 'society' in the context of social theory we usually mean 'modern society'. When it arrived, anonymously at first, people started talking about it immediately: that is how we know about it, of course.

– But if we do not know what it is, and it did not have its name yet, how do we know when it first arrived?

Well, this is a very good objection. The discourse on 'society' is a bit like the reconstruction of a murder mystery and involves some projection from the present into the past: we start with a certain idea of what it is *in the present* that we refer to as 'society', and then we try to clarify what 'it' is by tracing its emergence and development *over time*. We tend to look for evidence of its existence mostly in written texts, as – at least in the modern period – it is through texts that humans most explicitly try to give an account of social relationships.

One of the most celebrated early documents of the arrival of society is a perplexing, in fact very humorous poem that made a lot of people very angry when it was first published in 1705. It was written in London, a place with a good claim to being the birthplace of modern society. The author was an immigrant – unsurprisingly, as immigrants often make the sharpest observations – who had gone to London (from the Netherlands) for love of the buzz, the dirt and the chaos, and of an Englishwoman, apparently. Our witness (a medical doctor) took a rather dusty old metaphor, comparing society to a beehive. The special twist of his poem was that he used this old image to highlight and celebrate some very un-bee-like behaviour patterns that were typical in his exciting and much-loved modern environment. The doctor – by the name of Bernard Mandeville – diagnosed that the beehive in question (London) was a good place to be because its inhabitants did *not* behave like actual bees (Mandeville 1989). How then did they behave?

Mandeville's beehive was as crowded as it was productive: there were 'Millions endeavouring to supply/ Each other's Lust and Vanity' (note the rhyme!). Lust and Vanity, traditionally associated with the seven deadly sins, are treated in this satire as rather respectable. The poem tells us that society (alias the beehive) is full of dodgy characters – 'knaves' – who try to get rich without 'down-right working', exploiting the labour of others, including 'Sharpers, Parasites, Pimps, Players,/ Pick-Pockets, Coiners, Quacks, Sooth-Sayers'. Remarkably, though, Mandeville does not propose a dichotomy between 'knaves' and honest, hard-working folk, but argues quite to the contrary that 'The grave Industrious were the Same' as 'the knaves': 'All Trades and Places knew some Cheat,/ No Calling was without Deceit'. From a moral perspective, the place was rotten to the core. But, rather scandalously, from here Mandeville went on to formulate a shocking celebration of this 'beehive':

> Thus every Part was full of Vice,
> Yet the whole Mass a Paradice; ...
> Such were the Blessings of that State;
> Their Crimes conspired to make 'em Great ...

Society is something that – rather miraculously – turns a mess of crimes and vices into paradise. (Mandeville uses the word 'state' rather than society, but he means the same thing – the modern separation of state and society had not yet been followed through.) Virtue and Vice became friends, 'And ever since/ The worst of all the Multitude/ Did something for the common Good'. Although every individual member of society complains about it all, society turns all those complaints and moans into something like musical harmony, where opposed things serve each other. Envy and Vanity become 'Ministers of Industry' to the effect that 'the very Poor/ Lived better than the Rich before', something that defenders of capitalist development have claimed countless times ever since.

The most hilarious twist comes in Mandeville's description of how this paradise perished: disaster struck when the members of society, rather than enjoying these wicked modern ways, 'barb'rously' called for honesty and *condemned cheating*! Foolishly, they tried to have their cake and eat it – but as Mandeville reminds his readers, the idea of a convenient but also virtuous life is 'a vain/ Eutopia seated in the Brain': 'Fraud, Luxury, and Pride must live;/ Whilst we the Benefits receive'. Whereas in any number of classical and pre-modern political and moral theories, and still today in the view of many people, society falls apart when morality weakens, in Mandeville's modern beehive, society is destroyed by *invoking* morality. No surprise that Mandeville landed in some hot water.

Incidentally, scholars are still debating whether Mandeville *himself* was intending us to take his poem literally as an attack on the idea of morality: did he really mean we should take pride in subordinating virtue to wealth-production? Probably not, but this need not bother us here. Although it is in the form of a humorous poem, the 'Fable of the Bees' exhibits a wonderfully dark realism. Whatever the author's intentions, his text pointed its many readers rather brutally to the paradoxical character of this new thing that was not yet universally called 'society' at the time. For three centuries now he has reminded us that the traditional discourses of morality are not quite sufficient to talk about it. Hence the need for *social theory*. All modern social theory tries – with generally very good success – to translate the paradoxical point made by Mandeville into less poignant language. One could probably write a pretty good history of social theory by looking at all the authors who have commented on Mandeville's satirical poem.

In order to counter-balance the gospel according to Mandeville, I would like to quote briefly from another classic comment on the concept of 'society', by another wonderful writer, another Londondweller, writing two hundred years later, also polemical but quite different in attitude:

> The very word 'society' sets tolling in memory the dismal bells of a harsh music: shall not, shall not, shall not. You shall not learn; you shall not own; you shall not – such was the society relationship of brother to sister for many centuries ... Inevitably we ask ourselves, is there not something in the conglomeration of people into societies that releases what is most selfish and violent, least rational and humane in the individuals themselves? ... Inevitably we look upon society ... as an ill-fitting form that distorts the truth; deforms the mind; fetters the will. Inevitably we look upon societies as conspiracies that sink the private brother, whom many of us have reason to respect, and inflate in his stead a monstrous male, loud of voice, hard of fist, childishly intent upon scoring the floor of the earth with chalk marks, within whose mystic boundaries human beings are penned, rigidly, separately, artificially ... (Woolf 1998, pp. 307–8 and 313)

This is from Virginia Woolf's splendid diatribe *Three Guineas* (the same text that also contains the famous line 'as a woman, I have no country'), first published in 1938. (The quote is from the 'Third Letter'.) Although there are similarities to Mandeville's account – such as the account of the selfishness of people in society – the perspective on society is contrary: where in Mandeville, society composes out of the selfish behaviour of modern 'knaves' a wondrous, wealth-creating, multi-part harmony, for Woolf society turns perfectly decent people into childish, irrational, brutal monsters.

The two statements are, in spite of saying opposite things, equally true. They shine a light on two principal perspectives on society that one finds in the tradition of social theory: the more optimistic one answers the question what are the patterns or mechanisms that allow society to survive or even to flourish, whether one deplores or celebrates it. After all, given how *rare* riots, revolutions and high school shootings really are, society seems to function, by and large, most of the time! The more pessimistic perspective answers the question why and how society produces patterns of behaviour in humans that are far more horrible than humans would be (presumably) in a state of nature, i.e. outside or before (or after) society.

The meaning of 'theory'

So much for 'social' and 'society'. Let us turn now to 'theory'. Here the waters are even muddier, as the word 'theory' has quite a range of overlapping and related meanings, some more generic and some more specific. A sense of its complexity can be gleaned from the following statement by Auguste Comte (1798–1857), the man who did most to bring the word 'sociology' into circulation:

> For, if on the one hand any positive theory must necessarily be based on observation, it is equally true on the other that, in order to make observations, our minds require a theory of some sort. If, in considering phenomena, we did not relate them immediately to some principles, not only would it be impossible for us to connect these isolated observations, and in consequence to make any sense of them, but we should be quite incapable of remembering them; and, most often, the facts would remain unperceived. (Comte, quoted in Elias 1978, p. 34)

Comte makes a distinction here between what he calls 'positive theory' and more indistinct varieties of theory: 'theory of some sort'. By 'positive theory' he means a theory that is in keeping with the doctrine of 'positivism', i.e. the endeavour to formulate plans for the reform of society based on its systematic empirical observation. 'Theory of some sort' is involved in making perceptions and observations, relating these observations to 'some principles', connecting them, making sense of and remembering them. Whereas 'positive theory' is made and applied by (in Comte's conception, positivist) scientists and policymakers, 'theory of some sort' is made and applied by everyone all the time.

A more recent theorist has proposed a similar distinction. Percy Cohen called 'systematic theories' the kind of theories that a reader would expect to be covered in a book on social theory: 'general ideas consciously formulated for some purpose or purposes' (Cohen 1968, p. 2). In a textbook on social theory of 1968 that was of great influence in British sociology, Cohen distinguished four types of 'systematic theories' that I will discuss later on. For now, I would like to stick a bit longer with the garden variety of theory, 'theory of some sort' or *non-theory theory*, as it were: the mud from which 'systematic theories' somehow emerge, which they leave behind and negate, and to which they also return. Cohen said the following:

> The most elementary theories, which we use unconsciously, are those embedded in our language; for, all language must use certain universal categories; and to use a universal category is, in effect, to use a theory. (Cohen 1968, p. 2)

Cohen's example is the sentence 'This typewriter is heavy': it implies a theory of what 'heaviness' is. If we did not have a theory of heaviness, the sentence would be of no relevance. Our spontaneous theory of heaviness is responsible for certain practical implications, such as better make sure it does not drop on your foot. Cohen's suggestion that there is a theory of 'heaviness' is reminiscent of the famous examples given by the linguist Benjamin Lee Whorf. Drawing on his work experience as an insurance clerk, Whorf examined the implications of our using such phrases as 'empty drums of gasoline' or 'waste water': the former are not actually empty but tend to contain highly explosive vapours. The spontaneous application of emptiness theory to these not-so-empty drums cost his insurance company dearly: after all, why should I not light my cigarette next to an 'empty' drum? Industrial 'waste water' may be called 'water', but it can also be highly flammable: uncritical and unconscious application of water theory proved fatal when someone threw a cigarette end into it (Whorf 1956, pp. 135–7). From this kind of practical experience Whorf learned that the most innocent-looking everyday language can be a rather dangerous affair, as it is loaded with 'theories of some sort'. Similarly, when some talking head on TV mentions 'free markets', it might be a good idea to keep in mind that they are in fact about as free as those gasoline drums are empty – and about as explosive. Another example would be the humble statement 'I think'. We might be tempted to believe that our language uses two different words when there are two different referents of some sort, such as in this case, a subject 'I' and an activity 'think'. We assume spontaneously that the structure of the sentence 'I think' reflects the structure of a reality where there exists an 'I' that just happens to be engaged in an activity called 'think'. This implies logically that this activity 'think' likewise exists somehow independently from this particular 'I' and might attach itself to some other 'I' – you, for example – the next moment. Wrong: there may well be unthinking 'I's, but there is no 'think' without a subject that does the thinking. Lewis Carroll illustrated this issue when he wrote about the grin of the Cheshire-Cat in *Alice in Wonderland*: in the absurd dream-world of this book, the grin still hung in the air for some time after the cat had disappeared (Carroll 1992, p. 53). In a more complex sentence such as 'I do research on this', whereby 'this' might be, for example, 'society', we encounter the same problem: 'I', 'do research' and also 'this [society]' are *in the sentence* different things that just happen to find themselves in the same sentence, but *in reality* they are not different things. The 'sort-of-theory' that is embedded in language structure is contradicted by proper (systematic) social theory which tells us that 'I' and 'this', namely society, are neither entirely different, nor identical things: I am part of society, and society is very much part of what I am. My doing research is part of what I am as well as of what society is. Mediated through my person, society does research on itself. By doing research on society, I research myself.

Large areas of sociological research, under different names and with differing trajectories, are dedicated to the description and analysis of those 'theories of some sort' that we use in everyday life. These areas of sociological research lead into 'systematic theorizing' only if and when they inquire critically *which* 'spontaneous theories' (world-views, ideologies, imaginaries, patterns of culture etc.) emerge in *what kinds of* social constellations or types of society, and *why*. The latter are among the questions asked by systematic theory: they aim to move from spontaneous, automatic sort-of-theorizing to conscious, critical theorizing, and it is as a first step towards the latter that producing theory includes describing and analysing sort-of-theories. Systematic theory works its way out of the messy given-ness of spontaneous theorizing; the latter's description and analysis are its self-reflection, self-clarification and self-criticizing. Social theorists differ from their contemporaries 'only' by committing themselves to *systematically* examining a situation shared by all.

Spontaneous and systematic theories

Max Horkheimer, a Marxist philosopher who became one of the pioneers of systematic empirical social research in the middle third of the twentieth century, famously suggested that theory could be either 'critical' or 'traditional', whereby the latter meant as much as 'affirmative' or uncritical (see Chapter 12 on this.). Horkheimer illustrated what was to him an all-important distinction with a formulation by the idealist philosopher Johann Gottlieb Fichte (1762–1814): 'in constructing the world, one is not conscious of constructing, as it is done by necessity rather than out of freedom' (quoted in Horkheimer 2002, p. 245). This sentence, written more than two hundred years ago, needs some unpacking:

1. We – subjects, individuals, maybe also individuals constituted as groups – construct the world. Fichte meant that we construct it *in our minds*, through our intellect, imagination, speaking, writing, acting and so on. Without us doing all this, there is in fact no world – or at least no world that we know of: surely the world that we relate to and that we act on is the one we 'construct'. Whether there is another one we cannot know, and it does not really matter much in practice.
2. We do this constructing 'by necessity' – we do not *choose* to do it, it just happens: it is almost as if the world constructs itself through us, using us as its instrument or medium. If on first reading, the idea that we humans construct the world seems to turn us into mighty god-like creatures, this second point is quite a downer!
3. Because it is done 'by necessity', we are not conscious of it – which makes it sound even less glorious. *However:*
4. There is an implication, albeit only in the negative, that the constructing *could* perhaps also be done 'out of freedom', and would then be conscious. There seems to be some kind of link between *consciousness* and *freedom*.

And this is really why, according to Horkheimer, we need consciously developed theory. Theory is conscious – and thereby linked to freedom – when it is negative and critical of anything that obstructs freedom. Being conscious, negative and critical, however, does not occur spontaneously. Again for illustration, think of Snoopy's 'dog superiority theory': Snoopy famously had to address the essay question, 'Why dogs are superior to cats', and did so in only one sentence: 'They just are, and that's all there is to it!' (Schulz 2008, p. 158). Snoopy is so firm in his theoretical beliefs that he does not need many words to express what in his universe is blatantly obvious. To adapt Fichte, Snoopy constructs the world unconsciously and 'by necessity' – unthinkingly, spontaneously, automatically, organically. In this dog's mind, theory follows from and reflects societal practice – his own, anyway – in perfect harmony, undisturbed by any negative thoughts, easily stated 'short and to the point', as Snoopy himself comments in the last panel of this classic strip. Not being dogs, we need less convenient and comforting theories.

Wordy restatements of the obvious vs. theory as revelation

But there is also a lot of truth in another definition of social theory: 'endless pages of long words which, when we translate them, tell us the obvious' (Craib 1992, p. 13). Craib continues to say, however, that although the bulk of the output of social theorists might well be described as wordy restatements of the blatantly obvious, there are exceptions about which the opposite is true. They are what he describes as 'good theory'. Good theory 'tells us something we didn't know and couldn't discover by looking' (Craib 1992, p. 13): something that is not obvious, and that we cannot get to by way of some short cut. No amount of even the most highly organized data-crunching can discover or construct it. Theory is revelation.

Craib's point is that theory expresses things of which we have no direct experience. This goes for all sciences: few people have direct experience of the fact that the earth is round and travels around the sun. This idea ('heliocentrism') had to be argued for in the mode of theory, which is what Nicolaus Copernicus did in his book of 1543. It took about another century, due to a whole range of changing societal conditions, until it was generally accepted as true. Likewise, we have no direct experience of 'society' – is there such a thing? As was the case with heliocentrism, some people deny it. Those of us who believe it exists argue that without assuming its existence, a range of experiences could not reasonably be accounted for; this presupposes communication of and some amount of agreement on what those experiences ('data') are, and also on what should count as a reasonable way of interpreting them. The same goes for 'patriarchy' and 'class': social facts or just some interesting ideas? As theoretical concepts properly speaking, they are revelatory tools that make visible a reality that is otherwise not visible. Once we accept the theory, we will find that the data point to and confirm it. Without the context of a theory, however, the data do not point anywhere at all. Raw data *conceal* the reality 'behind' the data (patriarchy, class) which only theory can reveal.

Theory is about revelation of something mysterious, often the attempt to get to grips with something beyond our control. For social theory, this something is *society*, a something that is beyond the control of individuals, of course, but – perhaps increasingly so – also beyond the control of the totality of all those who constitute society. As Craib describes it, the process of producing theory in science – social or otherwise – is quite similar to that in everyday life (Craib 1992, p. 7): I try to explain something, so I look for patterns in my own experience or that of someone I know, or both. Then I also include some general ideas that I have picked up somewhere, perhaps consciously, perhaps not. I try to be systematic about it, and to reach some clarity in order to present the case to myself or to someone else. I do this through the use of logic which brings experiences and ideas into certain relationships, such as 'causality' or 'contradiction'. *Voilà*: theory. Every social theory 'makes some propositions which are counter to our immediate experiences and beliefs, and this is, in fact, the way in which we learn from them'. Craib uses the following two examples:

> The punk might believe that she is in full rebellion against the culture of her parents and authority, yet for the functionalist theorist she is setting in motion a series of adjustments by means of which that culture and society continue to survive in a smoother-running way than before. The worker might believe she is getting a fair day's wage for a fair day's work, but for the Marxist she is being systematically exploited. (Craib 1992, p. 7)

These examples show why theory can at times be unpleasant. The punk might tell the sociologist (her father, perhaps?) where to stick his functionalism, and indeed this sociologist seems to be missing something: the rebellion is surely not *only* a cunning mechanism by which society reproduces itself (to the tune of 'the more it changes, the more it stays the same'), but it does also constitute a moment of change. Maybe it needed to produce overblown illusions about its own importance in order to get off the ground in the first place, but that does not mean it is *exclusively* functional, self-defeating and affirmative of the system. The rebellion might, however, learn something about its own limitations from fatherly sociology, and be the stronger for it. Craib's second example helps explain why workers who buy into the liberal rhetoric of 'a fair day's work for a fair day's wage' will not be easily impressed by Marxist critical theory: these nasty party-pooping Marxists destroy a soothing ideology that makes life more bearable. Craib neglects to say, however, that the Marxist notion of a reality of exploitation that takes on the appearance of the 'fair wage' relation can only have emerged from the groping, growing reasoning of workers who *did* notice that this kind of fairness left one class much better off than the other. One such reasoning worker was indeed that impoverished refugee and precariously paid journalist, Karl Marx himself, his petty-bourgeois family background notwithstanding. The history of the labour movement is full of *déclassé* middle-class intellectuals who are in fact workers, whether they like it or not.

Cohen's four types of systematic theories

When it comes to theorizing theory, the distinction between everyday theories, or else 'elementary theories', and 'systematic theories' – 'general ideas consciously formulated for some purpose or purposes' (Cohen 1968, p. 2) – is only the first, most fundamental distinction. Cohen further divides systematic theories into four types: analytic, programmatic, normative and scientific. This book (like others on social theory) deals mostly with the second type, 'programmatic theory', but it seems useful to briefly outline what the others are in order to gain a clearer idea what we expect social theories to do.

Analytic theories explore the logical connections between axiomatic statements and are often implicitly used in social theory, but rarely explicitly. (An 'axiom' or postulate is a statement that is presupposed to be true as the basis for an argument.) They might occur at a highly formalized level of theory-formation, when one tries for example to clarify what one means by 'causality', 'reciprocity' or 'dialectics'.

Normative theories aim to formulate norms, most often in the context of ethics or aesthetics: how something ought to be or ought to be done. Social theories often have normative aspects, but again, they are rarely explicit; when social scientists admit their normative commitments – which they should do much more often – then they typically point to a normative theory that sits outside social theory, formulated somewhere else such as in the contexts of philosophy or religion. Social scientists invoke these, but do not normally formulate them (and if they do, then they will be perceived as part-time philosophers when they do).

Scientific theories, in Cohen's definition, are usually 'theories of' something in particular (say, the theory of youth delinquency) and look at causal connections: when this happens, then that must follow, as long as a certain set of conditions is given. This kind of theorizing is in fact quite rare in the social sciences; it is generally admired, when it succeeds, and is the jewel in the crown of any good positivist. (Note, however, that in the social sciences we tend to deal with a weak form of causality only, which is really just statistical probability.) Scientific theories must be empirically testable and refutable, which presupposes that we know what a refutation would look like even though there has not been one so far.

This leaves us with the *programmatic theories*, which Cohen also calls 'metaphysical theories'. Those who want to model the social sciences very narrowly on the natural sciences (or what they imagine the latter to be like) do not usually have much time for programmatic theories as they are not testable and do not set much store by causality. Still, programmatic theories are subject to rational appraisal. (Rational appraisal, of course, presupposes in turn a specific understanding of what constitutes logical thinking, such as dialectical or non-dialectical logic. Such discussions are done in the area of 'analytic theory'.) Programmatic or metaphysical theories shape, direct and give purpose to the social-scientific enquiry. Cohen writes:

> Some metaphysical theories ... constitute useful assumptions which have a programmatic or suggestive role: they may delineate a broad field in which more precise formulations can be made; they may provide ways of interpreting evidence which is used to test more precise theories; or they may sensitize an observer to the kind of factors

which are relevant to explaining a particular phenomenon. (Cohen 1968, p. 5)

Cohen names the theory of natural selection as an example, namely the idea that if a species survives for long, then it must possess characteristics that are well adapted to a particular environment. If the species disappears, then it must have been ill adapted. This is not a scientific theory, as it cannot be tested, verified or falsified; it does not even describe any kind of causality (or statistical probability) as on either side of the 'if – then' formula sits basically the same thing in a different formulation: disappearance points to a lack of adaptation, but 'lack of adaptation' can only be diagnosed since the species has disappeared. A is interpreted as B; there is not much point in claiming that A is *caused* by B because the concept of B already contains A. The theory is programmatic, however, in the sense that its 'value lies in directing the inquiries of the student of evolution' (Cohen 1968, p. 6): the theory invites the researcher to look at a set of phenomena in a particular way, and thereby directs the research. This it does very well, and therefore it is a good example of a programmatic theory.

The case is similar with a sociological theory like this one: 'The various parts of a social system are necessarily interdependent.' This could also be expressed like this: if something is a social system, then its parts are 'necessarily interdependent'. Again, this is almost a tautology: a social system is *defined* as something whose parts are 'necessarily interdependent'. This is surely not scientific; perhaps it has some similarity to an analytic theory, as it clarifies the meaning of a concept, and perhaps it is also secretly a little bit normative: the author of this theory (Talcott Parsons) perhaps quite *likes* his social world to be 'a system' in this specific sense, but that is not what the theory is designed to say. Programmatic it is, however: it allows us to ask a meaningful question, namely, what conditions determine to what extent the parts of a system are in fact interdependent? *Voilà*, we have a research programme.

Another example: 'Social order rests on the acceptance of common values.' Most social scientists would probably spontaneously agree to this, but few would mistake it for a scientific theory: there is no causality here – order does not necessarily follow simply from the fact that 'common values' are accepted. In British society, for example, this sentence is usually but not universally true. It contains perhaps a bit of wishful thinking, i.e., an unacknowledged normative element: it sounds like the kind of thing liberals *want* to believe about modern liberal society. But then again, liberals also call the police to restore order, either when common values are wanting, or when some subset of citizens maliciously misinterpret those values (liberty, equality, etc.) by taking them too literally, perhaps. The theoretical statement that 'social order rests on the acceptance of common values' is partly true, certainly one-sided, but makes a reasonably good sociological theory: it is useful to formulate questions with. And this is what we most want from a 'programmatic theory': it suggests problems, and points to where to look for solutions.

Theories are modified in the light of experience but 'they do more to structure experience than experience does to test them' (Cohen 1968, p. 10). From my own experience – or rather, from theoretically driven self-observation – I feel that I have only rarely, if ever, abandoned a theoretical idea because fresh data falsified it: I am quite resistant to data. It seems more likely to me that theoretical ideas are destroyed by other, more elegant or logically coherent theoretical ideas. But maybe that's just me. The fundamental dialectic that rules this relationship has been classically expressed by Immanuel Kant (1724–1804): 'Thoughts without contents are empty; perceptions without concepts are blind' (Kant 1976, p. 95; this is at the beginning of the chapter on 'transcendental logic' in the 1787 edition of *Critique of Pure Reason*, section B76). Knowledge and understanding are served neither by empty thoughts – concepts without experiential, perceptual, empirical contents – nor by blind, shapeless perceptions. *Concepts without empirical content are not really concepts, and perceptions that are not shaped by concepts are not really perceptions.* But what drives the constant to and fro between concepts and perceptions, theories and data? The Marxist theorist John Holloway suggested that

> the starting point of theoretical reflection is opposition, negativity, struggle ... dissonance ... discontent ... frustration ... rage ... unease, a confusion, a longing ... a dissonance ... that divides us

against ourselves ... a tension between that which exists and that which might conceivably exist. (Holloway 2002, pp. 1, 5, 6)

He refers to this tension as the 'dual dimension of reality': there is the reality of what exists and the reality of what does not exist. Holloway rejects the separation between, on the one hand, a (positivist, scientific) theory of reality and, on the other hand, a (normative, philosophical) theory of what might or should exist: this separation is untrue to 'dual reality' because what does not (yet) exist already exists as a potential, expressed in ideas. Ideas exist: they are the perceptible reality of things that do not (yet) exist except as possibilities. Theory in this perspective is a means to have at least a furtive glance at that side of our 'dual reality' that does not actually exist (yet).

Did someone ask why we need social theory? There are only two reasons, really:

1. to be able to imagine and think about that which does not (yet) exist but might exist one day; and
2. to be able to perceive and think about that which does exist.

Two pretty strong reasons to give it some thought.

References

Carroll, Lewis. 1992 [1865]. *Alice in Wonderland*. Ed. Donald J. Gray. New York, London: Norton.

Cohen, Percy S. 1968. *Modern Social Theory*. London: Heinemann.

Craib, Ian. 1992. *Modern Social Theory, From Parsons to Habermas*. New York: Harvester Wheatsheaf.

Elias, Norbert. 1978 [1970]. *What is Sociology?* New York: Columbia University Press.

Holloway, John. 2002. *Change the World Without Taking Power: The Meaning of Revolution Today*. London: Pluto Press.

Horkheimer, Max. 2002 [1937]. 'Postscript', in *Critical Theory. Selected Essays*. New York: Continuum, pp. 244–252.

Kant, Immanuel. 1976 [1781, 1787]. *Kritik der Reinen Vernunft*. Hamburg: Meiner.

Mandeville, Bernard de. 1989 [1705]. *The Fable of the Bees*. London: Penguin.

Schulz, Charles M. 2008. *The Complete Peanuts 1973–1974*. Seattle, WA: Fantagraphic Books.

Whorf, Benjamin Lee. 1956 [1941]. 'The relation of habitual thought and behavior to language', in *Language, Thought, and Reality, Selected Writings*. Ed. John B. Carroll. Cambridge, MA: MIT Press, pp. 134–159.

Woolf, Virginia. 1998. *Three Guineas*. Oxford: Oxford University Press.

2

The well-planned reorganization of society: Auguste Comte

Isidore Marie Auguste François Xavier Comte (1798–1857) was a child of the French Revolution of 1789–99. As one would expect from the child of such an exceptional, violent and inspirational parent, he both followed in the Revolution's footsteps and rebelled against it. As for his actual parents, they were fairly conservative Catholics: his father was a civil servant in Montpellier in the South of France. Auguste Comte was an extremely bright student, especially in maths, and completed school early. He was accepted right away by the École Polytechnique in Paris, at the time the most prestigious place to study mathematics, the natural sciences and technology. This institution had been founded during the Revolution and was still during the period of restoration (since 1814) shaped by the modernizing spirit of republicanism. As Comte was not only bright but also disinclined to obey authority, prone to throw tantrums and not entirely unaware of his own genius – some apparently called him arrogant – he was chucked out and had to move back in with his parents in Montpellier. This didn't go so well either, so he moved back to Paris and lived from occasional and precarious jobs. Sticking it out in the big city and the milieu of the Polytechnic paid off, however: Comte got to know one of the most charismatic and exceptional intellectuals of the time and became his personal secretary, a position that launched Comte himself as a leading light: during most of the nineteenth century, the French thought of Comte as their greatest philosopher – not bad for someone who was kicked out of both university and parental home. Being down and out in Paris was not such a bad situation for an emerging major intellect.

From 1817 to 1824, Comte was the secretary of Claude-Henri de Rouvroy, Comte de Saint-Simon (1760–1825). Their relationship ended when they fell out over the question of the authorship of the 'Plan of the Scientific Work Necessary for the Reorganization of Society', the text that laid out the overall direction for Comte's life-work, written and published in different versions between 1822 and 1824. Saint-Simon was an aristocrat who was in love with the modern world. He sided with the French Revolution, and accordingly led a rather adventurous and unsettled life, from fighting in the American War of Independence to a spell in prison during 'the Terror' under Robespierre. He had a strong interest in large-scale engineering and was involved in abortive attempts at canal building, including a project that anticipated what later would become the Panama Canal. The ending of the Revolution found him impoverished – but alive – and turning towards intense study. Although he remained poor, he became a hugely influential author – the kind who picked up what was in the air in this revolutionary period and gave ideas to others. Among those whom he inspired – apart from Comte – were Augustin Thierry (1795–1856), Comte's predecessor as Saint-Simon's secretary, and the group who became known as the Saint-Simonian 'school'. Thierry went on to become a leading liberal historian with a strong influence from Romanticism, which he also shared with Saint-Simon. The Saint-Simonian 'school' developed Saint-Simon's ideas into an influential form of 'utopian socialism'.

Saint-Simon and Comte were influenced by the same set of key thinkers of the time. First of all, they were students and followers of British empiricism in the vein of Francis Bacon (1561–1626) and John Locke (1632–1704), considering sense perceptions to be the source and means of all knowledge and believing that all theories needed to be tested against observed facts. In the more immediate French context, one of the principal influences was the liberal economist Jean-Baptiste Say (1767–1832), who was a popularizer of some aspects of the classical political economy of Adam Smith (1723–90). Saint-Simon borrowed from Say the concept of 'l'industriel', the industrialist, which refers to all those who are involved in production (as opposed to the clergy and the aristocracy, who are not). This concept is important, as Saint-Simon and Comte saw themselves as voicing the standpoint of 'the industrialists'. This concept is closely related to that of the 'Third Estate', which has roughly the same meaning. One of the most influential political pamphlets of the first stages of the French Revolution had the title *What is the Third Estate?*, published in 1789 by Emmanuel Joseph Sieyes (1748–1836), often referred to as Abbé Sieyes. (Sieyes was a minor cleric but was not religious – taking a low-ranking job in the Church was at the time one of the ways an intellectual could make a living.) Sieyes was a major influence on many theorists of the time, including Say, Saint-Simon and Comte: together with his fellow revolutionary, the philosopher and mathematician Condorcet (1743–94), Sieyes had coined the terms 'social science' and 'sociology', and founded in 1793 the *Journal d'instruction sociale*, the first journal of social science. They intended to promote a rationalist social science as the basis for the reconstruction of society, and in this context also pioneered quantitative methods.

Saint-Simon, who coined the word 'positivism', and Comte who followed him differed from their revolutionary predecessors Sieyes and Condorcet in taking a more sceptical view of the enthusiastic belief in progress that was characteristic of the protagonists of the French Revolution. In this they let themselves be inspired by some of those who opposed the Revolution, in particular the Catholic traditionalists Joseph de Maistre (1753–1821) and Louis de Bonald (1754–1840). They used some of the ideas of these counter-revolutionary thinkers, such as the notion of society as an organism that precedes the individual, without, however, adopting their sociopolitical perspective: Saint-Simon and Comte were dedicated modernizers who thought it worthwhile to try and learn from the enemy.

Although the 'Plan' was widely read and well received, Comte never achieved lasting academic employment, and from 1826 onward he gave lectures in his own flat. These resulted in the publication, between 1830 and 1842, of the six volumes of *Cours de philosophie positive*, the *Course in Positive Philosophy*. Progress on this work was initially interrupted by a severe mental crisis that lasted until 1828 (and recurred twice later in his life). The first three volumes are expositions of mathematics and the natural sciences, the last three are on 'la philosophie sociale', which is where 'sociology' is outlined. Comte was profoundly disturbed by the 1848 revolution in

France – he had hoped and expected that in the positive stage of human history nothing as violent and chaotic as a revolution would occur. He answered it with a change of tack in his work: positivism needed to become a positive social and political force in the form of an organization and a religion, which he founded in 1848 (Societé Positiviste) and 1849 (the 'Religion of Humanity'), respectively. The shift in emphasis was also reflected in his subsequent restatement of his theory in the four-volume *Système de politique positive* (*System of Positive Politics*) published between 1851 and 1854. Comte, then as before, rejected the liberal, individualistic notions of freedom of conscience and of pluralism and asserted the need for strong moral and spiritual authority, separate from temporal authority, which would give society a determinate common purpose. At the same time he thought – rather naively – that such authority could be warranted without any form of administrative despotism – as that would stifle progress – by way of voluntary moral assent.

Comte's 1824 'Plan of the Scientific Work Necessary for the Reorganization of Society' was the first public announcement of his research project, meant to result in the publication of a multi-volume series of books. These books would contain what he would later refer to as 'sociology'. The body of the 'Plan' is called the 'General exposé', or 'general exposition', and is framed by a 'Foreword', an 'Introduction' and a more detailed description of the first of the three parts of the project that Comte plans and announces here ('First series of works'). What the three parts of the 'Programme' are is explained at the end of the 'General exposé'.

Foreword

Comte begins the text by stating that his project has two principal goals, 'to establish that politics must today rise to the rank of the sciences of observation' and 'to apply this fundamental principle to the spiritual reorganization of society' (47). The key sentence is this:

> The goal of the first part [of the theoretical programme] is, properly, to establish on the one hand the spirit which should reign in politics, considered as a positive science; and on the other hand to demonstrate the necessity and the possibility of such a change. (47)

Structure of the selected text

Foreword (47–49)
Introduction (49–62)
1 The need for the reorganization of society (49–50)
2 The kings' plans for the reorganization of society (50–53)
3 The peoples' plans for the reorganization of society (53–57)
4 Both misconceptions are complementary and must be replaced by organic doctrine (57–62)
General exposé (62–86)
5 The slowness of social and intellectual change (62–65)
6 Fundamental change cannot be brought about without acknowledging the distinction between theoretical and practical works, their equal importance and the antecedence of theory (65–72)
7 Scientists are best qualified to develop the organic theory and alone have the authority to secure its acceptance (73–77)
8 Only scientists committed to the organic doctrine can create a unified general society in Europe and overcome patriotism (77–80)
9 The three different theoretical states of human knowledge culminate in the positive doctrine (80–84)
10 Why the moral revolution that is now needed has not been possible in the past (84–6)
[First series of works (86–144)]

Comte, Auguste. 1998 [1824]. 'Plan of the Scientific Work Necessary for the Reorganization of Society'. In Auguste Comte, *Early Political Writings*. Edited and translated by H. S. Jones. Cambridge: Cambridge University Press, 47–144.

This twofold perspective is repeated in Comte's description of the second part of the theoretical work to be written, which is supposed to outline 'the work that is needed to imprint this character on politics'. Such an outline of what needs to be done would be produced by studying 'the laws which have guided the general course of civilization' (47) and 'the social system which the natural development of the human race must bring to dominance today' (48).

An attentive reader can discern already on the very first pages a tension in Comte's conception that is characteristic of his entire work: the positive science which he will later call 'sociology' is to establish a spirit that *should* reign. Comte makes an argument for its possibility but also the *necessity* of its reign. He claims that a law-bound 'natural development of the human race' will *by necessity* bring about what people nevertheless have to 'imprint' on politics. The becoming positive of modern society is, on the one hand, a necessary development rooted in the course of human civilization and, on the other hand, something we have to work and struggle for. This ambiguity – we are sailing with the wind, but still need to do the rowing – will remain a characteristic of positivistic social theory far beyond and long after Comte himself.

In the remainder of the 'Foreword', Comte adds an acknowledgement of his intellectual debt to Saint-Simon and a nod in the latter's direction that the contribution of literature and the arts to the renewal of 'social sentiments' is as important as that of science; however in the present work, and until the last decade of his life, Comte kept quiet about literature and the arts.

Introduction
1 The need for the reorganization of society

Comte's starting point is his analysis of the period he lived in: a 'great crisis experienced by the most civilized nations' (49). His take is that this crisis is constituted by two opposed tendencies: 'A social system which is dying' coexists with 'a new system whose time has come and which is in the process of taking definitive shape'. The tension between them creates 'disorganization', anarchy and the threat of dissolution in tandem with 'reorganization'. By the latter, society 'is led towards the definitive social state of the human race, the one which best suits its nature, that in which all its means of prosperity are to receive their fullest development' (49).

Comte says that the crisis was useful in the first place as it weakened the old 'feudal and theological system' and helped modify it 'to allow us to proceed directly to the formation of the new'. Then, however, Comte adds a big 'but' (and sentences starting with a signal-word like 'but' always deserve special attention):

> But today, now that this condition is fully satisfied ... the predominance that the critical tendency still retains is the greatest obstacle to the progress of civilization, and even to the obstruction of the old system. It is the primary cause of the terrible and constantly recurring upheavals which accompany the crisis. (49)

It is interesting how Comte uses the word 'critical' here: 'the critical tendency' has brought about the crisis but if the crisis is now to be ended, critique has to end, too. Critique and crisis had their time and function, but now we have been through that and we need to move on. Enough of negativity – it is time now to become positive in order 'to stop the anarchy which is daily invading society'. The 'civilized nations' must now 'abandon the critical direction for the organic direction' (50) and form the new social system. Comte adopted the use of the word 'organic' from Saint-Simon whose research assistant he still was at the time of writing. It had for them a quite specific meaning that is related to, but also somewhat different from, how it came to be used later, when nineteenth-century romantics dreamed of 'organically grown' societies and twenty-first-century supermarkets offer organically grown vegetables. (The romantics implied that ideal societies evolved, like plants, spontaneously and without not-so-organic interference from human machinations such as the modern state and its planning commissions, while the supermarkets claim similarly that the organic veg grow untouched by not-so-organic pesticides, etc.). In Comte's day, 'organic' meant quite simply that something is 'organized' in a stable and functional manner: one could think perhaps of the way the pipes of a pipe organ are organized. This meaning of the word still resonates with the – distinctly unromantic – primary meaning of the Greek word *organon*: tool or instrument, also a set of tools, or a machine; for medieval Christians the pipe organ seems to have symbolized a well-organized *kosmos*, an ordered world. The design of a pipe organ also somehow evokes the human body, which suggests in turn that the imagery of 'organisms' and well-structured, functional machines are not a million miles apart.

Taking 'the *organ*ic direction' means the 're*organ*ization' and stabilization of society that is Comte's principal concern. In the next step in his argument, Comte states that the need for reorganization is generally felt. He writes that to date there have been two opposite sorts of endeavours to reorganize society, those by peoples and those by kings. Both are equally imperfect, and in combination prolong rather than end the crisis. That Comte puts 'peoples' and 'kings' in opposite camps points to the very important fact – certainly confusing for a twenty-first-century reader – that he was thinking of society not (yet) in a nationalist manner: kings still constitute (for Comte) a category of their own, they do not emerge out of and represent peoples. Only later in the nineteenth century, after nationalism had conquered and transformed traditional European political thought, would (nationalist) monarchists see kings as representatives of peoples. For Comte, still, there are 'the kings' on the one side, 'the peoples' on the other. His thinking is in this respect very close to that expressed in one of the chief pamphlets of the French Revolution, Sieyes's famous *What is the Third Estate?* (1789): Sieyes had argued that only the 'Third Estate' – the middle and working classes – constituted 'the nation', and the aristocracy was not actually a part of it.

2 The kings' plans for the reorganization of society

Comte argues that 'the kings' of the time (i.e. the allied European reaction against the French Revolution) mistook the reorganization of society for the simple re-establishment of 'the feudal and theological system' (50). Comte rather graciously suggests that the kings are not driven in this simply by self-interest, but rather fail to consider 'the general course of civilization' and 'the tendency of society towards the establishment of a new system, more perfect and no less solid than the old one' (51). From their 'vantage-point' (modern sociologists would say 'standpoint' or 'situatedness'), Comte writes, the kings quite understandably were not able to see beyond 'the anarchic state of society' whose nature they fail to understand. Comte gives at this point the first version of his theory of the present state of things, i.e., the crisis of French society, of which the French Revolution had been a major expression, making a bold and coolly scientific, macro-historical proposition:

The fall of the feudal and theological system does not stem, as they think, from recent isolated and so to speak accidental causes. Instead of being the effect of the crisis, it is on the contrary its source. The decline of this system has taken effect gradually over the preceding centuries, by a succession of modifications, to which, independent of any human will, all classes of society have contributed, and of which kings themselves have often been the primary agents or the most ardent promoters. It has been, in short, the necessary consequence of the course of civilization. (51)

This is how the emerging discipline of sociology, still busy being born and not yet going by that name, replied to reactionary critics of the French Revolution: it was not intellectuals and troublemakers who brought about the fall of the old regime, but rather the regime's disintegration produced the troublemakers. The protagonists and servants of the old regime undermined their own rule by promoting what later sociologists would call the process of modernization. A rather abstract and intangible force had driven them to do so, to which Comte refers as 'the course of civilization'. Comte points here – with an elegance that is rare in his later, more convoluted writings – to a problematic that still remains at the heart of modern social theory: the historical dialectic of (dynamic, socio-historical) structure – 'the course of civilization' – and (individual, social) agency – troublemakers. If this theoretical statement were to be translated into policy advice for 'the kings', the advice would be that locking up any number of troublemakers will not solve their problem: you cannot lock up the course of history.

Comte explains that no one can turn back the clock: to undo the Revolution, one would need to undo eighteenth-century philosophy; to do that, one would need to undo the Reformation of the sixteenth century; to do that, one would need to undo 'the progress of the sciences of observation introduced into Europe by the Arabs' in the eleventh and twelfth centuries. Furthermore, one would need to reintroduce serfdom because 'the enfranchisement of the communes [around the same time] was the first and general cause of the decay of the feudal system' (52). Even if some unimaginably powerful reactionaries were able to turn the clock back on all this, they would gain nothing, because they still 'should not have extinguished the principle of progressive civilization, inherent in the nature of the human race'. For Comte, this 'principle' is really the locomotive of history.

In his analysis of history, Comte shows here an acute sense of historical irony: 'the kings' who thought of themselves as defenders of the old regime, even when they reformed and reconstructed it, promoted the advancement of the arts and the sciences, presumably in the service of their old regime. But 'it is to the progress of the sciences, the arts and industry that the decay of the old system is to be traced' (52). The old regime, by trying to modernize and thereby save itself, created the conditions of its own downfall. This 'radical incoherence' demonstrates for Comte the absurdity of any attempt to bring back the old regime.

3 The peoples' plans for the reorganization of society

While 'the kings' react to the crisis incoherently and absurdly, in effect only temporarily slowing down the course of civilization, Comte writes that 'the peoples' are equally wrong in their reaction. On the positive side, Comte points out that at least they accept the fact that civilization leads them to a new system. They are not able to see what it is, though, and in their blindness they become just another obstacle to progress. Comte asserts that 'uprooting' the obstacle created by 'the peoples' is even much more important than sorting out 'the kings' (54).

At this point it is necessary once more to stop and reflect on the (for twenty-first-century readers) somewhat puzzling meaning of one of Comte's key words here: *peoples*. As he uses it in the plural, Comte's term 'the peoples' has something of the meaning of the then emergent concept of 'peoples' as 'nations'. However, Comte uses it in opposition to the aristocracy and 'the kings': he seems to think of 'the people', in the sense of 'the commoners', in all 'civilized' nations (read: in Europe) as being somehow the principal collective agent of social change in the period of crisis. 'The peoples' are the main carriers of the progress of civilization. (Comte sometimes also uses the terms 'the ruled' and 'the rulers', e.g. 60.)

Comte is not one to flatter his main agent of history, however. His judgement of 'the peoples' is almost as harsh as that of the kings: their thinking on the reorganization of society

has as its distinctive characteristic a profound ignorance of the fundamental conditions which any social system must fulfil in order to
have true solidity. It amounts to presenting as organic principles the
critical principles which have served to destroy the feudal and theological system. (54)

It is important to note that Comte changes gear here from a discussion of specific, European history to an assertion of general, sociological laws: he claims that 'any social system' must fulfil certain
'fundamental conditions', and positive science will tell us what they
are.

'The peoples' mistake the negative power of critique, which has
a rightful place only temporarily in the context of demolishing an
old system, with the positive power required for building a new one.
They have turned critique into a doctrine, a kind of anarchism the
main elements of which Comte identifies as hostility to government,
exaggerated individualism and the notion of the sovereignty of the
people. The critical doctrine divests government 'of any principle
of activity' and reduces it 'to a wholly negative role' (54):

Government is no longer conceived as the head of society, destined
to bind together all individual activities and direct them towards a
common goal. It is represented as a natural enemy, encamped in the
midst of the social system, against which society must fortify itself
by the guarantees it has won, keeping itself in a permanent state of
defiance and defensive hostility which is ready to explode at the first
sign of attack.

Relatedly, 'the dogma of unlimited freedom of conscience' initially
was but the expression of the decline of theological beliefs (55). It
was 'in line with the progress of the human mind' only in the specific context of the struggle against the theological system. Since
that struggle has been won, this 'dogma' has become an obstacle to
the reorganization of society, as it prevents 'the uniform establishment of any system of general ideas' without which 'there can be
no society'.

Comte argues that 'whatever level of education the mass of men
may reach, it is evident that most of the general ideas destined to
become commonplace will only be able to find acceptance on trust,
and not by means of proof'. Let us unpack this statement: there are

'general ideas' that are 'destined to become commonplace', and only a few people in society (scholars and specialists) will ever be able to work out which ones they are. Everyone else has to take them on trust. Freedom of conscience is applicable therefore 'only to ideas which are to disappear' and have 'become matters of indifference', such as theological ideas in a period when theology is no longer the predominant way of thinking about society and the world. Comte's argument on the freedom of conscience is, on the one hand, surprisingly anti-liberal, as he rejects the concept of such freedom; on the other hand, it contains an important sociological observation: the critique of a ruling ideology only emerges at the point when that ideology is already on the decline. Critique hastens rather than causes this decline.

Comte backs up his rejection of freedom of conscience with an analogy: there is no such freedom in astronomy, physics, chemistry or physiology either, where it would be 'absurd not to take on trust the principles established in these sciences by competent men' (56), and it should be no different in politics. It is important to note here that the concept of science employed by Comte differs from the twentieth-century idea of science as a realm in which everybody, no matter who they are, is allowed and in fact encouraged to test and question anything: our contemporary concept of science is much closer to what Comte dismissively calls 'the critical tendency'. It is good to keep this in mind: Comte as the classic advocate of 'scientific' social theory has a concept of science that itself would not really stand up to scientific scrutiny.

In a similar vein, Comte argues that 'the dogma of the sovereignty of the people' was created only to combat the principle of divine right, 'the general political basis of the old system'. With the defeat of feudalism, this dogma has also reached 'the natural end of its career' and needs replacing. Comte adds that the critical doctrines are in fact rather similar to the ones they helped to defeat: freedom of conscience simply means the substitution of individual infallibility for papal infallibility, whereas the arbitrary will of kings is substituted by the arbitrary will of peoples, which by implication means that of individuals. This aspect of Comte's argument contains important food for thought: 'freedom of conscience' and the 'sovereignty of the people' can in fact be used to defend irrational principles – religion, the nation – against rationalist critique, as later versions of the (self-)critique of the Enlightenment would come to assert. Then again, there is an interesting, and arguably anti-emancipatory, class aspect to his argument when Comte states that the critical doctrine has been 'leading us to confer power on the least civilized classes', 'investing the least enlightened men with absolute control over the system of general ideas determined by superior minds to serve as a guide for society' (56–57). Comte concludes that the critical doctrine is 'absolutely inapplicable to the reorganization of society', as 'weapons of war cannot … suddenly become building instruments' (57). Critique and reorganization are entirely different projects.

4 Both misconceptions are complementary and must be replaced by the organic doctrine

Both misconceptions, that of the kings and that of the peoples, are 'equally pernicious'. They would have disappeared by now, how-ever, were they not constantly reinvigorating each other – by threat-ening each other (58). The only escape route out of this deadlock is 'the formation and general adoption, by peoples and by kings, of the organic doctrine' which 'will lead society as a whole on the road to the new system' (59). In a characteristic move, Comte claims both the necessity and the timeliness, or feasibility, of the class-transcending organic project: 'the moment has at last arrived'. What defines this moment is a political event, the French Revolution some thirty years prior to when Comte was writing, which 'by the implementation of critical ideas deprived them of their chief influ-ence' (60): having destroyed the feudal order, the critical tendency has exhausted itself so that 'there is no longer any true critical pas-sion among the peoples', nor any true reactionary passion among the kings. Comte observes that the intellectual fashion of the day is 'a sort of hybrid opinion' that mixes reactionary and critical ideas. Comte refers here to the 'eclecticism' of the liberal philosopher Victor Cousin (1792–1867). Liberalism as a political-intellectual tradition emerged in the same socio-historical context and milieu as positivism, and shared with the latter the intention of preserving the achievements of the Revolution while ending the revolutionary period. Comte dismisses the liberal theory as incoherent and proposes positivism as a more powerful alternative.

General exposé
5 The slowness of social and intellectual change

Comte begins the main section of the text with the sarcastic remark that 'in a space of thirty years we produced ten constitutions, each in its turn proclaimed to be eternal and irrevocable' (63). The fact that these constitutions were not so eternal shows Comte that the human mind moves in slow and gradual transitions rather than at one fell swoop. Comte suggests an analogy between politics and physical astronomy: 'after Newton had discovered the law of universal gravitation', it took almost a century until all the parts of the science of physical astronomy had been coordinated into a system 'compatible with that law' (64). The process begins with the proposition of a general principle and proceeds through the reconstitution of all aspects of the science. Likewise, feudalism took its definitive form only in the eleventh century, 'more than five centuries after the general triumph of the Christian doctrine in western Europe'. Comte seems optimistic, on the one hand, that creating the organic doctrine and the society of the future will take much less time than that, as it is much simpler and more 'natural' than feudalism, but states that, on the other hand, 'as the course of society is necessarily always essentially the same, depending as it does on the permanent nature of the human constitution' (65), one cannot rush these things.

6 Fundamental change cannot be brought about without acknowledging the distinction between theoretical and practical works, their equal importance and the antecedence of theory

One key point of Comte's text is a plea on behalf of the importance of social theory and the demand for its strict separation from the more practical concern with political institutions:

> The formation of any sort of plan of social organization is necessarily composed of two series of operations, totally distinct in their object,

as well as in the kind of capacity they demand. One, theoretical or spiritual, has as its goal the development of the seminal idea of the plan, that is of the new principle according to which social relations must be co-ordinated, and the formation of the system of general ideas intended to serve as a guide for society. The other, practical or temporal, determines the mode of distribution of power and the system of administrative institutions which are in closest conformity with the spirit of the system as settled by the theoretical operations. (65)

First we need the big idea, and then we fill in the details. The theoretical work is 'the soul, the most important and the most difficult part, even though only preliminary' (66). Up to now in the critical period, or crisis, people have failed to develop the big idea and have instead attempted unsuccessfully to reorganize society by piecemeal reform. As a result, they 'have remained enclosed in the old system'. This could not have been otherwise because 'any system of society has as its final object to direct all individual powers towards a general goal' of activity – indeed, 'society only exists where a general and combined action is exerted'. (You can easily recognize here the source of Durkheim's concept of society.) Comte suggests that from this definition of 'society' it follows that its reorganization must begin by redirecting its general goal-orientation, and proceeds to argue that 'there are only two possible goals of activity for a society', just as for an individual, and that 'these are conquest, or violent action on the rest of the human race, and production, or action on nature to modify it to the advantage of man' (66–67). In between there can only be 'hybrid association[s] devoid of character'. The first, 'the military goal was that of the old system', while the second, 'the industrial goal is that of the new' (67). Comte proposes here a dichotomy of two, as it were, ideal-typical forms of society, with a transitory, unstable, hybrid form in between. The new society is prevented from being born properly by its failure to pronounce confidently what its essential principle is – *industry* – and to reorganize itself uniformly and consistently according to that principle.

Post-revolutionary society has so far failed to exit the period of critique and crisis because it has obsessively preoccupied itself with the reform of superficial details of political form, such as the constitutional division of powers, neglecting the reform of the spirit that would fill and animate these forms. 'Spirit' means roughly what we would call culture – so this is a sociological critique of politics as divorced from society and culture. Comte writes that society was led thereby to 'this monstrosity of a constitution without spiritual power' (67) – an early critique of modern liberal constitutionalism as soulless and 'merely' formal that still today informs discussions of citizenship, nationalism, 'constitutional patriotism', belonging and so on.

Comte spends several more pages hammering home his point that theory must precede praxis: 'there is never action without preliminary speculation' (69), and those who think they refuse theory in fact merely perpetuate 'superannuated theories', albeit without knowing it. One of his examples sounds particularly contemporary: 'those who proudly affect not to believe in medicine ordinarily hand themselves over with an eager stupidity to the crudest charlatanism'. Then Comte turns to celebrating the separation of theory from practice, arguing that it increased in tandem with 'the development of the collective and individual intelligence of the human race' to the effect that one can measure 'the degree of civilization of a people by how far the division of theory and practice is pushed, together with the degree of harmony that exists between them' (69–70). The European Middle Ages count for Comte as a particularly striking example at the macro level: theoretical, spiritual power was distinct from and independent of temporal, practical power, but they were in harmony. Their distinction-in-harmony was, to Comte's mind, the source of this period's splendour (70). This is the paradigmatic case of an organic period. Modernity must strive towards a similarly organic type of organization. Comte suggests that the full development of feudalism in the eleventh century was preceded and facilitated by the development of Christian theology in the centuries before, and that likewise in the present the development of the positive doctrine must precede and facilitate the emergence of positive society. As in the past 'spiritual anarchy preceded and engendered temporal anarchy', so now, likewise, the task of reorganizing spiritual power is more urgent and timely than that of temporal power: 'nothing essential and durable can be done for the practical part, until the theoretical part is established or, at least, very advanced' (72).

7 Scientists are best qualified to develop the organic theory and they alone have the authority to secure its acceptance

In the critical period, metaphysicians developed ideas and 'legists' – that is, lawyers and related professions – implemented them (73). In the organic period, legists will still make a 'potent' if 'subordinate … contribution to the adoption of the organic doctrine', whereas reasoning will be done by scientists:

> It is clear that men who make a living out of methodically forming logical theoretical combinations, that is the scientists engaged in the study of the sciences of observation, are the only ones whose type of ability and intellectual culture satisfies the necessary conditions. (75)

Comte adds here an interesting footnote, in which he qualifies and almost reverses this endorsement of scientists: he writes that most scientists 'are too absorbed by their particular occupations' and affected 'by certain pernicious intellectual habits which today result from this specialization' to play 'a truly active role in the establishment of political science' (75). The 'essential role in the formation of the new social doctrine' is therefore reserved for those few scientists 'who, without devoting their lives to the special cultivation of any science of observation, possess an aptitude for science, and have made a sufficiently close study of the general shape of positive knowledge to be penetrated by its spirit'. If we look here at, quite literally, the small print of Comte's argument, we see that the positivist spirit of the new society is not to be developed by *actual* scientists (in the sense of what we would now call the hard sciences) but by *meta-scientists*, as it were, that is, people who know a lot *about* the sciences – not coincidentally, people like Comte himself and subsequent practitioners of the discipline that Comte some twenty years later will call 'sociology'. This is interesting: the same Comte who, in the main text above the footnotes, invites 'the scientists' as a group to direct the spirit of the new society, expresses in a footnote on the same page the kind of disdain for specialists and their tunnel vision, scientific or otherwise, that was developed by many if not most social theorists in the nearly two centuries that followed, the present time included.

Contrary arguments in the footnotes notwithstanding, Comte

continues (upstairs in the main text) that 'in the system to be constituted, spiritual power will be in the hands of the scientists', whereas
'temporal power will belong to the heads of industrial works' (76),
who mostly take over from 'the legists': this brave new world is for
machers not *schmoozers*. Comte's plan is that 'the scientists' will go
ahead working out the theoretical framework of the new society,
while 'the most important industrialists' will 'organize the administrative system according to the bases laid down' by the scientists
(76).

This division and order of proceeding is 'indicated by the nature
of things'. Comte adds another argument, though, that tells us
something about the context in which he operated. He writes that
'the critical doctrine has produced in the majority of minds the
habit of setting oneself up as supreme judge of general political
ideas', and that 'this anarchic state of the intellect is an obvious
obstacle to the reorganization of society' (76). The 'true organic
doctrine' that will be able to 'terminate the present crisis' can
therefore only be developed by a group in contemporary society that enjoys 'uncontested authority in matters of theory', and
Comte suggests that 'the scientists' are the only such group (77).
Only they can defeat 'the critical prejudice that conceives moral
sovereignty as an innate right in each individual'. Because society
has already developed the habit of 'submitting itself to the decisions of scientists for all particular theoretical ideas', the scientists
will be able to extend this habit also to general theoretical ideas.
In other words, positive society, based on the authority of science
that overcomes anarchic individualism, is already a reality at the
micro level and merely needs to be expanded to the macro level
of society.

8 Only scientists committed to the organic doctrine can create a unified general society in Europe and overcome patriotism

Comte adds another rather remarkable aspect of his plan: 'a
European crisis needs European treatment', although 'all the peoples of western Europe' treat it 'as if it were simply national' (77).
This misconception and the national separation that it reflects are
recognized by Comte as modern phenomena:

This isolation of the peoples is a necessary consequence of the fall
of the theological and feudal system, a process which dissolved the
spiritual bonds which that system had established among the peoples
of Europe and which ... [t]he critical doctrine is incapable of re-
establishing. (77)

Intellectual anarchy, as Comte sees it, cannot produce social and
political unity, least of all at a supra-national level. Only the 'organic
doctrine' can 'produce this union, so imperiously demanded by the
state of European civilisation' (78). The new European union, based
on positivism, 'will be more perfect than that produced by the old
system' because the union of the Middle Ages 'existed only in the
spiritual domain' – in the form of Christianity – whereas today 'it
must equally come about in the temporal domain'. Careful reading reveals here again the slippage typical of Comte's argument:
civilization *demands* union, only positivism *can* deliver it (because
Christianity cannot any more), and thus it *will* deliver it. The possibility that civilization's demand for a European union might go
unheeded, and that things might go pear-shaped, is not contained in
the script: Europe's 'peoples are called upon to form a true general
society, complete and permanent' (78). If this sounds familiar, that's
because it is: current discussions around the 'deepening' or perhaps the disintegration of the European Union still revolve around
exactly the kind of problems described by Comte nearly 200 years
ago.

Each people, due to 'the particular variation of its state of civilisation', will take care of a particular functional part of the overall
system, so that all will benefit from cooperation. Here Comte echoes
ideas taken from the discipline of classical political economy: all
countries within an integrated economic system benefit from all
others if all produce what they are best at producing, reflecting
particular conditions. So far, this is all within the framework of
discussions of the time. Comte's very specific contribution is his
argument that there is only one force in Europe that can bring about
this project:

scientists alone form a true coalition, compact and active, all of whose
members understand each other and correspond easily and continuously, from one end of Europe to the other. They alone today have

> ideas in common, a uniform language, a general and permanent goal
> for their activity. (78)

Although most readers will probably feel that Comte overstates his case here, there is undeniably an element of valid sociological observation in his remarks on the communication and associational habits of scientists. The only other group 'pre-eminently directed towards union by the nature of their work and by their habits' are industrialists, whose profession it is to make other people work together. Even they, however, are unable to promote macro-level 'combination' because they 'still allow themselves to be too dominated by the hostile moods of a savage patriotism' (78). It is quite remarkable – and true – that Comte suggests that scientists can be expected to be less inclined to 'savage patriotism' than industrialists (the global character of capitalism notwithstanding), concluding that the scientists should therefore direct the industrialists. Comte is here at his anti-nationalistic best. His positivism reveals itself as a surprisingly naive form of idealism, however, as he seems content to derive the pre-eminence of the scientists from what he proposes is a 'law of civilization': theory precedes practice – that's just the way it is, always. The assumption of this alleged law prevents Comte from thinking about *how* and on what practical grounds the scientists and their organic theory could *become* the dominant force that would release Europe from the crisis. The flaw in Comte's reasoning becomes apparent from looking closely at how he formulates his thoughts, such as in the following sequence:

> It is without doubt superfluous to demonstrate that the current contacts between scientists will acquire a much increased intensity when they direct their general forces towards the formation of the new social doctrine. This consequence is obvious, since the force of a social bond is necessarily in proportion to the importance of the goal of the association. (78–79)

Comte formulates here another (assumed) law: the *force* of a social bond depends on its *goal*, so that – without doubt, obviously, necessarily – the ability of the scientists to be the force that creates the new society will increase as soon as they decide to take on the project of doing so. This is what logicians call a *non-sequitur* – it just does not follow. In compensation, however, I can offer here one iron law that has been proven beyond reasonable doubt: any sentence that starts with the words 'It is without doubt superfluous to demonstrate that...' should be doubted very strongly indeed.

The logic of Comte's argument is basically that 'the peoples' need a unifying force to defeat 'the kings' (who enjoy the advantage of being internationally organized anyway), and 'the scientists' are the only plausible force that can do this. The peoples *by necessity* will therefore elect the scientists as their spiritual, intellectual and moral leaders, and they will therewith become the carriers of the organic doctrine (79). This way they will form a 'spiritual coalition' that cannot but defeat the 'purely temporal coalition' formed by the kings (80): the spiritual always has the edge over the merely temporal (another of Comte's laws), and the organic coalition has its sails to the wind of the history of human civilization. Comte's theory is as positive as it is optimistic. Unfortunately, we might say with the benefit of hindsight, it is a bit too optimistic.

9 The three different theoretical states of human knowledge culminate in the positive doctrine

Comte sums up at this point what he thinks follows from his argument so far: '*the scientists must today raise politics to the rank of the sciences of observation*' (81; italics in the original). Adopting this doctrine permits 'the acceleration of the progress of thought' (81): theory is what we need, and we need it now. Because the production of theory takes such a central place in Comte's thinking, he moves now to a reflection on how thinking works, probably the best-known aspect of his work:

> By the very nature of the human mind each branch of our knowledge is necessarily liable in its course to pass in its turn through three different theoretical states: the theological or fictional state; the metaphysical or abstract state; the scientific or positive state. (81)

This is the famous 'law of the three states'. In English, the word 'stages' is sometimes used instead of 'states', which is unfortunate as it reduces the ambivalence of the word used by Comte, *états*: 'states' can be thought of as consecutive in time, like the word 'stages', but also as simultaneous, and both these meanings are clearly present in Comte's argument. The concept of the 'theological state' seems to cover everything from the early periods of human civilization to the Christian Middle Ages, and it is quite remarkable, setting a precedent for what later would become cultural anthropology, with what kind of detached friendliness Comte writes about these. He writes that in the 'theological or fictional state', 'supernatural ideas served to link the small number of isolated ideas which then constituted science': 'observed facts are explained in the light of invented facts'. In other words, Comte regards what anthropology would later discuss as mythology as an early form of science, and indeed argues that this state is 'necessarily that of any science at its cradle. However imperfect it may be, it is at that time the only way of connecting facts', that is, the only way of reasoning. By implication, the beginnings of a new science in the present would also have to show such characteristics.

The 'metaphysical or abstract state' is of a merely transitional nature and reflects a situation in which facts have 'become more numerous' (82). Reasoning takes place by way of drawing together these more numerous facts in the light of ideas which are no longer wholly supernatural but not yet 'positive' or fully scientific either. Comte writes that ideas are in this context personified abstractions *from* facts, whereas in the positive state ideas are themselves (very general) facts, not mere abstractions *from* facts. An abstract, metaphysical idea – Comte seems to be thinking of concepts like justice, for example – can be understood either as 'the mystical name of a supernatural cause or the abstract enunciation of a simple series of phenomena' (81), which means it partakes in both the theological and the positive modes of the human mind. This ambiguity makes them, for Comte, 'illegitimate'.

In the 'scientific or positive state' ideas or general laws are 'suggested or confirmed by the facts themselves' (82). They are treated as hypotheses that will be verified one day by observation, or falsified. Whereas in the metaphysical state, an idea or concept (justice, say) is imagined as having a reality of its own (or even agency: we say that 'justice rules', or demands something, etc.), in the positive state ideas are nothing more than 'means of general expression for phenomena'. Comte claims, of course, that his 'law of the three states' is such a positive idea: he has discovered it by way of observation, that is, by studying the history of the sciences, including astrology, physics, chemistry and physiology. He makes here some very interesting comments on what we would now refer to as psychology (considered then a part of physiology): in this particular science that was in the process of emerging at the time, all three 'states' of the mind coexist, to the effect that some of its practitioners think of psychological phenomena as somehow supernatural (theological state), some as 'the incomprehensible effects of the activity of an abstract being' (metaphysical state) or, finally, some as 'stemming from organic conditions susceptible to demonstration' (positive state). Arguably, this description still holds true in the twenty-first century: the three states of the mind coexist in how most people think about the soul or psyche.

In the case of 'politics as a science', Comte writes that 'the doctrine of kings represents the theological state' (the discourse of divine right, etc.), and the doctrine of the peoples the metaphysical one (social contract, sovereignty, natural right, human right), whereas 'the scientific doctrine' is now itching to be fully developed as an empirical science (82–83). It takes as its starting point 'the rung which man occupies in the system of nature' (83). This 'rung', or the position of humans within nature, i.e., humanity's relationship to the rest of nature, determines 'the constant tendency of man to act on nature, to modify it to his advantage', and considers 'the social order as having as its final object to develop collectively this natural tendency, to regularize it and to channel it so that the amount of useful action can be maximized'. This is what civilization is all about. Comte claims that this conception of the fundamental laws of human organization is derived from 'direct observation of the collective development of the species' and is thus positive, not metaphysical. The theory is entirely derived from empirical study of history, apparently innocent of any theoretical preconceptions – as having such preconceptions would be metaphysical.

10 Why the moral revolution that is now needed has not been possible in the past

On the last pages of the 'General exposé', Comte returns to the question of the timeliness of the positive doctrine, which underlines how important timeliness is to that doctrine itself: intriguingly, Comte undertakes here an effort to explain the emergence of his theory in terms of that theory itself. Its concluding comments are particularly interesting because they seem to contradict some of the more idealistic formulations found earlier in the text. Comte writes that

> the theory could not have been established until [now] because it would have been too far ahead of practice ... it could not have had an adequate experimental basis any sooner. A system of social order had to be established, accepted by a numerous population and composed of several large nations; and this system had to have lasted for an extended period so that a theory could be founded on this vast experience. (84)

Comte's earlier insistence on the priority of theory over practice is here reversed: he suggests now, much more plausibly, that theory must be based on an established societal practice and can only be slightly 'ahead of' that practice. Judging the text as a whole, Comte seems more or less aware of, but struggling with, what later social theorists would describe as the dialectical relationship of theory and practice.

This statement is followed immediately by Comte's next claim that 'the theological system, destined to prepare the human mind for the scientific system, has reached the end of its career' (84): the critical-metaphysical system has undeniably destroyed the theological system. It is worth noting that Comte suggests here this did not happen just by accident – it was destiny! Hidden in the harmless little word 'destined' is the notion that the course of human history was somehow written into its DNA from the word go. This is an idea most people would probably call metaphysical, if not theological... Comte concludes that 'scientific politics must therefore be founded' most urgently (85): society cannot do without a theory, but 'metaphysical politics' are only good for a transitional, negative period, so one has to fear that 'theological politics could be reconstituted' if positive politics are not developed right now.

> In summary, there has therefore never been a moral revolution at once more inevitable, more mature and more urgent than that which is now to elevate politics to the rank of the sciences of observation in the

hands of the combined scientists of Europe. This revolution alone can introduce into the great current crisis a truly dominant force, which is alone capable of regulating and preserving society from the terrible and anarchical explosions with which it is threatened, by placing it on the true path to an improved social system, which the state of its knowledge imperiously demands. (85)

The fundamental ambiguity of Comte's theory is encapsulated here in the word 'must': the new doctrine 'must therefore be founded' means, on the one hand, *we really need to get our act together because the situation is dangerous, and it could get even worse!*, but also, on the other hand, *there is an inner logic to this crisis that will inevitably result in the positive system.* This second meaning of the word 'must' undermines the first one: if the outcome is already predestined, why do we have to struggle so hard? The formula that the revolution is 'inevitable', 'mature' as well as 'urgent' is in this sense rather contradictory.

Perhaps this could be part of the explanation of its tremendous success as a theory: the impact of social theories does not necessarily come from their truth-content and consistency, but from how well they give expression to contradictions and ambiguities that are characteristic of a societal reality. Here is STOETZLER'S IRON IMPACT LAW OF SOCIOLOGICAL THEORY: the more ambiguous the theory and the more it allows itself to be interpreted in completely contradictory ways, the bigger its impact chances.

3
If you can't beat democracy, join it: Alexis de Tocqueville

Alexis de Tocqueville (1805–59) was a lawyer turned politician and writer from an aristocratic and ultra-royalist family who held, in sharp distinction from his family, a moderately liberal outlook. Although not at all a friend of the Revolution, he found the attempt of the Bourbon monarchy, after the defeat of Napoleon in 1814/15, to restore the 'old regime' a mission impossible. Things would never again be the way they had been, so he argued that it was much preferable to try and make the best of the new type of society that had resulted from the Revolution.

Still at an early stage of his career as a lawyer, Tocqueville managed in 1831 to be commissioned by the French government for a nine-month research trip to the USA. This was under the government of the 'bourgeois king' Louis Philippe, whose comparatively liberal, constitutional regime had resulted from the revolution of 1830 that ended the restoration period. The official purpose of the trip was to examine the American prison system with a view to reforming the French one, which had a reputation of breeding rather than reducing criminality. Tocqueville and his friend and collaborator, Gustave de Beaumont (1802–66), also a liberal, a lawyer and from aristocratic background, together travelled 7,000 miles in the USA and Canada and conducted hundreds of interviews, not only on prisons. Theirs was a packed itinerary, taking in the North East, Canada, the Great Lakes region, the Midwest – which at the time was the Western frontier – and the South all the way to New Orleans. Apart from interviewing experts, they compiled and studied large amounts of documents and literature. As a result of the trip, Tocqueville and

Beaumont co-authored an influential report on the American prison system and penal reform, published in 1833, and another book on America each: Beaumont wrote a social-critical novel dealing with slavery in the USA, published in 1835, and Tocqueville wrote the two volumes of *Democracy in America* of 1835 and 1840.

Both Tocqueville and Beaumont advocated prison reform and the abolition of slavery. They are also notable for having written some of the classic liberal critiques of colonialism, including a book by Beaumont of 1839 on Ireland. Beaumont there combined a scathing critique of British brutality and exploitation with a belief that the British political system also provided the tools to solve the very problem that British imperial rule created. This position was characteristic of the form of Anglophile French liberalism that both Tocqueville and Beaumont represented. Tocqueville authored several pieces on the colonization of Algeria which was underway at the time and also a book on Ireland, all based on visits to these countries, and taking a similar position: he spoke out against colonialism's murderous brutality but advocated a more gentle form of colonialism as an aspect of the spreading of liberal civilization and societal modernization. Tocqueville also published a book based on a trip to England in 1833. In this book he described the striking fact that the richest country in Europe had the greatest number of paupers, and then argued that this pauperism was created by public charity which subsidized low wages and idleness. Many of these themes of classical liberal discourse should sound remarkably familiar to contemporary readers.

Democracy in America was the book that made Tocqueville instantly famous. He became a politician soon after, but seems to have had a tendency to make enemies both on the right and the left – as befitting a proper liberal, perhaps, but unhelpful in the harsh world of politics. After the 1848 February Revolution, he was elected to the Constituent Assembly and was involved in drafting the constitution of the Second Republic, as well as in the crushing of the radical-democratic and socialist Paris insurrection of June 1848. He was a key figure in the defence of the ill-fated republican bourgeois regime, although he had never advocated the revolution that brought it about. The liberal republic defeated its proletarian opposition in Paris so thoroughly in June 1848 that it subsequently found itself at the mercy of the right-wing reaction that had its popular base in the country. Tocqueville became a member of the Legislative Assembly and briefly even Minister of Foreign Affairs, but resigned after the December 1851 *coup d'état* by Louis-Napoléon Bonaparte. Bonaparte, the nephew of Napoleon I, proclaimed himself Emperor Napoléon III a year later. Tocqueville rejected Bonaparte's regime, which developed into the paradigmatic case of industrial-capitalist modernization under an

---

Structure of the selected text

Introduction to book 1 (3–15):
1 The gist of the book (3)
2 A potted history of democracy (3–6)
3 The need for a new political science of society follows from the historical situation (6–8)
4 A quick look back on how good we had it in the Middle Ages (8)
5 The mess we are in now and the golden age that may lie ahead (8–10)
6 Ideas, sentiments and actions are now out of alignment (10–12)
7 In the United States one can study pure, undistorted democracy to prepare for the future (12–15)
The concluding three chapters of book 2 (661–676)
8 What kind of despotism do democratic nations have to fear? (661–665)
9 Continuation of the preceding chapters (666–668)
10 The individual and the press (668)
11 The importance of the judiciary and of forms (668–671)
12 Conclusion of this section (671–673)
13 General view of the subject (673–676)

Tocqueville, Alexis de. 2002 [1835, 1840]. *Democracy in America*. Translated, edited and with an introduction by Harvey C. Mansfield and Delba Winthrop. Chicago: University of Chicago Press.

---

authoritarian, anti-liberal political regime; today we still refer to
some dictatorial and fascist regimes of the twentieth century as
'Bonapartist'. Tocqueville went back to research and writing. His
Recollections from the 1848–49 revolutionary period were published
only posthumously, but in 1856 he published the second major work
he is mostly remembered for, *The Old Regime and the Revolution*.
This book revisits some of the themes of *Democracy in America*
and takes a similarly sociological perspective that is also reminiscent of Comte's interpretation of the 1789 French Revolution: the
political event 'The Revolution' is interpreted in the perspective of
the larger-scale revolution that consists in the societal changes that
Tocqueville associates with the concept of democracy.

In two respects Alexis de Tocqueville was a great writer: first,
his writing is enjoyable in a way that the more academic varieties of sociological writing often are not; this is especially true of
Democracy in America, which is as much a travel report by someone
who knew how to meet (and how to interview) numerous people
while travelling, as the product of extensive reading. Second, in his
writings something happens that – if one is lucky – can result from
the serious study of ideas and confronting them with their reality:
the text transcends, re-educates, perhaps refashions, its author, and
enriches itself with interesting contradictions. An aristocrat with
liberal leanings sets out to study something that puzzled him –
democracy – and ends up, affected by the inner logic of its object,
almost a democrat. Some journey!

Introduction to book 1
1 The gist of the book

In the first two sentences of *Democracy in America* Tocqueville gives
a masterful example of how one can set out the contents of a book
in its first paragraph:

> Among the new objects that attracted my attention during my stay in
> the United States, none struck my eye more vividly than the equality
> of conditions. I discovered without difficulty the enormous influence
> that this primary fact exerts on the course of society; it gives a certain
> direction to public spirit, a certain turn to the laws, new maxims to
> those who govern, and particular habits to the governed. (3)

Tocqueville announces as the subject matter of his book a 'new object', a 'primary fact' (fact as in 'social fact'), namely 'the equality of conditions', and how this 'primary fact' affects 'the course' (we would probably say the development, evolution or dynamics) of society. Tocqueville names four areas of society that are affected by the social fact of equality: 'public spirit' (we would say 'culture' for 'spirit'), the laws, 'maxims', i.e. rules and strategies, of government, and 'habits' developed by those who are being governed, i.e. the societal and interpersonal practices of everyday life. Tocqueville writes that he came to see in 'equality of conditions the generative fact from which each particular fact seemed to issue': a social fact that produces other social facts.

Tocqueville then describes something that is true of many travel reports (and in a way also applies to many travellers who don't write reports): writing about America was really a way of writing about something that had bothered him *at home*, and to examine which he had undertaken the journey in the first place. Although in Europe, 'equality of conditions' had not yet reached 'its extreme limits as it had in the United States', it was getting there, 'and the same democracy reigning in American societies appeared to me to be advancing rapidly toward power in Europe' (3). Tocqueville slips in, almost by the by, a highly original definition of the term 'democracy' as 'equality of conditions': a broad sociological rather than a political definition that would more narrowly refer only to a form of government. 'A great democratic revolution is taking place among us' that is still ill understood by his contemporaries.

2 A potted history of democracy

From this exposition of his project, Tocqueville moves to a short potted history of the progress of democracy in France since the twelfth century. An initial situation in which power resulted solely from either force or landed property was first challenged by the institution of the clergy: the history of equality begins when the clergy 'open its ranks to all, to the poor and to the rich', to the effect that 'he who would have vegetated as a serf in eternal slavery takes his place as a priest in the midst of nobles, and will often take a seat above Kings' (4). Society becomes in time more civilized, stable and complex, which leads to the need for civil law and the emergence of jurists. Alongside the priests, they form another group that challenges the aristocracy's erstwhile monopoly of power. A third group emerges from the fact that 'the Kings ruin themselves in great undertakings; the nobles exhaust themselves in private wars; the commoners enrich themselves in commerce', which means that the latter have money which they can lend to the former who need it. Next, 'enlightenment spreads', and 'the mind becomes an element in success; science is a means of government, intelligence a social force' (4), so that those with intelligence also enter the competition for power. The value of birth as the route to power is in relative decline. Forms of 'transferable wealth' eroded feudalism and produced power that did not result from feudal tenure; henceforth, any 'discoveries in the arts' ('arts' meaning technology) and 'improvements in commerce and industry' inevitably created 'new elements of equality among men' (5).

Discoveries, new needs, desires, tastes, fashions, passions, superficial or profound, 'seem to work in concert to impoverish the rich and enrich the poor'. Tocqueville suggests here that developments in poetry, eloquence, the arts, philosophy, 'even if they were found in the possession of its adversaries', still served the cause of 'the people' by 'putting into relief the natural greatness of man'. People power therefore spread in tandem with civilization and enlightenment, helped along by institutions such as 'the mail [that] comes to deposit enlightenment on the doorstep of the poor man's hut as at the portal of the palace' (5–6). Tocqueville sums up this enthusiastic, albeit one-sided, narrative by stating that there has been a 700-year social revolution 'in all the Christian universe' that had brought the nobles down and the commoners up, so that 'soon they are going to touch' (6). The progress of democracy has been aided by everybody, as 'all have been driven pell-mell on the same track, and all have worked in common, some despite themselves, others without knowing it, as blind instruments in the hands of God'. It is therefore 'a providential fact, and it has the principal characteristics of one: it is universal, it is enduring, each day it escapes human power; all events, like all men, serve its development' (6). Democracy is unstoppable and irreversible.

3 The need for a new political science of society follows from the historical situation

Tocqueville reveals that his book 'was written under the pressure of a sort of religious terror in the author's soul, produced by the sight of this irresistible revolution that for so many centuries has marched over all obstacles' (6). He emphasizes that a 'continuous tendency' in history such as this one can only be God's will, against which one must not struggle (7). However, people have quite rightly not yet given up the wish to *direct* 'the movement that carries them along', and it is in this tension between an objective, 'providential' fact and a wish to direct this fact that Tocqueville hopes to intervene:

> To instruct democracy, if possible to reanimate its beliefs, to purify its mores, to regulate its movements, to substitute little by little the science of affairs for its inexperience, and knowledge of its true interests for its blind instincts; to adapt its government to time and place; to modify it according to circumstances and men: such is the first duty imposed on those who direct society in our day.

A new political science is needed to 'instruct', 'purify' and 'regulate' democracy (7). This new science is one of society and history, but it is to be political in the sense of providing the grounds for devising appropriate policy. This is necessary because no government has prepared for the powerful tendency towards democracy that God in his typically unfathomable manner has unleashed on us:

> The most powerful, most intelligent, and most moral classes of the nation have not sought to take hold of it so as to direct it. Democracy has therefore been abandoned to its savage instincts; it has grown up like those children who, deprived of paternal care, rear themselves in the streets of our towns and know only society's vices and miseries.

Like a negligent father, the class of the great and the good have failed to educate democracy properly and to 'teach it to govern'. Tocqueville makes here an interesting distinction that almost seems to anticipate the Marxian one between 'base and superstructure': 'As a result, the democratic revolution has taken place in the material of society without making the change in laws, ideas, habits, and mores that would have been necessary to make this revolution useful' (7). He does not clearly say what 'the material of society' is, but we can infer that it is society minus 'laws, ideas, habits, and mores'; Tocqueville implies that a mismatch between the former and the latter causes the trouble, and policy informed by the 'new science' needs to address this mismatch.

4 A quick look back on how good we had it in the Middle Ages

As much as this statement embraces modernity, Tocqueville follows it up with an equally anti-modern, romanticized look back on the good old days of the Middle Ages when 'royal power, leaning on the aristocracy, peacefully governed the peoples of Europe', refrained from abusing its power and calmly looked after the flocks. Back then people did not have the idea of 'rights' because they in practice enjoyed quasi-rights established by custom. Tocqueville claims that there were 'inequality and misery in society at that time, but souls were not degraded' (8), and in this context he makes a sociologically interesting observation: 'It is not the use of power or the habit of obedience that depraves men, but the use of power that they consider illegitimate, and obedience to a power they regard as usurped and oppressive' (8). This sentence is well worth dwelling on a bit longer. From its context it is clear that Tocqueville means it both as a normative statement and a statement of fact: social hierarchy in the medieval society that he describes here was a good thing because it was considered legitimate by all involved. That is a value judgement (with which we might well disagree): as long as it was *considered* good, it actually *was* good. At the same time, though, it can also be read as an analytical statement, and as such it is not inaccurate: the historical study of social movements can demonstrate that people start to rebel not when things *are* very bad, but when they *think* things are very bad (even though they are perhaps less bad than at other times).

5 The mess we are in now and the golden age that may lie ahead

In the Middle Ages as imagined by Tocqueville, 'the social body could have stability, power, and above all, glory'; this is very different in the contemporary period:

> But now ranks are confused; the barriers raised among men are low-
> ered; estates are divided, power is partitioned, enlightenment spreads,
> intelligence is equalised; the social state becomes democratic, and
> finally the empire of democracy is peacefully established over institu-
> tions and mores. (8–9)

Tocqueville makes us feel the hectic, unsettling, transitional character of this period even through his use of grammar: a staccato of
short, non-subordinated sentences, urging forward to the grand
resolution offered in the following paragraph:

> I conceive a society, then, which all, regarding the law as their work,
> would love and submit to without trouble; in which the authority
> of government is respected as necessary, not divine, and the love
> one would bear for a head of state would not be a passion, but a rea-
> soned and tranquil sentiment. Each having rights and being assured
> of preserving his rights, a manly confidence and a sort of reciprocal
> condescension between the classes would be established, as far from
> haughtiness as from baseness.
>
> The people, instructed in their true interests, would understand
> that to profit from society's benefits, one must submit to its burdens.
> The free association of citizens could then replace the individual
> power of nobles, and the state would be sheltered from both tyranny
> and licence. (9)

This is as close as one can get to a classically liberal conception of
society in one short paragraph: because all see themselves as the
makers of the law, they don't mind submitting to it; there is love
for state and society, but it is cool, reasoned and well-instructed
rather than passionate; all are confident possessors of rights, and
class structure is stabilized by 'reciprocal condescension', a choice
of words that captures one of the key characteristics of modern
liberal society with sardonic elegance: *we don't like each other, but
harmony is warranted by the fact that we couldn't care less about it.* The
striking term 'free association' that wraps up Tocqueville's vision
was picked up and redeployed by others, most notably Karl Marx,
with different content, and is nowadays a marker of communist and
anarchist theories more than of liberalism.

 In Tocqueville's well-governed version of democracy, 'the social
body' will move in a 'regular and progressive' manner; there will

be less brilliance but also less misery, more vices but fewer crimes. People will understand that they need to cooperate, and that particular interest 'merges with the general interest'. They will be more prosperous, and more peaceful not due to fatalism, but 'because they know how to be well-off' (9).

6 Ideas, sentiments and actions are now out of alignment

After outlining his very liberal utopia, Tocqueville returns to the present poor state of things which evokes 'sadness and ... pity' in him (10). The old society is destroyed, but the new one is not yet in place. The only winner so far is a tyrannical and exploitative government lording it over ignorant, selfish, weak, hateful and insecure people. This post-traditional but not yet modern populace displays rather puzzling confusions: 'it seems that in our day the natural bond that unites opinions to tastes and actions to beliefs has been broken', 'sentiments' and 'ideas' that ought to go together, do not do so any more. ('Tastes' seems to mean here dispositions, or stable habits of acting that are informed by a world-view.) Tocqueville's first example is that of Christianity which in itself he argues favours 'freedom, the source of all moral greatness' (11): 'Christianity, which has rendered all men equal before God, will not be loath to see all citizens equal before the law.' Furthermore, 'the reign of freedom cannot be established without that of mores, nor mores founded without beliefs', and Christianity should therefore be a natural ally of democracy whose efforts it could 'sanctify'. In spite of all this, the 'partisans of freedom' have chosen to perceive 'religion in the ranks of their adversaries': the movement of freedom has somehow dissociated itself from its natural foundation in Christianity, Tocqueville is surprised to find.

Tocqueville continues to give us an extended list of contemporaries with twisted minds:

- 'naturally noble and proud men' who defend slavery;
- advocates of freedom who fail to understand 'what is holy and great in it', i.e., who do not perceive what Tocqueville thinks is the metaphysical or religious (Christian) foundation of the concept of freedom;

- 'virtuous and peaceful men' who sincerely love their country but are 'adversaries of civilization', i.e., of historical progress and the advent of democracy;
- those who advocate progress but strive 'to make man into matter', i.e., materialists and atheists, as a small number of eighteenth-century Enlightenment thinkers had been;
- those who 'want to find the useful without occupying themselves with the just', by which he probably means utilitarian thinkers, but perhaps also Comte who rejected the idea of 'justice' as dangerous metaphysical nonsense;
- those who want 'to find science far from beliefs' (atheists again) and 'well-being separated from virtue' (utilitarians again who argue for virtue only inasmuch as it results in utility).

All these are unworthy of being seen as 'champions of modern civilization' (11). From the standpoint of Tocqueville's cool liberalism, grounded in a rational form of Christianity, this is a topsy-turvy world 'where nothing is linked, where virtue is without genius and genius without honor; where love of order is confused with a taste for tyrants and the holy cult of freedom with contempt for laws' (12).

7 In the United States one can study pure, undistorted democracy to prepare for the future

On the last pages of the introduction, Tocqueville turns now finally to the country that is mentioned in the title of the book: the 'one country in the world' that displays 'the results of the democratic revolution operating among us without having had the revolution itself', and thus without resistances and counter-tendencies (12). Tocqueville describes the founding of America almost in terms of a laboratory experiment:

> The emigrants who came to settle in America at the beginning of the seventeenth century in some fashion disengaged the democratic principle from all those against which it struggled within the old societies of Europe, and they transplanted it alone on the shores of the New World. There it could grow in freedom, and advancing along with mores, develop peacefully in laws. (12)

A social historian of the United States would probably shake her head at this – Tocqueville here hardly describes history 'as it actually happened'. His method could best be described as the construction of a sort of ideal type (to use a term famously used by Max Weber more than half a century later), i.e., a thought-experiment that isolates one aspect of historical reality on the grounds of assuming that it is singularly important: for better or worse, this is why we see Tocqueville as a pioneer of sociology, rather than of history. A critic of Tocqueville's method would object that he writes here about democracy as if it was a thing that could have been cut out of its context, loaded on a boat and shipped to America like the potatoes that were sent back; in reality, however, a social fact like 'democracy' – in Tocqueville's sense of the word, a macro-historical tendency – only exists *in relation to* other social facts: as Tocqueville himself describes rather well, democracy *is* (or was then) the struggle against the hierarchical order of the old regime; one cannot take it away from that context and 'transplant' it elsewhere any more than one can take the donkey's shadow away from the donkey.

Tocqueville believes that in America there is 'almost complete equality of conditions' and that Europe will 'sooner or later' also arrive at such conditions. Importantly, though, he emphasizes that by 'democracy' he does not refer to a form of government: the American one is not 'the only form of government that democracy can give itself'. A study of America is worthwhile, however, because the 'generative cause of laws and mores' is the same in America and Europe (12). Tocqueville is not primarily interested in forms of government and legislation because, he writes, 'there is almost never any absolute good in the laws' (13), by which he means to say that law is always relative to historical and other conditions: his focus is on what he calls the 'generative cause', a kind of *generic and global principle* that generates all specific phenomena including 'laws and mores'. Tocqueville emphasizes his value-neutrality concerning that 'generative cause' itself, the 'social revolution' of democracy: he refuses to judge it; it is simply a social fact, thrown to us by God, to be dealt with 'rendering it profitable to men':

> I confess that in America I saw more than America; I sought there an
> image of democracy itself, of its penchants, its character, its preju-

dices, its passions; I wanted to become acquainted with it if only to know at least what we ought to hope or fear from it. (13)

While there is no point in judging an irreversible social fact, Tocqueville makes clear in this introduction what he thinks is a good form of society: before the age of democracy, the benign, patrimonial order of the Middle Ages had been good, while under conditions of democracy where things are a lot more complex, a modern, liberal class society held together by mutual, cool condescension based on rational embrace of the benefits of universal interdependence is an achievable form of a good society.

The concluding three chapters of book 2
8 What kind of despotism do democratic nations have to fear?

The second volume of *Democracy in America*, first published in 1840, addresses the same principal themes but is generally more analytical and reflective than the first volume of 1835. In its concluding chapters, Tocqueville sums up the ways in which his initial analysis as expressed in the first volume, after five more years of reflection, has shifted.

> During my stay in the United States I had remarked that a democratic social state like that of the Americans could singularly facilitate the establishment of despotism, and I had seen on my return to Europe how most of our princes had already made use of the ideas, sentiments, and needs to which this same social state had given birth to extend the sphere of their power. (661)

This formulation demonstrates clearly how Tocqueville uses the concept of 'democracy' as the name of a 'social state', not a form of government: the despotism that 'democracy' makes possible has in fact not (yet) occurred in the United States, but democratic despotism is in evidence in *European* states where the democratic revolution – a social, not a political revolution – has helped to consolidate princely rule. Tocqueville critiques his own earlier expectation that modern Christian nations could 'come under an oppression similar to that which formerly weighed on several of the peoples of antiquity'. Tocqueville finds now that on second thoughts things are far worse than that, as well as somewhat more benign: the bad news is that in antiquity there was never 'a sovereign so absolute and so powerful' as to 'administer all the parts of a great empire' and to 'subjugate all its subjects without distinction to the details of a uniform rule'. Tocqueville anticipates here elements of what twentieth-century theorists would describe as totalitarian rule. Such an endeavour, even if any ruler had conceived and wished it, would have been impossible in antiquity due to 'the insufficiency of enlightenment, the imperfection of administrative proceedings, and above all the natural obstacles that inequality of conditions gave rise to' (661). Even under the Roman Caesars, 'the details of social life and of individual existence ordinarily escaped' government control.

The *modern* kind of despotism that Tocqueville anticipates is determined, though, by these same three conditions: enlightenment, bureaucracy and democracy – the latter again in the sense of societal equality due to the disappearance of insurmountable class and caste barriers. The (relatively) good news is that this potential despotism would be 'more extensive' but also 'milder, and it would degrade men without tormenting them' (662). No crucifixions, apparently, are to be expected; while sovereigns will find it easier to concentrate power and 'penetrate the sphere of private interests' more regularly and more deeply, 'the same equality that facilitates despotism tempers it'; 'as men are more alike and more equal', there are no great personalities, no powerful groups, no very wealthy individuals who could resist the despot, and 'public mores become more humane and milder' as well. Tocqueville seems to think that hugely concentrated state power will simply find no objects for the tyranny that it will be capable of. It is a condition of the emergence of the modern state that there is no longer any enemy who would be worthy of the modern state's full force: 'tyranny in a way lacks an occasion and a stage'. He concludes: 'Democratic governments can become violent and even cruel at certain moments of great excitement and great peril; but these crises will be rare and transient.' More often than not, government will be by schoolmasters rather than by tyrants. When we look at present-day societies, we may be tempted to concede that Tocqueville had a point.

'I see an innumerable crowd of like and equal men' who 'fill their souls' with 'small and vulgar pleasures' (663). All are 'withdrawn and apart', considering family and friends as their only social world. Democratic man 'no longer has a native country' (663). 'Above these an immense tutelary power is elevated, which alone takes charge of assuring their enjoyments and watching over their fate. It is absolute, detailed, regular, far-seeing, and mild.' It would be wrong to call it 'paternal' as it does not seek to educate 'its objects' but 'to keep them fixed irrevocably in childhood': they are to enjoy themselves, but not have any wider ambitions. Tocqueville is so brilliantly sharp here, it hurts:

> It willingly works for their happiness; but it wants to be the unique agent and sole arbiter of that; it provides for their security, foresees and secures their needs, facilitates their pleasures, conducts their principal affairs, directs their industry, regulates their estates, divides their inheritances; can it not take away from them entirely the trouble of thinking and the pain of living? ... So it is that every day it renders the employment of free will less useful and more rare ... Thus, after taking each individual by turns in its powerful hands and kneading him as it likes, the sovereign extends its arms over society as a whole; it covers its surface with a network of small, complicated, painstaking, uniform rules through which the most original minds and the most vigorous souls cannot clear a way to surpass the crowd; it does not break wills, but it softens them, bends them, and directs them; it rarely forces one to act, but it constantly opposes itself to one's acting; it does not destroy, it prevents things from being born; it does not tyrannize, it hinders, compromises, enervates, extinguishes, dazes, and finally reduces each nation to being nothing more than a herd of timid and industrious animals of which the government is the shepherd. (663)

This 'sort of regulated, mild, and peaceful servitude' can go together well 'with some of the external forms of freedom' (663) as well as 'the sovereignty of the people' (664).

After this rather unflattering portrayal of the modern state, Tocqueville turns to the modern individual in whose conflicted psychology he suggests lies the root of the problem: 'our contemporaries are incessantly racked by two inimical passions: they feel the need to be led and the wish to remain free' (664). The synthesis of 'these contrary instincts' results in political democracy: 'they imagine a unique power, tutelary, all powerful, but elected by citizens'. They 'console themselves for being in tutelage by thinking that they themselves have chosen their schoolmasters'. Tocqueville takes a rather unenthusiastic view of voting – in fact he sounds more like an anarchist than a liberal: 'In this system citizens leave their dependence for a moment to indicate their master, and then re-enter it.' He concludes that 'the freedom of individuals' cannot be guaranteed by delivering it 'to the national power', and emphasizes once more his perspective: 'The nature of the master is much less important to me than the obedience.' Nevertheless, a political system in which the sovereign is 'elected or closely overseen by a really elected and independent legislature' is preferable to despotism, but not because it is less oppressive: Tocqueville asserts that it might even be more oppressive, but 'it is always less degrading' because the powerless individual 'can still fancy that in obeying he submits only to himself'. Tocqueville describes (and welcomes as a kind of lesser evil) in these words what one could call an ideological effect that obscures actual oppression.

He proceeds then to make a characteristic distinction: he argues that under representative government 'one preserves individual intervention in the most important affairs' – such as the election of the government – but suppresses it 'in small and particular ones':

> One forgets that it is above all in details that it is dangerous to enslave men. For my part, I would be brought to believe freedom less necessary in great things than in lesser ones if I thought that one could ever be assured of the one without possessing the other. (664–665)

In other words, freedom cannot be divided, but *if* one had to choose, Tocqueville argues that freedom in small, everyday societal matters is more fundamental than political freedom: 'subjection in small affairs' that 'manifests itself every day and makes itself felt without distinction by all citizens … constantly thwarts them and brings them to renounce the use of their wills. Thus little by little, it extinguishes their spirits and enervates their souls' (665). People will lose 'little by little the faculty of thinking, feeling and acting by themselves', and thus fall 'below the level of humanity'. Merely taking part in elections from time to time will not compensate for the damage done by an everyday life marked by obedience and dependency, and it is improbable that 'a liberal, energetic, and wise government can ever issue from the suffrage of a people of servants'. This system is unstable and people will either 'create freer institutions or soon return to lying at the feet of a single master'. The twentieth century has provided plenty of evidence for the second of these two options, and some for the first.

9 Continuation of the preceding chapters

The next chapter gives a handy summary of Tocqueville's views on despotism under social conditions of democracy. Despotism has always been a bad thing, but under modern conditions of equality – i.e., the absence of solid caste structures and other potential barriers to it – despotism can become absolute to the extent that 'men' could be robbed of their autonomy and freedom as completely as to lose parts of their humanity (666). Tocqueville is equally assertive, though, that 'reconstructing an aristocratic society' is not an option: as God himself made us live in a democratic society, we have only one option, namely making it a source of freedom. This is, however, a tricky assignment. The difficulty arises not least from the fact that it is 'at once necessary and desirable that the central power that directs a democratic people be active and powerful' (667): society and the state must make up for what modern individuals are now less likely to undertake. In spite of the great emphasis on freedom, Tocqueville's liberalism is not of the variety that advocates a minimal or 'night watchman' state. His point is that the strong state must be prevented from *abusing* its power: 'democratic procedures' must be found that do what pre-democratic social structures had done previously:

> Instead of handing over to the sovereign alone all the administrative powers that one takes away from corporations or from the nobles, one can entrust a part of them to secondary bodies formed temporarily of plain citizens; in this manner the freedom of particular persons will be surer without lessening their equality. (667)

Tocqueville argues that in the past hereditary officials at the level of provincial governments were independent from the central power because they did not receive their office from the latter. In modern society elections can fulfil the same function of granting independence from the central power. Likewise, aristocratic societies produced 'rich and influential particular persons' who were self-sufficient – independently wealthy – and 'whom one does not

oppress easily or secretly'. Democratic society does not produce
such individuals – so he thought – but 'when plain citizens associate, they can constitute very opulent, very influential, very strong
beings – in a word, aristocratic persons' (668). Such 'associations'
are, thus, the guarantors of freedom that can take the place the aristocrats had held – but without the injustices of actual aristocracy:

> A political, industrial, commercial, or even scientific and literary
> association is an enlightened and powerful citizen whom one can
> neither bend at will nor oppress in the dark and who, in defending
> its particular rights against the exigencies of power, saves common
> freedom. (668)

Tocqueville packs a lot of disparate bodies under the concept of
'association' ('political, industrial, commercial, or even scientific
and literary' associations), and expects a lot from them – to be
enlightened as well as powerful and opulent, to defend their particular interests against the modern state and society as well as to
defend 'common freedom'. Almost two centuries on we are reluctant to expect this much from associational life, or 'civil society' as
we would call it, but Tocqueville's enthusiasm on this matter is still
inspiring.

10 The individual and the press

In the next section, however, Tocqueville returns to the question
of whether and how the individual can defend his or her freedom.
This is a crucial issue for Tocqueville because unlike in the old days,
'[i]n centuries of equality, each individual is naturally isolated' as
there is no class of 'hereditary friends' who automatically will rush
to one's assistance (668): caste or status group solidarity has disappeared. Although Tocqueville probably thought of the solidarity of
networks of aristocrats, we might just as well think of the traditional
working-class milieu that used to be a basis of class solidarity but
lately has disintegrated to make way for pure, abstract class relations
between 'monadic' individuals. In the state of equality and democracy as Tocqueville understands it, 'a citizen who is oppressed has
therefore only one means of defending himself: it is to address the
nation as a whole, and if it is deaf to him, the human race'. This can

only be done – if at all – through the press, and therefore 'freedom of the press is infinitely more precious in democratic nations than in all others; it alone cures most of the ills that equality can produce'. Tocqueville expects a lot from 'the press':

> Equality isolates and weakens men, but the press places at the side of each of them a very powerful arm that the weakest and most isolated can make use of. Equality takes away from each individual the support of his neighbors, but the press permits him to call to his aid all his fellow citizens and all who are like him.

A more sceptical observer might want to ask how these isolated and weak individuals can get access to 'the press' and use it as an instrument. Does 'the press' – we would say, the media – allow itself to be used as an instrument by just anybody, even the most isolated and disempowered individuals? Hardly. Tocqueville must have thought of a very decentralized and accessible but at the same time globally connected form of 'the press'. We might think Tocqueville's very liberal ideas about the role of 'the press' are somewhat better matched by contemporary 'social media'. Still, the question remains why 'equality' – a societal state in which all are equal and identical – makes my neighbours uninterested in my case and destroys neighbourly solidarity, but allows me to invoke the global solidarity of 'all who are like me' through the media. Tocqueville indulges here perhaps in a bit of whistling in the dark. Anyway: although Tocqueville saddles 'the press' with a bit too much responsibility, he sums up his position in a very quotable statement: 'The press is the democratic instrument of freedom par excellence.'

11 The importance of the judiciary and of forms

From the press Tocqueville moves on to 'judicial power' which he sees in a similar light: it is elementary that it is 'constantly at the disposition of the most humble' of individuals (668). Individual rights are endangered by a typical trait of democracies: an 'instinctive disdain' for forms (669). Forms, including social forms that guarantee the rights of individuals, stand in the way of easy and instant enjoyment, and democratic people do not like delayed gratification. Forms, including legal forms, slow down the strong and give the weak 'time to recollect himself', and thereby warrant freedom. Tocqueville recommends not a superstitious but 'an enlightened and reflective worship' of forms. He adds that violating the rights of an individual is particularly damaging to 'national mores' (670) and puts 'society as a whole in peril' when society has just gone through an extended period of revolution. Revolution accustoms people to the fact that rules and forms can change at any time, and that particular interests are every so often sacrificed to some notion of the greater good (671). Revolutions are therefore particularly dangerous when they occur in democratic societies. Although there are situations in which revolutions are legitimate, Tocqueville argues that people in modernity should think twice before starting one.

12 Conclusion of this section

Tocqueville recapitulates that 'in most modern nations, the sovereign', whatever the political form, 'has become almost all-powerful', while society is characterized by 'unity and uniformity' (671). Policy and legislation should therefore defend whatever remains of individuality. Among his contemporaries, however, Tocqueville perceives two equally 'fatal' but contradictory attitudes: one rejects the modern state of equality in the conviction that it inevitably leads to 'anarchy', while the other, 'more enlightened', believes that equality 'invincibly' leads 'towards servitude' (672). This latter view is closer to Tocqueville's own, except that he does not believe in the inevitability of democratic servitude. He sharply criticizes fatalism: 'They bend their souls in advance to this necessary servitude; and despairing of remaining free, at the bottom of their hearts they already adore the master who will soon come.' This attitude of anticipatory submissiveness is surely a trait of many members of modern society. But there is hope, because modern people 'have the taste for independence naturally'. They (i.e. we) are by nature impatient with rule, they (we) 'love power' but 'are inclined to scorn and hate whoever exercises it' (673). 'These instincts ... come from the foundation of the social state', which means they are historically specific, modern but fundamental and stable 'instincts' that 'will furnish new arms to each new generation that wants to struggle in favour of men's freedom'. Tocqueville advocates on these grounds being afraid of the future insofar as it 'makes one watchful and combative', but counsels against 'that sort of soft and idle terror that wears hearts down and enervates them' (673).

13 General view of the subject

Here we come to the conclusion of the conclusion. Tocqueville rises to the occasion and makes quite a drama of it: 'confronted with so great an object', namely to sum up the gist of his argument, 'I feel my sight becoming blurred and my reason wavering' (673) – we have all been there. Anticipating criticism, perhaps, he points out that the object of his study – modern society – still 'is only being born'. Only one thing is sure: there has never been a revolution like this one (673). Tocqueville now gives a dense, two-paragraph-long shopping list of what is gained and what is lost in the emerging reality, observing that 'goods and evils are split equally enough in the world'. Had he been a lecturer and not a writer, he might have put it in a table like the one on the next page.

Luckily, however, he was not a lecturer, and therefore he goes on to describe with remarkable frankness his ambivalent feelings on this state of affairs:

> I let my regard wander over this innumerable crowd composed of similar beings, in which nothing is elevated and nothing lowered. The spectacle of this universal uniformity saddens and chills me, and I am tempted to regret the society that is no longer. (674)

In the olden days he used to see only the very great, rich and learned, and chose not to see at all the very small, poor and ignorant. Looking back, he writes, 'I understand that this pleasure was born of my weakness': young Tocqueville had been able to cherry-pick what to see and what not to see because human beings cannot see all. God, however, sees 'at once, the whole human race and each man'. And therefore, he concludes:

> It is natural to believe that what most satisfies the regard of this creator and preserver of men is not the singular prosperity of some, but the greatest well-being of all: what seems to me decadence is therefore progress in his eyes; what wounds me is agreeable to him. Equality is

In modern society we find . . .

Disappearing:	Increasing:
great wealth, extraordinary prosperity, irremediable misery	small fortunes, desires and enjoyments
vast ambitions	ambition (but not so vast)
	isolation and weakness of individuals
energetic souls, *great* devotions, *very* lofty, *very* brilliant, *very* pure virtues	society's ability to be agile, far-seeing, and strong; particular persons do small things, the state does immense ones
violence and cruelty	mildness of mores, humaneness of legislation
very delicate and *very* coarse pleasures, *very* polite manners, *very* brutal tastes	orderly habits
adorned life	long existence, safe property, easy and peaceful life
very learned men and *very* ignorant men	widespread enlightenment
the powerful impulsion of some men	the combined small efforts of all men
genius and perfection	fruitfulness in works
the bonds of race, of class, of native land	tightness of the great bond of humanity

perhaps less elevated; but it is more just, and its justice makes for its greatness and its beauty.

I strive to enter into this point of view of God, and it is from there that I seek to consider and judge human things. (674–675)

This evokes an old tradition of Christian literature, the confessional account of a subject's not quite successful striving to follow the straight and narrow path that would please the Lord: Tocqueville tries really hard to *like* democracy, not merely to understand and accept it, but it is not easy.

On the last page, Tocqueville rather surprisingly changes tack once more; the Christian-confessional section that clearly endorses democracy as God's preferred social state is followed by a strong statement of historical relativism that sounds more like a Comtean argument. Aristocratic and democratic nations both have their pros and cons, and are in fact not comparable: they constitute 'as it were, two distinct humanities' (675). It would be unjust to judge the one by the yardstick of ideas drawn from the other. Therefore we 'ought not to strain to make ourselves like our fathers, but strive to attain the kind of greatness and happiness that is proper to us'. Concerning whether this is possible, Tocqueville is 'full of fears and full of hopes', but tends towards (characteristically liberal) optimism: he declares himself 'firm in the belief that to be honest and prosperous, it is still enough for democratic nations to wish it'. He asserts this politics of the will explicitly against those who think that 'peoples are never masters of themselves here below' (676), but are subject to this or that 'insurmountable and unintelligent force born of previous events, the race, the soil, or the climate'. Such 'false and cowardly doctrines' – racism or any other forms of determinism or fatalism – cannot but produce 'weak men and pusillanimous nations'. Tocqueville concludes:

> Nations of our day cannot have it that conditions within them are not equal; but it depends on them whether equality leads them to servitude or freedom, to enlightenment or barbarism, to prosperity or misery.

Democracy and equality is the hand we have been dealt. Now the point is to make the best of it.

4

Pariahs of the world, unite!
Flora Tristan

Flora Tristan (1803–44), an early proponent of feminist and internationalist socialism, was a stubbornly independent-minded thinker, self-taught and with little formal education but widely acknowledged as a great writer, especially of travel narratives. Journeying and, in more senses than one, never being at home anywhere led her to sociological thinking, and resulted in her writing one of the key programmatic texts of the movement for social reform, *The Workers' Union* (1843). She emerged out of the context of the 'utopian' and Christian socialisms of 1830s France but advocated and conceptualized a rather hard-nosed, radically egalitarian reformism. She literally killed herself through exhaustion in the process of taking her reform programme on the road, engaging in an exploration of proletarian France that constituted a kind of ethnographic action-research.

Tristan was born in Paris to a French woman about whose background little is known and a Peruvian aristocrat who was a colonel in the Spanish army. Her father, Don Mariano de Tristan Moscoso, was a friend of Simón Bolívar, who subsequently emerged as a key figure in the Spanish-American wars of independence (1808–26) that led to the establishment of the republics of Venezuela, Colombia, Peru, Bolivia and Ecuador. These events in Latin America were triggered by the Napoleonic invasion of Spain, which weakened the Spanish Empire, but the Franco-Spanish war also had a profound impact on Tristan's personal life: when she was four years old, her father died from a stroke and their house just outside Paris was confiscated by the French state as he counted as an enemy alien. A comfortable early childhood was followed by a lifetime of struggling to make ends meet. At the age of about 15 she learned that she was illegitimate because her parents, who had married in Spain where Tristan's mother was a refugee from the French Revolution, did not have any legal documentation of their marriage. Flora Tristan started working for a painter and lithographer whom she married in 1821. The marriage was unhappy, and she left her abusive husband after four years. For the next thirteen years she had to fight for custody of her three children, and her right to leave the marriage (there was no right to divorce) and to make a living, often leaving her children with her mother. Apparently she mostly worked as a chambermaid for a number of English women, accompanying them on their travels in England, Switzerland and Italy. In 1829 she wrote a letter to a very wealthy uncle in Peru, hoping to receive an inheritance from her father. The uncle refused her legal claims, as she did not have the necessary paperwork, but embraced her as a family member and started sending her a regular pension. Encouraged by this semi-success in reconnecting with the aristocratic side of her family, and exhausted by the ongoing struggle with her husband over custody of her children, she travelled, without children, to Peru in 1833, leaving France on her thirtieth birthday. She spent three-quarters of a year in Peru, failed to secure her inheritance, but discovered something else: her own abilities as an observer and writer. An outcast at the bottom of society in France, in Peru she was acknowledged by her relatives as an intelligent, energetic, curious and brave individual and given access to all echelons of society. She returned with diaries that became the publication that made her name, *Peregrinations of a Pariah* (1838). It is a travel book very much in the romantic mode, a personal first-person narrative of a Quixotic quest, interspersed with ethnographic descriptions of what she had seen, from slavery in Cape Verde via the circumnavigation of Cape Horn to the political struggles in post-independence Peru and the customs of women in Lima. It also contained scathing reflections on her own marriage. Her Peruvian uncle did not like the way he was represented and terminated her pension. Immediately after her return from Peru she published a pamphlet called *On the Necessity of Giving a Warm Welcome to Foreign Women* (1835), in which she reflects on the importance and vulnerability of foreigners: 'foreign

women' meant here both visitors from abroad and women from the
countryside who might be looking for work in places like Paris or
be abandoned single mothers. The pamphlet pioneered the concept
of women as a class – central to French socialist feminism – and
argued for a feminist cosmopolitanism.

Tristan also visited England again and published travel pieces in
newspapers; she started attending feminist meetings and campaign-
ing for the legalization of divorce. She also studied the socialist
writers Saint-Simon, Fourier, Considérant (a disciple of Fourier)
and Robert Owen. In 1838, when *Peregrinations of a Pariah* was
published, her estranged husband shot her – she survived, with a
bullet stuck in her chest for the rest of her life – and was sent to
prison. The upside of this was that it resolved the custody issue.
The scandal also added to Tristan's celebrity and increased sales of
her book. In 1839, the year of the Chartist uprising at Newport, she
visited England again and published in 1840 another travel book,
Promenades in London, known in English as *The London Journal of
Flora Tristan*. The book on London is of a much more conceptual-
reflective character than *Peregrinations*. Especially in its second edition of 1842, it combines first-hand observation with use of sources
and theoretical literature. Its principal concerns are class, ethnicity
and the position of women; it contains sections on factory work,
prostitution, the Irish and Jewish quarters, the cross-class spectacle
of the horse races at Ascot, schools, a mental asylum, prisons, the
role of age, the display of manners in the Houses of Parliament,
the education of women, and the Chartists.

Following the examples of the Chartists, the Owenites and the
Catholic Association in Ireland led by Daniel O'Connell, Tristan
came in this period to see grassroots organization as a way to go
beyond socialist utopianism. Back in France, she engaged in establishing relations with the Owenites in England. In the process she
increasingly moved from mingling with 'utopian' socialists (who
were mostly intellectuals) to meeting and discussing with often illit-
erate workers, and from this emerged her most conceptual publication, *The Workers' Union* (1843).

The Workers' Union developed out of her critique of Owenism
which she found too environmentally deterministic and too little
concerned with the aspiration to freedom, for Tristan essentially a

spiritual, or perhaps even religious, factor. The concern with freedom led her to the notion of self-activity, the idea that social reform
must come from a union of the workers themselves, not from liberal
middle-class benefactors granting reform to them. As an aspect of
her religious romanticism, she cast herself as a sort of messiah, but
this messiah was not to lead the masses: she merely intended to
prod the workers to get organized and realize their own collective
strength. To create this unity, they needed to overcome the barriers
of nations, trades and sexes – hence the Union. The workers would
elect a leader who would be financed by their subscriptions and
accountable to them (this was apparently modelled on the formal
structure of the Catholic Association in Ireland at the time). The
Workers' Union would build and operate a 'workers' palace' in every
borough, serving as combined school, hospital, training, leisure and
retirement centre, all under the immediate control and ownership
of the Union. Workers would form corresponding groups internationally to develop their own values and objectives and defend
their interests, just like the bourgeoisie had done before them: this
process she referred to as 'constituting the working class'. This
means that 'class' is not a merely descriptive category but is one that
depends on agency. Tristan emphasized that 'it is up to you and
only you to act in the interest of your own cause … Workers, put
an end to twenty-five years of waiting for someone to intervene on
your behalf' (37–38). The insistence on self-activity and autonomy
is the central difference from the 'utopian socialists' of her day. This
is evident in a comment she made on a book by 'the former Saint-
Simonian leader' Enfantin (*The Colonization of Algeria* of 1843):

> Today, for Enfantin, labor organization simply means *regimenting* the
> workers in a regular manner. In his mind the term *labor organization*
> has the same meaning as military organization. Such a way of seeing is
> truly beyond words! May the Lord keep you, workers, from that kind
> of organization. Let the most populous class perish from misery and
> hunger before agreeing to be regimented, which means exchanging its
> freedom for assurance of rations. (71)

The workers should not be prepared to pay for welfare ('assurance of rations') by subordination. After *The Workers' Union* was
published (through a kind of crowd-funding campaign involving

workers all over Paris), Tristan took it on an extensive reading
tour throughout the South and East of France. Between April and
September 1844 she visited 19 industrial towns and in the process produced notes for what she meant to be her next book, a
report on working conditions and her meetings and conversations
with groups of workers and others. She died near Bordeaux from
exhaustion, probably typhoid fever; the drafts for this book, *Tour
de France*, were only published much later in 1973. Another draft,
edited by a friend from her notes, was published posthumously in
1845, entitled *The Emancipation of Woman.*

The selected text, 'Why I mention women', is the third chapter
of *The Workers' Union* in the 1842 edition.

Structure of the selected text

1 For the love of God and Woman (75)
2 Woman as a pariah (76)
3 The proletariat used to be denigrated similarly, but this
changed in 1789 (76–8)
4 The subdual of women is bad for all of society (78–9)
5 Women's reasons to be irritated (80–82)
6 Women's influence on men (82–3)
7 Where there are masters and slaves, there cannot be happiness (83–4)
8 The benefits of equality (84–6)
9 Women's equality is a men's issue (86–9)

Tristan, Flora. 1983 [1843]. 'Why I mention women'. In *The
Workers' Union*. Translated and with an Introduction by Beverly
Livingston. Urbana, IL: University of Illinois Press, 75–98.

---

1 For the love of God and Woman

The chapter begins with an appeal to the workers to take note of
the following argument because it was in their own interest. Tristan
refers to workers as 'the most vital, numerous, and useful part of
humanity' (75). 'Usefulness' obviously undergirds the workers'
right to resist domination. Tristan adds here a somewhat cryp-

tic, quasi-religious statement that seems to underlie her thinking: she writes that nothing ever happens 'in the moral and physical worlds' (i.e. the social-cultural and the material worlds) that is not determined by 'loving God' and 'loving Woman'. Loving God and loving Woman amounts to the same thing as loving and serving 'all men and women': general, universal social reform is a way of showing one's love of God as well as of Woman. She does not elaborate on this aspect of her thinking and indicates that she will only deal with the 'effects' of love of God/Woman, namely the practical social reform, not the metaphysical (or religious) question of that love itself. This reflects the fact that the sense of religiosity Tristan expresses here, including the sense that Woman (as opposed to 'all women') is also a kind of metaphysical notion, was fairly common in French socialism of the time. What makes Tristan stand out from her historical context is her emphasis on concrete analysis and practical measures.

2 Woman as a pariah

Tristan begins her argument with a summary appraisal of 'how for the six thousand years the world has existed, the wisest among the wise have judged the female race' (76). This needs some explaining. The idea that the world was only 6,000 years old was common at the time: modern archaeology and geology were yet to prove that the earth is much older than that. Contemporary readers might also find confusing Tristan's use of the expression 'the female race', *la race femme*: race and class were at this time still sometimes interchangeable to the extent that 'women' could be designated as either. (Victorian elites also sometimes referred to the working class as 'a race'. When reading historical documents from the nineteenth or earlier centuries it is important to keep in mind that words have an annoying habit of changing their meanings every so often!) Unlike English-language feminists, French feminists still today sometimes talk about 'the class of women' or 'the female race', chiefly to alert themselves and their readers to the fact that none of these words – race, class, sex – have fixed, unequivocal meanings.

Tristan states that 'up to now, woman has counted for nothing in human society', and this is reflected in the views promulgated by religion, law and philosophy: all have 'treated her as a true pariah'. Religion holds that woman represents temptation, sin, evil, flesh, corruption and rottenness, and she is therefore asked to 'mortify' and 'mutilate' heart and body (76). Law denies her any active role and demands that she 'serve as an appendage to your lord and master, man'. Philosophy holds woman to be inferior to man, lacking intelligence, logic and any 'ability for the so-called exact sciences', being 'feeble-minded', 'weak-bodied', cowardly, superstitious, like a child or a doll.

3 The proletariat used to be denigrated similarly, but this changed in 1789

The repetition of such ideas over thousands of years makes them hard to eradicate, but 'what must make us hope' is the fact that 'the wisest of the wise have also for six thousand years pronounced a no less horrible verdict upon another race of humanity – the proletariat' (77). (Note that also the proletariat is referred to as a 'race'.) Until the French Revolution of 1789, the proletarian had been 'a taxable, drudging beast of burden'. In the Revolution, 'all of a sudden the wisest of the wise proclaimed that the lower orders are to be called the *people*' and '*citizens*' enjoying '*the rights of Man*' (italics in the original). Tristan writes that two claims were made in the French Revolution of 1789: one, that the proletarian had equal 'civil, political, and social rights', and two, 'that he possessed a brain of the same quality as the royal prince's'. People realized quickly, though, that 'this second judgment on the proletariat was truer than the first': while civil, political and social equality remains contested, it is plain to see that as soon as they were permitted, out of the lower orders 'surged' the best generals, 'learned men, artists, poets, writers, statesmen, and financiers', which led to the increase of the French nation's glory, commerce and wealth. 'Everyone agrees today that men are born indistinct, with essentially equal faculties, and that the sole thing we should be concerned about is how to develop an individual's total faculties for the sake of the general well-being.' Tristan writes that these developments are 'a good omen for women' (77–78) whose 1789 is still to come. She writes from a very optimistic perspective: things have been very bad from the beginning of the world until 1789, but beginning with the Revolution they are now gradually looking up.

4 The subdual of women is bad for all of society

The denigration of women has had 'disastrous consequences ... for the universal well-being of all men and women' (78). Tristan's chief point is here about education: women have been, and still are, kept uneducated, which means a loss to society of half its constituents' capacities. She makes here an interesting and mordant distinction:

> Those who believed that woman by nature lacked the strength, intelligence, and capacity to do serious and useful work, very logically deduced that it would be a waste of time to give her a rational, solid, and strict education, the kind that would make her a useful member of society. So she has been raised to be a nice doll and a slave destined for amusing and serving her master. (78)

'[F]rom time to time', however, 'some intelligent, sensitive men, showing empathy with their mothers, wives, and daughters, have cried out against the barbarity and absurdity of such an order of things.' On such occasions, 'society has been moved for a moment' – but then has been 'pushed by logic' and has responded by excluding women from education even more forcefully. Society admitted that women do have the capacity for 'moral strength and intelligence' but noted that 'they would not be able to employ them usefully in this society which rejects them'. That same society then proceeded to save them from the 'awful torture' of feeling that 'one has force and power to act' while seeing 'oneself condemned to inaction'. Tristan's description of this 'logic' drips with sarcasm:

> This reasoning was irrefutably true. So everyone repeated, 'It's true, women would suffer too much if their God-given talents were developed, if from childhood on they were raised to understand their dignity and to be conscious of their value as members of society. Then never would they be able to bear the degradation imposed upon them by the Church, the law, and prejudice. It is better to treat them like children and leave them in the dark about themselves: they will suffer less.' (78–79)

From the biting sarcasm of this polemic, Tristan turns now in a more serious tone to the specific question of what women's lack of education means for working-class men in particular:

> In the life of the workers, woman is everything. She is their sole providence. If she is gone, they lack everything … However, what education, instruction, direction, moral or physical development does the working-class woman receive? None. As a child, she is left to the mercy of a mother and grandmother who also have received no education. One of them might have a brutal and wicked disposition and beat and mistreat her for no reason; the other might be weak and uncaring, and let her do anything … Instead of being sent to school, she is kept at home in deference to her brothers and so that she can share in the housework, rock the baby, run errands, or watch the soup, etc. At the age of twelve she is made an apprentice. There she continues to be exploited by her mistress and often continues to be as mistreated as she was at home. (79)

Tristan emphasizes the suffering of the children: 'Nothing embitters the character, hardens the heart, or makes the spirit so mean as the continuous suffering a child endures from unfair and brutal treatment' (79–80). Injustice first hurts and causes despair; then, 'when it persists', it makes one 'hardened, unjust, and wicked' (80). 'Such will be the normal condition for a poor girl of twenty.' Young women 'marry without love … in order to get out from under parental tyranny'. The children born in this situation will go through the same experience.

Tristan states repeatedly in the book that there is no point in flattering the working class – which she accuses some middle-class authors of doing – but that it must be critiqued sharply if things are to get better. She addresses working-class women directly at this point:

> Working class women, take note, I beg you, that by mentioning your ignorance and incapacity to raise your children, I have no intention in the least of accusing *you* or *your nature*. No, I am accusing society for leaving you uneducated – you, women and mothers, who actually need so much to be instructed and formed in order to be able to instruct and develop the men and children entrusted to your care. Generally, women of the masses are brutal, mean, and sometimes hard. This being true, where does this situation come from, so differ-

ent from the sweet, good, sensitive, and generous nature of woman? (80)

Tristan asserts the equality of women to men but at the same time asserts the idea of woman's 'sweet, good, sensitive, and generous nature', and her responsibility for the upbringing of children.

5 Women's reasons to be irritated

'Poor working women! They have so many reasons to be irritated! First, their husbands' (80). Tristan asserts that 'there are few working-class couples who are happily married', and she gives a graphic description of why, quite possibly drawing on some of her own experience: being more educated and better paid, 'the husband thinks he is (and he is, in fact) very superior to his wife, who only brings home her small daily wage and is merely a very humble servant in her home' (80). Therefore he treats her with 'great disdain', whereupon 'the poor woman either openly or silently revolts, depending upon her personality'. This results in 'an atmosphere of constant irritation between the master and the slave (one can indeed say slave, because the woman is, so to speak, her husband's property)' (80–81). This in turn causes the husband to spend much time and money in the tavern drinking cheap wine 'in the hope of getting drunk, with the other husbands who are just as unhappy as he' (80). The wife's irritation and her 'brutality and wickedness redouble'. On top of the irritation caused by the husband's behaviour, there are 'pregnancies, illnesses, unemployment, and poverty', as well as

> the endless tension provoked by four or five loud, turbulent, and bothersome children clamoring about their mother, in a small worker's room too small to turn around in. My! One would have to be an angel from heaven not to be irritated, not to become brutal and mean in such a situation. (81)

Tristan's refusal to flatter the workers is clearly on display in these accounts.

Next, Tristan discusses the impact on the children: they 'see their father only in the evening or on Sunday', always 'either upset or drunk', giving them 'only insults and blows':

Hearing their mother continuously complain, they begin to feel hatred and scorn for her. They fear and obey her, but they do not love her, for a person is made that way – he cannot love someone who mistreats him. And isn't it a great misfortune for a child not to be able to love his mother! If he is unhappy, to whose breast will he go to cry? If he thoughtlessly makes a bad mistake or is led astray, in whom can he confide? Having no desire to stay close to his mother, the child will seek any pretext to leave the parental home. Bad associations are easy to make, for girls as for boys. Strolling becomes vagrancy, and vagrancy often becomes thievery. Among the poor girls in houses of prostitution and the poor men moaning in jails, how many can say, 'If we had had a mother able to raise us, then we would not be here.' (81–82)

6 Women's influence on men

Tristan goes back now to her earlier statement that 'woman is everything in the life of a worker' (82). As mother, woman teaches children 'the science of life, which teaches how to live well for ourselves and for others, according to the milieu in which fate has placed us'. (Note the emphasis on the role of 'milieu' – social context – on what it means 'to live well', i.e. mores and morality.) 'As lover', woman has a powerful influence, and even more so as wife, and then finally as daughter. The sociological quality of Tristan's argument comes out well in the following passage on how these things differ depending on class:

Note that the worker's position is very different from an idle person's. If the rich child has a mother unable to raise him, he is placed in a boarding school or given a governess. If the young rich fellow has no mistress, he can busy his heart and imagination with studying the arts and sciences. If the rich man has no spouse, he does not fail to find distractions in society. If the old rich man has no daughter, he finds some old friends or young nephews who willingly come and play cards with him; whereas the worker, for whom all these pleasures are denied, has only the company of the women in his family, his companions in misfortune, for all his joy and solace.

She argues here that for working-class men, women replace the entire society from which they are excluded. Several things are surprising in this argument: unlike what one might have expected from a feminist argument, she does not denounce women's exploitation by this situation, but refers to women's roles in support of her argument for educating women to make them better at fulfilling these roles. Likewise, unlike what one might expect from a socialist argument, she does not so much denounce the exclusion of workers from society as argue for the creation of an autonomous parallel society managed, financed and controlled by workers themselves: the Workers' Union. This is her specific demand:

> The result of this situation is that it would be most important, from the point of view of intellectually, morally, and materially improving the working class, that the women receive from childhood a rational and solid education, apt to develop all their potential so that they can become skilled in their trades, good mothers capable of raising and guiding their children and to be for them free and natural school-teachers, and also as they can serve as moralizing agents for the men whom they influence from birth to death. (82–83)

The thrust of her argument is to argue for 'moral' improvement of the working class – 'moral' here in the sense of 'mores', i.e., social and cultural practices. However, her view differs from the more customary perspective of middle-class reformers who try to persuade workers to become more like themselves: she develops a 'workerist' perspective that tries to nudge workers to act in their own best interest and to 'constitute' themselves as a class through building a union.

7 Where there are masters and slaves, there cannot be happiness

Tristan again addresses her male audience directly:

> Are you beginning to understand … why I would like women placed in society on a footing of *absolute equality* with men to enjoy the legal birthright all beings have? I call for women's rights because I am convinced that all the misfortunes in the world come from neglect and scorn shown until now for the natural and inalienable rights of woman. (83)

Acceptance of women's equality is a precondition of woman's education, and the latter is a precondition of the education of all, especially all of the working class. (Note that the English translation is wrong here: Livingston mistranslates that 'woman's education depends upon man's in general'. The original French text has it the other way round.) Tristan provides two arguments in this context: the first is that women educate the children, and therefore are crucial for shaping the mentality of the next generation; the second, more originally perhaps, is that oppressed, ignorant, moody and resentful women are not much fun to be with *for the men*:

> Workers, in the current state of things, you know what goes on in your households. You, the master with rights over your wife, do you live with her with a contented heart? Say, are you happy? No, it is easy to see, in spite of your rights, you are neither contented nor happy. Between master and slave there can only be the weariness of the chain's weight tying them together. Where the lack of freedom is felt, happiness cannot exist. (83)

Tristan acknowledges that men 'always complain about the bad moods and the devious and silently wicked characters women show in all their relationships'. To this she replies that 'in the state of abjection where the law and customs place them' women are quite right not 'to submit without a murmur to the yoke weighing on them'. 'Their protest, since the beginning of time, has always been relentless' and has increased since the Declaration of the Rights of Man, which neglected to address the state of women. '[T]he slave's exasperation has peaked' (84).

8 The benefits of equality

Tristan appeals to workers again and makes a rare compliment in addressing workers as being those 'who have good sense and with whom one can reason, because, as Fourier says, you do not have minds stuffed with systems': workers are empirically minded, non-ideological, common-sense people familiar with the concrete realities of life. This is her pitch to the male workers:

> [Y]ou, men of the people, you would have clever workers for mothers, earning a good wage, instructed, well-raised and very able to teach and raise you, workers, as it is appropriate for free men; ... your sisters, lovers, wives, and friends would be educated, well-raised

women whose daily companionship would be most pleasant for you,
for nothing is sweeter or gentler to a man's heart than a woman's
conversation when she is well educated, good, and speaks with logic
and benevolence. (84)

It would make all the difference to the everyday life of a working-
class family: the husband would no longer treat his wife with disdain, so that she would no longer be irritated and 'appear brutal,
devious, grouchy, angry, exasperated, or mean'. No longer a servant, she would become 'his associate, friend, and companion' and
'employ all her intelligence to keep her house neat, economical, and
pleasant' as well as raising her children well (85).

Although mostly Tristan does not seem to challenge the division
of labour between the sexes in the family, there is at least a hint that
equality and education might soften it somewhat: 'The worker, also
educated and well brought up, will find it delightful to teach and
develop his young children' because '[w]orkers in general are kind-
hearted and love children very much':

> How diligently a man will work all week knowing that he is to spend
> Sunday in his wife's company, that he will enjoy his two little mis-
> chievous, affectionate girls and his two already educated boys who
> are able to talk with their father about serious things! How hard this
> father will work to earn a few extra cents to buy pretty bonnets for his
> little girls, a book for his sons, an engraving or something else which
> he knows will please them? With what joyful ecstasy these little gifts
> will be received, and what happiness for the mother to see the recipro-
> cal love between father and child! It is clear that this, hypothetically,
> would be the most desirable domestic life for the worker.

It is interesting to see how in this early text of feminist theory
the progressive aspects are mixed in with generally rather conservative ideas about gender roles: although the entire argument
is for the equal education of women, the notion that the girls will
receive 'pretty bonnets' and the boys books marks a fault-line in the
argument.

Next Tristan addresses a particularly divisive matter in the reality of working-class families then (and now, presumably):

> Comfortable at home, happy and satisfied in the company of his kind,
> old mother and young wife and children, it would never occur to [the

husband] to leave the house to seek a good time at the tavern, that place of perdition which wastes the worker's time, money, and health, and dulls his intellect. (85)

The money saved thus would allow working-class families to go 'for meals in the country in summer': 'So little is necessary for people who know how to live soberly' (85–86). Education and equality will, for Tristan, translate into a sensible form of ascetic discipline, and childlike fun for all:

Out in the open air, the children would all be happy to run with their father and mother, who would be like children to amuse them; and in the evening, with contented hearts and limbs slightly weary from the week's work, the family would return home very satisfied with their day. In winter, the family would go to a show. These amusements offer a dual advantage: they instruct children while entertaining them. How many objects of study an intelligent mother can find to teach her children in a day spent in the country or an evening at the theater! (86)

Family life like this will end profligacy because 'the married man who loves his family finds satisfaction in depriving himself and lives with exemplary frugality' (86).

9 Women's equality is a men's issue

In the concluding section, Tristan sums up her argument on why working-class men ought to support women's equality, and puts it into the context of her argument on the Workers' Union. The main point is that 'the law which enslaves women and deprives her of education oppresses you, proletarian men' (87). The rich have a whole range of 'elegant, witty, women' who 'make them into men who *know how to live*, the right kind of men', whereas 'you, poor workers, to rear and teach you, you have only your mother; to make you into civilized men, you only have women of your class, your companions in ignorance and misery'. Therefore, '[i]n the name of the universal well-being of all men and women', Tristan invites working-class men 'to appeal for women's rights'. From the perspective of subsequent forms of socialist theory, one might object that Tristan puts too much emphasis on the workers' responsibility for their own oppression, apparently ignoring the issue of systemic exploitation. On the other hand, though, she is surely right on two points: one is that oppression, exploitation and denigration of women by working-class men prevents any meaningful collective class action, and is also in this sense an issue of primary importance; and the second is that this is an issue that can be directly and immediately addressed through the activity of the workers themselves:

> Thus, workers, it is up to you, who are the victims of real inequality and injustice, to establish the rule of justice and absolute equality between man and woman on this earth. Give a great example to the world, an example that will prove to your oppressors that you want to triumph through your right and not by brutal force. You seven, ten, fifteen million proletarians, could avail yourselves of that brute force! In calling for justice, prove that you are just and equitable. You, the strong men, the men with bare arms, proclaim your recognition that woman is your equal, and as such, you recognize her equal right to the benefits of the *universal union of working men and women*. (87–88)

Recognition of women's equality would make the working class so strong that it could afford to avail itself of the use of violence which, to Tristan, is another key issue.

Tristan's argument implies that women will benefit from the workers' palaces to be founded by the Union equally with men, and argues that recognition of women's equality is an inheritance from the French Revolution of 1789. The chapter ends with a draft of a declaration that would become part of the charter of the Workers' Union:

> 'We, French proletarians, after fifty-three years of experience, recognize that we are duly enlightened and convinced that the neglect and scorn perpetrated upon the natural rights of woman are the only cause of unhappiness in the world, and we have resolved to expose her sacred and inalienable rights in a solemn declaration inscribed in our charter. We wish women to be informed of our declaration, so that they will not let themselves be oppressed and degraded any more by man's injustice and tyranny, and so that men will respect the freedom and equality they enjoy in their wives and mothers.
> 1. The goal of society necessarily being the common happiness of men and women, the Workers' Union guarantees them the enjoyment of their rights as working men and women.

2. Their rights include equal admission to the Workers' Union palaces, whether they be children, or disabled or elderly.

3. Woman being man's equal, we understand that girls will receive as rational, solid, and extensive (though different) an education in moral and professional matters as the boys.

4. As for the disabled and the elderly, in every way, the treatment will be the same for women as for men.' (88–89)

Again, it is worth noting that Tristan softens her demand for equal education by inserting that education for girls shall be 'rational, solid, and extensive (though different)' – whatever that might mean …

5

Capitalist modernity is the real savagery: Karl Marx

Karl Marx (1818–83) grew up in a reasonably well-to-do, caring and harmonious middle-class family in the Rhenish town of Trier, in the far west of Germany near the French border. His father was a lawyer, an enlightened man, and a moderate liberal. He had converted from Judaism to Protestantism only a short time before Marx was born. Trier had been conquered by Napoleon in 1794, bringing among other things Jewish emancipation. The French imperial government acted to reinforce the liberal traditions of the town before it fell to Prussia in 1815. The Prussian monarchy then reversed Jewish emancipation, which forced Marx's father to convert as he did not want to lose his career and livelihood.

Marx studied law, history and philosophy at the universities of Bonn and Berlin from 1835 to 1841 after initially also trying his hand at poetry. As he became more and more involved in the 'young Hegelian' circle of radical intellectuals, an academic career became unthinkable due to the anti-liberal political climate of the period, and Marx became the editor of a new, liberal-democratic journal based in Cologne. When this publication had to close down, he moved to Paris in 1843 and accepted a position as the editor of a German-language journal there. His journalistic work forced him to deal with social and political issues, while he continued to sharpen his philosophical critique – especially of Hegel – and began to study political economy as well as French socialist literature. His notebooks from that period, sometimes called 'the Paris manuscripts', were published posthumously and are often referred to as a help for unlocking philosophical implications in his work that are less obvious in his more polished writings. In 1845 he was expelled from France and moved to Brussels where he stayed until he was expelled from Belgium too, in March 1848. In these intense five years in Paris and Brussels, Marx published his first essays, including some of his most influential pieces such as 'A Contribution to the Critique of Hegel's Philosophy of Right. Introduction', and his first two books containing critiques of contemporary French and German socialist theories. He also started his collaboration with Friedrich Engels (1820–1903), whom he first met in 1844, and produced copious drafts that were to become highly influential after their posthumous publication, including *The German Ideology*. In 1849 Marx settled in England as a stateless person after a wild year of revolutionary activity in Germany. From 1851 onwards his principal source of income was his journalistic work for the *New York Tribune*. At the same time he engaged in the sustained research that resulted chiefly in the 1867 publication of the first volume of *Capital* and an enormous amount of draft material, some of which was edited and published by Engels as the second and third volumes of *Capital*. The most famous portion of the unpublished material of that period has, since its publication in 1939 under the name *Grundrisse* ('fundamental drafts' or 'groundworks'), come to be seen as perhaps the most profound and comprehensive statement of Marx's theory of capitalist modernity. *Grundrisse* is among the material that shows how much Marx in his 'mature' period studied European as well as non-European history and anthropology to put his theory of capitalist modernity, and how to overcome it, into a comparative perspective.

Marx was at no point an academic, however, a detached scholar or 'Great Thinker'. Primarily, throughout his life, he saw study and research as self-evidently important parts of the struggle for human emancipation. It is fitting therefore that the text most directly connected to his name is the *Manifesto of the Communist Party* which he co-wrote with Engels. Published just before the February 1848 revolution, it was of little influence at the time but later became probably the most influential political pamphlet of the twentieth century. A decade in which human emancipation remained off-stage ended when serfdom and slavery were abolished in Russia in 1861 and in the USA between 1863 and 1865, and in Europe things also started moving again. Marx was elected a member of the General Council of the International Working Men's Association (the 'First International') from its foundation in 1864, and remained its chief strategist until its dissolution in 1876, following a backlash in the aftermath of the military destruction of the Paris Commune of 1871, which Marx and the 'First International' had supported.

If one reads Marx in his historical context, one finds that a number of ideas that are generally held to be his are in fact quite common to a range of thinkers in the Enlightenment. These include the notion that history is the history of class struggles, or more generally, that conflict is the motor of history; that human beings are not isolated, Robinson Crusoe-like creatures but live in communities or societies and are shaped by them; that the first precondition for the formation of communities or societies is the production of necessities, such as food and shelter; that this production and its conditions determine, to an extent, social and intellectual forms; that God is a human projection, not a reality. By contrast, some important points that are in fact central to and *original* in Marx are that classes are relational, rather than stand-alone entities with an essence of their own; similarly, that human 'essence' or nature, insofar as it has to do with social behaviour, is nothing more than 'the ensemble of social relations', i.e., historically and socially constituted rather than fixed; and that 'men make their own history but not in circumstances of their own choosing', which points to the dialectic of what contemporary sociologists would call 'structure and agency'. Perhaps Marx's most important political principle – fuelling his countless polemics against fellow, or not-so-fellow, socialists – follows from this: this is, that humans must change their circumstances by changing themselves, rather than trusting that some kind of authority or intellectual leadership, or the state, will do it for them. 'Revolutionary change' in this sense means for Marx the human grassroots activity of *self-change*.

Marx's writings fill several metres of bookshelves. They consist of journalism (his day job), polemics against other socialists (his passion), letters (personal, scholarly and to do with political organizing within the labour and radical-democratic movements), drafts for works that remained unfinished, copious notes and excerpts from wide-ranging, life-long, thorough studying, and then the much smaller number of well-known works that he completed, polished and published. Among the latter, the one that stands out most is the first volume of *Capital. A Critique of Political Economy*. As it says on the tin, this book offers a 'critique' of 'political economy' – two terms that need clarification. 'Political economy' as a scholarly discipline was the first systematic attempt to understand the structure and dynamics of modern capitalist society and a key element of the eighteenth-century movement generally known as the Enlightenment. As well as a critique of the discipline of that name, Marx's *Capital* is also a critique of the object theorized by that same discipline: the term 'political economy' also denotes the reality of modern society itself, looked at under the particular perspective of how society organizes its own reproduction. (Concerning the words 'political' and 'society', it is worth keeping in mind that in the eighteenth- and nineteenth-century contexts the modern distinction between 'the political' and 'the social', as well as 'state' and 'society', was only gradually emerging. The word 'political' still resonated with its classical Greek root in *polis* – the city state – and *politeia*, which means society, community and the state all at the same time – not yet disaggregated as they are in modernity.)

The word 'critique' in the title of the book also deserves clarification, as for Marx and his peers this word meant two quite different things simultaneously: first, a close analysis of the internal logical structure of an argument or body of texts that shows up inconsistencies and logical errors, often vacillating between a coolly analytical and a polemical tone peppered with sarcasm and personal insults (a sport in which Marx was second only to Shakespeare); secondly, a form of contextualization and relativization that measures the validity of an argument or body of texts against the reality that produced it and that it refers to. This second meaning of 'critique' aims to demonstrate how and to what extent the argument that is being critiqued is situated in its context and what is the realm of its (relative) truth.

The first volume of *Capital* is the only one that Marx completed, although he had projected a comprehensive theoretical work of six volumes. The publication process for the unpublished material begun by Engels and others is still ongoing today, more than 130 years after Marx's poverty- and illness-ridden body ceased serving his cantankerous spirit. The first chapter of volume one of *Capital* is widely seen as the most difficult of any of Marx's writings – a good place to start, therefore, as the rest will be much easier once you got your head around the notorious first chapter. Marx himself writes in the preface that the difficulty comes from the fact that he begins the book with the simplest, most elementary form of capitalist society, and the most elementary form of any object is always the most difficult to research and explain. Marx presents as the most elementary social form of capitalist society the 'commodity-form of the product of labour': this is the subject matter of the present chapter. While difficult, the text is also very funny: it is as much sarcastic social commentary and polemic as it is a philosophically informed critique of some of the key ideas entertained by modern bourgeois society about itself. Marx explicitly states that he presupposes 'a reader who is willing to learn something new and therefore to think for himself' (Marx 1974, p. 19). We have been warned.

The chapter falls into four sections, the third of which is by far the longest and also the most technical (and will be treated

---

Structure of the selected text

1 The two factors of a commodity: use-value and value (43–48)
2 The twofold character of the labour embodied in commodities (48–53)
3 The form of value or exchange-value (54–75)
3.1 The elementary form of value (54–68)
3.2 Expanded, general and money forms of value (68–75)
4 The fetishism of commodities and the secret thereof (76–87)
4.1 On social relations that take the form of relations between things (76–80)
4.2 On scientific method: moving from complex to simple social forms in order to discover the historicity of social facts (80–87)

Marx, Karl. 1967 [1867, 1887]. *Capital. A Critique of Political Economy. Volume 1: The Process of Capitalist Production.* Translated from the third German edition by Samuel Moore and Edward Aveling. London: Lawrence and Wishart.

here more briefly). In the fourth section, entitled 'The Fetishism of Commodities and the Secret Thereof', Marx makes the most theoretically consequential aspects of his argument most explicit; this section is given the most detailed exposition here.

1 The two factors of a commodity: use-value and value

The first paragraph of *Capital* introduces three of the key terms of the text: wealth, the 'capitalist mode of production' and the commodity:

> The wealth of those societies in which the capitalist mode of production prevails presents itself as 'an immense accumulation of commodities', its unit being a single commodity. Our investigation must therefore begin with the analysis of the commodity. (43)

The first thing we are told about 'the capitalist mode of production' is that when it 'prevails' (implying that other social structures might well coexist with it) it makes wealth (the principal subject matter of the discourse of political economy) 'present itself', or appear, in a particular social form called 'the commodity': the commodity is the *form of wealth* in capitalist societies. It is worth noting here that Marx explicitly talks about a 'capitalist mode of production': this indicates that what we now address as 'capitalism' (a concept that became common only after Marx) is for Marx first of all about how society *produces* wealth, rather than, say, how it *distributes* wealth. This is important because it means that many popular issues such as justice, compassion and so on, let alone 'greedy bankers', that come with the discussion of distribution are not at the forefront of the Marxian critique.

There is a mildly sarcastic undertone in his description of wealth in capitalism as 'an immense accumulation of commodities' as it evokes the image of loads and loads of stuff; he put this phrase in quotation marks because he references here an earlier publication of his own – apparently he was very pleased with this neat little turn of phrase.

Marx goes on to define a commodity as 'a thing that by its properties satisfies human wants of some sort or another'. This also indirectly defines 'wealth' in terms of what satisfies 'human wants'.

'Wants' are defined quite broadly: they can 'spring from the stomach or from fancy', implying that they will vary depending on historical and social context, as do 'fancy' (the imagination) and wealth. Marx also adds that a commodity can satisfy wants 'directly as means of subsistence, or indirectly as means of production': a machine that I buy and then use to earn my living is also a commodity.

After these basic determinations, Marx introduces a first rendering of perhaps his most fundamental analytical distinction: 'Every useful thing ... may be looked at from the two points of view of quality and quantity' (43). Again, he emphasizes the historical character even of such a fundamental observation: the many potential uses of the many different properties that any one 'useful thing' may have are discovered by humans in the process of history, and the same is true of the different ways to measure the quantities of all kinds of things. Quality and quantity correspond to the two key terms that are the subject matter of the first section: the utility, or usefulness, of any one thing makes that thing a 'use-value'. (In the language of classical political economy, it is both possible to say that a commodity *is a value* and *has value*. Please note also that I have replaced throughout this chapter the old-fashioned expression 'value in use' with 'use-value'.) Every commodity is a use-value whereas not every useful thing is a commodity – some useful things are gifts, for example, or can be picked in forests for free. The utility of a commodity depends on what *concretely* that commodity-thing is, but not at all, for example, on how laborious it was to make it (44): water for example, supremely useful, just needs to be bottled, while an enormous amount of research and labour time went into the Korg Kaossilator (to name a random example), which is totally useless to most people. Whether a thing is a use-value or not again depends on historical context: no thing simply *is* a use-value as 'use values become a reality only by use or consumption'. Most importantly, use-values 'constitute the substance of all wealth, whatever may be the social form of that wealth'. Wealth means having access to plenty of useful things that cater to human 'wants' (those of the stomach or of the fancy).

'In the form of society we are about to consider', Marx continues, use-values 'are, in addition, the material depositories of exchange-value'. This is the second key term of this section. From the fact that it requires a 'material deposit', we can infer that 'exchange-value' must be something immaterial. 'Exchange-value, at first sight, presents itself as a quantitative relation, as the proportion in which [use-values] of one sort are exchanged for those of another sort, a relation constantly changing with time and place.' At one particular time and place, 'a given commodity, *e.g.*, a quarter of wheat' is exchanged for x amount of 'blacking' (an old-fashioned word for shoe or metal polish), y amount of silk or z amount of gold. All these are exchange values of a quarter of wheat, and as such are *in this respect* identical to each other as well as to the quarter of wheat. This is despite the fact that wheat, blacking, silk and gold are in their material reality, and concerning the uses to which they lend themselves, all entirely different. The first mystery Marx highlights in his critique of political economy is how a series of things that are totally different when looked at as concrete things can be treated as identical when looked at as being exchange-values. Marx infers that 'exchange-value, generally, is only the mode of expression, the phenomenal form, of something contained in it, yet distinguishable from it' (45): in these several different things, 'there exists in equal quantities something common' to all of them. All these equivalent things are, insofar as they are exchange-values, reducible to this something.

Marx starts his search for this mysterious something with an observation made by classical political economists: 'the exchange of commodities is evidently an act characterized by a total abstraction from use value' (45), whereby 'abstraction from' means something like 'bracketing out' or disregarding what one 'abstracts from'. Commodities must be use-values, i.e. they must have *some* utility, but exactly *which* utility they have is irrelevant. Commodity exchange abstracts from all concrete characteristics: £100 worth of lead is of as great a value as £100 worth of silver. Now, what is the mysterious substance of which £100 is a measurement? Marx takes on board here another discovery from classical political economy: if usefulness is disregarded, and with it all concrete characteristics of the commodity, as they all determine its usefulness, then the commodities 'have only one common property left, that of being products of labour' (45), to be precise, of 'labour in the abstract':

> Along with the useful qualities of the products themselves, we put
> out of sight both the useful character of the various kinds of labour
> embodied in them, and the concrete forms of that labour; there is
> nothing left but what is common to them all; all are reduced to one
> and the same sort of labour, human labour in the abstract. (46)

To illustrate this point, it is worthwhile to look at a passage from
one of the eighteenth-century sources that provided Marx with the
decisive clue:

> One man has employed himself a week in providing this necessary
> of life ... and he that gives him some other in exchange cannot make
> a better estimate of what is a proper equivalent, than by computing
> what cost him just as much labour and time; which in effect is no more
> than exchanging one man's labour in one thing for a time certain, for
> another man's labour in another thing for the same time. (quoted on
> p. 54, footnote)

This quote indicates nicely how the pioneers of the discipline of
political economy, the first 'social science', worked out one of its
central ideas.

Commodities, when 'looked at as crystals of this social substance', embodiments of 'homogeneous' or abstract human labour,
are 'values'. ('Exchange-value', expressing the proportion in which
commodities are exchanged, is the form of appearance of 'value',
its substance, which is 'crystallized' abstract labour; more on this
later.) The magnitude of this 'social substance', abstract labour, that
is contained in and that constitutes the value of the commodity, is
measured in time; the value of the commodity is determined by the
'labour time socially necessary for its production' (47), or else, in the
words of an eighteenth-century text quoted by Marx, 'the quantity
of labour necessarily required, and commonly taken in producing'
the commodity. The important point here is that this 'socially necessary' labour time is a *statistical average*, namely the time 'required
to produce an article under the normal conditions of production,
and with the average degree of skill and intensity prevalent at the
time'. Value is therefore an entirely societal category. The category
of value, central to capitalist society, logically presupposes that the
subjects of this society imagine '[t]he total labour power of society,
which is embodied in the sum total of the values of all commodities

produced by that society … as one homogeneous mass of human labour power, composed though it be of innumerable individual units' – although most people most of the time will not be aware of this logical presupposition (46).

The 'individual units' of the totality of society's labour power, whose carriers are otherwise known as human beings, are equal in the eyes of capitalist society as long as they perform their jobs with average skill and average intensity. Marx describes here, in his analysis of the logical structure of 'economic' concepts, characteristics of modern society such as a tendency towards a form of social equality and identity that represents a statistical average – a discovery that resonates with Tocqueville's analysis of 'democracy'. Should the 'individual units' fail to keep up with the statistical average of skill and intensity – as well as technological progress – they are in trouble:

> The introduction of power-looms into England probably reduced by one-half the labour required to weave a given quantity of yarn into cloth. The hand-loom weavers, as a matter of fact, continued to require the same time as before; but for all that, the product of one hour of their labour represented after the change only half an hour's social labour, and consequently fell to one-half its former value. (47)

Although the individual hand-loom weavers *concretely* work as hard and diligently as before, and although the *use*-value of their cloth is as high as before, *at the level of society* the value of cloth has fallen: they will see their income fall accordingly. (To avoid misunderstandings: some of these unfortunate weavers will be able to convince customers that their cloth is aesthetically or morally superior to the new-fangled, mass-produced stuff from the factories, so that these customers volunteer to pay a price above the new, reduced value of the cloth, but that would be another chapter; at the individual level, the *actual prices* of commodities tend to 'fluctuate around' their societally constituted *values* due to various, often subjective, reasons that are bracketed out of the present discussion of only the most abstract and simple concepts.) In general, the rise of productiveness of labour in society – due to increased knowledge and experience as manifested in better technology and social organization of work processes – will correspond to a fall in the production of value but an increase in use-values, i.e. concrete wealth. Therefore increased productiveness which allows us to produce *more concrete wealth* in capitalist society takes the form of *diminished abstract wealth* (value). It could be added that increased productiveness actually is only to be welcomed if it produces welcome products – but this cannot be discussed here.

Marx wraps up the first section by recapitulating that 'a thing can be a use value, without having value' (48), namely 'whenever its utility to man is not due to labour'. Furthermore, a thing 'can be useful, and the product of human labour, without being a commodity', as a commodity is defined as something that is produced for exchange with others. Lastly, nothing can be a value or a commodity without being useful: 'If the thing is useless, so is the labour contained in it; the labour does not count as labour, and therefore creates no value' (48). This last point again underscores the extent to which the concepts developed by Marx in this text are societal concepts.

2 The twofold character of the labour embodied in commodities

The observation that a commodity is a 'complex of … use value and exchange-value' (48) leads Marx to the further observation that 'labour, too, possesses the same two-fold nature; for, so far as it finds expression in value, it does not possess the same characteristics that belong to it as a creator of use values'. Marx emphasizes that 'this point is the pivot on which a clear comprehension of political economy turns' (49), and that he discovered it. The second section introduces this one, crucial argument and then recapitulates most of the contents of the first section from the new perspective on the twofold character of labour.

If you struggled in reading the very heavy first section, you will be grateful for the amount of repetition Marx provides in the second section: Marx's argument becomes clear only by revisiting the same theme in its variations. Learning to read the 'critique of political economy' is a bit like learning a foreign language – it won't suffice to *know* how it works, one needs to go through the motions. For the purposes of this introduction, however, I will in the following only discuss whatever new concepts are introduced in the text – this introduction is, of course, not meant to replace actually reading the primary text: you will not get the same out of reading a map as out of climbing a mountain.

Marx presents in the first chapter of *Capital* one of the chief results of his research in a very simple form: while his research proceeded from a complex reality to the most elementary forms, as scientific research typically does, the presentation of its results in book form begins with the most elementary forms and then proceeds, throughout *Capital* and the many posthumously published drafts that formed part of his overall project, to reconstruct – on paper – the complexity of societal reality. In the first two sections of the first chapter Marx therefore does something very simple: he takes two key observations central to eighteenth-century classical political economy, the twofold character of the commodity-form and the notion that labour is the essence of value – i.e., the point with reference to which it can be determined in which proportion commodities are exchanged – and puts them together. The second section, which Marx highlighted as containing his most important discovery, explores what happens when these two conceptions meet. This is how it goes.

A 'coat is a use-value that satisfies a particular want' (49). It results from 'a special sort of productive activity', coat-making, which is concretely and materially different from shirt-making, umbrella-making, pudding-making, or linen-making. 'The labour, whose utility … manifests itself by making its product a use-value, we call useful labour.' The utility of 'useful labour' is to make useful things and, like the utility of useful things, it depends entirely on its concrete qualities. Commodity production presupposes that a society has already developed 'social division of labour' as '[o]nly such products can become commodities … as result from different kinds of labour' – otherwise there would be no point in exchanging them. Marx adds that division of labour in the most general sense of the word does not necessarily presuppose a very high degree of specialization: 'the human race made clothes for thousands of years, without a single man becoming a tailor' (50). In a society not based on generalized commodity-production, persons who happen to be good at coat-making will not necessarily 'be tailors', but they will make the necessary coats and may then resume fishing, astronomy, DJ-ing, shepherding or whatever. Again, it is worth pointing out that Marx *historicizes* his concepts: the commodity-form has a history, a beginning and, probably, also an ending. By contrast, he emphasizes that 'useful labour', in spite of its ever-changing concrete form, is in fact 'eternal': 'special productive activity, exercised with a definite aim, an activity that appropriates particular nature-given materials to particular human wants' is 'a necessary condition, independent of all forms of society, for the existence of the human race' without which there can be 'no material exchanges between man and nature, and therefore no life'. He adds that useful labour is always labour *on something* particular, 'a material substratum' that is 'furnished by nature' and whose form is changed by labour, 'helped by natural forces' (such as water power or the power contained in fossil fuels, etc.): 'labour is not the only source of material wealth' (50).

Marx moves now from the discussion of use-value and useful labour to the much more thorny issue of value and *labour as creating value*: 'abstract labour', i.e., labour looked at in abstraction from its concrete form and specific usefulness.

> Productive activity, if we leave out of sight its special form, [namely] the useful character of the labour, is nothing but the expenditure of human labour power. Tailoring and weaving, though qualitatively different productive activities, are each a productive expenditure of human brains, nerves, and muscles, and in this sense are human labour. They are but two different modes of expending human labour power. (51)

'Labour in the abstract' is 'the expenditure of simple labour power, i.e., of the labour power which, on an average, apart from any special development, exists in the organism of every ordinary individual'. This average differs in accordance with geographical and histori-cal context. Marx recaps: just as 'in viewing the coat and linen as values, we abstract from their different use-values', so in viewing weaving and tailoring as abstract labour 'we disregard the difference between its useful forms, weaving and tailoring' (52).

3 The form of value or exchange-value
3.1 The elementary form of value

The third section of the text begins with a playful philosophical self-reflection on the presentation of Marx's argument that must seem rather puzzling for anyone not as well trained in classical German philosophy as Marx apparently assumed his readers would be. 'Commodities come into the world in the shape of use-values', their 'plain, homely, bodily form' (54). One imagines Marx giggling away while writing 'come into the world', as this phrase is used in German first of all for babies: German babies 'come into the world' which raises the question, of course, where, if not 'the world', do they come from? Marx has fun here with the implication that for denizens of capitalist society, commodities are some kind of spiritual, extraterrestrial beings (values) that 'become flesh' (use-values) in the way that, for pious Germans, babies do.

Commodities are only commodities if they have two forms, a 'physical' form and a 'value-form'. By contrast with the 'coarse materiality' of the former (the commodity flesh), the latter (the commodity soul) is entirely immaterial: 'not an atom of matter enters into its composition'. We cannot see or touch value: 'the value of commodities has a purely social reality', namely as 'embodiments of one identical social substance', human labour in the abstract (i.e. in abstraction from its concreteness). Marx has already discussed in the second section what this mysterious, immaterial substance *is*; now he asks how it can actually *appear* – a question of philosophical, if not theological character: what can possibly be the earthly *manifestation* of an abstract 'substance'? (If it helps, for comparison think of the notion of the God who became man in Christian theology.) The answer (already given earlier) is restated here: it 'can only manifest itself in the social relation of commodity to commodity' (54). Marx reminds his readers that he started in the first section 'from exchange-value, or the exchange relation of commodities, in order to get at the value that lies hidden behind it'. Translated into a more pedestrian version of the argument, this references the fact that – in the view of the political economists – two individuals who exchange commodities determine the proportion in which they will be happy to exchange their wares from a calculation of the labour time they exerted on producing them: the exchange proportion (exchange-value) is thus linked to the idea of labour expenditure (measured in units of time) as the essence of the value of the commodity. (This classical bourgeois idea is currently revived in so-called 'let-schemes': two individuals who exchange *x* amount of home-grown cabbages for a haircut will feel they have made a 'fair deal' when they both think that growing x amount of cabbages took about as much labour time as cutting the cabbage-grower's hair. It would be interesting to witness the haggling: 'What – such a quick cut for this many cabbages? Don't you know how much work goes into growing a cabbage?') At the more philosophical level at which Marx operates here, the argument is that value is a *socially consti-tuted abstraction* whose concrete reality lies in exchange value, which is a *practical, social relation*. The latter is the reality of the former. Value is therefore at the same time an abstraction and a reality – an *abstracting social practice*, one could say: a social practice that involves bracketing out some aspects of its own reality. After section two has established what value *is*, section three returns now to the argument begun in the first section on how it materially, practically, in reality, *appears* – 'comes into the world' – as exchange value. Marx's reflections are highly instructive beyond the role they play in his own overall argument, as the question, what kind of reality does an abstraction have, is fundamental to social theory: *what is the materiality of a social relationship?*

In the next paragraph, still on the first page of the third sec-tion, Marx points to something that he says even the most ignorant person knows well: money. Everybody knows – without ever having thought about it – that all commodities, in spite of their infinite variety in the concrete, can be reduced to 'their money form' in which they are all (substantially) equal: different amounts of the same slightly mysterious substance (54). Although this is an every-day experience – every child knows about it – the money form is in fact the most complex 'value form' of the commodity; Marx begins its exploration with the simplest 'value form', 'that of one com-modity to some one other commodity of a different kind' (54), and proceeds throughout the third section (some twenty pages long) to 'solve the riddle presented by money'. I will give in the following only the gist of it, before devoting a bit more detail to the fourth section, the famous discussion of 'commodity fetishism'.

When we state that 'x amount of commodity A is worth y amount of commodity B', which Marx calls the 'elementary or accidental form of value', we presuppose that we think of 'xA' and 'yB' as equivalents, and of A and B thereby as 'commensurable', i.e., things of the same essence that can be measured with the same measuring tool. The social process that puts certain amounts of A and B in a quantitative relationship automatically and unconsciously imagines the labour that went into the making of these *different* commodities as *identical*: this process (commodity exchange) abstracts from the specificities of the concrete labour processes. This automatically presupposed abstraction, which provides a notion of what is a 'fair deal', is exclusively characteristic of *commodity* exchange: in other forms of society people would have other forms of exchanging things that would also have other ways of creating in the exchangers the sense that an exchange went well, or not so well. Marx calls the defining, albeit merely implicit, reference point of *commodity* exchange 'abstract[ly] human labour' or 'human labour in the abstract' (57).

Although abstract human labour constitutes value, the product of that labour 'is a value' (or 'has value') only as a commodity, i.e., when it stands in an exchange relation with other commodities: value can only become actual ('enter into the world') as 'exchange-value', i.e. within exchange. Everybody and everything, however, must become flesh in order to 'enter into the world' – that goes for value as for babies or the Lord himself. Exchange-value becomes flesh in the 'relative value form', as Marx now terms what he has introduced already: the value of '*x* amount of A' appears (enters the world) in the form of '*y* amount of B', which means that '*y* amount of B' (B being some other commodity) is the 'value body' in which the 'value soul' of '*x* amount of A' can appear. This sounds weird only because it is formulated in a very formal manner; in fact the point is straightforward: it would not make any sense at all to say that 'five kilos of strawberries are worth five kilos of strawberries', but 'five kilos of strawberries are worth one gram of gold or one baseball cap or one half-hour massage' makes sense, at least in the context of a society that exchanges all kinds of things, including services, as equivalent amounts of 'abstract human labour'. (Whether that in itself makes sense is a completely different question.)

Something that is almost banal becomes, upon translation into formal, theoretical language, something quite bizarre: this is the welcome effect of making everyday things unfamiliar and strange by theorizing them, or rather, of showing how strange they really are by stripping them of their familiarity. One of the techniques Marx uses to this purpose is the application of heavy philosophical terminology to very mundane, everyday phenomena. He spends another page or so hammering home the point that the 'value soul' of commodity A can become visible only by taking on the 'value body' of another commodity, commodity B, and makes in passing here a few observations that served later social theorists as career-defining discoveries. Again, Marx emphasizes that things are what they are because of the relationships in which they stand to other things: a coat is 'just' a coat, a use-value, but can become something much grander, namely the 'equivalent form of value' for, say, fifty jars of strawberry jam. Marx compares this sarcastically to the difference between a man in civilian clothes and the same man in uniform, which latter increases his social standing, as the uniform is indicative of a particular social relation in which he stands to other people (58). What is puzzling here is that the value of the jam *can only* appear in the form of something that is not jam, such as the coat, and that this coat (think of it as a primitive form of money) is a use-value, a thing, that *is* the value, the (value-) soul of the jam (insofar as it serves as the 'relative value form' of the jam). Marx throws in a few analogies here for illustration: a person A, 'for instance, cannot be "your majesty" to [person] B, unless at the same time majesty in B's eyes assumes the bodily form of A': person B, the subject, must recognize that the concrete, bodily appearance of person A, the king, represents 'majesty' (a social relation) and needs to be able to recognize in all successors of King A the equivalent bodily forms of appearance of that same (somewhat mystical, but socially constituted) substance called 'majesty' (58). Marx adds an even more sarcastic comparison: when the 'value soul' of jam looks like a coat, then the fact that the jam 'is value, is made manifest by its equality with the coat, just as the sheep's nature of a Christian is shown in his resemblance to the Lamb of God'. The Christian recognizes his or her own soul in the materiality of the Lamb; the Lamb, a material being, expresses the spirituality of the Christian. (Note that Marx uses the word 'soul' consistently here for what he describes as the effect of a social relationship, i.e., what we would now call a 'social construct'.) Marx concludes the exploration of this point with another metaphor, saying that 'the body of commodity B acts as a mirror to the value of commodity A' (59), and adds a footnote that unpacks some of the philosophical subtext of the argument, although in characteristically tongue-in-cheek manner: 'In a sort of way, it is with man as with commodities' (as if it was not rather the other way round...): man does not come 'into the world ... with a looking glass in his hand', and therefore

> man first sees and recognizes his reflection in other men. Peter only establishes his own identity as a man by first comparing himself with Paul as being of like kind. And thereby Paul, just as he stands in his particular, Pauline physicality, becomes to Peter a form of appearance of the *genus homo*.

Marx plays a rather complex charade here: the footnote shows that the 'behaviour' of the commodities that recognize their own 'soul' in their mirror reflection in other commodities in fact mirrors the way human beings (as infants) establish their humanity (their soul, as it were) by mirroring themselves in each other. Something universal (the humanity of human beings/the value of commodities) becomes apparent and tangible only by becoming flesh in something particular (another human being/another commodity), whereby the particular comes to represent the universal. A few pages further down, this is restated as 'use value becomes the form of manifestation, the phenomenal form of its opposite, value' (62).

Inching closer to the concept of money, Marx now points out that we tend to think of the ability of 'commodity B' in its physical reality to represent the value of 'commodity A' as one of its 'natural' characteristics, like its weight, density or colour, whereas it is really only the effect of a societal relationship. Again he illustrates this – in another light-hearted footnote – with an observation that sounds as if it comes from mid-twentieth-century 'interpretative' sociology (but is actually borrowed from the philosopher Hegel): 'one man is king only because other men stand in the relation of subjects to him. They, on the contrary, imagine that they are subjects because he is king' (63). I once heard a very similar statement from an actress: on stage, 'the king is always played by the other actors', not by the actor who supposedly plays the king. Even if, say, everybody on stage was naked or wore identical black suits, as is sometimes the case in a modernist production, and even if 'the king' was entirely silent, one could tell who was the king just from watching how the others act towards him. On the stage that we call society, some of those 'other actors' may or may not believe in some kind of kingly essence that makes the king a king – it does not matter as long as they *do the acting*. In reality, of course, king-ness is nothing but a social relationship (just like commodity value) – a social construct, as it were.

Marx comments in this context on a passage from a work by the classical Greek philosopher Aristotle (384–322 BCE), the *Nicomachean Ethics*. (This work, one of the key texts of Western philosophy, is named after the person it was dedicated to, Nicomachus.) Aristotle made in this text an early attempt to explain what money is, and stated – two thousand years before modern political economy – that 'the money form of commodities is only the further development of the simple form of value – *i.e.*, of the expression of the value of one commodity in some other commodity'; Aristotle observed that equating 'five beds' with 'one house' is no different from equating 'five beds' with 'this amount of money'. (Apparently furniture was quite expensive in Athens back then, compared to houses!) Aristotle also observed that these equations imply equality and commensurability between the things that are being equated, but ended up saying that this implication must be a form of mistaken thinking as unequal things are not really commensurable. Marx's interpretation of Aristotle's failure to discover abstract labour – which is a truly modern idea – is most interesting:

> Greek society was founded upon slavery, and had, therefore, for its natural basis, the inequality of men and of their labour powers. The secret of the expression of value, namely, that all kinds of labour are equal and equivalent, because, and so far as they are human labour in general, cannot be deciphered, until the notion of human equality has already acquired the fixity of a popular prejudice. This, however, is possible only in a society in which the great mass of the produce of labour takes the form of commodities, in which, consequently, the dominant relation between man and man, is that of owners of com- modities. The brilliancy of Aristotle's genius is shown by this alone, that he discovered, in the expression of the value of commodities, a relation of equality. The peculiar conditions of the society in which

he lived, alone prevented him from discovering what, 'in truth,' was
at the bottom of this equality. (65–66)

Although some commodity exchange existed in classical Greek
society, most things were not produced as commodities, and most
people, most of the time, did not interact as owners, sellers and
buyers of commodities: slaves in particular were owners of nothing, not even their own labour power. It was therefore not possible
for an inhabitant of classical Athens to come up with the notion of
abstract labour as universally equal: it was not equal. Only the daily,
all-embracing, continuous practice of exchanging commodities in
modern society, where most things are produced and exchanged as
commodities, could create the mentality within whose framework
the concept of 'abstract labour' seems plausible: the idea, namely,
that there is a common substance to all those different commodities, and all the different acts of labour that produce them, that
makes them commensurable and exchangeable as equivalent por-
tions of an identical 'substance' – abstract labour. Marx's comment
on Aristotle illustrates well his method of critique: he applauds
Aristotle for going as far as he did, and then suggests a historical
explanation for why he could not go further.

3.2 Expanded, general and money forms of value

What Marx calls the 'elementary' or 'simple' form of value is a
theoretical category, not the description of an empirical reality: in
reality, no one exchanges linen for coats (and even if some people
do, it will hardly be of great societal importance). In reality, as
soon as exchanging commodities has become a generalized social
practice, all commodities are 'citizens' of a 'world of commodities'
in the sense that all commodities are related to all others through
multiple exchange relations that establish equivalences between all
and sundry: the values of commodities are therefore much less accidental, more societal, than the notion of its 'simple form' might suggest (69). This results in what Marx calls the 'general form of value'.
It 'results from the joint action of the whole world of commodities'
(71) – again, Marx talks about commodities, half tongue-in-cheek,
half seriously, as if they were active subjects, like the tin soldiers in

The Nutcracker or their descendants in *Toy Story*. And, again as in those fairy tales, their 'world' exerts compulsions just like ours does: 'every new commodity must follow suit'. The existence of commodities as values is 'purely social' and 'can be expressed by the totality of their social relations alone' – just like human existence in society. In the world of commodities, one commodity becomes 'the universal equivalent' whose 'bodily form' becomes 'the visible incarnation … of every kind of human labour' (72). The 'universal equivalent', generally known under the sobriquet 'money', is to the totality of commodities what the Pope is to all Catholics: there is only ever one Pope at a time (with very few historical exceptions), but all members of the faith recognize their own best self in His Holiness. The analogy goes even further: just as the election of a Pope settles and consolidates what the meaning of the Catholic faith is, so does the election of one commodity as the 'universal equivalent' of all other commodities consolidate their shared universal identity and exchangeability as commodities (73). It is the dotting of the 'i' (to borrow the phrase Hegel once used to describe the function of a monarch in modern society).

Marx only touches here on the subject of money, going no further than to give a most fundamental definition of money as the 'first among equals' in the world of commodities, and proceeds to wrap up the argument of the famously difficult first chapter of *Capital*. This first concluding section has the puzzling title 'The Fetishism of Commodities and the Secret Thereof' and no, it is *not* about how we fetishize certain commodities, such as fast sexy sports cars or Louis Vuitton handbags. We don't know how many handbags he had, but Marx was decidedly *not* a critic of 'consumerism'.

4 The fetishism of commodities and the secret thereof

In the first three sections of the first chapter of *Capital*, Marx as it were limbered up in mostly rather respectful and polite discussions of the basic concepts of political economy. Now, in the fourth and final section, Marx gets into his stride. The discipline of political economy is showered with sarcasms that ridicule a theory that uncritically reflects the superstitions of a society that is organized like a cargo cult, only bigger and bolder.

The fourth section falls into two halves, in the first of which Marx gives us a condensed version of his argument so far, whereas in the second he reflects once more on his own method in distinction to that of the political economists whose work he critiques.

4.1 On social relations that take the form of relations between things

Upon reflection, Marx writes, a commodity is 'in reality, a very queer thing, abounding in metaphysical subtleties and theological niceties' (76). Whereas its use-value side is a straightforward affair – humans change materials so as to make them useful – the value side gives it a 'mystical character'. The table, when it takes the social form of a commodity, 'evolves out of its wooden brain grotesque ideas, far more wonderful than "table-turning" ever was'. (Table-turning was a spiritualist fad popular in the restoration period of the early 1850s.) A thing, as commodity, i.e. a particular kind of social thing, assumes agency and has ideas of its own, apparently. Very strange indeed.

The factors that determine value are in themselves not mystical at all: labour is never anything but 'expenditure of human brain, nerves, muscles, etc.'. Also the fact that humans in whichever form of society are interested in the question of how long it takes 'to produce the means of subsistence' is unsurprising. And there is no mystery finally in the fact that 'from the moment that men in any way work for one another, their labour assumes a social form'. The mystery only starts at the specific historical point (quite recently, in terms of human history) when the products of labour assume the commodity form. It is only now that the 'equality of all sorts of human labour is expressed *objectively* by their products all being equally values' (76–77; italics added). Only now does the expenditure of labour power, measured in units of time, take 'the form of the quantity of value of the products of labour' (77), i.e. an objective form. Only now do 'the mutual relations of the producers, within which the social character of their labour affirms itself, take the form of a social relation between the products' – a relation between objects, that is. This is a most peculiar claim: the things have social relations, that is, they form, apparently, a kind of society, a society of things. And this society of things is our society. But the fault does not lie with the things themselves, but with us, the humans who *labour in a particular way*: the capitalist way. Marx inches now towards a first high point, and perhaps the key point of his argument, a critique of labour as practised in capitalist society:

> A commodity is therefore a mysterious thing, simply because in it the social character of men's labour appears to them as an objective character stamped upon the product of that labour; because the relation of the producers to the sum total of their own labour is presented to them as a social relation, existing not between themselves, but between the products of their labour. This is the reason why the products of labour become commodities, social things whose qualities are at the same time perceptible and imperceptible by the senses … [A] definite social relation between men … assumes, in their eyes, the fantastic form of a relation between things. In order, therefore, to find an analogy, we must have recourse to the mist-enveloped regions of the religious world. In that world the productions of the human brain appear as independent beings endowed with life, and entering into relation both with one another and the human race. So it is in the world of commodities with the products of men's hands. This I call the fetishism which attaches itself to the products of labour, so soon as they are produced as commodities, and which … has its origin … in the peculiar social character of the labour that produces them. (77)

It is perhaps worth recalling that this comes from a writer who belonged to the radical wing of the Enlightenment movement and was able to take atheism – his own and, presumably, that of most of his readers and interlocutors – for granted. (He was shocked when during his stay in Paris he realized how religious many French socialists were; see the previous chapter.) Given this context, it was not just a nice little metaphor to say that the only analogy apt to illustrate the most elementary social form of capitalist society is religion: it was a massive, deliberately polemical attack on a modernity that was nowhere near modern enough. Enlightenment critique had, after all, denounced religion as a mental practice of outward projection of illusions produced by deceived human minds. Marx says that exactly that kind of thing, delusional projection as we know it from religion, takes place at every minute of our apparently secular and enlightened social lives. This delusional projection is the mechanism at the centre of the elementary social form of capitalist society, the commodity form. And it gets even better: Marx describes the commodity form as *fetishism*, a term with which Christian 'explorers' and other pioneers of colonialism had denoted the 'primitive' religions of 'the savages' whom they encountered in the heart of darkness and which they smugly felt was so clearly inferior to their own. Comte and Hegel were among those who discussed fetishism as primitive religion. There is clear polemical intent in Marx's choice of words here: the apparently rational, enlightened mode of production central to European modernity is the real savagery.

Marx proceeds from here to flesh out his proposition that the 'fetishism of commodities' derives from 'the peculiar social character of labour' in commodity-producing society. He sets out from the observation that, 'as a general rule', commodities are produced by 'private individuals or groups of individuals who carry on their work independently of each other' (77). They 'do not come into social contact with each other until they exchange their products' – only at that point does 'the specific social character of each producer's labour' show itself:

> In other words, the labour of the individual asserts itself as a part of the labour of society only by means of the relations which the act of exchange establishes directly between the products, and indirectly, through them, between the producers. To the latter, therefore, the relations connecting the labour of one individual with that of the rest appear, not as direct social relations between individuals at work, but as what they really are, thingly relations between persons and social relations between things. (78)

The last half-sentence of this passage is one of the strangest in *Capital*, and perhaps one of the most important: the relations between the labour of one individual and all others 'appear … as what they really are'. Contrary to expectations, given the mockery of the commodity form as quasi-religious on the previous page, Marx states now that reality and appearance are in fact the same – but topsy-turvy: relations between persons are *really* thing-like rather than social, and relations between things are *really* social rather than thing-like. ('Thing-like' or 'thingly' is the literal translation of the word Marx uses here, *sachlich*; the standard English translation, 'material', is misleading.)

In order to unpack this seemingly absurd statement, we can easily agree that relations between things can be said to be social when these things are 'social things', which is indeed what Marx says. Relations between persons can be said to be 'thing-like' if they are dominated by things, which, again, is indeed Marx's argument: the productive activities of isolated commodity producers are regulated by the proportions in which their products 'exchange themselves'. The producers in question have no influence on this. At least subjectively, it may 'really appear' to the individual, isolated producers that the commodities have their own ideas about what they are worth, because the producers can never be aware of all the various factors that determine the exchange value of a commodity. Marx's continued play with 'reality' and 'appearance', including his ongoing spiel about things that act and form 'a world' of their own, destabilizes these concepts, and it becomes increasingly clear that what is 'real' at one level of analysis might be 'illusion' at another: after all, things *don't* in fact have minds of their own! Their apparently mystical activity must really be an effect of the activities of humans in society, but one that is neither transparent to these humans, nor intended, nor controllable. As these activities (capitalism) are real and the 'illusions' are their *necessary* effects, the 'illusions' are real, too – that is, they are not just illusions that would disappear if properly explained. Even if I fully understand how capitalism works, I am still forced to act in accordance with its 'real illusions'. If I practise these 'illusions' on a daily basis, I will also believe them to be realities – because they are…

Marx emphasizes that the 'division of a product into a useful thing and a value', i.e., the commodity form of the product, 'becomes practically important only when exchange has acquired such an extension that useful articles are produced for the purpose of being exchanged, and their character as values has therefore to be taken into account, beforehand, during production' (78). This underlines once more that Marx's argument is not so much about things but about the labour that produces them: this is why Marx talks about a 'capitalist mode of *production*', not generic 'capitalism'.

The twofold character of labour is reflected in the twofold character of the commodity: the duality of the socially useful character of concrete, particular forms of labour *versus* the socially equal character of all forms of labour in abstraction is reflected in the duality of the use-value *versus* the value of the commodity. In this sense, the commodity-form is secondary to, and derives from, the twofold form of labour (in a society dominated by generalized commodity production, i.e. a capitalist society).

Marx is, however, too much the dialectician to leave it at that; as so often, the argument is immediately followed by its reversal: *at the level of the consciousness of the individuals* who are involved in this societal practice, Marx hastens to add, it works the other way round. The particular labours that brought forth products as commodities are revealed as 'what they really are' – certain quantities of abstract labour – only at the point of exchanging these products. Although the individual producer of umbrellas or textbooks almost inevitably thinks of his or her labour as very specific, particular, skilled labour, at the point of exchanging the products as commodities he or she realizes that the exertion of concrete, particular labour was only the form of appearance of what in essence was already the exertion of abstract labour. (It would be different if umbrellas and textbooks had been produced only in order to be given away for free among friends, family or, in communism, the human commonweal, or posted for free on the internet.) One must read these passages very carefully, as Marx aims to describe at the same time what people in society *do* as well as what they *think* they do, and how both are related. He explicitly states that 'when we bring the products of our labour into relation with each other as values, it is not because we see in these articles the material receptacles of homogeneous human labour' (78): it does not matter whether we *know about* 'abstract labour' or not. Marx writes that '[w]e are not aware of this, nevertheless we do it'. Value, Marx writes, 'does not stalk about with a label describing what it is' but rather 'converts every product into a social hieroglyphic' (79). Humans 'try to decipher the hieroglyphic, to get behind the secret of [their] own social products', but even 'the recent scientific discovery' (by the pioneers of the bourgeois discipline of political economy) that commodities *as values* 'are but thingly expressions of [abstract] human labour spent in their production' fails to prevent 'the social character of labour' from appearing as its 'objective character'. Marx emphasizes here the limits of science and of what we might call the 'critique of ideology': although only in (generalized) commodity production does 'the specific social character of private labour' (the fact that it takes the form of abstract labour) assume 'in the product the form of value', the inhabitants of the world of capitalist production continue to think of this peculiar social fact as an eternal, unchangeable fact of nature, whatever social science and critique may tell them. Marx admonishes us here not to overestimate the efficacy of the 'scientific' critique of ideology: everyday life in capitalist society relentlessly trains people to think of the commodity form as the natural form of the products of labour, and even whole armies of scientists and critics will not change that. It could be added that even those of us who, after studying the critique of political economy for example, *are* aware of the historicity of the value form will continue to act as if it were a natural rather than a social fact as long as we, too, have to earn our living by exchanging labour power for money.

The everyday experience that cements the value form into people's brains is the need repeatedly to address 'the question, how much of some other product they get for their own?' (79). Exchange-values appear the more natural, the more they have attained 'by custom ... a certain stability': gold has always been more expensive than milk, so it seems that it is part of its nature to be expensive. Exchange-values therefore 'appear to result from the nature of the products'. (Should anyone finally discover the philosopher's stone and produce gold like popcorn, this supposed aspect of its nature will change.) The illusion of their naturalness is helped by the fact that exchange proportions 'vary continually, independently of the will, foresight and action of the producers' to whom then 'their own social action takes the form of the action of objects'. The fact that the magnitude of value is determined by what is the societally average necessary labour time asserts itself 'in the midst of all the accidental and ever fluctuating exchange relations between the products' like a 'law of nature', just as gravity does – except that gravity really *is* a fact of nature, whereas the law of value only looks like one.

4.2 On scientific method: moving from complex to simple social forms in order to discover the historicity of social facts

Marx begins the remainder of the first chapter with another methodological reflection. He observes that, in general, social science begins with what it finds in the present, that is, the results of the historical process, and then gradually moves backwards in time. In the highly developed present, the 'forms of social life' already appear stable and natural, and most social scientists aim to decipher their meaning but not 'their historical character' which has already become invisible. To destabilize the illusion of naturalness, Marx implies, one must study their emergence. 'The categories of bourgeois economy' are 'forms of thought expressing with social validity the conditions and relations of a definite, historically determined mode of production', generalized commodity production (80): when Marx writes that they are valid in their specific context, he means that they are the categories one *cannot but* live by in the type of society for which they are valid. In order to show that they are not valid outside this specific context, Marx suggests looking at 'other forms of production' (81). On the next several pages, he sketches out four different cases of 'other forms of production', one fictional, two historical and one utopian.

First, Marx has a laugh in describing the life of Robinson Crusoe in terms of a one-man economy that obviously involves neither division of labour nor any economic exchanges at all. This is Marx ridiculing those classical political economists who loved to use fictional accounts of life outside modern civilization such as the tale of Robinson Crusoe to illustrate their theoretical models. The point is, however, that in the novel by Daniel Defoe, Crusoe remains when marooned on his island 'a true-born Briton' and keeps 'a set of books' about himself, containing among other data the lengths of time that he needed to make various 'objects of utility'. (Luckily, Crusoe had salvaged a watch, a ledger and other key necessities from the wreck.) Marx points out that Crusoe has therewith at his command 'all that is essential to the determination of value' (81). The humour of this passage is that in the absence of any form of society, there is absolutely no point in keeping these books, and Crusoe does it only because he is, even on his desert island, really a member of British society temporarily isolated from it. Preoccupations that are normal in that society are absurd outside it, and their de-contextualized portrayal also tars that society itself with the brush of absurdity – the stuff of satire. In a more technical sense, one could add that although Crusoe is able to determine the magnitude of the value of various things he produces on the island, value is not able to 'actually appear' (in the form of exchange value) as there is no exchange: his products are not values as they are not produced for commodity exchange. An essence that does not actually appear, or materialize, does not in fact exist, which means that Crusoe can only measure the magnitudes of non-existent values. Instead of the ledger, it would have been better if he had taken a cookbook, something like 'Difficult dishes for singletons with lots of spare time to kill'. Marx's joke here is that a true Briton would always prefer a ledger over, say, a cookbook.

Marx's second and third cases are the feudalism of the European Middle Ages and the economy of the peasant family that stands in for what the early history of most of mankind everywhere might have looked like. Marx contrasts here the use of historical and contemporary empirical accounts of non-bourgeois economic forms with the construction of non-empirical, basically fictional models as used by the bourgeois political economists: while the latter only reproduce aspects of bourgeois society by projecting them into fictional, non-bourgeois contexts, actual historical-empirical research helps to show, by way of contrast, what are the historically specific characteristics of modern, bourgeois society. In European feudalism, 'we find everyone dependent, serfs and lords, vassals and suzerains, laymen and clergy' (81). All spheres of life are organized in terms of 'personal dependence'. Therefore

> there is no necessity for labour and its products to assume a fantastic form different from their reality. They take the shape, in the transactions of society, of services in kind and payments in kind. Here the particular and natural form of labour, and not, as in a society based on production of commodities, its general abstract form is the immediate social form of labour. Compulsory labour is just as properly measured by time, as commodity-producing labour; but every serf knows that what he expends in the service of his lord, is a definite quantity of his own personal labour power ... [T]he social relations between

individuals in the performance of their labour appear at all events as
their own mutual personal relations, and are not disguised under the
shape of social relations between the products of labour. (81–82)

A historically more ancient form of production, although still existing in Marx's day, is the 'directly associated labour' (82) of 'the
patriarchal industries of a peasant family, that produces corn, cattle,
yarn, linen, and clothing for home use'. These things are produced
in a kind of division of labour but not as commodities. The members of the peasant family, and other forms of 'primitive' community, probably negotiate somehow the lengths and the kinds of work
that every member has to contribute, but the 'distribution of the
work within the family, and the regulation of the labour time of the
several members, depend as well upon differences of age and sex as
upon natural conditions varying with the seasons'. The work you
do depends on who you are, i.e., your role and positioning in the
family, and what work there is to be done. The concept of 'abstract
labour' cannot emerge in this context, as concrete labour itself is
the social mediation. No mystery there: in both empirical-histor-
ical examples, feudal and 'patriarchal family' forms of production,
the organization of production, exploitation and dependency are
straightforward, in your face, unashamed. Only the modern period,
which likes so much to think of itself as the age of Enlightenment,
produces the real-life mysticisms of the 'fetishism of commodities'
and 'abstract labour'.

The following section, containing Marx's discussion of the
fourth case of a non-bourgeois form of production, constitutes one
of the very few examples in Marx's writings in which he hints at
what form of society would be desirable: 'an association of free
individuals, carrying on their work with the means of production
in common, in which the labour power of all the different individuals is consciously applied as the combined labour power of society'
(82–83), a formulation that could well serve as a basic definition of
'communism'. (The standard English text, clearly under the influence of English romantic socialism, mistranslates 'association' and
'society' as 'community'.) Marx was famously reluctant to elaborate
a detailed utopia, as he thought of his work as a *critical* theory,
not a prescriptive or normative one. This might explain why he is

extremely brief on this issue here, too: he does not say much, except that communism would be a bit like Robinson Crusoe's situation if only Crusoe was a society, not an individual. All products are produced as objects for use, not for exchange; the entire production of society is immediately 'a social product' (83), not a private product. Those products that will serve as 'means of production' remain social, those that are 'consumed by the members as means of subsistence' need to be distributed. Marx is uncharacteristically vague here: 'The mode of this distribution will vary with the societal organization of production, and the degree of historical development attained by the producers'. He probably had in the back of his mind the various (mutually hostile) tendencies among communist and socialist movements at the time, but avoided discussing any of their differing views on the distribution of wealth. He limits himself to making two points: the first goes back to Crusoe's ledger, the second to the issue of religion. Concerning book-keeping, Marx states that measuring labour time would have two roles to play in 'an association of free individuals': one, for the planning of production, which includes determining the adequate proportion of specific labours to social wants; two, for distribution, if society decides to link an individual's share in the social product to that individual's working contribution. (Among socialists at the time, some would have demanded 'to everyone according to their work', some 'to everyone according to their needs', irrespective of how much work an individual contributes to society; Marx belonged to the second group, but he is deliberately ambiguous here. Maybe he was trying not to alienate the majority of his potential readership in the first chapter!) The take-home point here is that although a communist society will measure and calculate labour time, it will not make use of the concepts of 'abstract labour' and value: the 'needs and wants' will be mediated with the labouring activities of society's members directly and concretely, through a process of deliberation and planning, not abstractly through commodity exchanges.

Marx concludes the section on the historicity of forms of production with a short reflection on religion. Marx paints here with a broad brush, making a number of statements that would each deserve a book of its own. First, here is Marx's theory of Christianity in one sentence:

For a society based upon the production of commodities, in which
the producers in general enter into social relations with one another
by treating their products as commodities and values, whereby they
reduce their individual private labour to the standard of homogeneous human labour – for such a society, Christianity with its *cultus*
of abstract man, more especially in its bourgeois developments,
Protestantism, Deism, &c., is the most fitting form of religion.

The English translators introduced this sentence with 'The religious world is but the reflex of the real world', which is not contained in the original German text and distorts the argument: Marx
writes that Christianity is the 'most fitting' form of religion for a
commodity-producing society, and points to the *analogy* between
the theological idea of 'abstract man' and a societal reality as structured by universally equal, abstract human labour. He does not
elaborate here on which way the causality between these two phenomena runs, but it is clear that he sees commodity production in
antiquity as a subordinate phenomenon that cannot have caused
the emergence of Christianity. Commodity production gradually,
in history, became a dominant phenomenon, in parallel with the
modernization of Christianity in the Reformation. Marx adds that
the absence of the abstract, universalist aspects of Christian theology in more ancient forms of religion correlates with the absence
of abstract, universalizing forms in their social organization, and
moves then from the question of the specific form of religion to that
of religion as such:

The religious reflex of the real world can, in any case, only then finally
vanish, when the practical relations of everyday life offer to man none
but perfectly intelligible and reasonable relations with regard to his
fellow men and to nature. The life-process of society, i.e. the process
of material production, will not strip off its mystical veil until it is
treated as production by freely associated men, and is consciously
regulated by them in accordance with a settled plan. (84)

Although Marx does not seem to be saying that the specific form
of religion must faithfully reflect a specific social reality, he sees the
general fact that there is religion *as such* as a reflection of the mastery
of an opaque, unintelligible society over the humans who created it.
The fact that Marx discusses this issue in such a prominent place

in his most prominent piece of writing shows that his fundamental concern is not just the overcoming of the capitalist mode of production – a quite recent historical phenomenon – but the wider character of human civilization of which capitalist society is only the most recent incarnation. The thrust against 'opacity', 'mystical veils', domination and religion clearly marks his effort as that of the continuation of the eighteenth-century Enlightenment.

This was the climax of the famously difficult first chapter of *Capital*; congratulations if you made it all the way to here. On the final pages Marx makes several more sarcastic comments on political economists and theologians, including a quotation from one of Marx's own earlier writings that is worth relating:

> Economists have a singular method of procedure. There are only two kinds of institutions for them, artificial and natural. The institutions of feudalism are artificial institutions, those of the bourgeoisie are natural institutions. In this they resemble the theologians, who likewise establish two kinds of religion. Every religion which is not theirs is an invention of men, while their own is an emanation from God … Thus there has been history, but there is no longer any. (85)

History is, for bourgeois economists, a movement from supposedly 'artificial institutions' – obstacles and fetters to human productivity such as under feudalism – to supposedly 'natural institutions' such as commodity exchange, exchange-value and abstract labour. Once these supposedly natural institutions have been achieved, history ends – there is nowhere else to go. For Marx, as has been shown, the appearance of naturalness is itself a product of a particularly complex society. No social fact is natural, just as 'no chemist has ever discovered exchange-value either in a pearl or in a diamond' (87).

6

The conflict of community and society: Ferdinand Tönnies

Ferdinand Tönnies (1855–1936) is famous for having coined one of the most often used, and perhaps also most contested, pairs of contrasting terms in modern social thought: community and society, a dichotomy so famous that even in English-language contexts it is often given in German: *Gemeinschaft* and *Gesellschaft*. Not coincidentally, Tönnies's background, too, is full of contrasting terms: he came from a small town in the northernmost part of Germany, an area that was actually a part of Denmark when he was born. His family were wealthy farmers, whose wealth stemmed from agricultural trade with England. Tönnies's father was a regular at the Hamburg stock exchange: a provincial kind of conservatism and commercial modernity were intertwined in their world. Tönnies studied classics and philosophy and moved towards social theory from political philosophy; he was a leading specialist on Thomas Hobbes (1588–1679), the rationalist theorist of the modern state whom he considered to be the most important founding father of sociology. He was familiar with the philosophers of the Enlightenment, such as Hobbes, Hume and Spinoza, but no less with romantic and historicist nineteenth-century *critics* of the Enlightenment. Tönnies visited England many times, on one occasion meeting Friedrich Engels there, and once (in 1904) he also visited the USA. Politically he was a liberal, although like most German thinkers of the time he was also influenced by the more conservative critics of modern civilization such as Nietzsche, and even studied medieval mysticism. Then again, unlike most liberals, he sympathized both with the labour movement and with the conservative theorists of state socialism who wanted the monarchical state instead of an independent workers' movement to bring about social reform and justice. (In Imperial Germany, the Social Democratic Party was banned from 1878 to 1890.) In short, Tönnies was a rather complex figure.

He published his best-known book, *Community and Society*, in 1887, with the subtitle *An Essay on Communism and Socialism as Historical Social Systems*. The subtitle was replaced in later editions by the less provocative *Fundamental Concepts in Pure Sociology*. The book was not very widely received initially, and as Tönnies was considered a sympathizer of social democracy he failed to secure an academic position until 1909, when he became assistant professor for political economy in Kiel, North Germany, and full professor in 1913. He retired in 1916, apparently for health reasons, and resumed teaching after the war in 1921. Although he lived most of his working life as a private scholar and writer, he was immensely productive in a wide range of sociological areas, produced many theoretical, historical and empirical studies and was widely regarded as the key figure of German sociology. In 1909 he co-founded with Georg Simmel, Max Weber and others the German Society for Sociology, whose president he was until 1933.

The context in which his career took off after the turn of the century was again most paradoxical: the spirit of the time in the decade before the First World War turned increasingly towards a nationalist form of discontent with capitalist modernity that ultimately fed into various fascist sects and small groups, including one led by a man called Hitler. Many in this increasingly right-wing youth movement embraced Tönnies as their prophet: they picked up on the more conservative elements in Tönnies's conception and reframed them in a way Tönnies himself would not have approved of. Tönnies in the same period gradually turned more left-wing and in fact joined the Social Democratic Party in 1930 as a vocal campaigner *against* National Socialism. The Nazis acknowledged the fact by dismissing him from his teaching job in 1933, immediately after taking power, and cutting his pension. He died impoverished three years later.

Ferdinand Tönnies's book *Gemeinschaft und Gesellschaft* of 1887, sometimes rendered in English as *Community and Association*, more often *Community and Society*, was one of the texts that helped establish the discipline of sociology in Germany and beyond. The book had a strange fate: on the one hand, its title became one of the signature phrases not only of the new discipline, but also of the zeitgeist of the period from the 1890s to the First World War, as it seemed to encapsulate in a neat, well-phrased formula the reservations that especially young people then had about the modern world and the nostalgia for a supposedly lost sense of community that came with it. It ticks all the boxes for a powerful slogan, as every PR specialist will confirm: it scans nicely, it has alliteration, and it yokes together two similar-sounding words that are meant to express extreme opposites, while offering nothing less than the key to understanding all the woes of the modern world: the book title from heaven. On the other hand, the book is written in such a dense, old-fashioned philosophical style that it is hard to imagine that many people actually read it. Indeed it remained mostly esoteric for its first two decades: a book that a few philosophers and other academics would read and comment on. Then something changed – debates concerning the nature of modern civilization started to grip much larger numbers of people in the decade leading up to the First World War. Intellectuals in Germany, France and Britain claimed to be giving spiritually differing answers to questions concerning the meaning of life (which they did not, really) and state elites happily endorsed these intellectuals' pretentious hyperbole as it came in handy in the process of laying the groundwork for their war mobilizations. *Gemeinschaft und Gesellschaft* saw a second printing in 1912, and from then on many more: it was understood, or perhaps misunderstood, to be supporting the trend of nostalgic critique of civilization.

Reading *Gemeinschaft und Gesellschaft*, which Tönnies wrote as a 30-year-old, is an exercise in studying ambivalence: whatever the author's intention may have been at the time, and perhaps against what the author of the youthful masterpiece came to stand for later in his life, no text can ever be entirely innocent of how its readers construct its meaning. This alone makes it a fascinating object of study. Beyond that, it is also one of the most complex works of the classical canon, quite short in fact, written in a condensed style and therefore hard work to read, but very rich in content: it is a rationalist work, but in the spirit of Spinoza, talking systematically about rational as much as non-rational things, including the relationships between reason, feelings and the imagination.

For practical reasons, I will use for the present introduction an article by Tönnies, also entitled 'Gemeinschaft und Gesellschaft', written in 1931 for a sociological handbook, which offers a condensed and much more easily readable version of the argument. It illustrates well the spirit out of which the discipline of sociology was born in Germany, and might whet your appetite to have a go at the real thing. Be warned, though, that reading Tönnies right after Marx will come as a bit of a shock to the system: Tönnies writes – dare I say it – in the dry and pedantic style of an archetypal German professor, entirely lacking the mischievous wit and élan of a freewheeling cosmopolitan troublemaker like Marx. You need some patience to get through the first pages of what follows – after a rather slow start, Tönnies does offer an argument that you cannot afford not to know.

Structure of the selected text

1 How we know other people, and how that affects our relationships with them (3–11)
2 Barter and exchange as the simplest type of social relation or bond (11–13)
3.1 Social entities (13–14)
3.2 Human volition (14–16)
3.3 *Gemeinschaft* and *Gesellschaft* (16–18)
4.1 Relationships, collectives, social organizations (18)
4.2 The social relationship (18–23)
4.3 The collective (23–25)
4.4 The social organization (25–28)
4.5 Capitalistic, middle-class or bourgeois society (28–29)

Tönnies, Ferdinand. 1955 [1931]. 'Gemeinschaft and Gesellschaft: Introductory Article'. In *Community and Association*. Translated and supplemented by Charles Loomis. London: Routledge and Kegan Paul, 3–29.

1 How we know other people, and how that affects our relationships with them

Tönnies defines sociology as the study of the 'social nature' of people, in particular 'the sentiments and motives which draw people to each other, keep them together, and induce them to joint action' (3). He emphasizes that common existence is made possible by 'the products of human thought' that result from these sentiments and motives. These 'find their consummation in such important forms as community, state, and church, which are often felt to be realities or even supernatural beings'. These fundamentals of Tönnies's sociology – widely shared by the founding generation of academic sociologists in Germany – form a kind of triangle whose corner points constitute each other mutually: motives and sentiments – thoughts and knowledge – social forms.

Questions of thought and knowledge are, for Tönnies, at the heart of social institutions. He therefore approaches the study of social relationships by asking, *How do I know other people?* As usual in Tönnies, his discussion of this question operates through pairs of opposed concepts. The first of these is 'acquaintanceship and strangeness'. The point of Tönnies's argument here is that degrees of acquaintanceship and strangeness correspond to degrees of *knowledge* about the other person: 'In a strange city one may by chance meet in a crowd of strangers an acquaintance', Tönnies begins. Starting from this simple situation, he adds conceptual distinctions referring to *how* I know the other person: the acquaintance could be casual or familiar. A casual acquaintance may be someone known to me 'in some special capacity such as that of being engaged in the same profession', or it may be that we 'have met once before and exchanged a few words' (4). In any case an acquaintance would be someone whom I know and who knows me. I also know many people who don't know me; they are not acquaintances. Tönnies adds that the concept of 'friends' needs to be distinguished from that of acquaintances, as the relationship with friends involves mutual approval. Approval is based on but goes beyond knowledge. Acquaintanceship tends towards friendship, however, and some people refer to their acquaintances as friends: the distinction is in fact rather fluid.

The second distinction is that between sympathy and antipathy. Sympathy and antipathy are feelings that are partly instinctual but also frequently connected with thought and knowledge (4). There is a clear hint in Tönnies's text that for him this distinction has something to do with gender: 'The more sympathy and antipathy are instinctive, the more they are related to outward appearance, especially where women are concerned' (4–5). Tönnies seems to believe that women are particularly likely to be impressed by the outward appearance of men, and adds: 'Men, too, often fall in love with women at first sight'. Knowledge counteracts instinct, though: instinctive sympathy is 'counteracted in actual experience, by a more intimate knowledge of the hitherto strange person' that may verify or falsify the first impression. 'Sympathies and antipathies can be of many different degrees' and kinds, including 'intelligent sympathy' rooted in 'thinking consciousness', or the sympathy one has with 'those who side with us' in a conflict or those who belong to the same faith, party, profession or class. Tönnies rejects in this context a clear-cut distinction between feeling and thinking.

The next pair of concepts is confidence and mistrust. These can be caused by knowledge of another person, but also by sympathy or antipathy 'which sometimes proves to be unwarranted' (6). Here Tönnies begins the discussion of modern society against the background of the very generic concepts discussed so far: 'On the other hand, confidence has become highly impersonalized through modern trade' (7) where it is assumed that 'even the personally less reliable businessman' will repay his debts out of self-interest. Usually a business, not a person, enjoys financial credit. In modern business, we tend to trust a business partner on the basis of institutional arrangements, without personally knowing him or her. 'Personal confidence' depends on the intelligence and experience of the person who trusts; 'rationalized confidence' depends on the formal position or authority of the person to be trusted, such as a pilot or a doctor. This is particularly relevant to modernity: our trust in pilots, doctors or lawyers relies on skill and volition. When we make a judgement on whether to trust in someone's skill, we rely on membership in the profession, evidence of examinations, experience and reputation (8), rather than personal acquaintance. Individual cases can be distinguished by asking which of these elements predominate. Concerning volition, i.e., decisions that the person to be trusted is able to take, we trust in the morality that we assume is connected to a profession, and the self-interest of the professional. Here we clearly move into the area of social things:

> But it can easily be seen that something else besides these reasons underlies our peace of mind, our feeling of security. Our confidence in that which is regular and safe, although we are rarely aware of it, rests upon the three great systems of social will which I define as order, law, and morality. The two functions last mentioned, the legal and the moral orders or systems, are the fully developed types of the first one. (8)

We are confident that we can predict the other person's volitions and actions because we trust that there is order which comes, among other things, in the shape of law and morality.

From here Tönnies moves to a discussion of interdependence. Interdependence refers to the degree to which a person's will is bound up through obligation or prohibition in a particular type of social relationship, i.e., the degree to which one's free will is in fact *unfree*. Again, for Tönnies this is a matter of knowledge and volition: 'He is bound in these social entities if he is conscious of being linked to them' (8). Tönnies seems to suggest that only consciousness of the relationship makes it operational – he does not seem to acknowledge as relevant social relationships of which one is not conscious. He mentions as extreme forms of dependence servitude, slavery, but also hypnosis and 'sexual slavery'. The distinction to be made is to what extent the dependency is literally binding – such as in the case of a slave – or 'merely' metaphorically binding, such as in psychological dependency or 'sexual slavery', which is, as it were, in the mind but no less – perhaps even more – effective.

'Social relationship or bond implies interdependence, and it means that the will of the one person influences that of the other, either furthering or impeding, or both.' The combination of several persons' volition results in common volition (9). If more persons are involved, a 'collective will' emerges (10). Again, Tönnies emphasizes knowledge as constitutive of volition and agency: the individual persons 'all know of their dependence on one another and thereby on the collective will', and 'it is through this very knowledge that they are connected with one another'. Every collective will is given a name, and the individuals tend to imagine the collective will to be a person like themselves. Every 'social entity' contains 'a social will which determines the co-operating individual wills by giving them rights as well as imposing duties on them'. Every person is obliged to follow both 'a moral imperative' imposed by the collective will and an imperative imposed by the individual will (11).

Tönnies does not give any concrete examples here, but when he talks about 'social entities' he means 'a society' or 'a nation', or other bodies and institutions. It is important to keep in mind that Tönnies was a specialist on Thomas Hobbes, and his sociology is distinctively Hobbesian: in Hobbes, society is constituted by a 'contract' – a decision, a volitional act – concluded by individuals. Tönnies is in this sense a key representative of the tradition of 'methodological individualism', which refers to any theoretical conception that takes the existence of individuals as its logical starting point and derives everything else – society, institutions, relationships, social dynamics – from the acts, thoughts and wills of those individuals. In Tönnies's conception this means that individuals gain knowledge of their interdependence, this knowledge translates into volition, which in turn leads to the creation of 'social entities' that are based on some kind of common will.

2 Barter and exchange as the simplest type of social relation or bond

Tönnies proceeds to look at what he thinks is the elementary 'and also the most rational' form of all social relationships: barter or exchange. 'Simple barter' means the exchange of two objects whereby the one becomes a means to obtain the other (11). Tönnies does not primarily think about material objects here: 'All acts of mutual aid and assistance' are forms of barter, and 'all living together is a continuous exchange of such aid and assistance'. While the degree of its intimacy depends merely on its frequency, which is a quantitative aspect, different types of relationships are determined by differing 'underlying motives'. The principal difference that, according to Tönnies, determines the character of different social relationships is that between *conditional* and *unconditional volition*. The most straightforward case of unconditional volition is the 'love of the mother for her infant, from whom she does not expect or require anything as long as he has not reached the age of reason'. The motive of the mother's volition is the desire to satisfy the desire of the infant, which is the opposite of the motive of the infant's volition: infants are absolute egocentrics. Tönnies treats altruistic motherly love as a rare, extreme case of volition: generally speaking, in the context of society, 'love alone does not bind'. The individual is bound to society by something other than love. Tönnies seems to imply that motherly love survives just long enough to allow the infant to turn into a child. Henceforth, exchange relations – which are conditional – are predominant: 'Thus definite liking and benevolence, even though it be love, becomes atrophied when one party fails to return it' (12), i.e. it is conditional. '[O]ne party may make the welfare of the other his own will, as it is true especially in the case of sexual love', but this can turn to hatred if it is not reciprocal. The more passionate the unrequited love, the more violent the hatred that may result. Tönnies adds the observation that the same goes for self-love: extreme self-love easily results in extreme self-hatred and suicide.

Tönnies argues that the 'higher type of social bond' differs from these simple and somewhat ideal-typical cases. More complex or 'higher types' contain two elements: first, that which can be described 'as containing mutual advantage, assistance, or amicable activity', as discussed above; secondly, that which contains 'an element of binding social will which works on and controls the individual will'. The example of marriage can illustrate this dialectic: marriage is, on the one hand, an exchange relation between two individuals (exchanging all kinds of 'things', material, emotional, spiritual, etc.) but also a social form that is 'willed' – i.e. promoted, formalized, institutionalized, supported, enforced, controlled, warranted – by society. Depending on what particular kind of society we look at, the 'higher will' of society might overrule the wills of the two individuals involved and either prevent their marriage, or perhaps prevent the dissolution of the marriage. The first element, the element of bartering and rationally mutual advantage, makes itself felt whenever an 'inadequate and opposing action of the partner' or member 'calls forth a counteraction' as long as 'this whole' continues to exist. When the social entity entirely depends on the partner, as in marriage, both partners need to conform, or else the entity will dissolve even though it is 'conditioned by an existing social will of a higher type', by which Tönnies means society at large. The relationship between majority and minority in society differs from the relationship between two individuals in marriage: differing scales of magnitude create a different dynamic between, on the one hand, a bond by bartering and, on the other hand, a bond by 'higher social will'.

3.1 Social entities

Tönnies summarizes his argument so far:

> Sociology as a specialist science has as its subject the 'things' which result from social life, and only from social life. They are products of human thinking and exist only for such thinking; that is, primarily for individuals themselves who are bound together and who think of their collective existence as dominating them and as a something which is represented as a person capable of volition and action, to which they give a name. (13)

Slightly rephrased, this means: sociology deals with (social) things that are products of the thinking of individuals about their collective existence as a (kind of) person that has a will, acts and dominates these individuals, and to which they give a name (such as 'society').

Tönnies compares but also contrasts these social things to the things that are the subject matter of religion: '[t]he manner of existence of this social thing or person is not unlike that of the gods, which, being imagined and thought of by men who are bound together, are also created in order to be glorified'. The difference, however, is that 'the gods disappear for the people to whom they belong when their existence is no longer believed in', whereas 'social "entities", as we call them, do not require such belief or delusion' (13). The social things can survive and flourish without (fraudulently) being ascribed a metaphysical nature and godlike characteristics (14). Tönnies shows himself here as a classical rationalist:

> The scientific critical attitude destroys all of these illusions. It recognizes that only human thought and human will are contained in all of these imaginary realms, that they are based upon human hopes and

fears, requirements and needs, and that in their exalted forms they
are comparable to poetical works of art on which the spirit of the ages
has worked.

This is the central idea of Tönnies's sociology: social institutions
('entities', 'social things') are essentially works of the social imagination created by thinking and willing, which in turn are driven by
hopes, fears and needs. The central question that must guide their
analysis is therefore: *what, why, and how do thinking human beings
will and want?* This is the central question of Tönnies's sociology.
Tönnies argues that people 'want to attain an end and seek the
most appropriate means of attaining it'. Such means–ends-directed
behaviour 'has through the ages been directed and made easier by
pleasure and devotion, by hope and fear, by practice and habit, by
model and precept': culture and tradition in society stand in the
service of means–end rationality, and that's all there is to it. In this
respect, at least, and contrary to the overall impression, Tönnies is
not a romantic thinker.

3.2 Human volition

The central distinction in Tönnies's conception, leading directly
to the dichotomy of *Gemeinschaft* and *Gesellschaft*, is that between
'natural will' and 'rational will'. It is here that a more typically nineteenth-century critique of rationalism asserts itself. 'Natural', or
else 'general', 'original', 'integral' or 'essential' will, is 'conditioned
through reciprocal interaction with' knowledge and ability (14–15),
expressing the 'whole intellect' of a person, including traditions,
'mind and heart' and conscience (15). 'Natural will' expresses who
or what a person *is* in his or her entirety. 'Rational will', by contrast,
is characterized by 'deliberation', the conscious thinking about
ends and means. In it, 'the thinking has gained predominance' (15),
and that creates a problem. Tönnies emphasizes that the 'rational
will is to be differentiated from intellectual will': intellectual will
'gets along well with subconscious motives which lie deep in man's
nature and at the base of his natural will, whereas rational will
eliminates such disturbing elements and is as clearly conscious as
possible' (15). In other words, in the rational will an integrated,

well-balanced wholeness has been disturbed – an idea with clear roots in the romantic critique of rationalism. For Tönnies, the problem with 'deliberation' (as opposed to the more general concept of 'the intellect') is that it is able to separate means and ends, and infers 'that the means are not fundamentally connected to the end', not 'allied, interwoven, or identical'. Means could even 'stand in strong opposition to the ends'. Deliberation in this sense 'permits no consideration of means other than that of their perfect suitability for the attaining of the end'.

> The principle of the rationalization of the means develops everywhere as a necessary consequence the more thought, in accordance with the desire and intention, is intensively focused on the end or the goal. This signifies, therefore, an attitude of indifference to the means with respect to every consideration other than their greatest effectiveness in attaining the end. This indifference is frequently attained only by overcoming resistance resulting from motives other than the consideration of the end, which motives may hinder, dissuade, or frighten one from the application of this means. (15–16)

Basically Tönnies describes here unscrupulousness, sometimes, as he writes, combined with 'bravado and arrogance' and 'in conflict with the feelings': a *macho* attitude, as it were. Tönnies provides here the original formulation of a critique of one-sided 'means–end rationality' that is more often associated with the names of Max Weber, Jürgen Habermas and others. Tönnies refers to natural and rational will as 'normal concepts' that represent 'ideal types' (in the sense of the term as later defined by Max Weber) in between which 'all real volition and action takes place' (16). They 'serve as standards by which reality may be recognized and described'.

3.3 *Gemeinschaft* and *Gesellschaft*

From here, Tönnies moves to his chief pair of concepts, 'community and society'. '[I]ntellect in natural will attains its fruition in the creative, formative, and artistic ability and works and in the spirit of the genius' (17). 'In its elementary forms natural will means nothing more than a direct, naive, and therefore emotional volition and action, whereas, on the other hand, rational will is most frequently

characterized by consciousness.' Tönnies suggests in these formulations that there is not necessarily a split between intellect and emo-
tions, which are interacting in 'natural will'. Only in 'rational will'
has intellect driven out emotion.

Natural will is about creating, rational will is about manufactur-
ing, i.e. 'bringing forth the means'. The two types of volition also
lie at the basis of different types of association, although no particular association entirely belongs to one or the other category. This
leads Tönnies to his key formulation on 'community and society':
'I call all kinds of association in which natural will predominates
Gemeinschaft, all those which are formed and fundamentally conditioned by rational will, *Gesellschaft*' (17). These concepts denote
how individuals tend to be 'bound together' in an association. In
reality, both types of volition are 'interwoven in all kinds of associations' (18). Tönnies emphasizes that *Gemeinschaft* and *Gesellschaft*
are ideal-type concepts that are meant only to help describe realities
that contain both to varying degrees.

4.1 Relationships, collectives, social organizations

In the fourth and final section of the article, Tönnies describes
three types of 'social entities' that differ with respect to the extent
to which they are capable of volition: social relationships, collectives and social organizations (18). The 'social organization' is
'thought of as a kind of human person capable of creating a definite unified will' which 'binds and constrains' its members. The
members, though, maintain their individual wills as well. At the
other end of the scale, the 'social relationship' does not create a
collective will. It comes into existence when those who constitute
it do so consciously: they have to will it 'affirmatively'. It is the
'embryonic or emergent form' of the 'social organization'. The
'collective' lies between the two: it consists of 'a multitude of persons so held together that there result common intentions, desires,
inclinations, disinclinations – in short, common feelings and ways
of thinking', but not, however, common volition. 'It can reach no
decision as long as it does not "organize" itself into a committee,
special-interest group, or council' (18). Tönnies describes in the
next three sections these three concepts in more detail, and then

adds one final concept in which the entire discussion culminates: bourgeois, or civil society.

4.2 The social relationship

The 'social relationship' is the 'most general and simplest' social form and rests on two sets of foundations: on the one hand, it rests on 'the original, natural, and actual conditions as the causes of connections, of mutual dependence, and of attachment' (18), such as the fact that one is born into a particular family. On the other hand, it rests on 'the most fundamental, most universal, and most necessary requirements of human beings' (18–19). Tönnies thus begins his determination of the concept of 'social relationship' by distinguishing a particular and a universal dimension: *specific conditions* that I find myself in, and *general human needs* that I must fulfil like every other human being.

In the next step of the argument, he distinguishes between 'natural' and 'contract relationships'. The principal example of the former is the family relationship that involves feelings of intimacy, affirmation of each other's existence, ties, as well as 'a certain extent' of mutual sympathy and trust. Tönnies emphasizes that the family relationship does not necessarily have to be based on blood relationships but also applies, for example, to an adopted or foster brother: from this fact it can be inferred that it must be based on shared values, not 'blood' (19). The members of the family are conscious of their relationship and know 'that definite mutual action must regularly result therefrom'. Each expects and demands certain actions from all the others and from themselves: in this 'lies the embryo of "rights" which each claims for himself but also concedes', along with duties.

The concept of 'contract relations' is introduced with the observation that at some point needs will emerge 'that I can neither satisfy … out of my own volition nor out of a natural relation': I must find a way to satisfy those needs through actions that are conditioned by my need, 'not by consideration for other people':

> Soon I perceive that I must work on other people in order to influence them to deliver or give something to me which I need. Possibly in restricted individual cases my mere requests will be granted, as, for

example, in the case of a piece of bread or a glass of water. However, as a rule when one is not receiving something in a *Gemeinschaft*-like relationship, such as from within the family, one must earn or buy it by labor, service, or money which has been earned previously as payment for labor or service. (19)

I have now engaged in a *Gesellschaft*-like relationship, whose 'prototype is barter or exchange' (20). Such relationships require comparison and thinking and are thus 'oriented by reason'. They are 'primarily momentary' and 'come to have duration' only 'through repetition resulting in regularity' or through 'postponement of fulfillment' of the exchange act in the form of a promise: contract or exchange relationships, unlike 'natural relationships', are not durable by nature.

The 'natural relationship' precedes 'its subjects or members'. It also involves 'reason or intellect', but these are 'contained in the feeling of duty': in the 'natural relationship', unlike the 'contract relationship', reasoning is a subordinate, not a determining aspect. The contract relationship posits the contracting parties as strangers, or even enemies, and is entirely based on a logic of *do ut des*, the Latin legal formula meaning 'I give so that you will give in turn'. What I give is (for me) only a means to attaining what you will give in response. 'This is the simplest form of rational will' (21). In this way, Tönnies connects the concepts of exchange, contract and reason.

As the next step of his argument, Tönnies introduces a further distinction that is used to differentiate sub-categories of these two 'ideal-type' forms of social relationship. Tönnies asks to what extent there is 'equality in knowledge and volition, in power and authority on the part of the participants'. This distinction applies to *both* community- and society-type relationships. Concerning each type respectively, Tönnies distinguishes 'fellowship-type' relationships from 'authoritative-type' relationships, which are again understood as 'ideal types' that hardly ever occur in pure form in reality. The simplest fellowship/community-type relationship 'is represented by a pair who live together in a brotherly, comradely, and friendly manner, and is most likely to exist when those involved are of the same age, sex, and sentiment, are engaged in the same activity or have the same intentions, or when they are united by one idea' (21).

Tönnies illustrates this ideal type with the friendship of the mythical Greek warriors Achilles and Patroclus, as depicted in Homer's
Iliad. (When I read the *Iliad* as a teenager I had a strong feeling the
relationship between these two classical superheroes was somehow
more than strictly 'comradely', but I am sure no sexual undertone is
intended by Tönnies.)

Tönnies's prime example for the authoritative/community-type
relationship is that of father to child. It is characterized by authority in the service of protection (22). 'Although all authority has a
tendency to change into the use of force, in the case of the father as
well as the mother relationship such a tendency is arrested by love
and tenderness.' The authority of the father being 'the prototype of
all *Gemeinschaft*-like authority', Tönnies discusses priesthood as a
second key example. Priestly authority rests on 'mythological conceptions which place the father in Olympus or in heaven'. Tönnies
hints at the fact that in Christianity a very particular father–son relationship plays a central role, but it is not a relationship of authority:
instead, the god/father and his only son are almost identified with
each other, arguably as a result of a struggle to overcome polythe-
ism. His (or their) chief earthly representative, like priests more
generally, is again called 'father': *papa*, or pope.

Beyond ideal types, in reality most community-type relationships
contain a mixture of fellowship and authority elements. 'This is
the case in the most important of the relationships of *Gemeinschaft*,
the lasting relation between man and woman which is conditioned
through sexual needs and reproduction, whether or not the relationship is called marriage' (22–23). Perhaps surprisingly, this is
all Tönnies has to say here on this 'most important' relationship;
presumably he did not see any need to elaborate on how authority
and fellowship go together in marriage ('like horse and carriage', as
the poet says).

The distinction between the fellowship and authority types of
relationship can also be made concerning society-like social relationships, although Tönnies does not say anything at all here about
fellowship/society-type relationships: these would be contractual
relations based on equality of knowledge and power. In authority/
society-type relationships, authority is based on contract (23) but
actually results 'from the difference in the power of two parties, as

in the labor contract' between the (more powerful) employer and the (less powerful) employee. This seems to be for Tönnies the paradigmatic case of a 'society-like social relationship'. Tönnies adds that 'peace treaties' (which he puts in inverted commas) 'between victor and conquered' belong in the same category: 'Apparently it is a contract, but in actuality it is coercion and abuse.' (This aside on 'peace treaties' might be a reference to the Versailles Treaty that resulted from Germany's defeat in the First World War; this comment appears only in the essay from 1931, not in the book from 1887. Doubts about the political wisdom of the Versailles Treaty were widely shared at the time across political divides.) Tönnies also notes here that '*Gesellschaft*-like authority attains its consummation in the modern state' (23), which, however, belongs under the category of 'social organization', not simple 'social relationship', as the modern state clearly is a body that has, and articulates, a will (volition). Tönnies implies that contractual social relationships based on power differentials, like the labour contract, are the societal basis of the modern state.

4.3 The collective

In Tönnies's system of social forms, between mere 'social relationship' and full-blown 'organization' stands 'the collective'. He argues that 'natural and psychological relationships' form the basis of a collective as soon as they are 'consciously affirmed and willed' (23), without, however, going as far as forming a body that has volition, volition being the hallmark of 'social organization'. Tönnies argues that such 'natural and psychological relationships' constitute the characteristics that give 'certain classes ... prominence, nobility, and authority' (23). Any such characteristic is 'partly an objective phenomenon and partly something positive in the people's consciousness'. As an example Tönnies names the 'pride and haughtiness' of the members of 'a controlling estate' and the corresponding 'submission and modesty' of the lower classes (24).

Tönnies goes on to argue that 'the concepts of *Gemeinschaft* and *Gesellschaft*' should also be applied to 'the case of the collective': 'The social collective has the characteristics of *Gemeinschaft* in so far as the members think of such a grouping as a gift of nature or created by a supernatural will, as is expressed in the simplest and most naïve manner in the Indian caste system' (24). Membership in a *Gemeinschaft*-type collective such as a 'caste' is seen as 'something inherited' and to be retained and nurtured. It does not preclude 'intellectual self-consciousness': members of a lower caste or estate can affirm its existence by way of praising it for the virtues, special knowledge or skills that it possesses, which the higher castes or estates are lacking. Traces of the *Gemeinschaft*-type of collective are to be found in 'all systems of ranks or estates'.

Tönnies distinguishes from this the case of class struggle or the struggles of estates that aim at attaining equality. In such struggles, he writes, the estates – fighting merely for equal opportunity – tend to describe themselves in terms that resemble *Gemeinschaft*, while classes – which recognize 'no estates, no natural masters' – tend to describe themselves in terms that resemble *Gesellschaft* (25). Class struggle is 'more unconditional', 'more conscious' and more general. Perhaps the most intriguing point in Tönnies's argument on class struggle is that the class that describes itself as propertyless and oppressed, and recognizes 'no natural masters', thereby constituting a *Gesellschaft*-type collective, puts forward 'the ideal of the *Gemeinschaft* of property in field and soil and all the implements of labor'. This argument points to a key characteristic of Tönnies's conception: while community-type relationships are more traditional and society-type relationships more contemporary and relevant to current social struggles, in the context of contemporary society there emerges, *as a normative idea*, the notion of a rebirth of community in different, higher form.

4.4 The social organization

The principal characteristic of a 'social organization' or 'social body' is that it 'is never anything natural' (25), nor 'merely psychical' (26), but entirely social. It is characterized by its 'capacity for unified volition and action' based on a 'definite will' reflecting 'sufficient consensus'. Tönnies describes three cases which are, at the same time, stages that follow each other in a historical process and types that could, at times, coexist: first, the kinship group or clan; second, social organization defined by 'common relation to the soil' or geographical neighbourhood, such as the village community; and third, the town, out of which developed the modern state, 'the mightiest of all corporate bodies' (27). The clan is 'the embryo of a consciousness which matures into something beyond a mere feeling of belonging together' (26), but is still more 'natural' than 'social'. Tönnies does not seem to think that there is much room for 'fellowship' in the clan, but he writes that the village community can lean towards either fellowship or authority types of relationships. In the village, a shift takes place from 'the natural' to 'the social': 'The bond of field and soil and living together first takes its place along with and later more and more supplants the bond of common ancestry' (27). The actuality of village life gradually makes ancestry irrelevant. More and more alien members are incorporated into the village community. These tendencies are intensified in the town, which is initially a fortified village.

The main theoretical question here is, how does Tönnies relate these types of social organization to his main dichotomy, that of *Gemeinschaft* and *Gesellschaft*? He addresses this issue in the following passage that concludes the section on 'social organizations':

> These social bodies and communities retain their common root in that original state of belonging together which according to our concept is the *Gemeinschaft*. Indeed, although the original state of common being, living, and working is changed, it retains and is able to renew its mental and political forms and its co-operative functions. Thus a people which feels itself bound together by a common language, when held together within a national association or even when only striving to become a nation, will desire to be represented in a unity or national community, which may become intensified by national consciousness and pride, but may also thereby lose its original genuineness. (27–28)

Tönnies's argument on 'becoming a nation' emphasizes that the modern nation, in its tendency to constitute itself as a state, is not a form of community but of society. At the same time, however, he emphasizes here, as before in the context of his discussion of class struggle, that modern society has an intrinsic tendency to retain and reproduce *Gemeinschaft* in a changed form – basically, to borrow a term that Talcott Parsons later introduced, a 'societal community'. Society tends towards being higher-level community, as it were; perhaps society has never really stopped being community. The modern form of community, though, is not understood by Tönnies to be 'genuine' in an unequivocally romantic, nostalgic, backward-looking sense.

4.5 Capitalistic, middle-class or bourgeois society

After this long procession of 'normal concepts' and ideal types, Tönnies finally, on the last one-and-a-half pages of the article, arrives in the present and reveals what it all means – for us, here and now. The 'consummation' of the entire process described by Tönnies is 'what is frequently designated as individualism' (28). Out of 'the needs, interests, desires, and decisions of persons who previously worked co-operatively together', and who now interact on the basis of individualism rather than cooperation, arises the new phenomenon of 'capitalistic society'. 'Tending as it does to be cosmopolitan and unlimited in size, it is the most distinct form of the many phenomena represented by the sociological concept of the *Gesellschaft*.' In the first place, it is 'essentially a collective of economic character composed primarily of those who partake in that wealth which, as land and capital, represents the necessary means to the production of goods of all kinds': this means that 'capitalistic society' is initially the 'collective', or rather, the class, of landowners and capitalists. Having grown in strength, capitalistic society proceeds to build the modern state:

> Within narrow or far-flung borders which are determined by actual or supposed kinship bonds, of the existence of which the language group is the most valuable sign, it constructs its state, that is to say, a kind of unity resembling a town community which is capable of willing and acting. It develops as the capitalistic middle-class republic and finally probably will attain its perfection in the social republic. (28)

'Capitalistic society' morphs from being a 'collective' – the second 'social form' – to being a proper social organization – the third 'social form' – as a state, i.e. a social body with volition, in which it resembles the town community. It is important to note that, according to Tönnies, the modern state does not derive from or develop out of kinship or language community: the latter is merely used by 'capitalistic society' in its becoming a modern state.

Since Tönnies considers 'capitalistic middle-class society' a 'collective', i.e. a class or estate, he sees it inevitably as standing in opposition to 'the people'. This fact it cannot admit, however, because in society, where mastery is no longer considered natural, oppression and exploitation need to be camouflaged: 'it can only assert its existence through claiming to be identical with ... the whole people' (28–29). For Tönnies, the modern state is therefore essentially a charade. It involves 'conferring equal political rights on all citizens' (29) and some degree of social redistribution, but it cannot overcome the gap in wealth. Tönnies describes in these very condensed final paragraphs of the article a strange and rather surprising dialectic: the predominance of 'capitalistic society' strengthens 'the consciousness of the "social question"'. In the process, a *Gesellschaft* type of consciousness 'gradually becomes the consciousness of an increasing mass of the people': they increasingly come 'to think of the state as a means and tool to be used in bettering their condition, destroying the monopoly of wealth of the few, winning a share in the products' (29). In other words: the more the entire society becomes *like* the capitalists, the more they learn to turn the state as the most powerful tool in society *against* the capitalists. Tönnies basically provides here a philosophical foundation for the social-democratic project of gradual reform of capitalistic society.

The development depicted by Tönnies is deeply ironic: the society-type consciousness of means–end rationality that developed the modern state as a tool for capitalistic class-rule spreads throughout 'the people' to the effect that they give the 'capitalistic collective' a taste of its own medicine, using the modern state to recreate a more community-type form of society. Tönnies does not elaborate, though, how this reversal of fortunes can come about – he seems to believe that it is somehow inherent in the modern state itself and the political equality it warrants.

7
There is some Thing out there: Emile Durkheim

Only in France did the discipline of sociology have a real 'founding father': Emile Durkheim (1858–1917). As a young man, Durkheim had intended to become a rabbi like his father, but then he turned to studying philosophy. He did not become a philosopher either, however, as he looked for something more practical and more directly relevant to the political needs of the unsettled time he lived in: so he became a prophet as well as a *macher* of sociology, and a key figure in the reorganization of the French education system. As its 'founding father' he authored four of the most canonical books of French sociology, founded France's first university department of social science, became the first professor of sociology and founded the first journal of sociology in France. His writing as much as his knack for institution-building allowed him to build an actual 'school' of like-minded social researchers who were united by a common approach – something that did not come about elsewhere, except in Chicago. (The universities of Chicago and Kansas beat Europe narrowly in founding the very first sociology course, department and academic journal, on theoretical grounds that were initially more influenced by British and German than French traditions of social thought.) The Durkheimians sometimes referred to themselves as a 'clan', and Durkheim was the founder, leader and totem all in one. This happened for a reason, though, and as he would surely have agreed, it was society that did it.

Durkheim saw himself as continuing the work set out by Comte concerning the reorganization of society in the post-revolutionary situation. Although the socio–economic processes of modernization had advanced considerably since the middle of the nineteenth century in France, culturally and politically the situation was still as unstable in Durkheim's time as it had been in Comte's. As was obvious to many contemporaries, this was ever more a time for a renewed effort to promote and develop the Comtean programme of positivism.

The Franco-Prussian war of 1870–71, which Durkheim experienced as a boy, ended the imperial regime of Napoleon III, a type of governance that we still today call 'Bonapartist': a kind of military-bureaucratic dictatorship, based on a stalemate between the main organized class forces of society and in this sense 'above the parties', strongly nationalist and imperialistic, enjoying popular support due to charismatic leadership and some degree of social reform and welfare, and with a commitment to capitalist modernization. The regime of Napoleon III had resulted from the defeat of the revolutionary attempt at establishing a republic in 1848–52, and the 'Bonapartist' model was to become a characteristic of many of the darker sides of the twentieth century all over the world. What looked like a pretty stable and glorious regime was defeated with embarrassing ease in 1870, however, by proverbially well-disciplined Prussian troops, ushering in the Third Republic that lasted until the First World War. This is the republic of which Durkheim was a pre-eminent defender. Its fundamental predicament was that it was born not out of a strong, grassroots republican movement but out of devastating military defeat, which inevitably hurt the self-esteem of many in a strongly nationalistic society that had spent two decades idolizing the military. The confusion and discontent with the modernity of the Third Republic resembled that in the situation after the 1789 Revolution and the rule of Napoleon I which Comte had witnessed. Durkheim's work in establishing the new science of society was similarly motivated as a contribution to the consolidation of the new order. Politically, he was a liberal-conservative-positivist-socialist republican: he was conservative only in the sense that he defended a liberal republic that actually existed – a situation very different from, say, neighbouring Imperial Germany where a liberal republic was what a minority were dreaming about. He was a liberal as a defender of the rights of individuals – most prominently as a key figure in

the struggle against antisemitism during the Dreyfus affair (1894–
1906) – and also a socialist in the sense that he thought individuals
owed these rights, and everything else, to society, which therefore
should command their loyalty and solidarity.

Philosophically, Durkheim was most strongly influenced by
Kant, especially his 'deontological' ethics, which means ethics
based on a notion of absolute, non-negotiable duty (from Greek:
to déon, 'duty'), rather than on notions of virtue, greatest utility for
the greatest number or consideration of the specific consequences
of one's actions. Durkheim would have thought of ethics as the
most important philosophical discipline, and of sociology as a kind
of science of ethics. The principal way in which academia could
contribute to the consolidation of the republic would therefore be
the formation of duty-bound, ethically minded citizens through a
modern, secular and republican educational system.

Durkheim produced three of the key works of classical sociology
while he was still in his thirties: *The Division of Labour in Society*
(1893), *The Rules of Sociological Method* (1895) and *Suicide* (1897).
One of his late works, *The Elementary Forms of the Religious Life*
(1912), also counts among the classics of the discipline. *The Division
of Labour in Society* is a book of two arguments that can be seen as
contradicting or else complementing each other. Throughout by
far the longest sections of the book he turns the then widely shared
idea – reflected for example in Tönnies' writings – that traditional
society is organic and meaningful, and modern society somehow
cold and mechanical, on its head. In the process, he translates arguments from modern political economy into sociological arguments:
traditional society is characterized by what he calls 'mechanical solidarity' based on a strict moral consensus among people who are all
very much like each other, doing the same things in the same way,
mechanically obeying laws that repress difference. Not a good place
to be! Modern society, by contrast, is characterized by 'organic solidarity' based on a developed division of labour, functional intercon-
nectedness, cultural diversity and individualism. Modern society
enjoys laws that aim to reconcile, restitute and repair rather than
punish. Although Durkheim borrows – metaphorically, as he asserts
– the zoological argument about the increasing complexity of the
physiology of animals in the course of evolution, the word 'organic'

is here best understood in the sense of 'organized'. The concept of 'organic solidarity' is the centrepiece of Durkheim's defence of capitalist modernity at a time when right-wing defenders of the old regime were attacking it for destroying what they thought of as the substance of society. (At the same time, the emerging labour movement formulated its own critiques that sometimes overlapped with that of the conservatives, sometimes with that of the liberals.)

On the last thirty or so pages of *The Division of Labour in Society*, however, as well as in the widely discussed 'Preface to the second edition' of 1902, Durkheim accepts that capitalist modernity is not quite yet the best of all possible worlds and turns to discuss 'abnormal forms' of the division of labour, or else its 'pathologies' and 'anomies', which are those forms that fail to produce social solidarity. Durkheim mentions, for example, the 'hostility of capital and labour'. Quite in the Comtean spirit, he proposes to build ethically driven regulatory institutions that could heal 'illnesses' such as class struggle.

The Rules of Sociological Method is the founding manifesto of sociology as a scientific discipline (although it was not the first book on social science method – this honour goes to Harriet Martineau's *How to Observe Morals and Manners* of 1838). Durkheim sets out here what it means to be a 'science': the science of society should 'cause us to see things in a different way from the ordinary man, for the purpose of any science is to make discoveries, and all such discoveries more or less upset accepted opinions' (Durkheim 1982, p. 31). Science is meant to be a critique of received wisdoms – it is meant to rock the boat. Apart from the concept of 'society' as a 'social fact' as discussed below, Durkheim's most famous methodological statement is perhaps the following:

> [W]hen one undertakes to explain a social phenomenon, the efficient cause which produces it and the function it fulfils must be investigated separately. We use the word 'function' in preference to 'end' or 'goal' precisely because social phenomena generally do not exist for the usefulness of the results they produce. We must determine whether there is a correspondence between the fact being considered and the general needs of the social organism, and in what this correspondence consists, without seeking to know whether it was intentional or not. (Durkheim 1982, p. 123)

There are two important points here: first, the study of intentions and subjective meanings is best left to philosophy and literature as it cannot be done 'scientifically'. Durkheim also makes the point that people act in society for reasons of which they are not aware, so that what they *think* they are doing is not necessarily the best indication of what it actually *is*. This is a crucial aspect of a critique of society, although one could object that society's members' thoughts on society can surely give us important clues to work with. Secondly, social science must observe a division of labour between explaining *historically* how a social fact – say, an institution – came about, and explaining what function supports its continued existence *in the present*. Sociologists should always do historical and functional analysis in separate chapters, as it were. Whereas few would nowadays agree with Durkheim that we should bracket out intentions and meanings, the second point is methodologically extremely helpful: knowing how and why a social institution *evolved over time* does not necessarily tell us all about how and why it *works in the present*. However, what is special about the present only becomes clear when we know about the past.

Suicide is Durkheim's most enjoyable book to read, and his most popular. It is a very focused book as it is about one specific thing only, but Durkheim throws at this one thing all he has got – history, theory and, famously, statistics. He shows that the apparently most private thing is actually also a social thing, and that only a society with a good balance of social solidarity and respect for individuality is likely to keep suicide rates in check.

The last of Durkheim's major books was *The Elementary Forms of the Religious Life* (1912), in which he worked on two principal themes: first, he developed the argument that religion is a way in which society celebrates its own conception of itself, and thereby energizes the individuals who constitute it. Secondly, he tries to go beyond the classic philosophical question whether the categories of thought and perception derive from experience (empiricism) or are hard-wired into the human mind (idealism) by stating that they derive from society, which amounts to a sociological revision of Kantian epistemology. This book is crucial to both the sociology of religion and the sociology of knowledge. A key problem in Durkheim's developed position remains that it cannot account for the possibility of *critique* of society: if morality and all forms of thought, including religion, originate in society, how can society be criticized? On the other hand, where else could thought, critical or otherwise, originate, if not in society? Durkheimian sociology opens up the question of how we have to think about society in order to account for the fact that society *critiques itself*, which seems to imply that the existence of conflicting perspectives within society is normal, and desirable, rather than a case of 'anomie'.

The selected text is a section from the first chapter of *The Rules of Sociological Method*: 'What is a social fact?'

Structure of the selected text

1 Social facts as established beliefs and practices (50–52)
2 Social facts as social currents (52–53)
3 Education as the creation of a social being (53–54)
4 Social facts as distinct from their individual incarnations (54–56)
5 The collective origin of social facts (56)
6 Coercion and constraint as main characteristics of social facts (56–57)
7 Ways of being are consolidated ways of acting (57–58)
8 Concluding definitions (59)

Durkheim, Emile. 1982 [1895]. 'What is a social fact?' In *The Rules of Sociological Method and Selected Texts on Sociology and its Method*. Edited with an introduction by Steven Lukes. Translated by W. D. Halls. New York: The Free Press, 50–59.

---

1 Social facts as established beliefs and practices

Durkheim's book on the method to be applied by the new science of sociology begins with a discussion of its object. He points to a general consensus that 'social facts' are the object, but this term is 'used without much precision': 'there is, so to speak, no human occurrence that cannot be called social' (50) as practically anything has a social dimension to it, including drinking, eating and sleeping.

Durkheim rejects such a loose understanding of the term, and looks to develop a narrower and more precise definition. He begins with an example of what he thinks is a 'social fact' properly speaking:

> When I perform my duties as a brother, a husband or a citizen and carry out the commitments I have entered into, I fulfil obligations which are defined in law and custom and which are external to myself and my actions. Even when they conform to my own sentiments and when I feel their reality within me, that reality does not cease to be objective, for it is not I who have prescribed these duties; I have received them through education. (50)

Durkheim here sounds right away most of the themes that are relevant for his concept of 'social facts': it is about duties, commitments, obligations, law, custom, something that is external and objective even when it seems to be internal and subjective, something that is being prescribed and received through education. Although there is undeniably something social about how and what we eat and drink, the latter do not qualify as 'social facts' for Durkheim.

Durkheim adds that one often consults legal codes about the details of the law, and one is born into a religion which as a system of beliefs obviously pre-exists the believer (50). Then he turns to language and the economy:

> The system of signs that I employ to express my thoughts, the monetary system I use to pay my debts, the credit instruments I utilise in my commercial relationships, the practices I follow in my profession, etc., all function independently of the use I make of them. Considering in turn each member of society, the foregoing remarks can be repeated for each single one of them. Thus there are ways of acting, thinking and feeling which possess the remarkable property of existing outside the consciousness of the individual. (51)

These sentences are of the greatest importance for the history of social theory and, although they look innocent enough, they had enormous repercussions. The notion that language is a system that exists independently of the use anyone makes of it and 'outside the consciousness of the individual' anticipates the principal insight of structuralism in linguistics. Durkheim's text might well have inspired some of the famous formulations of the linguist Ferdinand de Saussure (1857–1913), first published in 1915, that revolutionized the social sciences when social scientists re-imported them in the middle of the twentieth century. The fact that Durkheim mentions money and, more generally, economic structures in the same breath with language is also worth mentioning and anticipates some of the themes that were later developed by structuralism in social theory. Durkheim's suggestion that the proper object of sociology is something that exists 'outside the consciousness of the individual' must have been quite a provocation at the time, although for us today, more than a century after Freud's theorization of the unconscious, it hardly sounds scandalous.

We have today come to take for granted that sociology talks about 'social things', but we should take the time to pause and think: what could it possibly mean that 'there are ways of acting, thinking and feeling' that exist outside consciousness? Are 'acting, thinking and feeling' not very much the stuff of consciousness? The more one thinks about this strange proposition the more paradoxical it must seem. Rather than rushing to take sides – are you with Durkheim or with Tönnies and Weber? – we should sit back and look at this crucial question: what kind of societal experience would lead one to make the Durkheimian statement? What is true about it, and how does it perhaps resonate with other, competing perspectives in social theory?

Apart from being external, the 'social facts' are 'endued with a compelling and coercive power' (51). As long as I conform to them, the coercion is not felt, but 'it asserts itself as soon as I try to resist'. The first example is again the law, where this is most obvious. The second example is that of 'moral rules', which are surveyed and enforced by 'public conscience', with or without the use of violence. Here Durkheim mentions 'ordinary conventions' such as those concerning 'mode of dress': if I ignore 'what is customary in my country and in my social class', I am ridiculed and kept at a 'social distance'. 'I am not forced to speak French with my compatriots, nor to use the legal currency, but it is impossible for me to do otherwise.' Again, language and the economy are singled out as 'social facts'. Durkheim here goes quite far in the direction that he seemed to reject at the outset: any kind of custom now seems a 'social fact', if you look closely. Durkheim adds another, much more specific example from political economy: 'As an industrialist nothing prevents me from working with the processes and methods of the previous century, but if I do I will most certainly ruin myself.' Then he adds another statement that makes the category of 'social fact' extremely broad again: even when I manage to 'struggle free' from the coercion of a custom or rule, the very fact that I had to struggle at all proves that this custom or rule is a social fact – as in the saying that the exception proves the rule (51). Durkheim sums up: the social fact 'is a category of facts which consist of manners of acting, thinking and feeling external to the individual, which are invested with a coercive power by virtue of which they exercise control over him' (52). They are neither 'organic phenomena', by which he seems to mean material or bodily phenomena – to do with the body, the human organism minus its psychological and social dimensions – nor 'psychical phenomena' which only exist in the individual consciousness. As for eating, drinking and sleeping, Durkheim would probably agree that they can be looked at *either* as 'organic', bodily phenomena *or* as 'social facts', insofar as they are regulated by customs and other social rules *on top of* the demands that the body itself makes. Durkheim adds that social facts can have as their 'substratum' either 'political society in its entirety', which seems to mean society in the sense of '*a* society', i.e., a national society as defined by state borders, 'or one of the partial groups that it includes – religious denominations, political and literary schools, occupational corporations, etc.'

This introductory section of the chapter ends on an interesting aside in which Durkheim tries to defuse criticisms that he anticipates will be directed against himself. He writes that 'this word "constraint" … is in danger of infuriating those who zealously uphold out-and-out individualism' (52), which points to his commitment to a not-so-zealous form of individualism. Durkheim rejects the notion 'that the individual is completely autonomous': since 'most of our ideas and tendencies … come to us from outside, they can only penetrate us by imposing themselves upon us'. Durkheim presents this crucial statement as if it were self-evident: 'This is all that our definition implies.' It is quite a momentous statement, though: the second half of this statement (those outside influences can only 'penetrate' us by 'imposing themselves upon us') does not necessarily follow from the first half (the individual is not completely autonomous). Could not the not-quite-autonomous individual *seek out* the influences and ideas it lacks? The question here is can we *choose* or are we just passively being 'penetrated' by whatever comes along? A lot is at stake here in terms of how we think about the balance between freedom and necessity in human society, and Durkheim is surely aware of this – as he adds: 'Moreover, we know that all social constraints do not necessarily exclude the individual personality' (52), and in an endnote he promises to discuss later whether 'all constraint is normal', or perhaps not. Durkheim's apparently neat definition of 'the social fact' is in reality rather the opening of a very big question. That is, of course, what makes it a useful concept for theorizing.

2 Social facts as social currents

Durkheim points out that all the examples discussed up to this point presuppose the existence of 'a well-defined social organization' (52). There are also, though, other social facts which 'do not present themselves in this already crystallized form but which also possess the same objectivity and ascendancy over the individual'. These he calls 'social currents'. His first example is that of 'the great waves of enthusiasm, indignation and pity' that can occur in 'a public gathering' (52–53). These come to the individual 'from outside' and 'can sweep us along in spite of ourselves'. Again, the coercion is felt only when the individual attempts 'to struggle against them', but it exists whether we are aware of it or not. If we deny it, 'we are the victims of an illusion which leads us to believe we have ourselves produced what has been imposed upon us externally', in the same sense that 'air does not cease to have weight, although we no longer feel that weight'. Durkheim describes here a feeling of unreality that is probably familiar to most of us in some form:

> Once the assembly has broken up and these social influences have ceased to act upon us, and we are once more on our own, the emotions we have felt seem an alien phenomenon, one in which we no longer recognize ourselves. It is then we perceive that we have undergone the emotions much more than generated them. These emotions may even perhaps fill us with horror, so much do they go against the grain. Thus individuals who are normally perfectly harmless may, when

gathered together in a crowd, let themselves be drawn into acts of atrocity. And what we assert about these transitory outbreaks likewise applies to those more lasting movements of opinion which relate to religious, political, literary and artistic matters, etc., and which are constantly being produced around us, whether throughout society or in a more limited sphere. (53)

Durkheim addresses here the theme of alienation that is common currency, in one form of another, among practically all the canonical writers of classical social theory. Like the weight of air or gravity, we are not able to feel the coercion of all the 'currents' that society produces around us, and we like to think of ourselves as much more our own persons than we really are. Once we step outside their range of influence, we notice them and are perhaps embarrassed by how outer-directed we really are. (Stepping outside is, of course, very tricky in the case of gravity, and, given globalization, increasingly difficult in the case of society too, but still possible to an extent when crossing borders and boundaries of some sort.) It is not clear what Durkheim was referring to when he mentioned crowds that commit atrocities, but in France at the time of writing there were incidents of antisemitic crowd violence in the run-up to the Dreyfus affair as well as anti-immigrant violence, for example against Italian and Belgian migrant workers. It seems likely that these were the kinds of events he was thinking of here.

3 Education as the creation of a social being

Crowd atrocities are an example of what Durkheim surely regarded as the darker side of the reality of 'social facts'. In the following paragraph he discusses a social fact of which he seems to approve, by and large, namely education. He writes that his definition of the concept of the 'social fact' can 'be verified by examining ... how children are brought up' (53):

If one views the facts as they are and indeed as they have always been, it is patently obvious that all education consists of a continual effort to impose upon the child ways of seeing, thinking and acting which he himself would not have arrived at spontaneously. From his earliest years we oblige him to eat, drink and sleep at regular hours, and to observe cleanliness, calm and obedience; later we force him to learn

how to be mindful of others, to respect customs and conventions, and
to work, etc. (53–54)

Subsequently, constraint is replaced by 'habits' and 'inner tendencies which render [the constraint] superfluous … because they are
derived from it' (54). Durkheim describes here a reality of education as coercion and imposition that was surely experienced by
many at the time (and maybe still is). In the positivist manner,
however, Durkheim derives from his claim that these are 'the facts
as they are', and always have been, the notion that the reality is a
desirable reality, too – it is just 'patently obvious'.

As a rule of thumb, it is a good idea to be suspicious of any author's
rhetorical demonstration of extreme confidence: it may point to a
wish to deflect from a point of contestation. And indeed Durkheim
engages here in a polemic with an important competitor in the arena
of theory: the British liberal theorist Herbert Spencer (1820–1903).
Durkheim follows up his, as he writes, 'patently obvious' observation with the admission that 'in Spencer's view, a rational education
should shun such means and allow the child complete freedom
to do what he will'. The position described here by Durkheim as
Spencer's is in fact also that of Emile Rousseau (1712–78), the key
contributor to Enlightenment educational theory. Durkheim dismisses this position: 'Yet as this educational theory has never been
put into practice among any known people, it can only be the personal expression of a *desideratum* and not a fact which can be established in contradiction to the other facts given above' (54). In other
words, Durkheim argues here that theorists – like Rousseau and
Spencer – should not be taken seriously when they simply *criticize*
the way certain things are being done (and perhaps have always
been done) without being able to point to alternative *social facts*.
This is indeed an important point concerning the methodology of
theoretical reasoning: Durkheim argues that facts must only be critiqued with the help of other facts, not by expressing a '*desideratum*',
i.e. something that would be desirable. This polemic against the
somewhat more utopian-liberal aspects of Spencer and Rousseau
is an expression of Durkheim's form of positivism: do not criticize based on some normative, utopian – Comte would have said
metaphysical – ideas but instead back up your critique by reference

to social facts. In the case of education, this would mean that I can criticize the existing education system only if I can point to some other society, somewhere, where things are done better, or some other area of society where the alternative principle that I want to advocate is already a reality. According to Durkheim, Rousseau and Spencer have to be asked where they find the grounding in reality for the critiques that they formulate.

Durkheim argues that the example of education is 'particularly illuminating' because 'education sets out precisely with the object of creating a social being':

> Thus there can be seen, as in an abbreviated form, how the social being has been fashioned historically. The pressure to which the child is subjected unremittingly is the same pressure of the social environment which seeks to shape him in its own image, and in which parents and teachers are only the representatives and intermediaries. (54)

The education of an individual human being, understood as 'unremittingly' subjecting this human being to pressure in order to shape him or her in the image of society, repeats at the micro level the historical process that created human society.

4 Social facts as distinct from their individual incarnations

Durkheim moves from here to a more abstract level of discussion. He insists again on a narrow definition of 'social facts', asserting that not all general facts such as 'thoughts to be found in the consciousness of each individual and movements which are repeated by all individuals' constitute 'sociological phenomena' (54). Durkheim introduces here a distinction crucial to his conception: social facts are to be distinguished from 'their individual incarnations'. Social facts 'are the beliefs, tendencies and practices of the group taken collectively', whereas 'the forms that these collective states may assume when they are "refracted" through individuals are things of a different kind':

> What irrefutably demonstrates this duality of kind is that these two categories of facts frequently are manifested dissociated from each other. Indeed some of these ways of acting or thinking acquire, by dint of repetition, a sort of consistency which, so to speak, separates

them out, isolating them from the particular events which reflect
them. Thus they assume a shape, a tangible form peculiar to them and
constitute a reality *sui generis* vastly distinct from the individual facts
which manifest that reality. Collective custom does not exist only in a
state of immanence in the successive actions which it determines, but,
by a privilege without example in the biological kingdom, expresses
itself once and for all in a formula repeated by word of mouth, trans-
mitted by education and even enshrined in the written word. (54)

Careful reading is required to follow the method of Durkheim's
argument here. He makes an observation about *some kinds* of social
facts that he seems to perceive as particularly telling examples:
those, that is, where the social fact is so consistently 'dissociated'
from its individual 'manifestations' as to 'assume a tangible form'
and 'constitute a reality *sui generis*', which means 'of its own kind'.
This is the case of collectively shared customs once they are written
down, codified and handed down the generations by way of tradition which becomes part of education. Importantly, Durkheim does
not claim that *all* social facts are so clearly 'dissociated' from their
manifestations. He does claim, however, that those that 'can even
exist without being applied at the time' (55) are the most clearly
developed examples. They tell us something also about all other
'social facts' that are less clearly 'dissociated' from their manifestations. The key philosophical term used by Durkheim in this passage is 'immanence': it means that a more abstract or more spiritual
entity is 'inherent to' a more concrete or more material entity, as
opposed to being external to it. This concept is perhaps best illustrated by looking across to the field of theology: there the question
would be whether God is *immanent to*, residing in, the world, or is a
separate entity 'of its own kind', outside and overlooking the world.
A theology of the first kind would argue, for example, that cutting
down a tree is cutting down a piece of God him/herself, rather than
just an act that she or he would look down on, favourably or not,
from somewhere high above. Sociological theory, in which theological concepts often resonate between the lines, asks a similar question: Durkheim thinks that 'social facts' have a reality of their own,
separate from how they manifest themselves here and there in different ways as observable phenomena, whereas for most other writers in the classical canon of sociological theory they are *immanent* to

the world of individual, observable phenomena, existing only in and through their individual manifestations. As *theologians* ask whether God exists separate from and prior to 'the creation' or is merely a name for the creative force of creation itself, *sociologists* ask whether society exists separate from and prior to concrete, warm, breathing individuals, families etc., or is simply our name for the societal dimension of these individuals, families etc. themselves.

Durkheim admits that 'this state of dissociation does not always present itself with equal distinctiveness' (55). Whenever a social fact has not taken on an observable separate existence (such as a legal code), methodology has to be applied that makes the social fact emerge from the mass of its individual manifestations. Durkheim uses here a metaphor from industrial chemistry: it is necessary to 'refine out the social fact from any amalgam and so observe it in its pure state'. The production of statistics is such a methodology:

> Thus certain currents of opinion, whose intensity varies according to the time and country in which they occur, impel us, for example, towards marriage or suicide, towards higher or lower birth-rates, etc. Such currents are plainly social facts. At first sight they seem inseparable from the forms they assume in individual cases. But statistics afford us a means of isolating them. (55)

Statistics provide purified social facts, with 'individual circumstances' washed away, expressing 'a certain state of the collective mind', 'social phenomena ... stripped of all extraneous elements'. The individual or, as Durkheim here writes, 'private manifestations' do 'in part ...reproduce the collective model' but also depend 'upon the psychical and organic constitution of the individual, and on the particular circumstances in which he is placed' (55–56). These phenomena 'could be termed socio-psychical'; they are 'of interest to the sociologist without constituting the immediate content of sociology'.

5 The collective origin of social facts

In the next step of his argument, Durkheim once more refutes the possible objection that 'a phenomenon can only be collective' if it is shown by each individual member of society, or at least most of them (56). Durkheim asserts again (as at the beginning of the preceding section above) that being general does not make a phenomenon a social fact. He does not give an example here, but one might think of the fact that all human beings feel thirsty from time to time. This is a general fact shared by every single individual of the human species, but it is not a social fact: it is directed entirely from within the genetic make-up of humans and would happen even to an individual abandoned at birth on a desert island. (By contrast, the phenomenon of people becoming thirsty immediately when they enter a pub *is* a social fact.) A social fact 'is general … because it is collective (that is, more or less obligatory)', not the other way around. 'Collective' means here as much as 'social'. Again, the aspect of coercion is predominant in Durkheim's definition: 'It is a condition of the group repeated in individuals because it imposes itself upon them.' Durkheim makes a distinction between *obviously* social facts which are 'invested with a special authority that our education has taught us to recognize and respect', and *less obviously* social facts that are not immediately recognizable as such: the latter are 'partly due to our direct co-operation' and were called 'social currents' by Durkheim earlier in the same chapter; they could perhaps also be described as social facts in the making, or emergent social facts:

> An outburst of collective emotion in a gathering does not merely express the sum total of what individual feelings share in common, but is something of a very different order … It is a product of shared existence, of actions and reactions called into play between the consciousnesses of individuals. If it is echoed in each one of them it is precisely by virtue of the special energy derived from its collective origins. If all hearts beat in unison, this is not as a consequence of a spontaneous, pre-established harmony; it is because one and the same force is propelling them in the same direction. Each one is borne along by the rest. (56)

Durkheim's second type of social facts is quite close to what Simmel or Weber would recognize as the stuff of society: interaction between individuals produces an effect that did not pre-exist the interaction in any way. The social fact is produced *in the social interaction* – it is not 'a consequence of a spontaneous, pre-established harmony'. (The word 'spontaneous' means here 'acting of its own accord', like a script that has been inserted into the individuals and runs on its own.) Durkheim argues here that the individuals have not been pre-programmed by some higher instance to react to each other in a particular way. His point is that the social fact emerges in a space *in between* the consciousnesses of the individuals, not *in* those individual consciousnesses. If, to take an example of the time, a political gathering turns into an antisemitic lynch mob, then we cannot assume that the individuals went into the meeting anticipating that this might happen. They might have been surprised by their own actions.

In terms of critique, this raises the question: weren't the rioters perhaps disposed to riot, after all? Surely it would be worthwhile to ask whether there was already at least a general *readiness* to run wild? Not all participants in a meeting react in the same way to the same influences. Why do things kick off on one occasion but not on another? Again, Durkheim's definition of the 'social fact' more resembles a research question than an answer – and that's all for the better.

6 Coercion and constraint as main characteristics of social facts

Durkheim at this point gives himself a pat on the back, stating that 'we have therefore succeeded in delineating for ourselves the exact field of sociology'. He recapitulates: 'A social fact is identifiable through the power of external coercion which it exerts or is capable of exerting upon individuals', which is 'recognizable because of the existence of some pre-determined sanction, or through the resistance that the fact opposes to any individual action that may threaten it' (56–57). A 'second essential characteristic' is that it 'exists independently' of its manifestations (57). Constraint can be 'manifested externally … as in the case of law, morality, beliefs, customs and even fashions', or be 'merely indirect' as in the case of 'an economic organization'. Of these two criteria, Durkheim clearly prioritizes the first, as the 'second definition is simply another formulation of the first one: if a mode of behaviour existing outside the consciousnesses of individuals becomes general, it can only do so by exerting pressure upon them' (57). Constraint and externality are therefore really the same.

7 Ways of being are consolidated ways of acting

In the final step of his argument, Durkheim reflects on a further distinction, that between social facts that are 'ways of functioning' and those that are 'collective ways of being' (57). Again borrowing terms from the natural sciences, Durkheim calls these 'physiological' and 'morphological' or 'anatomical', respectively: physiology is – in biology – the study of the *functioning* of organisms, morphology and anatomy are the study of their form and *structure*. Another term he uses in the same paragraph is 'substratum', which in geology denotes the 'underlying structure' or base layer, for example a layer of rock upon which sits the soil: the social ways of being are the 'substratum' of the social ways of functioning. It could be objected at this point that the 'social ways of being' are, of course, social facts, but they are not mere 'ways of acting, feeling or thinking', which is part of Durkheim's definition of 'social facts'. Is the definition of the social fact therefore inconsistent? Durkheim anticipates this possible critique and argues that in the case of society, physiology and morphology – functioning and structures – are in fact not entirely different: also 'the substratum of collective life' can be addressed as a set of social facts in keeping with his own definition of that concept. Durkheim gives the following examples of social facts that are 'ways of being' more than 'ways of functioning':

> the number and nature of the elementary parts which constitute society, the way in which they are articulated, the degree of coalescence they have attained, the distribution of population over the earth's surface, the extent and nature of the network of communications, the design of dwellings, etc... (57)

These formulations are quite abstract, but from Durkheim's subsequent explanations, what they mean can be inferred. The 'elementary parts' are human beings as individuals but also as groups, such as ethnic groups, for example. How they are 'articulated' means how they relate to each other. Their 'coalescence' refers to how well they gel or amalgamate into a coherent (for example, national) society. Durkheim clearly also envisages transnational aspects of society to be subject matter for sociology: he mentions the distribution of humanity over the surface of the planet and how all humans communicate and interact, nationally as well as globally, as well as more micro-sociological things such as the 'design of dwellings'. All these are 'social facts' because '[t]hese ways of being impose themselves upon the individual just as do the ways of acting' described above. When we wish to study the political structure of a society, Durkheim argues, we need to study its social divisions, not its geography, although the social 'may have some physical basis'. Durkheim singles out 'public law' as a privileged object of study because public law 'determines' the structures of political society as well as 'domestic and civic relationships' (57–58). These are social facts because they are external, coercive and indeed depend on 'ways of acting, feeling or thinking':

> If the population clusters together in our cities instead of being scattered over the rural areas, it is because there exists a trend of opinion, a collective drive which imposes this concentration upon individuals. We can no more choose the design of our houses than the cut of our clothes – at least, the one is as much obligatory as the other. The communication network forcibly prescribes the direction of internal migrations or commercial exchanges, etc., and even their intensity. (58)

These social things are in fact 'ways of being' as much as they are 'ways of acting': the making of 'political structures', such as state- and nation-building, operates in pretty much the same way as tastes in clothes and dwellings are made. Durkheim concludes that 'these ways of being are only ways of acting that have been consolidated':

> A society's political structure is only the way in which its various component segments have become accustomed to living with each other ... The type of dwelling imposed upon us is merely the way in which everyone around us and, in part, previous generations, have customarily built their houses. The communication network is only the channel which has been cut by the regular current of commerce and migrations, etc., flowing in the same direction.

Fluidity and historicity are as central aspects of Durkheim's concept of the 'social fact' as relative permanence, coercion and externality: 'a legal rule is no less permanent an arrangement than an architectural style'; a 'moral maxim' is more malleable, yet 'cast in forms much more rigid than a mere professional custom or fashion':

Thus there exists a whole range of gradations which, without any break in continuity, join the most clearly delineated structural facts to those free currents of social life which are not yet caught in any definite mould. This therefore signifies that the differences between them concern only the degree to which they have become consolidated. Both are forms of life at varying stages of crystallization. (58)

Durkheim concludes that those social facts that could be called 'morphological' – ways of being – are 'of the same nature as' those that could be called 'physiological' – ways of functioning.

8 Concluding definitions

Durkheim is now happy to give his final summary definition of the social fact: '*A social fact is any way of acting, whether fixed or not, capable of exerting over the individual an external constraint*'; or: '*which is general over the whole of a given society whilst having an existence of its own, independent of its individual manifestations*' (59). Durkheim has demonstrated that the fixity of social facts varies, from very fixed ('morphological') to very fluid ('social currents'), and that the two alternative definitions given, one emphasizing constraint, the other externality, amount to saying the same thing, as long as it is understood that the social fact is a way of 'acting, feeling or thinking'. (In this final definition on the last page of the chapter [59], Durkheim left out the 'feeling or thinking' bit, writing only 'acting', but this was probably just an omission.)

8

The double-consciousness: W. E. B. Du Bois

William Edward Burghardt Du Bois (1868–1963) had an unusual upbringing that, against a grim background, was also shaped by some benign aspects of American society of the time. He grew up in a small but prosperous, mostly white Anglo-Saxon industrial town in Massachusetts, New England, where only very few African-Americans lived, mostly as domestic servants. His own family background included black, Dutch, French and English ancestors. His father left him and his mother when Du Bois was still a small child, and she lived with the support of the local white upper class, who provided her with small jobs as well as charity, including a house to live in. She died when Du Bois was a teenager. Objectively, Du Bois and his mother were poor, but subjectively he grew up feeling almost a member of the local elite, where he seems not to have experienced much racial or even class discrimination. He is said to have assimilated well into the habitus of the Anglo-Saxon upper class: controlled manners, stiff white shirts and all that. He was a top student at high school and was given a scholarship to go to college. This was when reality kicked in: the college he attended was Fisk University, Nashville, Tennessee, a 'historically black' college in the segregationist South. (In the USA, a college is called 'historically black' if it was founded before the Civil Rights Act of 1964 and had then been primarily for African-Americans.) He commented later that leaving small-town New England and moving to Nashville was what made him 'a Negro'. The contrast between the two sets of social experiences also provided him with the principal theme of his life work: suddenly it was not his intelligence and genteel manners but his skin colour that placed him socially.

He received his BA within three years, during which time he also studied the reality of the black population by working as a volunteer schoolteacher, and then won a scholarship to go to Harvard where he did a second BA in philosophy. At Harvard, black and white students did not mix much but many of the professors received him warmly. He continued to an MA and a PhD at Harvard, including a two-year stay at the University of Berlin from 1892–94, where he studied with some of the same teachers who had taught Max Weber only a few years earlier, in particular the historical economist Gustav Schmoller. He was the first black student to receive a PhD from Harvard in 1895 for a historical study of *The Suppression of the African Slave-trade to the United States of America, 1638–1870* (published in 1896). His first teaching position was in Classics at Wilberforce College, a black university in Ohio. It was a strictly religious school, which he did not like at all, but on the positive side this was where he met his wife. He soon left and took up a research contract at the University of Pennsylvania, Philadelphia, in 1896. Here he produced one of the classic works of American urban sociology, *The Philadelphia Negro* (published in 1899), the first systematic study of blacks in the USA. Poorly paid and without any research support, or many signs of appreciation from the sociology department, he and his wife moved into a room in what was then the black slum area of Philadelphia (the 7th ward). His self-chosen mission was to prove empirically that the black population of Philadelphia were driven to destitution and criminality by environment and circumstance, not because of their 'racial essence', which was the predominant view back then among liberal reformers and social scientists alike, including his current employers. Methodologically, he built on the slightly earlier studies by Charles Booth on London and Jane Addams on Chicago, combining personal observation, mapping, census data, statistics and in-depth interviews. Du Bois's theoretical starting point was something he might well have picked up from German liberals like Max Weber: he discerned a contradiction in the behaviour of the American capitalists. Although capitalist rationality would have demanded the hiring of the cheapest workers able to do the job, they refused to hire black people. Employment, albeit highly exploitative, was the only route to emancipation for the latter, however, as only capitalistic work would allow them to pick up the necessary work ethic and 'better' themselves. Du Bois described a vicious circle that kept the black population captive: anti-black racial prejudice was reinforced by the assumption that the former slaves lacked the ability to engage in capitalist, 'free' work relationships and were therefore inefficient workers. As this kept them out of employment, the prejudice was further solidified. Furthermore, Du Bois discovered that at times a fairly well-to-do black middle class of doctors, lawyers, businessmen, caterers and barbers was in the process of developing, but their progress was halted by successive waves of European immigration, since white Americans preferred a recently arrived European over a black barber or doctor, no matter how talented. The resulting demoralization manifested itself in alcoholism, gambling and crime. Du Bois's conclusions are at this point still not much more than moralistic: he asks white capitalists not to exclude black people, and demands that talented and successful black people provide leadership to their community towards 'uplift'. In this context, Du Bois formed the twofold position that he stuck to throughout his long life: on the one hand, African-Americans have something important to contribute to American society and should be allowed fully to partake in it, as black people more generally should be part of global human society. On the other hand, in order to achieve this they also needed to organize themselves apart from wider society. Du Bois was neither an advocate of individualistic assimilation nor of fully separatist black nationalism, but held a position somewhere in between these extremes. He rejected the ideological essentialization of 'race' but warned against denying or ignoring the fact, as he saw it, that different 'races' actually existed in the world. 'Races' had been constituted historically and by human society and were therefore also subject to change. One should not conclude, though, from Du Bois's use of the word 'race' that he was somehow a racist. It is important to keep in mind here that only in the 1940s did all scholars and intellectuals opposed to racism come to agree that no 'human races' existed. Before that time, talk of 'races' did not necessarily make one a racist, as long as it was clear from the context that 'race' was meant as a historically and socially constituted grouping or category, not a hereditary, allegedly biological one. Words and how we use them have a history! When Du Bois writes 'race' we should perhaps read 'ethnicity' in the contemporary sense of that word: not racism, but an element of ethnocentrism can be found in Du Bois's position.

Structure of the selected text

Du Bois, William Edward Burghardt. 2007 [1903]. 'Of Our Spiritual Strivings' and 'Of the Sons of Master and Man'. In *The Souls of Black Folk*. Oxford: Oxford University Press, 7–14 and 111–127.

From 1897 Du Bois held an academic position at Atlanta University, from which he retired in 1944. In 1900 he helped organize the first Pan-African Conference in London, beginning a life-long commitment to the project of organizing global solidarity between all black people, which involved a great amount of travelling and lecturing. The huge success of the essay collection *The Souls of Black Folk* in 1903 brought him nationwide fame, and henceforth he divided his time between academic, political and journalistic work, as well as writing several novels. His most important political involvement was with the National Association for the Advancement of Colored People, which he helped found in 1909, the principal organization of the early Civil Rights movement before the 1960s. Later in life he also played a role in the international peace movement and became a sympathizer of the Soviet Union. In 1961 – aged 93 – he moved to Ghana where he intended to work on a global encyclopedia of African Studies. He died there 27 October 1963 – rather uncannily, just the night before Martin Luther King gave his celebrated 'I have a dream' speech at the Civil Rights march on Washington, DC.

I have chosen for close analysis two chapters from *The Souls of Black Folk*, the first and most famous chapter and the ninth chapter.

Chapter 1 'Of Our Spiritual Strivings'

The opening essay of *The Souls of Black Folk* (the revised version of an article first published in 1897) is a richly condensed exposition of the various themes of the book, written more in the literary style of a montage than a scholarly treatise. It showcases the different writing styles employed by Du Bois in the different chapters of the book: autobiography, commentary, conceptual-theoretical writing, historiography, anecdote. I will go through this chapter paragraph by paragraph, following the changes the text undergoes.

0 The crying of water

'Of Our Spiritual Strivings' begins, like all the chapters in *The Souls of Black Folk*, with a poem and a line of music. The music is the beginning of 'Nobody Knows the Trouble I've Seen', a 'sorrow song' as Du Bois calls it: 'The Sorrow Songs' is in fact the title of

the last chapter of the book. The lines of music at the beginning
of each chapter are taken from 'negro spirituals', the specifically
American form of 'spiritual songs' developed by African-American
slaves which combined work-song and church hymn. After emancipation both 'the blues' and gospel music derived from these. The
notes are given without words or titles, indicating that Du Bois
trusted that the wide, non-academic readership that he wrote for
would be able to read the music – a telling hint about the cultural
context he worked in. If the choice of music is perhaps unsurprising
given the subject matter of the book, the choice of poem is anything
but obvious. It is a work by Arthur Symons (1865–1945), an important English modernist poet, translator of French symbolist poetry
and literary critic, as well as a bohemian character or, as it was called
then, a 'decadent'. The poem is entitled 'The Crying of Water' and
was first published in 1901:

> O water, voice of my heart, crying in the sand,
> All night long crying with a mournful cry,
> As I lie and listen, and cannot understand
> The voice of my heart in my side or the voice of the sea,
> O water, crying for rest, is it I, is it I?
> All night long the water is crying to me.
>
> Unresting water, there shall never be rest
> Till the last moon droop and the last tide fail,
> And the fire of the end begin to burn in the west;
> And the heart shall be weary and wonder and cry like the sea,
> All life long crying without avail,
> As the water all night long is crying to me.

The first thing that seems significant here is that a book called *The
Souls of Black Folk*, a classic of American social theory, begins with
a poem by an English writer who lived in Wales and was famous for
being an intermediary between contemporary English and French
avant-garde poetry. The poem is about restlessness and crying (the
words 'cry' or 'crying' occur seven times), and then about the soul
and the sea. The speaker cannot understand the voice in his heart,
or the voice of the sea, both of which melt into one in the poem.
The sea is, of course, 'the biggest thing on earth' as (in a different
context) A. R. Ammons wrote, and for humans, therefore, pretty

much the closest thing to eternity and infinity. It seems to have moods and occasionally gets violent, but we cannot understand it: all this makes it a very plausible symbol for the soul. In addition, in the context of *The Souls of Black Folk*, the sea might also resonate with memories of the Atlantic slave trade and give a hint as to what caused all the crying and sorrow. The poem itself, however, is silent on causes: sorrow and restlessness are abstracted from their specifics and transposed into being aspects of a universal human condition, a kind of metaphysical sorrow, and I guess this is why Du Bois put it here. The *particular* issue of the condition of black people in the USA is framed, right from the first page, in *universalistic* terms.

1 How does it feel to be a problem?

After the poem and the line of music, Du Bois begins the essay with a reflection on the difficulty of asking, as well as answering, the 'unasked question' that is always there 'between me and the other world': 'They approach me in a half-hesitant sort of way, eye me curiously or compassionately, and then, instead of saying directly, How does it feel to be a problem? they say, I know an excellent colored man in my town…' (7). All his interlocutors 'flutter around it' instead of asking it directly, and he, with whom the others do not quite know how to interact, responds in equally polite and evasive ways. Nevertheless, Du Bois writes, this unasked question is the real question, and the starting point of the book.

2 Shut out from their world by a vast veil

Du Bois describes the day 'when the shadow swept across me', the day that brought the 'revelation' of his being 'a problem', during his childhood in New England. The scene happened at school – the schoolchildren exchanged 'visiting-cards', and one girl refused to accept his card: 'Then it dawned upon me with a certain suddenness that I was different from the others; or like, mayhap, in heart and life and longing, but shut out from their world by a vast veil' (8). The 'revelation' is ambivalent: maybe he is in fact different, or maybe he is similar – 'like' – as far as 'heart and life and longing' are concerned, but nevertheless 'shut out'. This is how Du Bois describes his initial reaction:

> I had thereafter no desire to tear down that veil, to creep through; I
> held all beyond it in common contempt, and lived above it in a region
> of blue sky and great wandering shadows. That sky was bluest when I
> could beat my mates at examination-time, or beat them at a foot-race,
> or even beat their stringy heads.

He accepts the separation in a detached, idealistic sort of way: young Du Bois is above the white racists' world and confronts it with his own sense of superiority: he 'beats' them, intellectually, in sports, or even in a schoolyard fracas. In adolescence, all these were still possible. 'Alas, with the years all this fine contempt began to fade; for the worlds I longed for, and all their dazzling opportunities, were theirs, not mine.' The reality principle sets in and breaks the boy's spontaneous sense of superiority. But this did not mean, in his case, that he would give up: 'But they should not keep these prizes, I said; some, all, I would wrest from them.' He considered becoming a lawyer, a doctor or a writer. Here Du Bois stops and points out that his own story is not typical, as other kids reacted differently:

> With other black boys the strife was not so fiercely sunny: their
> youth shrunk into tasteless sycophancy, or into silent hatred of the
> pale world about them and mocking distrust of everything white; or
> wasted itself in a bitter cry, Why did God make me an outcast and a
> stranger in mine own house? (8)

While he had the strength to continue the effort to beat the whites at their own games, basically by going to university and becoming a writer, other black boys resigned themselves to their situation and chose either 'tasteless sycophancy' or 'silent hatred', or probably a combination of both.

3 Double-consciousness

The third paragraph needs to be quoted in full – it introduces the concept Du Bois is most famous for:

> After the Egyptian and Indian, the Greek and Roman, the Teuton
> and Mongolian, the Negro is a sort of seventh son, born with a veil,
> and gifted with second-sight in this American world,—a world which
> yields him no true self-consciousness, but only lets him see himself
> through the revelation of the other world. It is a peculiar sensation,
> this double-consciousness, this sense of always looking at one's self

> through the eyes of others, of measuring one's soul by the tape of
> a world that looks on in amused contempt and pity. One ever feels
> his twoness,—an American, a Negro; two souls, two thoughts, two
> unreconciled strivings; two warring ideals in one dark body, whose
> dogged strength alone keeps it from being torn asunder. (8)

These are some of the most famous lines in African-American literature. Self-consciousness can be attained only by looking at oneself 'through the eyes of others', to the extent that these others
have been internalized: they have immigrated into one's own inner
life – they constitute a second soul – hence the plural of *The Souls
of Black Folk*. The two souls, represented in twofold thoughts,
strivings and ideals, are conflicting, and it takes 'dogged' physical strength to stop these conflicting souls from tearing the body
asunder. Du Bois makes use of two different mythical ideas here
to underline the particularity of the situation: one is the notion
that a child 'born with a veil' (a membrane of placenta covering the
newborn's face at birth) enjoys 'second-sight', namely particularly
acute perceptiveness (this seems to have been at the time a popular
folk belief among African-Americans); the other is the notion of 'the
Negro' as 'a sort of seventh son'. This notion is rather obscure but,
once you understand the reference, quite revealing: it is a reference
to Hegel's *Lectures on the Philosophy of History*, something Du Bois
probably studied during his stay in Berlin, in which the philosopher
of German idealism pronounces that there are, or rather have been,
six so-called 'world-historical peoples': Egyptians, Indians, Greeks,
Romans, the Germanic peoples and Mongolians. For Hegel, these
peoples – or rather, the cultures they produced – historically and
successively have been the focal points of the gradual evolution
of 'world spirit', i.e., the ultimately irrepressible drive of humanity towards civilization, reason and emancipation. Hegel left out
Americans, whom he expected to become a 'world-historical people'
in the near future, and Africans, of whom he had a notoriously
low opinion. Du Bois now adds African-Americans as the seventh
group to carry forward world history, thereby both accepting and
revising Hegel's famous scheme. Du Bois accepts both its nationalism and its cosmopolitanism: the nationalism of Hegel's notion of
the 'world-historical peoples' is sometimes understood as racialism,
as the 'world-historical peoples' can also be understood as racial

groupings; it is cosmopolitan, though, as these 'peoples' are only important in the Hegelian perspective inasmuch as they were protagonists of the shared and progressing history of humanity. And that is just how Du Bois sees African-Americans.

At the same time as being a specific characteristic of African-Americans, the 'double-consciousness' is also something any reader of the book will probably be able to relate to: Du Bois's usage of the concept of 'double-consciousness' is as much descriptive of a universal experience typical of the modern world as it is particular to the situation of African-Americans. The situation of African-Americans is not in itself entirely exceptional, but rather *exceptionally typical* of the situation of modern humans, similar to the weariness and restlessness described by Symons. Du Bois himself is no exception: his own position, in particular his usage of a philosophical-sociological language that resonates with themes in the wider tradition of (post-Hegelian) social theory, not only names and describes but *expresses* the 'double-consciousness'. This undergirds the nearly poetic, literary quality of the text, and surely contributed to its longevity as a classic.

4 To merge his double self

In the next paragraph, Du Bois moves from the description of the 'double-consciousness' to a dialectical account of how 'longing' drives 'the American Negro' to overcome 'double-consciousness' and achieve a more coherent form of self-consciousness that would consume but also preserve the elements that go into it. These are clearly elements of the Hegelian liberalism that was still in existence when Du Bois studied in Berlin: 'The history of the American Negro is the history of this strife,—this longing to attain self-conscious manhood, to merge his double self into a better and truer self. In this merging he wishes neither of the older selves to be lost' (9). Du Bois asserts that 'the American Negro' would not 'Africanize America' (which was hardly an option anyway), 'for America has too much to teach the world and Africa'. Du Bois rejects in this formulation any kind of mystical or ethnic anti-Americanism – his is a position that aims to defend modernity by improving it. Importantly, though, he 'would not bleach his Negro soul in a flood of white Americanism, for he knows that Negro blood has a message for the world'. The particular, here represented by 'Negro blood' (which formulation stems from the language of 'race' but in fact means what we would call 'ethnicity'), speaks to and must be included in the universal, modernity. 'Americanism' is likewise a particular that feeds into a universal, but cannot realize its potential universality if it remains 'white', i.e. limited and particular. Modernity needs a non-exclusive Americanism, and therefore it must be made 'possible for a man to be both a Negro and an American, without being cursed and spit upon by his fellows, without having the doors of Opportunity closed roughly in his face' (9).

5 To be a co-worker in the kingdom of culture

African-Americans' principal aim is to be 'a co-worker in the kingdom of culture' (9), but the racism of post-emancipation America prevents them from fulfilling their potential. This is to the detriment of 'culture'. Their 'best powers' and 'latent genius' have 'in the past been strangely wasted, dispersed, or forgotten'. Their failure to achieve much has been caused not by inherent weakness but by circumstance, namely by 'the contradiction of double aims': on the one hand, 'to escape white contempt', on the other, to serve 'a poverty-stricken horde'. Serving the needs and living up to the expectations of 'black folk' as well as 'the whites' is difficult to reconcile. Du Bois gives four examples, representing four different professional groups, or, to be more precise, four different fractions of the black (lower) middle class – artisans, ministers/doctors, scholars and artists:

– 'The double-aimed struggle of the black artisan—on the one hand to escape white contempt for a nation of mere hewers of wood and drawers of water, and on the other hand to plough and nail and dig for a poverty-stricken horde—could only result in making him a poor craftsman, for he had but half a heart in either cause.' The artisan has to serve the immediate needs of his primary constituency, but thereby inevitably confirms the prejudices of the whites.

– 'By the poverty and ignorance of his people, the Negro minister or doctor was tempted toward quackery and demagogy; and by the criticism of the other world, toward ideals that made him ashamed of his lowly tasks.' Du Bois seems very critical of the black upper-middle-class groups who give in to temptation and deliver bad work, while at the same time feeling ashamed about it as the whites – rightly, in Du Bois's view – criticize them.

– 'The would-be black savant was confronted by the paradox that the knowledge his people needed was a twice-told tale to his white neighbors, while the knowledge which would teach the white world was Greek to his own flesh and blood.' Intellectuals are more like the artisans in this respect: they do the right thing by teaching at the level the tutees find themselves at, but this cannot possibly make them look good in the eyes of the whites.

– 'The innate love of harmony and beauty that set the ruder souls of his people a-dancing and a-singing raised but confusion and doubt in the soul of the black artist; for the beauty revealed to him was the soul-beauty of a race which his larger audience despised, and he could not articulate the message of another people.' This last point reflects the race-thinking of the time: an artist can only ever 'articulate' the 'soul-beauty' of his or her own racial group – something that commentators have sometimes called 'cultural insiderism'. Black artists can therefore neither address larger (white) audiences nor offer to 'their own' folk something that is alien to their 'racial makeup'. This is one of the passages in which Du Bois sounds rather conservative and 'culturally racist'. The statement is also rather biased in the way it depicts 'the ruder souls of his people' – i.e. the lower classes – as naively enjoying their own 'soul-beauty' without complications, whereas intellectuals and artists cannot: the latter carry the burden of being 'the seventh sons', i.e., the carriers of the world-spirit that propels humanity forward in the march towards universal civilization, which requires them to look at their own 'soul-beauty' rather sceptically through the eyes of 'double-consciousness'. It seems much more fun to enjoy life as one of those 'ruder souls'!

The uneven development of American society forces African-Americans to work at two different levels simultaneously, to the effect that they fail at both. The 'double-consciousness' is in the fifth paragraph the opposite of the blessing it seemed to be in the third paragraph: the two half-consciousnesses undermine and sabotage each other, leading African-Americans into dead ends and even at times making them 'ashamed of themselves' (10).

6–7 The disappointment with emancipation

In the next two paragraphs Du Bois comments on another, more psychological aspect of the contemporary misery of African-Americans: during slavery, 'the American Negro' had 'worshipped Freedom with ... unquestioning faith' and had thought of slavery as 'the sum of all villainies'. Freedom and emancipation seemed to promise the end of all sorrows. When they were achieved, however, no promised land was delivered, and bitter disappointment set in: after 'forty years of renewal and development ... the swarthy spectre sits in its accustomed seat at the Nation's feast' (10). The 'forty years' resonate with the biblical notion of the forty years spent in the wilderness on the way to the Promised Land, and even the notion of a spectre at a feast seems to echo a biblical text (Daniel) where a ghost writes an ominous message on the wall of a palace during a feast. The spectre here does not write a message – it *is* the message: Du Bois implies that the 'swarthy spectre' – the continued misery of black folk – is a punishment for the nation's murderous sin by quoting a line famously addressed by Shakespeare's Macbeth to the ghost that haunted him: 'Take any shape but that, and my firm nerves/ Shall never tremble!' (Macbeth Act 3 scene 4). The nation can face any social problem, *but not this one*. It is worth noting that Du Bois seems to refer by 'us' and 'we' to the American nation as a whole. Like the murderer Macbeth, '[t]he Nation has not yet found peace from its sins' (slavery); 'the shadow of a deep disappointment rests upon the Negro people,—a disappointment all the more bitter because the unattained ideal was unbounded save by the simple ignorance of a lowly people'. The implication here is that it was unrealistic to expect with the ending of slavery the ending of the entire social misery. Having unrealistic expectations in the first place, it is implied, leads to depression even in the case of success (emancipation) and thwarts subsequent progress.

8 From political power to the power of education

Here Du Bois moves to a more historical account. The American Civil War (1861–65) was followed by a decade-long period of reform and attempted emancipation, the 'Reconstruction'. This period was marked by another illusion that ended in disappointment: all hopes were invested in the ballot when '[a] million black men started with renewed zeal to vote themselves into the kingdom' (11). When this period ended in 1876, hopes shifted on to education as 'the mountain path to Canaan'. A 'new vision began gradually to replace the dream of political power', that of 'book-learning' (put in inverted commas by Du Bois), 'the curiosity, born of compulsory ignorance, to know and test the power of the cabalistic letters of the white man, the longing to know'. The 'highway of Emancipation and law' was blocked, so a people hungry for knowledge thrust themselves on to the 'mountain path' of learning. It can be inferred that Du Bois considers that this 'steep and rugged' path is more likely to lead to the goal.

9 The dawning of self-consciousness

While the previous three paragraphs describe in a somewhat distanced tone the inevitable failure of the – perhaps equally inevitable – illusions held by the former slaves who expected too much from emancipation and the vote, the next paragraph is written as if with a sigh of relief: finally people begin to face the problem with a sense of realism. Education was indeed the way forward:

> Up the new path the advance guard toiled, slowly, heavily, doggedly; only those who have watched and guided the faltering feet, the misty minds, the dull understandings, of the dark pupils of these schools know how faithfully, how piteously, this people strove to learn. It was weary work. (11)

Du Bois seems to speak here from his experience as a Tennessee schoolteacher, and the culture shock suffered there by the educated young (black) gent from Massachusetts reverberates through these lines. We also hear the Berlin- and Harvard-trained sociologist speak: 'The cold statistician wrote down the inches of progress here and there, noted also where here and there a foot had slipped or someone had fallen.' It was a tough hike to Canaan, but

> the journey at least gave leisure for reflection and self-examination; it changed the child of Emancipation to the youth with dawning self-consciousness, self-realization, self-respect. In those sombre forests of his striving his own soul rose before him, and he saw himself,— darkly as through a veil; and yet he saw in himself some faint revelation of his power, of his mission. He began to have a dim feeling that, to attain his place in the world, he must be himself, and not another.

Education becomes self-discovery, and thereby produces the energy necessary for its continuation. With self-awareness also comes analysis of the social situation:

> For the first time he sought to analyze the burden he bore upon his back, that dead-weight of social degradation partially masked behind a half-named Negro problem. He felt his poverty; without a cent, without a home, without land, tools, or savings, he had entered into competition with rich, landed, skilled neighbors. To be a poor man is hard, but to be a poor race in a land of dollars is the very bottom of hardships. He felt the weight of his ignorance,—not simply of letters, but of life, of business, of the humanities; the accumulated sloth and shirking and awkwardness of decades and centuries shackled his hands and feet.

Du Bois reproduces here a line of argument that had been characteristic of most liberal emancipation discourses of nineteenth-century Europe (whether concerning Jews, workers or women): the damning judgement of the group to be emancipated is accepted (ignorance, sloth, shirking, awkwardness), but explained in terms of circumstance and thus to be overcome *gradually*. Education makes the freemen understand why political emancipation on its own could not but have failed. Du Bois tells a story of people who had to hit rock bottom – a state almost worse than slavery – to get better, and adds another aspect to cultural and economic underdevelopment, the problem of the dissolution of the traditional family among African-Americans:

> Nor was his burden all poverty and ignorance. The red stain of bastardy, which two centuries of systematic legal defilement of Negro women had stamped upon his race, meant not only the loss of ancient African chastity, but also the hereditary weight of a mass of corruption from white adulterers, threatening almost the obliteration of the Negro home. (12)

In this sentence the remnants of a culturalist race-thinking that still characterised Du Bois's early writings – in keeping with both American and German intellectual life of the time – can be felt. Du Bois defends here the family, which is of course a social institution, but his use of the words 'race' and 'hereditary' give this particular paragraph an uncomfortably racial undertone: 'ancient African chastity' had been destroyed by corrupt white men who for two centuries had legally raped enslaved black women. It is as if the brutality of the fact that is being named infiltrates the language that does the naming: the corrupt white genes produce the inauthentic 'bastardy' of a mixed, corrupted race.

10–11 Justified versus unfair prejudice

The 'very soul of the toiling, sweating black man is darkened by the shadow of a vast despair': prejudice (12). Du Bois writes that 'men ... learnedly explain [prejudice] as the natural defence of culture against barbarism, learning against ignorance, purity against crime, the "higher" against the "lower" races'. He points out that there are two kinds of reaction from 'the Negro' to prejudice: to the extent that 'this strange prejudice ... is founded on just homage to civilization, culture, righteousness, and progress, he humbly bows and meekly does obeisance'. It seems that this is also Du Bois's own position: he fully embraces the idea of civilizational progress, and the necessity for the more cultured to defend culture against those still more 'barbarian'. However, he distinguishes from this, as it were, justified form of 'prejudice' an unfair, malicious kind: 'that personal disrespect and mockery, the ridicule and systematic humiliation, the distortion of fact and wanton license of fancy'. Before this malicious kind of prejudice 'he stands helpless, dismayed, and well-nigh speechless'. It brought 'self-questioning, self-disparagement, and lowering of ideals which ever accompany repression' and produced 'an atmosphere of contempt and hate' – a defeatist attitude: 'what need of education, since we must always cook and serve?' And 'the Nation' happily echoed this sentiment, asserting that 'half-men' have no 'need of higher culture'. Nevertheless, Du Bois concludes, 'out of the evil came something of good,—the more careful adjustment of education to real life, the clearer perception of the Negroes' social responsibilities, and the sobering realization of the meaning of progress'. He seems to be saying here that the more malicious prejudice was thrown at African-Americans, the more realistic they became, shedding over-ambitious expectations of themselves.

12–13 Work, culture, liberty

The concluding section of the essay begins with yet another reference to German intellectual history, and also takes up again the image of the wild, restless sea that was introduced by the poem at the beginning:

> So dawned the time of *Sturm und Drang*: storm and stress to-day rocks our little boat on the mad waters of the world-sea; there is within and without the sound of conflict, the burning of body and rending of soul; inspiration strives with doubt, and faith with vain questionings.

Sturm und Drang, 'storm and stress' or 'storm and urge', was the moniker of a late eighteenth-century German literary movement that emphasized emotionality and individuality, not without a hint of romantic proto-nationalism, as complementary to rationality. It was typical of the late Enlightenment period to which it belongs. Incidentally the phrase was taken from a play of the same name that dealt with the American Revolution – which surely motivated Du Bois's borrowing of the phrase here: he re-imports a phrase from a German cultural movement that was itself inspired and enthused by the American revolutionary experience.

Du Bois sees his own present as a time of 'storm and urge', a time of conflict, uncertainty and restlessness. 'The bright ideals of the past' including 'physical freedom, political power, the training of brains and the training of hands' were 'over-simple and incomplete as long as they were pursued in isolation; as such they were 'the dreams of a credulous race-childhood'. This 'race' is now in the stormy process of growing up, and in that process overcomes those one-sided strategies of emancipation:

> Work, culture, liberty,—all these we need, not singly but together, not successively but together, each growing and aiding each, and all striving toward that vaster ideal that swims before the Negro people, the ideal of human brotherhood, gained through the unifying ideal of Race; the ideal of fostering and developing the traits and talents of the Negro, not in opposition to or contempt for other races, but rather in large conformity to the greater ideals of the American Republic, in order that some day on American soil two world-races may give each to each those characteristics both so sadly lack.

'Human brotherhood' is the cosmopolitan goal that is to be achieved through 'fostering and developing' the condition of the black 'race' to the point that the 'two world-races' – in the sense of the expanded Hegelian list of six, now seven world-historical peoples – complement each other to form an ever-more 'world-historical' American nation. A combination of 'work, culture, liberty' – i.e. economic development, education, political emancipation – is the means to achieve this. It is important to keep in mind that in the Hegelian meaning of this terminology, peoples and 'races' are 'world-historical' because they are, in a particular period of world history, at the forefront of the human struggle for emancipation and humanity. The cosmopolitan ideal of unity is 'gained' through, rather than against, that of 'racial unity': puzzling though this might sound to readers in the twenty-first century, the idea is that through the process of ethno-national unification the people learn to love the idea of unity that will inevitably lead them on to the ideal of universal humanity. Du Bois rearticulates here a conception that was very common in liberal nineteenth-century European discourses on nation and 'race'. Although there are complicated overlaps, it must be distinguished from those unequivocally racist discourses of the time that posited 'race' as an unchanging, extra-historical, biological essence immune and opposed to civilizational progress.

Du Bois continues by emphasizing that the two 'races' already in the not-so-emancipated present complement each other advantageously:

> We the darker ones come even now not altogether empty-handed: there are to-day no truer exponents of the pure human spirit of the Declaration of Independence than the American Negroes; there is no true American music but the wild sweet melodies of the Negro slave; the American fairy tales and folklore are Indian and African; and, all in all, we black men seem the sole oasis of simple faith and reverence in a dusty desert of dollars and smartness. Will America be poorer if she replace her brutal dyspeptic blundering with light-hearted but determined Negro humility? or her coarse and cruel wit with loving jovial good-humor? or her vulgar music with the soul of the Sorrow Songs?

This passage pushes the argument about the 'complementarity' of the two 'races' quite a bit further: in fact, the African-Americans are

already in their disabling condition a lot more humane and, in terms
of America's own ideals, more American than the white majority of
America. They embody the spirit of America better, as they have
faith, humility, humour and soul where white America has 'dollars
and smartness'. Du Bois sneaks in here a powerful bit of cultural
critique of capitalist civilization, again something that was central to
the thinking of the 'founding fathers' of social theory in Germany.
Lastly, it is worth noting that Du Bois here also mentions 'Indians' –
i.e. native Americans – in the same breath with 'Negroes'. He surely
had in mind an alliance in pursuit of emancipation. This brings us
to the closing sentence of the essay:

> Merely a concrete test of the underlying principles of the great repub-
> lic is the Negro Problem, and the spiritual striving of the freedmen's
> sons is the travail of souls whose burden is almost beyond the measure
> of their strength, but who bear it in the name of an historic race, in
> the name of this the land of their fathers' fathers, and in the name of
> human opportunity.

'The Negro Problem' is a test for the American republic as the
African-Americans fight simultaneously for their 'race', the father-
land and humanity – in this ascending order.

Chapter 9 'Of the Sons of Master and Man'

'Of Our Spiritual Strivings' is followed by thirteen essays, each
opened by a poem and a line of music, that develop different aspects
of the argument as set out in the lead essay of the book. I will now
look at the argument of Chapter 9, 'Of the Sons of Master and
Man', which is one of the more strictly sociological pieces.

1 The problem of 'race contact': the meeting of civilization with 'undeveloped peoples'

The title 'Of the Sons of Master and Man' indicates that the chapter
deals with the period after emancipation, i.e. after 'Master and Man'
– slaveholder and slave – have been replaced by their descendants.
The word 'son' in the title also indicates that there is not much about
daughters in this chapter. In the first section Du Bois spells out
the larger historical framework of his argument: 'the characteristic

of our age is the contact of European civilization with the world's undeveloped peoples' (111). This is the phenomenon usually addressed as 'imperialism' or 'globalization', depending on perspective. Importantly, Du Bois frames this phenomenon as 'the contact of diverse races of men'. This does not mean, however, that 'the contact of races' is driven by a racial dynamic (as European imperialist and proto-fascist forces of the time would have had it), as Du Bois uses 'race' (almost synonymous with 'a culture' or 'a civilization') as a descriptive concept, not an explanatory one. Up to the present, 'race contact' has led to results 'not pleasant to look back upon': '[w]ar, murder, slavery, extermination, and debauchery' have again and again been the results of the expansion of modern civilization and 'the blessed Gospel', neither of which he rejects in principle. He explicitly rejects, however, the 'complacent' narrative of imperialism as 'the fated triumph of strength over weakness, of righteousness over evil, of superiors over inferiors', and although he acknowledges that 'there are many delicate differences in race psychology … which explain much of history and social development', they fail to explain the crucial fact of 'the triumph of brute force and cunning over weakness and innocence'. Du Bois takes at this point the language of social Darwinism and gives it a characteristic twist:

> It is, then, the strife of all honorable men of the twentieth century to see that in the future competition of races the survival of the fittest shall mean the triumph of the good, the beautiful, and the true; that we may be able to preserve for future civilization all that is really fine and noble and strong, and not continue to put a premium on greed and impudence and cruelty. (112)

Perhaps not without a hint of sarcasm, Du Bois basically says here that the 'survival of the fittest' might not be such a bad idea if 'the fittest' simply meant 'the good, the beautiful, and the true' (another formula from German idealism, although the Germans usually put 'the true' first and 'the good' last). To ensure the triumph of 'the good, the beautiful, and the true', Du Bois asserts one must study 'the phenomena of race contact' in a manner that is conscientious, frank, sober and fair, for which the American South provides a fine field: 'we must ask, what are the actual relations of whites and blacks in the South? and we must be answered, not by apology or fault-finding, but by a plain, unvarnished tale'. And this is just what he aims to provide in this chapter.

2 The different dimensions of social relations in civilized life

Du Bois's account of 'race contact' is organized in terms of a general sociological conception: he writes that '[i]n the civilized life of to-day the contact of men and their relations to each other fall in a few main lines of action and communication' (112), namely 'the physical proximity' of dwelling-places and neighbourhoods; economic relations (the 'mutual satisfaction of wants' and 'production of wealth'); political relations (concerning 'social control', government and taxation); 'intellectual contact' and relations, including 'public opinion'; social contact; and religion. 'These are the principal ways in which men living in the same communities are brought into contact with each other. It is my present task, therefore, to indicate, from my point of view, how the black race in the South meet and mingle with the whites in these matters of everyday life.'

2.1 Physical space

Concerning 'physical dwelling', Du Bois states that it is 'usually possible to draw in nearly every Southern community a physical color-line on the map, on the one side of which whites dwell and on the other Negroes' (113). Importantly, 'segregation by color is largely independent of' what Du Bois calls 'that natural clustering by social grades common to all communities': 'a white slum' might often lie 'in the heart of a respectable Negro district'. The effect most emphasized by Du Bois is that 'the best of the whites and the best of the Negroes almost never live in anything like close proximity' so that 'both whites and blacks see commonly the worst of each other'. This emphasis follows from Du Bois's central interest in education and mutual cultural betterment through both 'races' learning from each other: the structuring of space prevents this from happening.

Du Bois contrasts the contemporary situation he witnessed with that before emancipation. He claims that 'in the patriarchal big house' masters and house-servants were in 'close contact' so that 'the best of both races' knew and had sympathy for each other, while 'the squalor and dull round of toil among the field-hands was removed from the sight and hearing of the family'. Making use here of his sociological imagination, Du Bois tries to understand the attitude of contemporary whites who had taken a liking to their father's house-servants (back in the day) but disliked the black people they observed on the streets of the post-emancipation city. The point for Du Bois here is that spatial separation after emancipation had negative effects, whereas spatial proximity had some advantages, even under conditions of slavery. He adds that 'the better class of blacks' also form their view of white people from their encounters 'with the worst representatives of the white race' which Du Bois deplores: it hinders civilizational progress which can only come from some form of mixing.

2.2 Economic relations

The decisive factor in Du Bois's interpretation of the economics of the South is the mind-set and mentality that centuries of slavery have produced in the African-Americans, which prevents them from succeeding in the entirely different conditions of a modern capitalist democratic environment: 'they are willing and good-natured, but not self-reliant, provident, or careful' (114), a situation which is 'the very opposite to that of the modern self-reliant democratic laborer'. They need to be trained towards 'foresight, carefulness, and honesty' so that they can survive 'relentless competition with the workingmen of the world'. Du Bois emphasizes that one does not need to take recourse to 'fine-spun theories of racial differences' to make an argument for the need for training 'after the brains of the race have been knocked out by two hundred and fifty years of assiduous education in submission, carelessness, and stealing'. He notes that 'after Emancipation', the African-Americans should have been given a legally protected space 'to settle down to slow and careful internal development'. Instead, they were 'thrown almost immediately into relentless and sharp competition with the best of modern workingmen under an economic system where every participant is fighting for himself, and too often utterly regardless of the rights or welfare of his neighbor'. Without using exactly these words, Du Bois argues for a reformed, softened down, less rapid form of capitalist development in which the state would protect the most vulnerable and secure their chance to catch up with the more advanced sectors of society. Neither the former slaveholders nor the Northern 'philanthropists' nor the National Government fulfilled their moral and historical duty in this respect.

The next paragraph provides a description of two types of capitalist regime, one more benign, the other, being more modern and more backward at the same time, less benign:

> For we must never forget that the economic system of the South to-day which has succeeded the old *régime* is not the same system as that of the old industrial North, of England, or of France, with their trade-unions, their restrictive laws, their written and unwritten commercial customs, and their long experience. It is, rather, a copy of that England of the early nineteenth century, before the factory acts,—the England that wrung pity from thinkers and fired the wrath of Carlyle. (114–15)

Du Bois argues that 'long experience' has established in the Northern states of the USA, as in England or France, a system where capitalism is tamed by trade unions, law and customs, whereas the South is in the more backward stage resembling England during the industrial revolution – that of raw and untrammelled capitalist exploitation. The reference to Thomas Carlyle (1795–1881), the main representative of the conservative, 'ethical critique' of capitalist modernity, is somewhat odd, as Carlyle had been a defender of slavery; but then Carlyle had many admirers in the sociological tradition. Du Bois writes that power in the South 'passed from the hands of Southern gentlemen' in 1865 'to those men who have come to take charge of the industrial exploitation of the New South,—the sons of poor whites fired with a new thirst for wealth and power, thrifty and avaricious Yankees, shrewd and unscrupulous Jews'. Du Bois, who was of course anything but a nostalgic defender of the slaveholders' regime, uses language here that makes the new regime seem even worse than the old: the invading 'sons of poor whites' from the North surely were no gentlemen, and as if 'thrifty and avaricious' Northerners were not bad enough, they brought with them 'shrewd and unscrupulous Jews', a formulation that reproduces the kind of social antisemitism that was common at the time in the context of both American and European 'populist' critiques of unrestrained capitalism. It is important to note that Du Bois himself noted and corrected this rather embarrassing aspect of his text: in later editions of the book, 'Jews' was replaced by 'immigrants', and Du Bois wrote in a letter of 1953 concerning these changes that on re-reading these words he saw 'that harm might come if they were allowed to stand as they are':

> First of all, I am not at all sure that the foreign exploiters to whom I referred in my study of the Black Belt, were in fact Jews. I took the word of my informants, and I am now wondering if in fact Russian Jews in any numbers were in Georgia at the time. (quoted in the introduction to the Oxford edition, page xxvi)

Irrespective of whether these 'unscrupulous immigrants' were Jews or not, he notes that 'I did not, when writing, realize that by stressing the name of the group instead of what some members of the [group] may have done, I was unjustly maligning a people in exactly the same way my folk were then and are now falsely accused'. Although one might still wonder whether it is quite right to blame 'immigrants' for the post-emancipation hyper-exploitation in the South, these remarks certainly demonstrate that Du Bois had the rather rare ability to correct his own mistakes. They also reflect the fact that he was one of those exceptional thinkers who become more critical and radical with age.

Du Bois writes that 'the Southern laborers, white and black' fell into 'the hands of these men ... to their sorrow':

> For the laborers as such, there is in these new captains of industry neither love nor hate, neither sympathy nor romance; it is a cold question of dollars and dividends. Under such a system all labor is bound to suffer. Even the white laborers are not yet intelligent, thrifty, and well trained enough to maintain themselves against the powerful inroads of organized capital. The results among them, even, are long hours of toil, low wages, child labor, and lack of protection against usury and cheating. But among the black laborers all this is aggravated, first, by a race prejudice which varies from a doubt and distrust among the best element of whites to a frenzied hatred among the worst; and, secondly, it is aggravated, as I have said before, by the wretched economic heritage of the freedmen from slavery.

Du Bois's account of society subjected to 'organized capital' is, at this stage of his writing career, rather simplistic: the 'new captains of industry' are unsympathetic, cold, usurious and cheating – by implication, more so than the gentlemen slaveholders of old – but, as capitalists, in principle colour-blind: all labourers suffer. The suffering is aggravated by race prejudice as well as the slavery-induced incongruous mentality of the African-Americans.

The next paragraph illustrates this state of affairs further: the blacks in the South are '[l]eft by the best elements of the South with little protection or oversight', victims of 'the worst and most unscrupulous men in each community' (115). Du Bois mentions again an 'enterprising Russian Jew' (116) who cheated 'an ignorant, honest Negro' (115) out of his property. (In later editions of the text the 'enterprising Russian Jew' becomes an 'enterprising American'.) There are good and bad 'elements' among blacks as well as whites, but the 'best' (i.e. the most educated) in 'each community' do not care much about the poor.

All this results in a situation where 'escape is impossible, further toil a farce, and protest a crime'. Du Bois concludes that 'such proceedings can happen, and will happen, in any community where a class of ignorant toilers are placed by custom and race-prejudice beyond the pale of sympathy and race-brotherhood' (116). There are positive signs, though: there is now 'a class of black landlords and mechanics who, in spite of disadvantages, are accumulating property and making good citizens' (116). They are less numerous than they would be under 'a fairer economic system', however, and 'above all, the personnel of the successful class is left to chance and accident, and not to any intelligent culling or reasonable methods of selection'. Du Bois seems to assume that in a more developed and fairer system – such as in his native Massachusetts or in Imperial Germany, perhaps – the most ethical and educated would constitute the social elite. This thought resonates with the idealistic notion expressed at the beginning of the first essay that 'survival of the fittest' should really mean 'survival of the most ethical'. Du Bois asserts that leadership towards betterment 'must come from the blacks themselves': no one doubts any more that 'individual Negroes' are able 'to assimilate the culture and common sense of modern civilization, and to pass it on, to some extent at least, to their fellows'. Leadership by such individuals 'is the path out of the economic situation' (116): it takes

Negro leaders of character and intelligence,—men of skill, men of light and leading, college-bred men, black captains of industry, and missionaries of culture; men who thoroughly comprehend and know modern civilization, and can take hold of Negro communities and raise and train them by force of precept and example, deep sympathy, and the inspiration of common blood and ideals. (117)

Such men must be brought into positions of power within the 'communities', and must have 'such weapons as ... are indispensable to human progress', first of all the ballot.

2.3 Political relations

The section on political relations is a plea for the universal franchise, but it is one of the least straightforward parts of the book. It begins with a reminder of the idealist rationalism of the period until the Civil War, still influenced by the discourses of the revolutionary period, when the belief in universal suffrage was unqualified: 'We argued ... that ... in every state the best arbiters of their own welfare are the persons directly affected' (117). In addition, it was thought that possession of the ballot by the emancipated slaves 'would compel their fellows to educate this class to [the ballot's] intelligent use': the more educated and enlightened classes – black and white – could not afford not to contribute to the former slaves' uplift, the argument went. This expectation did not survive the disappointment with the reality of post-emancipation society, culminating with a 'movement for disfranchisement' in the present period (118). Du Bois urges resistance of this movement because 'the modern organization of industry' presupposes 'the power and ability of the laboring classes to compel respect for their welfare', which in turn necessitates the ballot (119). It is worth noting that Du Bois's concept of 'the modern organization of industry' – modern capitalism – is intrinsically connected to that of democracy in this way, a notion that remained characteristic of American sociological theories of modernization and economic development. As capitalism is based on wage labour – i.e. contractual social relationships – it is conceptually thought to be irreconcilable with slavery and disfranchisement. However, Du Bois explicitly – and somewhat confusingly – grants that the argument *against* the universal franchise – at the time still typical of most forms of liberalism, and certainly of conservatism – is not without merit:

> I should be the last one to deny the patent weaknesses and shortcom-
> ings of the Negro people; I should be the last to withhold sympathy
> from the white South in its efforts to solve its intricate social prob-
> lems. I freely acknowledge that it is possible, and sometimes best, that
> a partially undeveloped people should be ruled by the best of their
> stronger and better neighbors for their own good, until such time
> as they can start and fight the world's battles alone. I have already
> pointed out how sorely in need of such economic and spiritual guid-
> ance the emancipated Negro was, and I am quite willing to admit that
> if the representatives of the best white Southern public opinion were
> the ruling and guiding powers in the South to-day the conditions
> indicated would be fairly well fulfilled. (119)

Du Bois's argument is: if only 'the best' (educated) among the whites were ruling the South, then he would welcome a patrimo-nial, educational regime that would ameliorate the blacks and guide them to bourgeois maturity. 'The best' are not in charge, however, and therefore there is no alternative to black self-emancipation:

> in any land, in any country under modern free competition, to lay
> any class of weak and despised people, be they white, black, or blue,
> at the political mercy of their stronger, richer, and more resourceful
> fellows, is a temptation which human nature seldom has withstood
> and seldom will withstand. (120)

The Southern whites lack the moral and civilizational righteous-ness to withstand the temptation of lording it over the blacks so that black disfranchisement would only allow the whites to get away with murder (literally and metaphorically).

2.4 Crime

On the next page and a half Du Bois sketches out some key ideas towards an African-American criminology. He starts out from the observation that since emancipation, 'crime among Negroes' has increased and 'a distinct criminal class among the blacks' of the slums of the great cities has emerged (120). Du Bois writes that 'under a strict slave system there can scarcely be such a thing as crime'. He does not explain this statement, but probably plays here on the idea that slaves are considered to be things, and things cannot commit crimes: committing a crime presupposes subjectivity, freedom of will and responsibility. Correspondingly, 'the police system of the South was primarily designed to control slaves', not to deal with crime. It was simply assumed that blacks would quite naturally commit criminal acts, and that whites would be their victims. The system did not change as radically as would have been necessary to reflect the social revolution that was emancipation, and was therefore not able to deliver 'discriminating treatment, firm but reformatory, with no hint of injustice' (120). (By 'discriminating treatment' Du Bois means 'treatment that discriminates, i.e. distinguishes, between guilty and innocent individuals' – the opposite of what we mean when we talk about 'discrimination' today!) As a result of this situation, whites did not care about the guilt or innocence of individual African-Americans, and the latter 'refused to believe the evidence of white witnesses or the fairness of white juries, so that the greatest deterrent to crime, the public opinion of one's own social caste, was lost'. 'Caste' means here what in contemporary language would be called 'community': according to Du Bois, neither punishment nor public morality in general but the judgements of 'one's own people', as it were, are 'the greatest deterrent to crime'. The lack of a functioning judicial system 'stir[red] up all the latent savagery of both races and [made] peaceful attention to economic development often impossible' (121).

2.5 Schooling
This leads Du Bois to the next issue on his list, education, the one of which he has most direct experience. However, he does not say much on this as it is discussed in several other chapters of the book: he merely points out that the public school system especially, but not only for blacks, is so bad that 'the nation' cannot expect anything but 'crime and listlessness' (122).

2.6 Intellectual atmosphere
Du Bois's final point is on 'the atmosphere of the land, the thought and feeling, the thousand and one little actions which go to make up … group life taken as a whole' (122) – 'the culture', that is, in the sense with which this word is used by cultural anthropology. He

describes the South as 'a land of mingled sorrow and joy, of change and excitement and unrest' (123). Nevertheless, there appears to be a 'conspiracy of silence' that hides from view the fact that there are two contrasting realms, one of mixing, one of separation. Du Bois describes this from the perspective of a casual visitor who at first does not notice the racial segregation:

> [S]ilently, resistlessly, the world about flows by him in two great streams: they ripple on in the same sunshine, they approach and mingle their waters in seeming carelessness,—then they divide and flow wide apart. It is done quietly; no mistakes are made, or if one occurs, the swift arm of the law and of public opinion swings down for a moment, as when the other day a black man and a white woman were arrested for talking together on Whitehall Street in Atlanta. (123)

The 'two great streams' mingle without touching. People mix without mixing: 'between these two worlds, despite much physical contact and daily intermingling, there is almost no community of intellectual life'. Du Bois again makes the point that until emancipation, 'all the best of the Negroes were domestic servants in the best of the white families' (124) which had led to 'bonds of intimacy, affection, and sometimes blood relationship, between the races'. After emancipation, the 'color line' has grown more forceful, not less. Although 'the increasing civilization of the Negro' has now created a class of black 'ministers, teachers, physicians, merchants, mechanics, and independent farmers, who by nature and training are the aristocracy and leaders of the blacks', they are more than ever isolated from their white equivalents. The following passage illustrates well the somewhat idealistic attitude of the then 35-year-old Du Bois:

> In a world where it means so much to take a man by the hand and sit beside him, to look frankly into his eyes and feel his heart beating with red blood; in a world where a social cigar or a cup of tea together means more than legislative halls and magazine articles and speeches,—one can imagine the consequences of the almost utter absence of such social amenities between estranged races, whose separation extends even to parks and streetcars. (125)

Du Bois expresses here the idea that there seems to be more reality and existential weight to the micro-level world of immediate

everyday social interaction – eye to eye, red blood warm and throb-
bing, hearts beating in the rhythm of life – than to the political
world of legislation and the public sphere. This is an idea quite
characteristic of American sociology at the time. At the very end of
this section, however, Du Bois gives this argument a specific class
twist:

> And here is a land where, in the higher walks of life, in all the higher
> striving for the good and noble and true, the color-line comes to sepa-
> rate natural friends and co-workers; while at the bottom of the social
> group, in the saloon, the gambling-hell, and the brothel, that same
> line wavers and disappears.

According to Du Bois's observation, race segregation is most effective, and most damaging, among the middle and upper strata, and
least effective among the poor who seem to visit the same saloons,
gambling-hells and brothels. In terms of the argument's implicit
value judgements, Du Bois does not seem to be singing the praises
of the red light district, but rather regrets that the fellowship of sin
is stronger even than race.

3 Conclusion: reciprocity of cause and effect

In his concluding section, Du Bois first of all asserts that he 'sought
to paint an average picture' of the situation, slanted neither towards
its most extreme nor its most benign aspects (125). This statement
is followed by his endorsement of the principal characteristics of
modern American civilization and the assertion of his belief that the
solution of the social problem of the South lies in both communities
accepting and realizing the precepts of that civilization:

> Deeply religious and intensely democratic as are the mass of the
> whites, they feel acutely the false position in which the Negro prob-
> lems place them. Such an essentially honest-hearted and generous
> people cannot cite the caste-levelling precepts of Christianity, or
> believe in equality of opportunity for all men, without coming to feel
> more and more with each generation that the present drawing of the
> color-line is a flat contradiction to their beliefs and professions.

This statement on 'the mass of the whites' seems a more enthusiastic endorsement of equality than is suggested by Du Bois's repeated
references to the role of 'the best' and the leaders of the two com-

munities earlier in the text. Christianity is not only shared between
the racial groups but also across classes, and Du Bois seems to see
here a root of evolving American democracy. Du Bois makes a point
of acknowledging that white racism has some justification in reality:
he writes that 'the present social condition of the Negro stands as
a menace and a portent before even the most open-minded' (126).
Du Bois paraphrases the whites' answer to this 'menace': black
'ignorance, shiftlessness, poverty, and crime' forces them to avoid
any 'fellowship with such persons' in self-defence. Du Bois writes
that their argument 'is of great strength, but it is not a whit stronger
than the argument of thinking Negroes': the latter argue that there
are historical causes for the bad condition of black folk, and that 'no
small number have, in spite of tremendous disadvantages, risen to
the level of American civilization'. Racism, though, thwarts, drawing 'lines of crime, of incompetency, of vice … tightly and uncompromisingly' (126). Du Bois concludes:

> In the face of two such arguments, the future of the South depends
> on the ability of the representatives of these opposing views to see
> and appreciate and sympathize with each other's position,—for the
> Negro to realize more deeply than he does at present the need of
> uplifting the masses of his people, for the white people to realize more
> vividly than they have yet done the deadening and disastrous effect of
> a color-prejudice that classes Phillis Wheatley and Sam Hose in the
> same despised class.

Phillis Wheatley was an eighteenth-century black poet (and a slave),
Sam Hose was a black farm labourer who was lynched with particular cruelty in 1899 after he had apparently killed his employer. Du
Bois's point here is that race prejudice fails to differentiate between
the poet and the murderer. (It seems a bit strange that Hose is here
quoted as a representative of the bad side of the black community,
in contrast to the poet Wheatley, because it is well documented that
Du Bois was deeply shocked by the lynching of Hose.)

Du Bois ends the chapter on a more theoretical note on the
reciprocity of prejudice and social condition:

> It is not enough for the Negroes to declare that color-prejudice is the
> sole cause of their social condition, nor for the white South to reply
> that their social condition is the main cause of prejudice. They both

act as reciprocal cause and effect, and a change in neither alone will bring the desired effect. Both must change, or neither can improve to any great extent. (127)

Discrimination must lead the blacks to 'retrogression', which in turn 'is ever the excuse for further discrimination'. The concept of 'reciprocity' captures well Du Bois's sustained attempt in this early, but most famous text to give a committed but well-tempered picture that goes to considerable, sometimes surprising lengths to portray the perspective of white American society along with that of African-Americans.

From good to bad capitalism and back: Max Weber

Max Weber (1864–1920), although born in the city of Erfurt in the middle of what was soon to become the German Empire, grew up in a leafy suburb of the capital Berlin in the milieu of the National Liberal Party of which his father was an important functionary. As a teenager he channelled a somewhat rebellious personality, and a dislike of schoolteachers, into intensive reading, to the effect that he already had a solid philosophical and literary education before he began studying law, history and political economy at university. Some of the themes of his later scholarship seem to reflect the contrasting influences of his parents: his mother was from a Calvinist family, a sober, passionate, pious and intelligent woman, while his cold and authoritarian father, a professional politician, enjoyed being part of the German Imperial establishment and seemed to his son intellectually rather shallow. In the heady, politicized period of the 1880s when Weber was a student (first in Heidelberg, then in Berlin) he developed a strong dislike of politicking professors who seemed to subordinate intellectual to propagandist concerns, and became a highly regarded practitioner of meticulous, heavily footnoted scholarship in legal and economic history. After receiving his PhD, still living in his father's house, he held down a lecturing job, a full-time job as a barrister and in between produced a massive empirical study of economic relations in East Prussian agriculture. The latter was an important contribution to the development of empirical social research out of 'historical economics', the empirically oriented tradition of economic science predominant in Germany at the time that was widely understood as an alternative to 'political economy'. In the German context of the time, 'political economy', of which Marx had been both a critic and a classical practitioner, was seen as an abstractly rationalist discipline, derived from the Enlightenment, against which the 'historical school' of law and economics emphasized the historical specificity and uniqueness of empirical phenomena, refusing to judge historical particulars in the light of universal reason. In reality, the difference between 'political economy' and 'historical economics' was not quite so clear-cut, and Weber developed his conception of the new science of sociology out of overcoming this (actually non-existent) dichotomy of theoretical and empirical reasoning.

Weber's highly disciplined postdoctoral work effort paid off: he gained a professorship in economics at Freiburg University in south-west Germany in 1893, and got married, too, to a woman who emerged later as a leading intellectual and sociologist. Max and Marianne Weber developed an intense companionship that seems to have been a rather different kind of marriage from what Max had experienced in his parents' house. After just three years he was appointed professor of economics in Heidelberg, the most prestigious German university at the time apart from Berlin – not bad for a 32-year-old high flyer. His rise to academic superstardom was cut short, however, by his own constitution: Weber suffered a mental breakdown in 1897, soon after the death of his father, which rendered him unable to work until 1903, when he began gradually to pick up again his previous levels of enormous productivity. For the rest of his life he remained mostly a private scholar, and died soon after the First World War at the age of only 56. Although Weber came from the bourgeois elite of German society, his life was no less troubled than, for example, Comte's.

In 1904 he was invited to give a paper at a conference in the USA, and the Webers used the opportunity to travel the country for slightly more than three months. Max Weber had done a lot of travelling in the years of his enforced down-time, but this trip seems to have energized him tremendously. He encountered many things that confirmed hunches and ideas that he had been working on already. US society was radically different from any European society, but at the same time was also quite European: the contrasting experiences could illuminate each other and throw into sharp relief the specifics of either. Extensive travelling, seeing things with eyes wide open and talking to lots of different people has repeatedly been at the centre of the renewal of social theory: the journeys of Tocqueville and Harriet Martineau to the USA, of Flora Tristan to Peru and England a bit later, of the Webers and others to the USA around 1900, and then later, of course, the enforced 'travelling' of a multitude of intellectuals fleeing European fascism.

Weber's visit to the USA confirmed the importance of a number of themes that had been on his mind: the role of religion in a modern society, the relationship of state, economy, technology, the bureau- cracy and the individual, and the different forms that power and governance take in modernity. No better place could have been found for someone thinking about the social meaning of rationaliza- tion: the USA was at the time in the midst of the Fordist revolution of industrial production – the assembly line and all that it meant for labour relations – which was also widely discussed in Europe.

Back in idyllic medieval Heidelberg, Weber produced several famous essays on methodology, *The Protestant Ethic and the Spirit of Capitalism*, studies on Russia after the 1905 revolution and on industrial relations in a modern factory, and co-founded with Simmel and Tönnies the German Sociological Association in 1909. In *The Protestant Ethic*, first published in the form of two long essays in 1904 and 1905 and then in revised form as a book in 1920, he claimed that Calvinism had helped prepare the ground for the development of modern capitalism in Europe. He followed up this claim with a series of studies of the respective ethical implications of all the world religions, trying to show why all *other* religions had helped *prevent* capitalism from emerging everywhere else. These studies do not provide a general sociology of religion in the sense that Durkheim produced, nor should they be seen as attempts to explain capitalism: Weber deliberately focused on one specific issue, the link between religion and economic ethics. It is obvious that an analysis of religious ethics *on its own* can explain neither the emer- gence nor the non-emergence of a new mode of production such as capitalism, but people's attitudes to organizing everyday life do play a part, and often are religiously determined. Weber's general outlook in this respect is well expressed in this statement (found in his late essay 'The Social Psychology of the World Religions'):

> Not ideas, but material and ideal interests, directly govern men's con-
> duct. Yet very frequently the 'world images' that have been created
> by 'ideas' have, like switchmen, determined the tracks along which
> action has been pushed by the dynamic of interest.[1]

This is central to Weber's sociology: people are 'pushed' to action
by social forces that manifest themselves in interests, but *which
action* we are pushed to is determined by how we *interpret* and *comprehend* these forces and interests, and here is where world-views,
including religious ones, come into play.

Comprehension needs concepts, and Weber is famous for having
theorized the concept of the concept. He defined sociological
concepts as 'ideal types', that is, conceptual tools created by the
researcher by selecting those aspects of the reality of a social thing
that appear particularly relevant to the researcher. Weber argued,
for example, that capitalism as an ideal type is about the accumulation of capital as an end in itself, rather than for consumption or
ostentation. This is irrespective of the fact, not denied by Weber,
that most capitalists do consume a lot, have all kinds of purposes
apart from a quasi-religious drive for accumulation, and that some
certainly like to show off their wealth. Showy capitalists are *lesser
capitalists*, though, in terms of the ideal type, and if their consumption habits get the better of their core commitment to eternally
expanding accumulation they might end up being *former capitalists*, as their forebears ended up being *former* feudal lords – 'former
people' as in the phrase coined by Maxim Gorky.

Although social action has causes, the direction of the action
is mediated by the actors' *interpretation* of these causes in their
situation. Weber distinguishes therefore different types of action
according to how the actor gives meaning to his or her actions:
action can be instrumentally rational, value-rational, traditional or
affectual. These are, again, ideal types, i.e. not likely to occur as
such in reality. One of the key issues in Weber's view of modernity
is that Western civilization since the sixteenth century has been
increasingly characterized by instrumental rationality, manifested in
social institutions such as markets, money, formal legal procedures

[1] In H. Gerth and C. Wright Mills (eds), *From Max Weber: Essays in Sociology*,
London: Routledge & Kegan Paul, 1948, p. 280

and bureaucracy. A preponderance of these can flush out value-rationality, the orientation of action towards goals and values. Social research that does not want to be just another cog in the machine must therefore be value-relevant. The question is, which values are relevant? Weber made quite clear what *his* values were – the flourishing of the German nation, for example, which he promoted often through a harsh critique of a national elite that he considered incompetent and backward, and the values of Western civilization, although they included that unstoppable trend towards rationalization through which this civilization seemed to be eating itself. He refused, however, to allow social science to assess or critique these values, or to make a scholarly claim that one set of values was superior to another. For Weber, there seems to be no rational basis on which we choose our values, which some critics held against him as a dangerous form of value-irrationalism. Through all this, Weber made a crucial contribution to translating a generally felt discontent with modern capitalist civilization into a theme for sociology.

For this chapter I have elected to look at the first half of the second chapter of the *Protestant Ethic*, 'The Spirit of Capitalism', and the second half of the last, fifth chapter, 'Asceticism and the Spirit of Capitalism'. These are the key passages in which Weber develops his understanding and critique of capitalist modernity.

Structure of the selected text

1 Individuality and uniqueness of spirits (47–48)
2 A provisional description of the capitalist spirit by Benjamin Franklin (48–52)
3 Utilitarianism versus calling in Franklin (52–54)
4 Capitalism, duty and greed (54–59)
5 Asceticism and the spirit of capitalism (175–178)
6 Two types of capitalistic attitude (178–183)

Weber, Max. 1978 [1920, 1904, 1905]. *The Protestant Ethic and the Spirit of Capitalism*. Translated by Talcott Parsons. London: Allen & Unwin.

1 Individuality and uniqueness of spirits

In the first section of the text, Weber outlines a definition of what he means by 'the spirit of capitalism'. In the German original, the word 'spirit' is put in inverted commas, to indicate that it is to be taken with a grain of salt. To our ears, the word 'spirit' sounds, of course, rather old-fashioned: today we generally use the word 'culture' to express roughly the same idea, except in some hackneyed phrases like 'the spirit of the times'. Weber starts out from defining a 'spirit' as a historical phenomenon 'significant for its unique individuality': 'a complex of elements associated in historical reality which we unite into a conceptual whole from the standpoint of their cultural significance' (47). In other words, a 'spirit' consists of several elements that form a 'complex', i.e. they occur together in reality, but are united by 'us' – presumably that means 'us historical sociologists' – into a concept. The reason that 'we' bother to do this is that these interconnected 'elements' seem to 'us' culturally significant. After this first definition of what he means by 'spirit', Weber helpfully throws in a definition of 'definition'. To underscore the importance of the individuality and uniqueness of 'spirits', he rejects what could be called the 'taxonomic' way of defining phenomena that is common, for example, in modern biology: a catalogue-style classification. He refers to this as the '*genus proximum, differentia specifica*' kind of definition, which means 'nearest fitting family & specific difference'. If a botanist defines a newly discovered plant, she will look for the best-fitting existing definition of an already known plant and then add in what respect the new plant differs from the already known ones in the same 'family' or *genus*. Weber signals here that he is not aiming to be a 'botanist' of forms of society – i.e. a positivist scientist. Such a scientist would define 'the spirit of capitalism' by first finding a definition of another 'spirit' that is quite similar – perhaps the 'spirit of feudalism' as a fellow member of the family of 'spirits of European forms of society' – and then describe how 'the spirit of capitalism' differs. Weber aims to operate the other way around: he wants to address himself right away and *exclusively* to looking at the unique *individuality* of 'the spirit of capitalism', without first looking at what it shares with other, kindred 'spirits'. A critic could object that, logically speaking, the description of the uniqueness of a historical-social phenomenon must also take account of what is *not* unique about it; Weber would probably grant that. Weber's point seems to be about where to start, and where to put the emphasis.

Weber argues that the kind of investigation that best captures the uniqueness of a phenomenon has to start with only a sketchy, provisional definition, whereas 'the final and definitive concept' can only be the *result* of the investigation: finding 'the best conceptual formulation ... from the point of view which interests us here' is the goal of his book (48). Weber adds that the point of view taken by him is not the only one possible: other perspectives would be just as valid. These opening paragraphs of the chapter give a clear indication of Weber's methodology: start from a particular point of view, i.e. take a value decision first of all on what is 'interesting', then look for a provisional definition, and then work through and elaborate on this definition to arrive at a 'definitive concept'.

2 A provisional description of the capitalist spirit by Benjamin Franklin

Following on from these methodological remarks, Weber begins the journey with a text extract that provides him with the 'provisional description' of the 'spirit of capitalism' that will in the course of the book be tested and refined. In a nutshell, Weber interprets this extract as describing capitalism as the psychologically anchored drive to increase capital as an end in itself. The extract used by Weber comes from two publications by the American writer, scientist, engineer and politician, Benjamin Franklin (1706–90), of 1736 and 1748, respectively. Two things need to be mentioned concerning this source. One is that the standard English-language edition of *The Protestant Ethic* would easily win the prize for the most embarrassing editorial blunder ever, as the translation attributes the quoted text to a 'Benjamin Ferdinand' (50) rather than Benjamin Franklin. The translator of the text was, by the way, no lesser figure than the American sociologist Talcott Parsons, who was instrumental in making the English-speaking world familiar with Max Weber. The mistake was corrected only in editions from the late 1970s onwards, almost half a century after the translation's first publication; if you use an older edition, watch out for 'Benjamin Ferdinand'! This teaches us something about how much we can trust books by even the finest academic presses.

The fictional 'Benjamin Ferdinand' was brought forth by Talcott Parsons's hard-working, sleep-deprived brain because Weber indicated in the next line that he took the quotation from a popular German novel by a now forgotten writer called Ferdinand Kürnberger. Of course Weber checked and corrected the quoted text with the help of a scholarly edition of Benjamin Franklin's writings, as you would have expected, but it seems that he first encountered it in Kürnberger's novel. This is the equivalent of your getting an idea from some YouTuber's rant and then tracing down the sources properly. It is good to know that the great Max Weber was happy to take inspiration from his favourite pulp fiction. The reference to this novel is in fact very interesting, because through it, Weber gives us a hint as to what prompted his interest in the question: the novel, published in 1855 under the telling title *The One Who Got Tired of America*, is the semi-fictional account of a journey to America by a German mid-nineteenth-century writer who tries to find out what the future of German society will be by looking at emerging modern American society. This theme is in keeping with the widely shared belief at the time that America shows Europe its own future. It has echoes from Tocqueville and indeed resonates with the fact that Weber himself visited the USA for an extended trip in 1904. The character in the novel goes to America in the hope of finding the democratic republic he might have wished Germany would become at the time, and is horrified to find what in the novel is called 'the Yankee spirit'. In the novel, the extract from Benjamin Franklin is used to illustrate this spirit and is contrasted with what the novelist thinks of as 'the German spirit', a romantic-nationalist vision of a modernity free of contradictions, conflict, ugliness and exploitation. Weber, who very much enjoyed his trip to America, now uses the same text extract for a different purpose, out of his rejection of the particular type of romantic German nationalism represented by Ferdinand Kürnberger: Weber's own nationalism was of a more hard-nosed, *realpolitik* variety, but that is a different story. The first, most obvious difference is that it is now presented as exemplary not of 'the Yankee spirit' versus 'the German spirit' as in the novel, but of 'the capitalist spirit' versus what could be called 'the traditionalist spirit'. Weber shifts emphasis from 'national spirits' to the 'spirits' of different types of society, although careful reading reveals that the re-coded 'spirit' still retains nationalist connotations.

Throughout *The Protestant Ethic* it is worth keeping in mind that a lot of interesting material is exiled into the notes, many of which were added by Weber after the original publication to reflect criticisms he had received. Many of the notes clarify points that remain less than clear in the main text – therefore it is important to pay attention to them. In a note containing details on Kürnberger's novel Weber writes that 'the German ... outlook' as expressed by Kürnberger 'has remained common to all Germans, Catholic and Protestant alike ... as against the Puritan capitalistic valuation of action' (192, n. 3). This is an important corrective to the title of the book: Weber in fact correlates the 'capitalist spirit' (what Kürnberger had called 'the Yankee spirit') to Puritanism, not to Protestantism in general: Weber knows very well that most German Protestants (who were Lutherans, not Puritans) had more in common with German Catholics than with English Protestants. In this sense the issue indeed remains one of national culture.

Now what does the extract from Franklin actually say? Its first point is that '*time* is money': taking half a day off work means throwing away half a day's earnings (48). Secondly, '*credit* is money': being able to use another person's money (by borrowing it as capital) allows one to make money, and therefore it is good to be creditworthy. This is because 'money can beget money, and its offspring can beget more, and so on' (49). The language here is quite graphic: 'He that kills a breeding sow, destroys all her offspring to the thousandth generation'. The next point is that paying back a loan on time increases one's creditworthiness, so that 'punctuality and justice', by which Franklin seems to mean the keeping of promises, are most important virtues next to 'industry and frugality'. Furthermore, when one has debts, being seen at work from early until late, rather than in the tavern, again keeps the creditors sweet: one should always be seen as careful, mindful and honest (50). Finally, Franklin recommends keeping account of even the smallest expenses, as seeing how they add up makes one save more in the future. Whatever amount of money one manages not to spend can be used in business for making a profit and will multiply accordingly. Weber sums up the 'spirit' of this at first sight rather banal list of recommendations for aspiring capitalists in these words:

> The peculiarity of this philosophy of avarice appears to be the ideal of the honest man of recognized credit, and above all the idea of a duty of the individual toward the increase of his capital, which is assumed as an end in itself. Truly what is here preached is not simply a means of making one's way in the world, but a peculiar ethic. The infraction of its rules is treated not as foolishness but as forgetfulness of duty. That is the essence of the matter. It is not mere business astuteness … it is an ethos. This is the quality which interests us. (51)

The last sentence of this passage points back to Weber's methodological emphasis on wanting to focus entirely on what is 'unique' about the chosen object of study, and the fact that he cannot but start from having a pretty developed, albeit provisional, idea of what it is that 'interests us'. In a sense, Weber uses the text only as an illustration for a point he wants to make: this is the point that 'interests us'.

I need to add here that there is a huge critical literature that discusses how well Weber understood any of the numerous sources that he used in *The Protestant Ethic*. If this is something that interests you, you will need to read his whole book, obviously, as well as the sources he used. For the limited present purpose of introducing Weber's sociology I have to refrain from discussing whether Weber's claims and interpretations are historically tenable or not – I am here only trying to establish what Weber's argument is, and how he approaches it. I will keep schtum on whether Benjamin Franklin actually meant what Weber thought he meant, as this is not relevant here.

Weber writes that Franklin's text formulates 'an ethically coloured maxim for the conduct of life' (51–52), and that this is 'the spirit of modern capitalism' (52). Weber writes that only modern, namely 'Western European and American' capitalism is characterized by 'this particular ethos'. In Weber's view, in the past there has been capitalism 'in China, India, Babylon, in the classic world, and in the Middle Ages' but without 'the capitalist spirit'. Weber is concerned with distinguishing different types of 'capitalism', opposing a modern to a traditional type. He is interested in the question of 'ethics' because he starts from his observation that *modern* capitalism is historically unique in being driven by a particular ethic: *other* capitalisms are just about making money.

3 Utilitarianism versus calling in Franklin

In the next paragraph, Weber points out that the quoted extract from Franklin sounds rather utilitarian, by which he means that certain virtues are extolled because they are useful: 'Honesty is useful, because it assures credit; so are punctuality, industry, frugality, and that is the reason they are virtues' (52). Weber admits that Franklin's recommendations may seem, at face value, hypocritical rather than particularly spiritual. However, 'the matter is not by any means so simple': Weber interprets the text against the grain, as it were, and looks for an explanation for the moral tone that seems to contradict the seemingly utilitarian *content* of the text. He finds the explanation in Franklin's autobiography: 'The circumstance that he ascribes his recognition of the utility of virtue to a divine revelation which was intended to lead him in the path of righteousness, shows that something more than mere garnishing for purely egocentric motives is involved' (53). Weber observes that in Franklin's ethic, 'the earning of more and more money' is 'combined with the strict avoidance of all spontaneous enjoyment of life' and 'completely devoid of any eudaemonistic, not to say hedonistic, admixture'. ('Eudaemonism' is a moral philosophy that posits happiness to be the highest goal of life, and virtue therefore to be in the service of happiness. 'Hedonism' posits enjoyment as the highest good.) Franklin's 'Puritan ethic' is entirely conceived of as 'an end in itself', and in this sense is the opposite of a utilitarian ethic: there is no utility in it, it does not serve the individual's benefit in any way. (Utilitarianism is a form of eudaemonistic ethics.) This 'Puritan-ethic-driven' capitalism is about duty, not about having a good time:

> Man is dominated by the making of money, by acquisition as the ultimate purpose of his life. Economic acquisition is no longer subordinated to man as the means for the satisfaction of his material needs. This reversal of what we should call the natural relationship, so irrational from a naïve point of view, is evidently as definitely a

leading principle of capitalism as it is foreign to all peoples not under
capitalistic influence. (53)

Weber added here a note relating to his use of the word 'irrational'.
He writes that 'a thing is never irrational in itself, but only from
a particular rational point of view', and that likewise there can be
'rationalization towards an irrational mode of life'. He writes that
he hopes that in this essay he will manage to 'bring out the complexity' of the 'concept of the rational' (194, n. 9). Weber indicates
here that there does not exist, in his view, one rationality surrounded by many forms of irrationality (the perspective of classical
Enlightenment rationalism), but he seems to think that there are
many forms of rationality, each of which considers all others as irrational: 'for a hedonist' (a person who believes that the meaning of
life is to enjoy life's pleasures), asceticism – the avoidance of joy, fun
and luxury – is irrational, whereas a Puritan embraces asceticism
because it is a form of rationalization 'with respect to its particular
basic values', namely the values of Puritan religiosity. This comment reflects well one of Weber's fundamental propositions: people
somehow, at some point, choose some basic values, or, more likely,
choose to accept those they grew up with, and from these basic
value decisions follows what *for them* counts as rational, and what
does not. *Which* values one chooses is, for Weber, not a matter for
academic exploration; instead, our discussions in the social, political
and cultural sciences are essentially about the relationship between
one's values and one's rationality.

Weber writes that the apparently irrational principle of modern
capitalism at the same time 'expresses a type of feeling which is
closely connected with certain religious ideas' and values, *in relation
to which* the 'irrationality' of the capitalist spirit might actually be
rather rational. Weber writes that Franklin was 'a colorless deist'
– meaning a man of the Enlightenment who liked his religion cool
and sober – but he related in his autobiography a quotation from the
Bible 'drummed into him' by 'his strict Calvinistic father':

> 'Seest thou a man diligent in his business? He shall stand before kings'
> (Prov. xxii. 29). The earning of money within the modern economic
> order is, so long as it is done legally, the result and the expression of
> virtue and proficiency in a calling; and this virtue and proficiency are,

as it is now not difficult to see, the real Alpha and Omega of Franklin's ethic. (53–54)

Weber claims that this 'peculiar idea ... of one's duty in a calling, is what is most characteristic of the social ethic of capitalistic culture, and is in a sense the fundamental basis of it' (54). It is important to note what Weber means by 'most characteristic': he does not mean *empirically* most characteristic, but *ideal-typically* most characteristic. A non-utilitarian sense of the 'duty' to make money as an end in itself is not necessarily the most obvious aspect *to be observed* when one goes around and looks at capitalism as it presents itself empirically, but it is *the unique aspect* of it, i.e. the one thing that distinguishes the 'capitalist spirit' most definitely from the spirit of any other form of society. This is the claim Weber makes.

4 Capitalism, duty and greed

In the next step of the argument, Weber grants two likely objections to his thesis: one, that the feeling of 'duty in a calling' can be traced back to the period before the advent of capitalism, and two, that present-day, fully established capitalism does not in fact rely on such a sense of duty:

> The capitalistic economy of the present day is an immense cosmos into which the individual is born, and which presents itself to him, at least as an individual, as an unalterable order of things in which he must live. It forces the individual, in so far as he is involved in the system of market relationships, to conform to capitalistic rules of action. The manufacturer who in the long run acts counter to these norms, will just as inevitably be eliminated from the economic scene as the worker who cannot or will not adapt himself to them will be thrown into the streets without a job. (54–55)

This is an example of how Weber describes the *empirical reality* of the capitalism he experienced, which is quite recognizable even to us more than a century later. There will be further examples later in the text, and they are similarly unflattering: Weber is not an enthusiastic defender of *present-day* capitalism, a monstrous system that denies individuals their sense of freedom. His argument in *The Protestant Ethic and the Spirit of Capitalism* is, however, principally

about the historical emergence of one particular aspect of capitalism *in its early days*. It will become clear later on that his intention
is to contrast the spiritually driven golden days of Puritan, ideal-
type capitalism to its present-day version and to suggest that his
contemporaries should try to reform capitalism by reconnecting to
(what he claims are) capitalism's spiritual roots. Weber proposes
this programme of ethical rejuvenation of capitalism as an alternative to trying to abolish it, as Marxist social democracy at the time
was still committed to doing.

Weber argues that describing the structural-functional workings
of a phenomenon in the present is different from describing its origins, an argument that closely resembles one of Durkheim's main
points in *The Rules of Sociological Method*. In order that 'a manner
of life so well adapted to the peculiarities of capitalism' can become
the dominant manner of life, it first 'had to originate somewhere,
and not in isolated individuals alone, but as a way of life common to
whole groups of men' (55). This origin of the 'capitalist spirit' that
must predate actual capitalism is what Weber aims to explain. He
does not claim, however, to be able to *explain capitalism* as such: he
is only exploring one of the factors that contributed to the emergence of capitalism – the one factor that is to Weber the most interesting and that is therefore central to the 'ideal type' of capitalism.
Although Weber does not say so explicitly, it seems that he finds the
spiritual aspect 'most interesting' because he hopes it can play a role
in the regeneration of the decadent capitalism of the present.

Weber points to New England, where Franklin was born, as a
context where the 'spirit of capitalism' as he understands it was in
evidence as early as the first third of the seventeenth century in a
society dominated by craftsmen, yeomen and preachers (55–56).
By contrast, some of the neighbouring colonies, the future southern
states of the USA, were less capitalist in spite of the fact that they
'were founded by large capitalists for business motives' (55). In
other words, what the 'large capitalists' in the southern colonies did
was less capitalistic, from the perspective of Weber's interest in the
'spirit of capitalism', than the small-scale, petit-bourgeois economy
that characterised the New England colonies. Clearly Weber constructs here two types of capitalism, even within the realm of the
(emergent) USA, only one of which deserves to be called capi-

talism proper. Weber emphasizes that the 'spirit of capitalism' as expressed in the text extract from Franklin 'had to fight its way to supremacy against a whole world of hostile forces' (56): it 'would both in ancient times and in the Middle Ages have been proscribed as the lowest sort of avarice', and even today, many social groups 'least involved in or adapted to modern capitalistic conditions' continue to see it that way. Against 'the illusions of modern romanticists', though, Weber argues that 'the instinct for acquisition' and the 'greed for gold' were, or are, not at all unknown outside the context of capitalism – quite to the contrary. Weber gives us a substantial list of eastern and southern figures famous for greed, both ancient and modern, including Chinese Mandarins, Roman aristocrats, modern peasants, Neapolitan cab-drivers or boatmen, their 'Asiatic' colleagues and 'the craftsmen of southern European or Asiatic countries' in general. Weber writes that their greed is 'very much more intense, and especially more unscrupulous than that of, say, an Englishman in similar circumstances' (56–57). Although these stereotypes would surely qualify as racist by contemporary standards, Weber's point is that all these people's greed is traditional as opposed to capitalist, and the worse for it:

> The universal reign of absolute unscrupulousness in the pursuit of selfish interests by the making of money has been a specific characteristic of precisely those countries whose bourgeois-capitalistic development, measured according to Occidental standards, has remained backward. As every employer knows, the lack of *coscienziosità* [Italian for conscientiousness or diligence] of the labourers of such countries, for instance Italy as compared with Germany, has been, and to a certain extent still is, one of the principal obstacles to their capitalistic development. Capitalism cannot make use of the labor of those who practice the doctrine of undisciplined *liberum arbitrium* [Latin for 'free will'], any more than it can make use of the businessman who seems absolutely unscrupulous in his dealings with others, as we can learn from Franklin. Hence the difference does not lie in the degree of development of any impulse to make money. The *auri sacra fames* [Latin for 'holy, or cursed, hunger for gold'] is as old as the history of man. But we shall see that those who submitted to it without reserve as an uncontrolled impulse … were by no means the representatives of that attitude of mind from which the specifically modern capitalistic spirit as a mass phenomenon is derived, and that is what matters. (57)

This passage adds a lot to the conception of what Weber now more specifically refers to as the 'bourgeois-capitalist' spirit: conscientiousness, moral standards or scruples, the ability to control the 'impulse to make money' but also to discipline the '*liberum arbitrium*'. The latter, which in Christian theology as well as in classical philosophy means 'free will' in the sense of the ability to make decisions as the arbiter of one's own affairs, is of course, from an employer's perspective, a rather inconvenient aspect of the human condition.

Weber notes that not only have all periods of history seen 'ruthless acquisition, bound to no ethical norms whatsoever' (57), but '[a]bsolute and conscious ruthlessness in acquisition has often stood in the closest connection with the strictest conformity to tradition' (58). 'Moreover, with the breakdown of tradition', ruthlessly unethical acquisitiveness was tolerated as either ethically indifferent or unavoidable, but it still 'has not generally been ethically justified and encouraged'. This only changed with the emergence of 'the conditions of an ordered bourgeois-capitalistic economy' characterized by 'the rational utilization of capital in a permanent enterprise and the rational capitalistic organization of labor'. The 'spirit of capitalism' was radically new insofar as it meant claiming 'ethical sanction' for a disciplining of the greed for wealth (58).

Just to be on the safe side, Weber added here a long note explaining what 'the point of the whole essay' was, written in response to critics who seemingly failed to get the point (197, n. 12). Weber goes back to his observation concerning the ethical tone of Benjamin Franklin's text: 'A lack of care in the handling of money means to him [Franklin] that one so to speak murders capital embryos, and hence it is an ethical defect' (196). He then acknowledges the point made by a critic that modern economic *theory* derives from rationalist and Enlightenment sources and has nothing to do with 'the Protestant ethic'. Fair enough, Weber writes, but his point was not to describe the emergence of the *theory* of capitalism but that of its everyday *practice*, and here he makes a very interesting point that clarifies his overall interest: a theory, he writes, cannot 'develop into a revolutionary force', but a 'religiously oriented rationalization of conduct' that provides 'psychological sanctions' *can*. The history of the emergence of capitalism did, of course, also involve the schemes of modernizing statesmen and princes who were influenced by rationalism and Enlightenment thought, but the transformation of the mentality and daily conduct of entire *populations* – as opposed to elites only – can best be explained by the ethos-driven, irrationally motivated, middle-class 'capitalist spirit' that Weber is interested in exploring. Rationalization needed to take irrational motivations into its service, as it were, as rationality on its own would not have been powerful enough to break down the muck of ages that safeguarded 'traditionalism'.

This is the argument of roughly the first half of chapter 2 of *The Protestant Ethic and the Spirit of Capitalism*. The remainder of the chapter elaborates on the points made so far, but you get the gist of it if you read up to this point. I will now turn to the concluding section of the book's fifth and final chapter, entitled 'Asceticism and the Spirit of Capitalism', which contains the book's most powerful and best-known passages.

5 Asceticism and the spirit of capitalism

Weber discusses a number of ways in which he believes Protestant asceticism anticipated, or first formulated, aspects of what he calls the 'spirit of capitalism'. Then he moves towards drawing the conclusions from the overall argument beginning on page 176, after a long quote from John Wesley (1703–91), one of the founders of Methodism.

Wesley argues in the quoted passage in a strikingly pessimistic tone that 'any revival of true religion' (175), by which he in fact means Methodism, cannot last long, as true religion 'must necessarily produce both industry and frugality' (whereby 'industry' means industriousness or diligence), and therefore wealth. With wealth come 'pride, anger and love of the world in all its branches' which in turn cannot but destroy 'true religion'. Wesley's own solution lies in the advice that those who become rich through their ascetic, hard-working lifestyle should donate their wealth in order to avoid the decline of their religiosity. Apparently not convinced that this could solve the problem, Weber ignores the bit about donating one's wealth and picks up only Wesley's description of the self-defeating tendency of Puritan religiosity. He concludes:

the full economic effect of those great religious movements, whose significance for economic development lay above all in their ascetic educative influence, generally came only after the peak of the purely religious enthusiasm was past. Then the intensity of the search for the Kingdom of God commenced gradually to pass over into sober economic virtue; the religious roots died out slowly, giving way to utilitarian worldliness. (176)

In the process, not much more remained of the 'Puritan ethic' than the comfort of having 'a good conscience', in fact 'an amazingly good, we may even say a pharisaically good, conscience in the acquisition of money, so long as it took place legally'. The reality of capitalist practice, though, had become utilitarian, i.e. driven by considerations of utility rather than spirituality. Weber adds that 'every trace of the "Deo placere vix potest" has disappeared', a formula that expresses the traditional Catholic opposition to making money from trade. Literally the Latin formula means 'he [referring to a trader or businessman] can hardly please God'. (Careful reading is here again rewarded with the sublime joy of discovering another hilarious typo that survived many decades of lazy proofreading, as Parsons's translation gives us 'deplacere' instead of 'Deo placere'. There is no such word as 'deplacere', but you will find that many fine scholars have faithfully quoted the completely meaningless phrase 'deplacere vix potest' in their treatises and textbooks.)

Even though now underpinned *in fact* by utilitarian capitalist practice, Weber concludes that '[a] specifically bourgeois economic ethic had grown up' (176) that was not simply a reflection of that practice. As economic success counted as visible evidence of God's grace and blessing, 'the bourgeois business man', as long as he followed established morality, could think of money-making as a religious duty. In addition, Weber mentions – with a hint of sarcasm – that the 'power of religious asceticism provided him ... with sober, conscientious, and unusually industrious workmen, who clung to their work as to a life purpose willed by God' (177). He continues, now with manifest sarcasm, that 'it gave him the comforting assurance that the unequal distribution of the goods of this world was a special dispensation of Divine Providence, which in these differences, as in particular grace, pursued secret ends unknown to men'. Weber supports this observation with a quote from Calvin stating that 'only when the people, i.e. the mass of labourers and craftsmen, were poor did they remain obedient to God'. He suggests that the idea of the 'productivity of low wages' – popular in capitalist economics – that 'the mass of men only labour when necessity forces them to do so', is in fact a 'secularized' version of the Calvinist idea just quoted: this is, to Weber, another case of a utilitarian *reinterpretation* of an originally religious idea following 'the dying out of the religious root'.

6 Two types of capitalistic attitude

Weber now recapitulates his argument on the specificity of *Protestant* ascetic religiosity in distinction from the ascetic traditions that exist within other religions: after all, one of the guiding interests of his research is why capitalist modernity emerged in 'the West' rather than anywhere else. He writes that the mere idea that 'faithful labour, even at low wages, on the part of those whom life offers no other opportunities, is highly pleasing to God' (178) is common to all ascetic traditions. *Protestant* asceticism added two things: first, it psychologically sanctioned this 'through the conception of this labour as a calling', i.e. a 'means of attaining certainty of grace'; secondly, 'it also interpreted the employer's business activity as a calling' and thereby legalized the exploitation of the workers' specific willingness to work: labour was treated as a calling, but so was the businessman's 'attitude toward acquisition' (179).

In the next passage, Weber undertakes a very interesting shift in his argument: from a discussion of 'the spirit of capitalism', he moves to an argument on 'two types of capitalistic attitude' (180). He contrasts the bourgeois capitalist attitude connected to the 'Protestant ethic' with a form of capitalism based on political privilege that he clearly finds objectionable:

> Calvinism opposed the 'organic' social organization in the fiscal-monopolistic form which it assumed in Anglicanism under the Stuarts … this alliance of Church and State with the monopolists on the basis of a Christian, social-ethical foundation. [Calvinism's] leaders were universally among the most passionate opponents of this type of politically privileged commercial, putting-out, and colonial capitalism. Over against it they placed the individualistic motives of

rational legal acquisition by virtue of one's own ability and initiative. And, while the politically privileged monopoly industries in England all disappeared in short order, this attitude played a large and decisive part in the development of the industries which grew up in spite of and against the authority of the State. (179)

Weber constructs here two types of capitalism: the one is individualistic, rational, legal, based on personal ability and initiative, and anti-state. The other is 'organic' (in the original German text, this word is put in inverted commas, indicating Weber's reservations about the concept), namely based on the 'alliance' of Church, state and big business, the latter of which enjoys monopolies granted by the state. This 'organic' capitalism is also based on (more traditional) Christian social ethics which are paternalistic, that is, obliging state, Church and other elites to look after the welfare of the poor (in exchange for their obedience). 'Organic' capitalism is also characterized by Weber as being about trade, distribution and colonialism, i.e. not primarily concerned with production. Puritan capitalism, by contrast, was productive without being protected by privileges and monopolies: the Puritan capitalists 'repudiated all connection with the large-scale capitalistic courtiers and projectors as an ethically suspicious class'. Weber claims that '[t]he difference of the two types of capitalistic attitude went to a very large extent hand in hand with religious differences': the nonconformists were 'again and again ridiculed' for 'personifying the spirit of shopkeepers, and for having ruined the ideals of old England' (180), namely the 'organic', traditionalist constitution of society. It is impossible not to be reminded here that the terms in which Weber constructs his two types of capitalism strongly resonate with political debates in Weber's own time: the alliance of Church and state, complete with Christian social ethics, colonialist adventures and state-directed development initiatives, were very much on the agenda in the German Empire at the time, and the 'spirit of shopkeepers' was certainly ridiculed both by those politically to the right of Weber, and to the left. Weber is clearly on a mission here to defend the proverbial shopkeepers and their spirit.

Weber now inches towards the grand finale of his book, taking up once more what he now calls the spirit of *modern* capitalism, namely the middle-class, Protestant-inspired variety, as opposed to the traditionalist capitalism 'from above' as one might call it:

> One of the fundamental elements of the spirit of modern capitalism, and not only of that but of all modern culture: rational conduct on the basis of the idea of the calling, was born – that is what this discussion has sought to demonstrate – from the spirit of Christian asceticism. (180)

He refers again to the extract from Franklin discussed earlier, describing it now as representing 'the content of the Puritan worldly asceticism, only without the religious basis, which by Franklin's time had died away'. Again this comment makes clear that Weber does not think that *actual* capitalists are typically religiously driven Puritans: only *one aspect* of the 'spirit of capitalism' – the defining, most interesting aspect – originated from the Puritan ethic, namely the *psychological* condition of obsessively having to make money and then more money and even more money *as if* it were a moral duty. We can assume that Weber was not so naïve as to believe that many capitalists *actually* think it is a duty. To understand this, it is important to keep in mind that Weber more often than not discusses 'ideal types', not empirical realities. Remember: the construction of an 'ideal type' rests on the theorist's prior decision about what is 'value-relevant'. In the concluding section of *The Protestant Ethic* Weber comes clean about what it is that makes him tick.

When some years back, at my secondary school, students were asked to choose and learn a monologue from Johann Wolfgang Goethe's great work *Faust* (written in 1806), by far the most popular was Faust's brilliantly depressed rant about not being able to have it all (*Faust*, Part 1, scene IV, 1548–1551):

> What from the world have I to gain?
> Thou shalt abstain – renounce – refrain!
> Such is the everlasting song
> That in the ears of all men rings.

Chances are that this might also have been one of Weber's favourites. Weber makes two references to Goethe's *Faust* in the following passage in which he claims that 'renunciation', which he sees as a secularized form of asceticism, is the spirit of our time: 'Limitation to specialized work, with a renunciation of the Faustian universality of man which it involves, is a condition of any valuable work in the modern world' (180). There is no valuable work without specialization and renunciation: the 'fundamentally ascetic trait of middle-class life' means 'a renunciation, a departure from an age of full and beautiful humanity, which can no more be repeated in the course of our cultural development than can the flower of the Athenian culture of antiquity' (181). Weber suggests that even Goethe himself, often seen as the last of the Renaissance men, resigned himself to accepting the unheroic and not so magnificent quality of modern life in capitalist society. Weber emphasizes the systemic, compulsory character of this situation:

> The Puritan wanted to work in a calling; we are forced to do so. For when asceticism was carried out of monastic cells into everyday life, and began to dominate worldly morality, it did its part in building the tremendous cosmos of the modern economic order. This order is now bound to the technical and economic conditions of machine production which today determine the lives of all the individuals who are born into this mechanism, not only those directly concerned with economic acquisition, with irresistible force. Perhaps it will so determine them until the last ton of fossilized coal is burnt.

Although the 'Protestant ethic' made a contribution to the emergence of modern capitalist industrial society, the latter has entirely transformed the former. Irrespective of what exactly are the various factors that brought it about, 'machine production' has become a totalizing force that subdues all members of society, not only those who build and operate the machines themselves. Weber's is a resigned, unhappy affirmation of this societal condition that is suffused with a suppressed nostalgia for both the blooming, broad-minded humanity of Renaissance men and the deliberate asceticism of the Puritans that opposed it.

Weber follows this up with a quote from one of the seventeenth-century Puritan theologians he discussed in detail in the first half of the fifth chapter, Richard Baxter (1615–91). He points out again the difference between the Puritan lifestyle and that of actual modern capitalism: 'In Baxter's view the care for external goods should only lie on the shoulders of the saint "like a light cloak, which can be thrown aside at any moment." But fate decreed that the cloak should become an iron casing' (181). (I have here substituted the word 'casing' for 'cage', as the latter is a mistranslation of the German word that Weber uses, *Gehäuse*, which evokes the image of the house of a snail, for example, not a cage. Parsons's famous formulation 'iron cage' is, of course, in itself a very powerful and inspired choice, but it is not what Weber wrote.) Weber goes on to describe in more detail what 'fate' did to us humans:

> [M]aterial goods have gained an increasing and finally an inexora-
> ble power over the lives of men as at no previous period in his-
> tory. To-day the spirit of religious asceticism – whether finally, who
> knows? – has escaped from the iron casing. But victorious capitalism,
> since it rests on mechanical foundations, needs its support no longer.
> The rosy blush of its laughing heir, the Enlightenment, seems also to
> be irretrievably fading, and the idea of duty in one's calling prowls
> about in our lives like the ghost of dead religious beliefs. (181–82)

This is Weber at his most delightfully dystopian: for a while, at least, there was some spirituality inside the 'iron casing', but that is long gone. Puritanism was then temporarily replaced by the Enlightenment, but that is over, too: modern capitalism is a fully mechanized machine and no longer needs any spiritual or philo-sophical props at all. There is only one survivor that gets people out of bed in the mornings: duty, the grey ghost of a dead religion. The only glimmer of hope seems to rest in Weber's telling interjec-tion 'whether finally, who knows?', which leaves the door open to the possibility that the Puritans' spirit might return to the scene of the crime. Weber's entire project of celebrating the Puritan ethic is ultimately motivated by what he thinks is the last hope for a dismal modernity: the return of a not-so-mechanical form of capitalism.

Weber adds that whenever 'the fulfilment of the calling cannot directly be related to the highest spiritual and cultural values', as in the Puritan ethic, it can only either be experienced 'simply as eco-nomic compulsion' or else 'the individual generally abandons the attempt to justify it at all'. In the latter case, the pursuit of wealth simply takes on 'the character of sport' (182). The current develop-ment may result in the rise of 'entirely new prophets', or 'a great rebirth of old ideas and ideals', or else 'mechanized petrification, embellished with … convulsive self-importance'. The inhabitants of this last, dystopian world could be described, Weber writes, as 'specialists without spirit, sensualists without heart', forming a 'nullity' that 'imagines that it has attained a level of civilization never before achieved'.[1] These formulations suggest that Weber did not have too high an opinion of most of his contemporaries, but he quickly adds: 'But this brings us to the world of judgments of value and of faith, with which this purely historical discussion need not be burdened.' Value judgements? *Surely not!* Weber quickly, as if slapping his own wrist, closes this little window on how he *really* felt about the modern world and outlined for himself – in truly ascetic manner – a gigantic future research programme: it would begin with the relevance of 'ascetic rationalism' for 'practical social ethics', then trace the evolution of rationalism from 'ascetic rationalism' through 'humanistic rationalism' and empiricism to utilitarianism, and how all of these were in turn influenced 'by the totality of social conditions, especially economic' (183). This is important to note, as Weber explicitly states: 'it is, of course, not my aim to substitute for a one-sided materialistic an equally one-sided spiritualistic causal interpretation of culture and of history'.

---

[1] The historian Hans-Christof Kraus discovered only recently that Weber adapted this famous formulation from a book by his teacher Gustav Schmoller (see *Frankfurter Allgemeine Zeitung*, 30 March 2016; thanks to Stefan Machura for this information).

10

Strangers who are from here: Georg Simmel

Georg Simmel (1858–1918) was born in, and remained for almost his entire life a dedicated resident of, Berlin, one of the fastest-growing and most rapidly changing cities in Europe at the time. His father, who owned a chocolate factory, was a Jewish convert to Catholicism, while his mother, likewise of Jewish background, was a Protestant, as was Georg Simmel himself. His father died when Simmel was still a child. He grew up solidly middle class, but not particularly wealthy. Simmel studied history and philosophy at Berlin University, where he began to be interested in epistemological questions of historiography: *how can we know and write about history?* Philosophically he was fundamentally a Kantian, but the decisive influence for his work was Moritz Lazarus (1824–1903), the pioneer of cultural anthropology. Simmel adopted from Lazarus the idea that individuality develops in 'interaction' (sometimes translated as 'reciprocal action') with the 'totality' of society and its 'spirit'. What nineteenth-century writers called 'spirit' – still reflected in Max Weber's concept of the 'Protestant spirit' – corresponds to what modern anthropology calls 'culture'. Simmel also picked up from Lazarus his central idea that individuals stand in the 'intersections of social circles', partaking in more than one social circle (or group, or societal category), and that in modernity the number of intersecting circles increases, resulting in more space for individuality in society. For Lazarus, a member of a generation of Jews who still had to fight for legal emancipation, this was an entirely positive development. Simmel in principle agreed but added an element of critique of modern civilization and the degree of alienation and oppression that it brings. Lazarus had been a key figure in Berlin's Jewish community and the fight against the emerging movement of political antisemitism in the 1880s. Simmel never entered the fray in the way Lazarus did, or indeed Durkheim during the Dreyfus affair, but his continuous engagement with the question of individuality in modern society must also be seen in the context of the contemporary antisemitic attack on liberal modernity.

Simmel received his PhD in 1881 for a thesis on Kant, and published in 1890 his first contribution to sociological theory, *On Social Differentiation*. In this book he developed an aspect of Herbert Spencer's sociology, namely the notion of the centrality of social differentiation as a means by which modern society warrants integration. It was followed in 1892 by *The Problems of the Philosophy of History* which contained a critique of aspects of Spencerian positivism that he disagreed with, such as the idea that there is an intrinsic tendency towards progress in history. In 1892–93 he published *Introduction to the Science of Ethics*, a sociological critique of Kantian ethics. Simmel emphasized the role of society in the constitution of ethics, anticipating some of Durkheim's arguments on the same matter.

After setting out the basic starting points of his sociology in these early works, Simmel began to produce a continuous stream of lectures and essays on a hugely diverse range of topics, many of which no philosopher or social scientist of the time would have touched: sex, money, dinner parties, feminism, fashion, conflict, 'the metropolis and mental life', borders and boundaries, 'the stranger', honour, the differences in how power plays out in a relationship between two as opposed to between three individuals, to name just a few. He also published a number of more conventional monographs on themes in philosophy and cultural history, including on Kant, Goethe, Rembrandt, Schopenhauer, Nietzsche, and religion, but most of his sociological writings are on much more narrowly demarcated subjects. Simmel always developed general, abstract concepts out of close analysis of specific, particular objects, a distinctively modern method of writing that confounded many of his more conventional colleagues, who regularly failed to see the wood for the trees in Simmel's work.

Many of his articles were immediately translated and published

abroad, most prominently in the USA, where Simmel was a decisive influence on the 'Chicago school'. In Germany, as internationally, he quickly achieved fame, not least because he was a skilled
lecturer who was able to hold the attention of large audiences. None
of this impressed the institutional gatekeepers of German imperial
academia, and in spite of the support of key figures like Max Weber,
who was a close friend, Simmel failed to secure regularly paid university employment until 1914, at Strasbourg, painfully far from
his Berlin home turf, shortly before the outbreak of the First World
War (when teaching ceased) and a few years before his death.

One of the reasons for Simmel's persistent outsider status seems
to have been that his contemporaries considered him to be Jewish.
Besides that, Simmel broke academic etiquette by publishing widely
and successfully in general interest journals and magazines, being
something of a man about town, hanging out in Berlin's bohemian
and artistic circles, and every now and again commenting on the
women's and workers' movements. He was also married to an independent-minded, highly regarded writer and philosopher, Gertrud
Simmel: more than enough to send shivers down the spines of many
German professors. Politically he was a reform-minded, somewhat
left-of-centre liberal, save that he published some wildly patriotic
articles at the beginning of the First World War – but then so did
Weber and Durkheim, for example. Many if not most progressive
intellectuals of the time failed to oppose the war when it mattered,
and the same is true of the labour movement. A lot of ink was spent
afterwards rowing back from the notion that rationality, culture and
civilization needed to be defended from their enemies by industri-
alized mass slaughter: people discovered the dialectic of modern
rationality the hard way.

Simmel's two main sociological works are *The Philosophy of Money*
(1900) and *Sociology: Investigations on the Forms of Sociation* (1908).
Simmel's core concept of 'sociation' refers to any kind of coming
together of people in social interaction. Sociation has content –
interests, wishes, feelings – and a form. The relationship of form
and content of sociation is the principal matter of sociological analysis: society consists of relations, intersections and interactions. The
point here is that the same form can have different contents, and the
same content can take different forms. A formal dinner is a social

form that either satisfies hunger or the need for sociability (or both at the same time). These are contents. The religious impulse (a social content) can be realized in the form of religion or find expression in some other social form. Simmel echoed the way Kant put human agency at the centre of perception, making the perception of things an activity: according to Kant, our mind, with the help of in-built concepts and categories, 'creates' (what we think of as) reality. Likewise, Simmel argues that we create society: Simmel describes society as a product of human mentalities, dispositions, sociation skills and interaction. They 'make society possible'.

One of Simmel's key themes is the dialectic of objective and subjective culture in modern society. One of the key instances of 'objective culture' is money, which Simmel discusses in a way that resonates with Marx's concept of the 'fetishism of the commodity'. For Simmel, modern individuals are, on the one hand, emancipated but, on the other hand, bound by an impersonal order, the 'laws of things'. The 'money economy' has created a distance between person and possession: a person living in Berlin can own something or a share of something, such as a factory or a gold mine, on a different continent without ever actually having been there. At the same time, the neutral character of money also makes possible cooperatives and associations, for example workers' syndicates, between people who don't (want to) share anything beyond an economic interest: a very private, unsociable or shy individual who would be unlikely ever to become an active member of a political group can still 'do something' by being a member of a trade union, for example, simply paying the monthly fee.

The division of labour creates a situation in which we do not know those on whom we depend. They are anonymous, not particular persons. Individuality is likewise separated from objective economic activity: my profession is certainly part of what I am as an individual, but most people no longer define themselves in terms of their profession. I can therefore begin to think of myself as different from my economic function, which is liberating at the same time as it creates indifference and alienation.

The pessimistic side of Simmel's account of modernity is best captured in his concept of the 'colonization of ends by means': all ends in modern society require complicated constructions of means and apparatuses, whose construction occupies us so much that we can easily forget what their purpose was. The best example is again money, the most universal means in modern society: in the process of raking it in, we may forget what it was meant for (although some of us unfortunately do not have *that* problem...). According to Simmel, the chasing after means produces a tense feeling of permanent expectation: we achieve something but we know, somehow, that it is a mere means to some end that is still unachieved.

The text examined in the following is a chapter from Simmel's 1908 *Sociology*, entitled 'The Stranger'.

Structure of the chosen text

1 The concept of the stranger (402–403)
2 The stranger as trader (403–404)
3 The objectivity of the stranger (404–405)
4 The abstractness of the relationship to the stranger (405–407)
5 Strangeness based on the denial of individuality (407–408)
6 The stranger as an organic member of the group (408)

Simmel, Georg. 1950. 'The Stranger'. In *The Sociology of Georg Simmel*. Translated, edited and with an introduction by Kurt H. Wolff. Glencoe, IL: The Free Press, 402–408.

---

1 The concept of the stranger

Simmel's short but hugely influential essay begins with the statement that the 'sociological form' of 'the stranger' unites two concepts: 'wandering', which means detachment or 'liberation from every given point in space', and its opposite, namely 'fixation at such a point' (402). 'The stranger' as a 'sociological form' is construed by Simmel as the unity of two opposite concepts, 'detachment' and 'fixation'.

The term 'sociological form' needs some explanation, as it is specific to Simmel. 'Form' implies that a social fact also has a content that is not necessarily sociological: 'the stranger' is for Simmel an object of sociology only regarding its form, while otherwise 'the stranger' is also a biological, psychological, physical fact. Durkheim surely would have agreed with this distinction. The concept of 'social form' shares with Weber's concept of the 'ideal type' that it does not exist *as such* but only in its actual forms of appearance: a form needs a content to become actual.

Unlike the way in which the word 'stranger' may be used elsewhere, as a person 'who comes today and goes tomorrow', Simmel defines the stranger as 'the wanderer who comes today and *stays* tomorrow' (italics added), 'the potential wanderer' who *might perhaps* leave tomorrow: on the one hand, he or she is 'fixed within a particular spatial group'; on the other hand, he or she 'has not quite overcome the freedom of coming and going'. The stranger's 'position in this group is determined, essentially, by the fact that he has not belonged to it from the beginning', and that 'he imports qualities into it, which do not ... stem from the group itself' (402).

Simmel writes that '[t]he unity of nearness and remoteness' is an aspect of 'every human relationship' but is most palpable in the figure of 'the stranger'. The distance in the relationship to the stranger 'means that he, who is close by, is far', while his or her strangeness 'means that he, who also is far, is actually near'. Strangeness is 'a specific form of interaction': 'The inhabitants of Sirius are not really strangers to us, at least not in any sociologically relevant sense: they do not exist for us at all; they are beyond far and near.' Should we humans ever interact with the inhabitants of Sirius, if there are any, we will thereby *become* strangers to each other. Simmel compares the stranger to 'the poor' and various kinds of 'inner enemies' as they belong but do not belong to the group at the same time. Simmel puts 'inner enemies' in inverted commas, indicating that he does not necessarily agree that the groups labelled in this way are indeed enemies at all. It is not clear who he is thinking of, however: German nationalists at the time would often have denounced Jews and Catholics in this way, or ethnic minorities such as those of Polish background. Simmel writes that his essay is about the ways in which a community of interaction is produced by 'elements which increase distance and repel' (403).

2 The stranger as trader

Simmel begins his exploration by taking an economic perspective. He states that throughout economic history, traders have tended to be strangers, and strangers traders. In the past, traders as middlemen were needed only for products that were imported from outside the social group. They had to be strangers, almost by definition. Simmel emphasizes that the group becomes more conscious of the strangeness of the trader once the trader settles down instead of being constantly on the move: the stranger who stays becomes a conscious presence. This can only happen once the group itself is developed enough to allow the trader to make a living without moving around. The trader expands the horizon of the existing group: the goods imported by the trader do not, for Simmel, fulfil essential demands or provide necessities, as he thinks of the group as self-sufficient in the first place:

> For in trade, which alone makes possible unlimited combinations, intelligence always finds expansions and new territories, an achievement which is very difficult to attain for the primary producer with his lesser mobility and his dependence upon a circle of customers that can be increased only slowly. (403)

The trader changes the group's idea of what is necessary and desirable. New demand is created, and thereby new opportunities for more traders emerge. New immigrants to the group will therefore find employment most easily in trade. Simmel adds that the classical example of the stranger is that of the European Jews who were for a certain period in history legally banned from owning real estate.

Simmel picks up this fact in the next step of his argument and plays on the double meaning of the notion of 'ownership of soil': 'The stranger is by nature no "owner of soil" – soil not only in the physical, but also in the figurative sense of a life-substance which is fixed, if not in a point in space, at least in an ideal point of the social environment.' The stranger, on the one hand, literally does not own soil, and on the other hand, is seen and denounced as someone who (figuratively) is un-grounded or rootless: 'Although in more intimate relations, he may develop all kinds of charm and significance', the stranger is landless and, in a sense, does not 'have a stake' in the same sense that the landowners do. This common English phrase – 'having a stake' – expresses the observation made by Simmel very well: it derives from the practice of claiming land ownership and connected rights by driving a stake into the ground. If I 'have a stake' in something, I am 'grounded', as it were.

Simmel concludes this step of the argument by saying that restrictions on intermediary trade and, even more so, finance, give the stranger 'the specific character of mobility' which 'embodies that synthesis of nearness and distance which constitutes the formal position of the stranger' (404).

3 The objectivity of the stranger

Simmel moves from here to another 'expression of this constella-tion' (404), 'the objectivity of the stranger'. The 'attitude of "objec-tivity"' is 'a particular structure composed of distance and nearness, indifference and involvement'. Simmel defines 'objectivity' along the same lines as 'strangeness', namely as the formal characteristic of being near and far at the same time.

The meaning of Simmel's concept of 'formal sociology', or the sociology of social forms, can be discovered best by paying attention to how Simmel constructs his essay. His 'formal' approach allows him to discuss a variety of very different contents in the same breath: to a reader who is inattentive to the notion of 'social form', the essay would appear as a merely impressionistic assemblage of various bits and pieces. Only the concept of 'form' holds the argument together: the 'excursus' is designed as an exploration of the dialectic of 'dis-tance and nearness' and how it shapes social relationships. It uses various specific contents to demonstrate this 'social form'.

Simmel introduces his argument on objectivity with a historical example: certain Italian cities used 'to call their judges from the outside, because no native was free from entanglement in family and party interests'. A judge needed to be as 'objective' as possible and therefore had to be a stranger. Another example is the fact that the stranger 'often receives the most surprising openness – confidences which sometimes have the character of a confessional and which would be carefully withheld from a more closely related person'. Simmel could have mentioned priests and psychoanalysts as further examples. He adds that objectivity does not mean non-participation, but rather 'a positive and specific kind of participation', and underlines that in the context of scholarship also, the production of objectivity is a specific, active process: the mind does not work like an empty slate 'on which things inscribe their qualities', as unreconstructed empiricists or strict positivists would have it. On the contrary, following Immanuel Kant's account, the mind actively 'operates according to its own laws' by eliminating accidental 'individual and subjective differences' that distort different people's perceptions of 'the same object'. One could perhaps say that the human mind is able to produce objective representations of reality because it is a stranger to that reality. This argument is not totally different from Durkheim's notion that reality is strange and thing-like to us. (It is worth noting in passing that this conception of how we make perceptions of the world is both anti-positivist and positivistic at the same time: it is based on Kantian idealism – i.e. a synthesis of rationalism and empiricism – and in this sense differs from positivism, but it is still positivist to the extent that it presupposes an objective and knowable reality out there of which we are able to produce 'objective' representations and judgements.)

Simmel continues, in the spirit of idealism and classical liberalism, to define objectivity in terms of freedom: 'Objectivity may also be defined as freedom: the objective individual is bound by no commitments which could prejudice his perception, understanding, and evaluation of the given' (405). This freedom to be objective, and thereby to enjoy privileged access to truth 'as though from a bird's-eye view', comes at a price, however: the stranger is often made a scapegoat. Simmel writes that since time immemorial, 'in uprisings of all sorts', the attacked rulers claimed the troubles had been provoked 'from the outside' by instigators. Simmel responds to this claim in two steps. First, he grants that there is some truth to this:

> Insofar as this is true, it is an exaggeration of the specific role of the stranger: he is freer, practically and theoretically; he surveys conditions with less prejudice; his criteria for them are more general and more objective ideals; he is not tied down in his action by habit, piety, and precedent.

Secondly, he writes that insofar as this is *not* true, i.e. insofar as a rebellion was *not* instigated by objective, truth-seeking, liberally minded strangers (think of Jews, travellers, students, artists, intellectuals, etc.), blaming them anyway serves to rebuild the peace between the actual rebels and those they attacked:

> But where the attacked make the assertion falsely, they do so from the tendency of those in higher position to exculpate inferiors, who, up to the rebellion, have been in a consistently close relation with them. For, by creating the fiction that the rebels were not really guilty, but only instigated, and that the rebellion did not really start with them, they exonerate themselves, inasmuch as they altogether deny all real grounds for the uprising.

By way of making the strangers scapegoats, the rulers build the rebels a golden bridge back home into the previous state of being loyal subjects of the rulers and exploiters whom they rebelled against. Both, rulers and rebels, can avoid asking themselves painful questions as to what really were the reasons of the rebellion. (Rather strangely, Simmel exiled the second part of this argument into a footnote.)

4 The abstractness of the relationship to the stranger

Simmel's next point is that the relationship to strangers is more abstract than other social relations due to its peculiar dialectic of 'nearness and remoteness' (405). He argues that all personal relationships can be explored by asking whether the commonality that sustains them is based on a particular or a universal. The more particular and exclusive the commonality, the warmer and more organic is the relationship; the more generic and universal the commonality, the more the relationship is abstract and cool. For example, 'with the stranger one has only certain more general qualities in common, whereas the relation to more organically connected persons is based on the commonness of specific differences'. The wider the social circle is in which a characteristic is shared, the weaker is its cohesive power: the characteristic of being human is shared by all of humanity, the widest possible social circle, and provides therefore only rather cool and abstract commonality. The most exclusive social relationship, say, that with one's mother, accordingly is the warmest and least abstract (406). The relationship with the stranger sits somewhere in between, but more at the abstract end of this scale:

> The stranger is close to us, insofar as we feel between him and ourselves common features of a national, social, occupational, or generally human, nature. He is far from us, insofar as these common features extend beyond him or us, and connect us only because they connect a great many people.

Rather intriguingly, Simmel argues that the dialectic between nearness and remoteness 'enters even the most intimate relationships':

> In the stage of first passion, erotic relations strongly reject any thought of generalization: the lovers think that there has never been a love like theirs; that nothing can be compared either to the person loved or to the feelings for that person. An estrangement – whether as cause or as consequence it is difficult to decide – usually comes at the moment when this feeling of uniqueness vanishes from the relationship. A certain scepticism in regard to its value ... attaches to the very thought that ... they experience [something] that has occurred a thousand times before; that, had they not accidentally met their particular partner, they would have found the same significance in another person. (406)

The dialectic of nearness and remoteness translates here into that of intimacy and strangeness, or perhaps estrangement. It is unclear whether Simmel thinks of this dialectic as an anthropological universal or a characteristic of modernity: the latter would surely make more sense, as the romantic celebration of the uniqueness of one's love is rare outside the modern context. Modernity created thereby a psychologically rather complicated demand that it is difficult for individuals to fulfil: everybody is expected to have absolutely unique experiences, but these experiences in fact follow a script that seems hard-wired into the libidinal structure of humans. It is a recipe for disappointment.

Simmel continues that an intimation of the falseness of the claim to uniqueness manifests itself in a feeling that is similar to jealousy (407). The estrangement, or strangeness, that is at the centre of this feeling is not due to growing or newly discovered differences between the partners, but to the discovery of 'the fact that similarity, harmony, and nearness' are not unique. The relationship loses thereby its quality of 'inner and exclusive necessity' and its intensity: it becomes more ordinary and therefore disappointing.

5 Strangeness based on the denial of individuality

Following on from this, Simmel discusses the opposite extreme: a kind of strangeness that *precludes* shared 'commonness based on something more general' (407), to the point of denying the stranger the quality of being human. Simmel mentions here the classical Greek word 'barbarian', which denoted not-quite-human strangers with whom no community was supposed to be possible at all. He points out that his own discussion of 'the stranger' is not about the stranger in this exclusionary sense: the relation to 'the barbarian' 'has no positive meaning' as 'the relation to him is a non-relation; he is not … a member of the group itself'. The people whom the classical Greeks called 'barbarians' fall into the same category as the inhabitants of Sirius mentioned by Simmel earlier in the text. They fall outside his concept of 'the stranger'.

The stranger as a group member, however, 'is near and far at the same time', an ambivalence that is characteristic of relations founded on nothing more than 'generally human commonness' (407). Here Simmel makes what is perhaps the most interesting observation in this context: this 'specific tension' arises because 'the consciousness that only the quite general is common, stresses that which is not common'. When all we share is our humanity, a rather abstract and generic thing, then we perceive our differences ever more sharply. This would not be such a bad thing if the differences in question were those of individuality: after all, all human beings are different from each other and we want to be perceived in our individuality – assuming that we stand, as does Simmel, in a philosophical tradition that prizes individuality over against conformity. This is not what happens to the stranger, though – on the contrary: the perception of 'the stranger' obliterates his or her individuality:

> In the case of the person who is a stranger to the country, the city, the race, etc., however, this non-common element is once more nothing

individual, but merely the strangeness of origin, which is or could be common to many strangers. For this reason, strangers are not really conceived as individuals, but as strangers of a particular type: the element of distance is no less general in regard to them than the element of nearness.

Theirs is a *generic* otherness, not a *particular* otherness. The stranger is perceived as a representative of a different *type* of human being, not a *particularly* different, concrete, individual and unique human being. Simmel's argument suggests that the full members of the group have a better chance of having their individuality recognized: the more similar I am to other full members of society, the more they will be prepared to view the remaining *minor* differences as my individuality and value them as such. If I wear the same *prêt-à-porter* business suit as all my colleagues but with a different coloured tie, everything else being equal, I will be celebrated as a real character. If I come to work in a kaftan, I am a kaftan-wearing *type of person*, not an admirable individualist.

Simmel illustrates his argument with a less silly example, namely the historical case of a type of poll tax that was levied differently for Christians and Jews in many German-speaking lands in the Middle Ages: whereas the Christian citizens paid an amount that varied depending on their wealth *at any particular point in time*, Jews paid a fixed amount because

> the Jew had his social position as a Jew, not as the individual bearer of certain objective contents. Every other citizen was the owner of a particular amount of property, and his tax followed its fluctuations. But the Jew as a taxpayer was, in the first place, a Jew, and thus his tax situation had an invariable element. (408)

Simmel adds that the amount of individuality that was granted a stranger in different taxation systems varied from case to case: sometimes the amount of tax that a stranger, such as a Jew, had to pay was fixed for every individual stranger – albeit once fixed, it was invariable irrespective of changes in the individual's fortune – and sometimes the amount was levied generically for the entire *category* of strangers, so that all Jews resident in a particular polity, for example, always paid the same amount of poll tax.

6 The stranger as an organic member of the group

In the last paragraph Simmel sums up the gist of his argument in a strictly formal manner: 'the stranger' is 'inorganically appended' to the group – i.e. did not emerge from it – but nevertheless is 'an organic member of the group' (408). The existence of strangers is part of the group's 'uniform life' – the stranger is an organ of the group, as it were. The relation to 'the stranger' is 'composed of certain measures of nearness and distance': this is what defines this particular 'social form'. However, Simmel adds that 'some quantities of them characterize all relationships': the dialectic of nearness and distance is thus not exclusively a characteristic of the social form of 'the stranger', it is only particularly characteristic of it.

11

Love, marriage and patriarchy: Marianne Weber

Marianne Weber (1870–1954) was born in a small German town in Westphalia just at the beginning of the Franco-Prussian war of 1870–71 that resulted in the founding of the Bismarck Reich. Her father was a country doctor, her mother, who died when Marianne was two years old, was from the much more prestigious family of her future husband, Max Weber, who was a second cousin. Her childhood was pious and austere, then increasingly unsettling and impoverished when her father and his two brothers became mentally ill. The experience turned her into an extremely organized, resourceful, self-reliant girl with stress-tested coping mechanisms in place that must have come in handy later in her marriage to Max Weber, who also had a mental breakdown: she must have been a tough cookie. After finishing school she played the role of the poor relative in an aunt's middle-class household in another small town. She learned to get by: while always keeping up appearances, she developed a secret determination to become the opposite of her petty, dull, provincial relatives who surrounded her. In 1891 she was invited to Berlin to spend a few weeks with the wealthy and elegant family of Max Weber Sr, his wife Helene and their eldest son, also Max. She returned for a second stay a year later, and soon enough, Max Weber Jr proposed to her. They got married in 1893. The following year they moved to Freiburg where Max became professor. Like Max, she was very close to Helene who was a pious, warm person and became an ersatz mother to Marianne – the three of them seem to have formed a kind of coalition against the cold, domineering patriarch of the Weber family.

In Freiburg, Marianne Weber began to study philosophy and took part in feminist discussions. After the Webers moved to Heidelberg in 1896, she continued to study philosophy, became involved with a feminist discussion organization and started writing – on top of her regular marital duties as manager of a professorial bourgeois household. In 1897 Max suffered a breakdown after the death of his father, entering years of serious depression until 1903, a period during which Marianne must have been first of all preoccupied with looking after him. Nevertheless she published her first book in 1900, *Fichte's Socialism and its Relation to Marxist Doctrine*. She hinted later, in a famous biography of Max that she wrote after his death, that the sudden eclipse of his public life and of his incipient superlative career had brought them very closely together as a couple: the illness provided them with an unexpected kind of happiness. They seem to have understood how to use the illness as an opportunity. In that period, Marianne also cut her teeth in political meetings while Max stayed home and rested. During their visit to the USA in 1904 she met leading American feminists such as Jane Addams. Weber's two key publications in that period are classics of feminist literature: a historical study on *Marriage, Motherhood and the Law* (1907) and her collection of essays *Reflections on Women and Women's Issues* (1919). During the war years both Marianne and Max seem to have been firing on all cylinders, engaging in politics and scholarship like there was no tomorrow. In 1919 Marianne Weber became the first female member of a German parliament: she represented the liberal German Democratic Party in the federal state parliament of the Republic of Baden, but gave up her seat when she moved with Max to Munich in 1920 where he took up a professorship. In 1920 she became president of the Federation of German Women's Organizations.

After Max's unexpected death in 1920, it was Marianne's turn to fall into a depression which she overcame by editing ten volumes of Max's works and writing his biography (published in 1926). Without this work, Max Weber hardly would have come to be seen as the giant of sociology we know now – in this sense, she *created* 'Max Weber' in those years. During the remaining years of Weimar Germany until the Nazi takeover in 1933, she continued to be increasingly important as a prolific writer of liberal feminist

social and legal theory and a public speaker. During the Nazi period (1933–45) she went into a resigned state of 'inner exile' like many other defeated liberals, and again suffered from depression. She published her memoirs in 1948.

The selected text is an essay from 1912 that was included in her volume *Reflections on Women and Women's Issues* of 1919.

Structure of the selected text

1 Woman as the property of man in primitive patriarchalism and the gradual shift towards milder domination (86–87)
2 Legal monogamy in Greek and Roman antiquity and religious consecration of marriage in Judaism (87)
3 Continuing patriarchy, the cultural-spiritual deepening of monogamy and the suppression of sex in Christianity (87–88)
4 Further spiritualization of marriage and the first recognition of the spiritual equality of woman in Puritanism (88–89)
5 Autonomy and equality of woman are recognized theoretically but practically given up in the marriage contract in German idealist philosophy (89–90)
6 In the industrial age, woman is freed from protection/domination through marriage while legal domination by the husband is still preserved (90)
7 Case study: the legal regulation of marriage in the German Civil Code and its reform (90–92)
8 Patriarchally disposed husbands counter the challenge to their authority through recourse to moral pressure (92–93)
9 Women can make marriage meaningful as an ethical institution only by refusing to violate their own ethical autonomy (93–94)
10 Marriage as the highest ideal of human community ought to resist suffocation by everyday life routine (94–95)

Weber, Marianne, 2003 [1912]. 'Authority and Autonomy in Marriage. Translation with Introduction and Commentary by Craig R. Bermingham'. *Sociological Theory* 21.2: 85–102.

1 Woman as the property of man in primitive patriarchalism and the gradual shift towards milder domination

Weber begins the text with a methodological statement: in order to understand 'the inner structure of marriage', one needs to look at its history, and especially 'the leading ideas through which it has been defined' (86). Weber engages thus in a form of historical sociology that aims to pay particular attention to how people in history have reflected on the forms of their living together.

At 'the beginning of all history the woman was the property of the man': this is, for Marianne Weber, the starting point of her history. This means, by implication, that she rejects any of the anthropological theories that see some form of 'matriarchy', or at least anything other than straightforward patriarchy, at the origin of mankind. Few if any contemporary anthropologists – a century later – would agree with this aspect of her argument, but it provides her with the fairly linear narrative of human progress that is characteristic of the classical liberal framework of her theoretical perspective. Man, she continues, was able to do with woman as he pleased: buy, sell, expel, or own a number of women. Weber asserts that this original condition of 'primitive patriarchalism' was simply based on 'the right of the stronger', adding that this was still the case among 'uncivilized peoples' of the present (86). For this claim she also fails to provide any specific reference; again, it is contrary to the findings of more recent anthropology that generally have a far more favourable view of so-called 'primitive peoples'.

Weber argues that one can talk about marriage strictly speaking only from the point at which the man is beginning to be bound by some kind of obligation towards the woman. The woman's family earns for her the legal position of wife, and for her children that of 'legitimate heirs', by equipping her with a dowry. From this starting point, civilization developed everywhere in the same direction, namely the aspiration 'to somehow protect the woman from the barbaric arbitrariness of the husband' (87). Civilization moved towards 'humane patriarchy' and 'milder domination of the wife'. Weber constructs here a simple evolutionary theory that is clearly in line with contemporary aspirations to overcome patriarchal domination.

2 Legal monogamy in Greek and Roman antiquity and religious consecration of marriage in Judaism

In the next step of her historical sketch, Weber briefly states that ancient Greeks and Romans created monogamous marriage, which legally solved the question of the legitimacy of children, but at the same time imposed marital fidelity, through the threat of severe punishment, only on women. This is how Weber sums up this process: 'She alone was the one who had to answer for the realization of a social and ethical ideal which antiquity already revered and recognized, but yet without making the attempt to force the sexually "needier" nature of the man under its sway' (87). She constructs here the process of civilization as a struggle by an emerging 'social and ethical ideal' against 'nature', in this case the 'needier' nature of the man. Men, on this view, seem naturally predisposed towards polygamy and had to be subjected to the process of civilization.

Weber adds that ancient Judaism 'still permitted polygamy' but invented something else of 'world-historical significance' that would become relevant in the civilizing process: it 'surrounded marriage for the first time with the *religious* consecration' (87). This is the starting point of the spiritual 'deepening' of marriage that is central to Weber's understanding of it. Unfortunately, the *specific* form of marriage that was consecrated was still entirely patriarchal: woman was created as a helper to man.

3 Continuing patriarchy, the cultural-spiritual deepening of monogamy and the suppression of sex in Christianity

In the next step, Weber moves to a discussion of Christianity. She notes a contradiction between, on the one hand, 'the lofty Christian teachings of religious equality of the woman', and on the other hand, emphasis on the woman's obligation of obedience: as Paul, 'the bearer of Christian propaganda', wrote, 'the woman is created for the good of the man' (87). She interprets the continuation of patriarchy as a failure to break with Judaic traditions. The innovation that is most important to the history of marriage, though, is the following: 'Christianity created a large, new cultural product: the deepening of the demand of legalized monogamy into

an indispensable religious-cultural imperative, that now was not
only directed toward the woman, but rather, for the first time in
history, emphatically toward the man as well' (87). Christianity
turned monogamy from a *legal* form that is concerned with the
legitimacy of heirs (and allows men to be polygamous outside the
legal form) into a *spiritual* form and cultural 'imperative'. Weber
argues that this was the origin of marriage understood as 'a *spiritual* relation between man and woman' that grows out of 'the
natural element of fleeting sexual love' (88). This big step forward
in the process of civilization was spoiled, however, not only by
the continuation of patriarchal domination of women but also by
a new form of domination: reacting against 'the sexual excesses of
the cultural world of late antiquity', the Church 'exaggerated the
ideal of controlling one's sex life to the point of despising' and sup-
pressing 'all that is natural' (88). While Weber seems to applaud
the Church's opposition to 'sexual excesses' (the German word
she uses here literally means 'unbridledness' or 'promiscuity'), she
maintains that even 'spiritualized' marriage has to have a basis in
sexual love. Sexuality and sensuality, however, were condemned by
the Church as sinful and connected to the figure of Eve. Luther's
Protestantism stuck to this doctrine, suggesting that God tolerates
sex in marriage only because it is compensated for by all kinds
of 'listlessness and torment' – a distinctly unenthusiastic view of
marriage.

4 Further spiritualization of marriage and the first recognition of the spiritual equality of woman in Puritanism

In Weber's narrative, more civilizational progress was made only
by the Puritans. She portrays a rather peculiar dialectic in the
Puritan conception of marriage, or, as she calls it, 'a detour':
Puritan asceticism meant the strict suppression of sensuality even
within marriage – unlike Luther's God, the Puritan God no longer
turned a blind eye. Sex was strictly for procreation only. This doctrine resulted in 'a never-before-achieved disciplining of the man'
and 'a deepening of the spiritual and ethical relation between man
and woman' (88). Spiritual intimacy became the sole meaning of
marriage for the Puritans. Weber quotes from a rather romantic

letter by the Quaker William Penn (1644–1718) to his wife, in which he points to her inner virtues and their love relationship as 'a work of Providence': it was 'God's likeness in each of us' that had 'attracted us to one another the most' (89).[1] Weber argues that it was in this particular context that 'the thought of religious equality of the woman was taken seriously for the first time'. The Quakers' acceptance of the individual's freedom of conscience 'against every earthly authority' also applied to the case of the wife with respect to the husband: 'Freedom of conscience, the mother of all civil rights of the individual, stood across the ocean [i.e. in America] at the cradle of women's rights as well' (89). It is implied in Weber's argument that men's polygamous drives first had to be subdued by strict asceticism in order to make further civilizational progress possible.

5 Autonomy and equality of woman are recognized theoretically but practically given up in the marriage contract in German idealist philosophy

In the next step of her argument, Weber turns to the strand of Enlightenment philosophy that most strongly influenced her own thinking, the German idealism of Kant and Fichte. (She had written her first book on Fichte and Marx.) Idealism secularized the – originally theological – idea of inalienable human rights and asserted them against the worldly authorities of state and society (89). The essential point of idealist philosophy was that the 'human being is, as a bearer of reason, intended to govern himself', i.e. to act 'in accordance with a conscience'. Conscience in turn is in tune with 'the moral law' as expressed in the Kantian 'categorical imperative'. This moral or ethical conception of reason is the ground for human beings' capacity for 'autonomy' and freedom and the idea of human dignity: humans as bearers of *reason* have *dignity* due to their capacity for *autonomy*. The human being in

---

[1] This seems to be a re-translation from the German by the translator of Weber's article, not Penn's actual wording. Weber seems to quote from Penn's letter to his wife Gulielma [available here: http://www.qhpress.org/quakerpages/qwhp/pp340.htm].

this sense is 'a personality' and an end in him- or herself (89). It follows that human relationships must be shaped in such a way that no human being uses another human being merely 'as a means for his personal ends' (90). This should obviously include the relations between the sexes: according to the principles of idealist philosophy, the wife 'may not be used as a mere means to the husband's ends'. Unfortunately, this was not the conclusion Kant and Fichte actually drew: they 'did not even think about laying a hand on the patriarchal system' (90). Instead, they managed through 'a clever chess move of reason' to reconcile the new philosophy with the old system of domination: although man and woman are 'originally equals', marriage is 'a contract through which the wife voluntarily subordinates herself to the husband'. Weber adds that Fichte, in spite of his generally patriarchal perspective, at least supported the woman's right to divorce.

6 In the industrial age, woman is freed from protection/ domination through marriage while legal domination by the husband is still preserved

'But that which was denied the woman in the realm of the idea was soon forced upon her in the realm of realities' (90): the idealist philosophy of freedom failed to take a stand for women's equality, but the reality of industrial society did. 'Technical and economic forces' reduced the 'household economy' (the English translation wrongly gives 'household work') and forced more and more women to 'stand on their own feet outside the home' which had previously provided protection as well as male domination. Intellectually also, her horizons were blown open. The combination of economic and intellectual change 'must fundamentally shift her position within our social community and her relation to the other sex' (90). Customs and views are shifting, opportunities have expanded, but 'the legally protected predominance of the husband' is still unbroken. Weber makes a distinction here between individual experience – including her own – and a structural problem: many men are ready 'to value their own wife as a personality' but 'only very few today agree to the fundamental renunciation of the rights of authority with regard to the entire female sex' (90).

7 Case study: the legal regulation of marriage in the German Civil Code and its reform

This general characterization of the contemporary situation as one of change is followed by a discussion of the regulation of marriage in the reformed German Civil Code as valid at the time. I do not want to give much space to this section as it is mostly specific to the historical context. Weber's principal point is that the legal situation is contradictory, based on a 'compromise between irreconcilable principles' (91): patriarchal authority and equality. Many things are reformulated 'politely' in the language of the modernized Civil Code: the words 'paternal authority', for example, have been replaced by 'parental authority' but on closer inspection only the family father in fact exerts the 'parental authority'. The words suggest a degree of equality that does not actually exist. Weber asserts that 'modern women … protest against these carryovers from the patriarchal system' (91). She demands that the protection of women should be a priority for marriage legislation as women are 'normally much more strongly bound' by marriage than men are. '*Companionship of the partners*' should replace the principle of authority (92). She points to three fundamental ways in which the Civil Code should be reformed: the husband's 'general, legal decision-making authority' is to be eliminated; parental rights should be divided up fairly; and women need financial independence (92).

8 Patriarchally disposed husbands counter the challenge to their authority through recourse to moral pressure

Weber describes now what this contradictory form of modern marriage looks like, in which the man asserts his authority but the woman already has a concept and consciousness of her own autonomy. It is not a nice picture!

First, Weber discusses household affairs. Her point here is that the woman is the more competent person, but nevertheless has to submit to male authority. She describes the psychological effect as follows:

It is clear that the constant bending of the wife's will without her
inner consent and conviction can either be a mere feigned submission
on her part, from which she, in turn, underhandedly frees herself
behind her husband's back, or it actually achieves a suppression of
her ability to reason – that is, the atrophy of her entire intellectual and
spiritual development. (92)

Beyond the household, Weber suggests that the patriarchally disposed husband will also 'want to dictate and control the inner life
of the woman' because 'marital relationships encompass the entire
person':

For this reason, strong aspirations toward self-reliance and intellectual development necessarily fill a husband who is bent on authority
with a severe uneasiness. He will not rest if he is not constantly secure
also in his position as the master of her most personal inner life. He
will feel the need to monitor her readings, her friendships, her interests outside the home. (92)

The husband will be suspicious of anything the wife does outside
the house, and Weber suggests that he has good reason to be so:
outside the house the wife is removed from personal domination
(93). 'The inner protest of the patriarchally disposed husband' will
normally come dressed up in the form of a moral concern that the
woman is neglecting family life and her children. Weber concludes
that the happiness of women is incompatible with men's assertion of
'the fundamental privileges of authority' (93).

9 Women can make marriage meaningful as an ethical institution only by refusing to violate their own ethical autonomy

Weber comes now to the high point of her argument. She introduces
a distinction between voluntary and compelled subordination (93).
The autonomous woman may well *choose* to subordinate her wishes
and interests under her husband's if she finds he commands 'higher
insight', 'more mature judgement', 'greater completeness' of personality or 'higher aspirations'. She can decide to do so, however,
only 'before the forum of her own conscience', and only 'from case
to case'. 'It may absolutely not be decided for all time at the very

beginning of their relationship, as the principle of authority would require.' Not blanket subordination, but '[o]nly the free sacrifices of love for the aspirations of a greater person possess beauty and dignity'. While she may have been thinking here of her own husband, she adds, perhaps a bit sarcastically: 'A husband's offer of these to the wife is also no disgrace.' This comment clearly indicates that, when writing this, she was aware that 'voluntary subordination' in reality tends to come more often from women than from men.

These rather traditional-sounding comments are followed by her critique of *involuntary* subordination:

> But if, instead of such free giving of one's self, the woman obliges his needs and everyday goals against her inner voice, simply because it is comfortable, for the sake of outward peace, or to please her husband, then she commits *blasphemy* against her own human dignity; then she devalues herself to a second-class being. (93)

Such subordination damages not only the woman herself, but also the husband: the wife will be 'almost a child, naive to the world, intellectually contented, enclosed in the circle of the household, fixed in her interests on the purely personal and trifling'. Weber writes that there is a kind of 'tragic irony' at work here: the so-called 'model-housewife' fails to provide any intellectual stimulations to the husband, and the 'relationship to her requires absolutely no effort from his side' (93) to the effect that 'everyday life's thick dust of boredom covers the relationships and turns to grey that which was once colourful and shining' (94).

Alternatively, the woman may mature 'in spite of her authoritarian boundedness' and 'one day her aspirations and reason will break through their bounds'. She will then find it very difficult to assert herself against a husband who has been accustomed to her submissiveness, so that she is likely to pretend submissiveness 'but to secretly circumvent such submission'. Her individual life will then become 'a strange hostile element that disturbs the marital happiness'. Trust will vanish, the marriage will break up, 'and all of this just because the wife first found herself so late, and because the husband did not learn to value the being at his side as "destined for self-determination" just as he is' (94). The implicit advice given by Weber here seems to be not to lose time, but to find one's autonomy at the earliest possibility: submission once established is difficult to break out from.

10 Marriage as the highest ideal of human community ought to resist suffocation by everyday life routine

This plea for autonomy is followed in the concluding section of the essay by some more moderate tones. First Weber provides a summary of her concept of marriage:

> Modern women value marriage as it should be – that is, a life's partnership that is founded on the affinity of souls and senses, and on the desire for full responsibility, as the highest ideal of human community that stands as an unshakable guiding star above the sexual life of civilized humanity. (94)

This is very much a definition in the spirit of Kantian idealism and classical liberalism: marriage is equally about 'souls' and 'senses', the spiritual-intellectual-ethical as well as the sensual, whereby the ethical ideal of community guides and directs sexual life. The physical is acknowledged but integrated and subordinated. Next she confirms that modern women are, 'like the women of all times', prepared to make 'those sacrifices that, as family members, marriage now demands from them'. She adds that these sacrifices are now more difficult to make than in the past 'because our time is the first to know the conflict between marriage and career, and between the special family tasks of the woman and her inner drive to contribute to the construction of the superpersonal cultural world'. In the modern context, woman like man must 'prove herself in the world', and women demand that men acknowledge this:

> They demand the trust that the female sex can learn to keep the balance between natural and self-selected tasks just as well as the male sex between its various obligations and interests. And they are convinced that only where this occurs can marriage be more than an institution of social expediency. (94)

The point of this argument is that Weber acknowledges that there is a conflict between 'natural' tasks – presumably this refers to child-rearing and perhaps also more generally household-related tasks

– and 'self-selected' tasks in the 'cultural world', including scholarship, the arts, civil society and politics. This conflict is not, however, specific to women: she states that men face similar conflicts as they too have to 'balance' 'various obligations and interests'. Unfortunately she fails to elaborate on this, but she might have on her mind the conflict between having to earn money for a family, and committing oneself as much as possible to writing poetry, playing in a band or overthrowing the government.

The last paragraph of the essay takes up again the 'critique of civilization'-theme from the previous section: she asserts that it is 'no small task to keep the marital partnership free from the suffocating ash of everyday life and habit through all of the phases of a long life' (94), from youthful passion through a busy mid-life to the long decline of old age:

> More dangerous than all the suffering and strife that destiny imposes from without, more fearful than the problems that arise out of the struggle of souls, is the endless chain of satisfied, comfortable, struggle*less* everydays, in which the partners have one another effortlessly in possession. (94)

Weber's metaphor of the 'suffocating ash of everyday life' is very similar to, and no less powerful than, her husband's famous metaphor of the 'casing hard as steel' (aka the 'iron cage'). The romantic aspect of both Webers' writings, their rejection of bourgeois smugness, rigour and complacency, seems to have been fed by their experience of the Puritan-driven warmth and inwardness of Max's mother, Helene, which might partly account also for the religious undertones: the force that can resist the onslaught of the 'suffocating ash' is, for Marianne Weber, 'the holy flame of tender and deep sensitivity' that is a reflection of 'the eternal' in the 'human soul' (95). Her principal proposition is that this flame can only prosper under conditions of equality.

12
Critical versus traditional theory: Max Horkheimer

Max Horkheimer (1895–1973) was born to a conservative Jewish family in the south-west German city of Stuttgart. His father was a textile manufacturer, a conservative, German-patriotic, hard-working, rationalistic self-made man who expected his son to take over his business. Horkheimer left school at the age of 15 to become an apprentice in his father's factory. During this period, he was introduced to literature and philosophy by his best friend, Friedrich Pollock (1894–1970), also the son of an industrialist but a well-read grammar-school boy. They remained close friends throughout their lives, and Pollock later played a key role in the development of 'Frankfurt School' Critical Theory alongside Horkheimer. Horkheimer's thinking, and Critical Theory in general, was shaped by three key historical determinants: the failure and defeat of working-class revolutions in 'advanced' capitalist societies at end of the First World War; the regression of the Russian Revolution of 1917 into an authoritarian-bureaucratic regime; and the failure of the working class and its organizations to resist fascism.

The young Horkheimer's thinking was strongly influenced by some philosophical ideas from Arthur Schopenhauer (1788–1860): the rejection of overly systematic philosophy, a negative view of bourgeois society as 'living hell' and the notion of compassion as the central concept for ethics. Rather exceptionally at the time, Horkheimer rejected the First World War from the outset and initially avoided the draft by working as a manager in his father's factory while writing social-critical novellas. At this time he also acquired another fundamental aspect of his outlook that he never

abandoned, in reaction to Social Democracy's support of the war
effort in 1914: he despised political parties, which to him were
like religious cults. He was drafted after all in 1916 but discharged
in 1918 due to illness, whereupon he lived as a writer in Munich
in a milieu of political radicals and bohemian artists, an important aspect of the Munich environment at the time. Admirers of
the revolutionary socialist Rosa Luxemburg (who was murdered in
1919 by proto-fascist militias backed by the new Social Democratic
government), Horkheimer and Pollock were sympathetic to, but
sceptical of, the short-lived Bavarian workers' council republic of
April 1919. Later the same year, Horkheimer started to study psychology, philosophy and political economy at the newly founded,
liberal University of Frankfurt/Main. He retained, though, the
contempt for academia and formal authority that he had picked
up from his reading of Schopenhauer. His inner distance from the
smug self-importance of academic life in fact served him quite well,
in combination with a useful skill that he had acquired through his
previous work experience as a trainee factory manager: to keep the
father sweet and the financial support coming, he needed to disguise
both his politics and his poetic leanings. Horkheimer was a right old
geezer in the literal meaning of that word – someone who does not
easily show his cards.[1] In Frankfurt he met Felix Weil (1898–1975),
the son of a grain merchant who had been radicalized in the failed
1918 revolution and was to become, with Pollock, the key figure in
the founding of the Frankfurt Institute for Social Research in 1923
(using money given by Weil's father). Horkheimer wrote his disser-
tation on Kant's *Critique of Judgement*, studied Marx from around
1920 and was involved in the discussions of Marxist theory that led
to the formation of the Institute, but then had no further involvement in it. Horkheimer studied Hegel from 1925 and in the process
turned towards the study of history and society. He acquired a
reputation for being an excellent lecturer and when the position of
director of the Institute became vacant in 1930, Horkheimer was
given the position – along with a professorship at the university
– partly because he was untainted by any apparent political affilia-
tions. His first publication that related directly to Marx, defending

[1] The word 'geezer' is presumed to stem from French *se guiser*, to disguise oneself.

Marx's concept of ideology against Karl Mannheim's sociology of knowledge, also appeared in 1930. Horkheimer's first book of social theory was published in 1934 – when he was already in exile – under a pseudonym. Entitled *Twilight: Notes from Germany*, it consists of aphorisms and short pieces that are based on micro-level observations of themes of social domination in capitalism. (It is available in English in a volume called *Dawn and Decline*.)

From his reading of Schopenhauer, Horkheimer retained the notion that society is able to put 'man's need for metaphysics' to work for many different ends. If one substitutes 'eros' or 'libido' for 'need for metaphysics', one arrives at the version of this idea that Critical Theory adopted from Freudian psychoanalysis. The integration of psychoanalysis into Marxian social theory was arguably Horkheimer's most momentous contribution to social theory, although it was not an idea he came up with on his own. In 1928 Horkheimer underwent psychoanalysis with Karl Landauer (1887–1945; Landauer died in the Bergen-Belsen concentration camp), a trainee of Freud and a member of the Vienna Psychoanalytic Society, who had opened a practice in Frankfurt in 1923. Horkheimer took part in a working group on psychoanalysis that also included Erich Fromm (1900–80), a trainee of Landauer, and helped found in 1929 the Frankfurt Psychoanalytic Institute, housed in the same building as the Institute for Social Research. Through Horkheimer's mediation, Fromm began in 1929 to work on the first empirical study undertaken by the Institute for Social Research, a study of German workers' political attitudes 'on the eve of the Third Reich'. Crucial to Fromm's and Horkheimer's appropriation of psychoanalysis was the distinction between self-preservation, or 'ego-drives', and 'libidinal drives' that aim for enjoyment (according to Freud's early drive theory). It allowed the addressing of the question why people acted in ways that *contradicted* their own material interests. The drive to self-preservation would command one to keep out of trouble, to avoid warfare or antisemitic pogroms, and instead to fight for one's rights and material interests. The 'libidinal drives', however, might command one to try to be 'loved' by a charismatic leader, and thus to do things that under rational analysis would seem damaging to one's self-interests: the emerging Critical Theory observed that there is a strange kind of pleasure to be had from obeying authority, even when this authority is irrational, violent and oppressive. This is the way in which society exploits people's drive for libidinal gratification, similar to the way it 'makes use of' the 'need for metaphysics', according to Schopenhauer. The study demonstrated unconscious authoritarian attitudes even among politically organized workers. This allowed the Institute to predict that there would be no widespread workers' resistance to a fascist takeover of power. The research seems to have contributed to Horkheimer's not harbouring any illusions about the danger of the situation: he transferred the Institute's money out of the country before the Nazis took power, so that it was able to continue its work in exile (first briefly in Switzerland, then in the USA). The exiled Institute published a more sophisticated and broad-based study along similar lines in Paris in 1936, called *Studies on Authority and Family*.

Next to its empirical work, the Institute published the highly regarded *Journal for Social Research* which existed from 1932 to 1941. After the Nazi takeover of power in 1933 it was published in exile. All theoretical aspects of 'Frankfurt School' Critical Theory were developed in the form of essays in this journal during this period, including several written by Horkheimer. One of the key texts, next to 'Traditional and Critical Theory' (1937) which is discussed below, was Horkheimer's 'Egoism and Freedom Movements: On the Anthropology of the Bourgeois Epoch' (1936). This essay starts out from Hegel's observation that there is an antagonism between the principles of 'self-assertion and self-interest' on the one hand, and subjective freedom, on the other, both of which are characteristics of modern bourgeois society: egoism and freedom are dialectically interwoven, but the former tends to destroy the latter. Horkheimer discusses a number of historical cases from the fourteenth century to the present and develops an 'anthropology of the bourgeois character' around the notions of cruelty against oneself and others. This essay provides an alternative account of the role of asceticism to that of Max Weber, emphasizing the importance of actively – for example, through oratory – working towards changing the personality structures of people in the process of building modern society. This essay in particular anticipates some of the themes of the highly complex book *Dialectic of Enlightenment*, co-authored with Theodor W. Adorno and first published in 1944, which is often considered one of the central works of social philosophy in the twentieth century. Another key work by Horkheimer, *Eclipse of Reason* (1947), consists of a series of lectures that provide a rather more accessible version of many of the same themes treated in his essays from the 1930s as well as in *Dialectic of Enlightenment*.

The decisive stages in the formation of the so-called 'Frankfurt School' type of Critical Theory happened in exile in New York and Los Angeles. Several major empirical studies, including most famously *The Authoritarian Personality* (1950), and most of the theoretical texts were produced in exile. The moniker 'Frankfurt School' was invented by commentators after Horkheimer, Adorno and Pollock returned to what was now the Federal Republic of Germany after the Second World War. Horkheimer remained the key player of the newly founded Institute in Frankfurt until 1953, after which he gradually withdrew, handing over the key role to Adorno. The most important 'Frankfurt School' publication in the immediate post-Second World War years was a large-scale study of the political consciousness of the West German population, including their attitude towards fascism, based on a massive programme of focus groups.

The selected text is the 1937 essay 'Traditional and Critical Theory', the most influential exposition of Horkheimer's understanding of Critical Theory. The essay sketches out on the first pages what the traditional understanding of 'theory' is (I refer to this part as sections 1.1–4), and then develops the concept of 'Critical Theory' as an alternative conception of theory. It is a theoretical essay that discusses the meaning of the word 'theory', and is in this sense an exercise in self-reflection. Self-reflection is in fact one of the characteristics of Critical Theory as conceived by Horkheimer: it always and ever anew reflects on its own possibility, function and task in society. Another characteristic is that it tends to define itself, and other things, in the negative by saying what it is *not*: this is part of what the word 'critical' means – it operates 'negatively' through *critique* of concepts rather than through positive definitions of concepts. In this essay, discussions of 'traditional' and 'critical theory' are therefore not strictly divided from each other: the sections that develop the concept of 'Critical Theory' (2.2–4.3) also bring back time and again aspects of the concept of 'traditional theory' as outlined in the beginning of the essay. Not unlike Marx's writing style in *Capital*, Horkheimer's essay may seem repetitive as similar ideas are presented, and negated, several times over, each time from a slightly different angle. Also as in Marx, however, most readers will be grateful for the repetitions, as this is rather dense and difficult material. The general rule for reading this more philosophical kind of text applies: initial incomprehension is a vital part of the process of understanding – so when you don't understand one thing, just smile, nod and carry on, as everything in the text comes around a second and third time. What you do not understand the first time

---

Structure of the selected text

Horkheimer, Max. 1972 [1937]. 'Traditional and Critical Theory'. In *Critical Theory, Selected Essays*. New York: Continuum, 188–243.

around, you will get the next time, but the process requires you gradually to get under the skin of the text. And even in spite of the repetitions, you will need to read the article several times, probably over many years – that is how it was for me, anyway. This is the department of heavy theory, which provides no shortcut to enlightenment.

1.1 The traditional concept of theory

Horkheimer begins his discussion with the concept of theory as it is commonly understood in the context of contemporary science, whereby 'contemporary' means here the 1930s when this text was written. Scientists mean by 'theory' a set of propositions that are consistent with each other in the sense that 'a few are basic and the rest derive from these', and the theory as a whole is consistent with the reality of 'actual facts' (188): 'If experience and theory contradict each other, one of the two must be re-examined. Either the scientist has failed to observe correctly or something is wrong with the principles of the theory.' Theory 'always remains a hypothesis': for modern science, theory has no legitimacy in itself. The facts have the last word, as long as *we-the-observers-of-facts* are convinced that our observations were not technically flawed. Horkheimer quotes from a book first published in 1902 by the French mathematician and physicist Henri Poincaré (1854–1912) who compared science to a ceaselessly expanding library: empirical sciences such as experimental physics put new books on the shelves – the 'data' whose assiduous accumulation also keeps the social scientists on their toes – while theoretical disciplines such as mathematical physics keep 'the catalogue': a large library without a catalogue would be useless, but the catalogue is only a means towards finding knowledge that is in the books (read: the data): there is no truth in the catalogue itself. The image of theory as nothing more than the library catalogue is the first determination of the 'traditional' concept of theory that Horkheimer sets out to challenge in this essay.

It is important to note that Horkheimer illustrates 'the traditional concept of theory' with a reference to the mathematician Poincaré: mathematics, in modernity generally understood to be a product entirely of the human mind, is mostly a domain of rationalist philosophers, who from the perspective of philosophy, are the opposite of empiricists: where empiricists believe that all knowledge stems from experience and sense data, rationalists believe that some if not all knowledge stems from the activity of human reason itself, theoretical mathematics being the principal case in point.

The rub is that Horkheimer does not take the perspective of a philosopher, but that of a theorist who has stopped believing in the relevance of some of the concerns of academic philosophy. An implicit goal of his argument is to show that there is a shared area between empiricism and rationalism, both of which *together* he addresses as 'traditional theory': empiricism and rationalism share the same reductionist concept of theory. In the next step of his argument, he quotes therefore a text by the founder of modern rationalist philosophy, and also a prominent mathematician, René Descartes (1596–1650), who argued in 1637 that all human thinking should be organized in the way of geometrical demonstrations: in the form of chains of reasoning that start out from 'simple and easy' propositions and move to the most complex in an orderly manner. For Descartes, deductive reasoning was a way to discover and understand remote and recondite things. For illustration, one might think here of modern physics, which shows by way of mathematical reasoning that, for example, a certain particle must exist, and then builds the machines that can empirically discover what the theoreticians have proposed *must* (probably) exist. If the experimental physicists cannot find it after a while, the theoretical physicists have to go back to the drawing board and think again, or build a better machine (if they can still get the funding).

It is important to keep in mind that Horkheimer's critique of the 'traditional' concept of theory does not take sides in the philosophical dispute between empiricism and rationalism, or inductive and deductive reasoning. Horkheimer emphasizes that rationalists have a variety of answers to the question of what the 'most universal propositions from which the deduction begins' should be: for some, deduction begins from 'experiential judgments', or inductions, for others from 'evident insights', or from 'arbitrary postulates' (189– 190). The situation is similar in the social sciences: 'The difference between those schools of social science which are more oriented to the investigation of facts and those which concentrate more on principles has nothing directly to do with the concept of theory as such' (190). The theoretical thinking involved in the 'assiduous collecting of facts' and in 'the analysis of basic concepts by an armchair scholar' differs less than is generally assumed:

> There can be no doubt, in fact, that the various schools of sociology have an identical conception of theory and that it is the same as theory in the natural sciences. Empirically oriented sociologists have the same idea of what a fully elaborated theory should be as their theoretically oriented brethren. (191)

The two camps only differ as to *when* the theorizing should be done, and *how much* of it is really helpful or necessary. Only the most strictly empiricist scholars – extremely rare among social scientists – would in fact insist that 'only complete inductions can supply the primary propositions for a theory', while most others allow other methods for the formation of the 'primary categories and insights' that are needed to construct scientific theories. Horkheimer points to Durkheim who 'agrees with many basic views of the empirical school but, in dealing with principles … opts for an abridgement of the inductive process', where theoretical concepts allow one to decide which phenomena matter and which do not.

Irrespective of how the 'primary principles' of a (traditional) theory were produced in the first place (empirically, intuitively, by deductive reasoning, or by stipulation), the theory remains a mere hypothesis that needs to be tested by new facts:

> There is always, on the one hand, the conceptually formulated knowledge and, on the other, the facts to be subsumed under it. Such a subsumption or establishing of a relation between the simple perception or verification of a fact and the conceptual structure of our knowing is called its theoretical explanation. (193)

The main target of Horkheimer's critique is the rigid relationship between theory and facts in traditional science: theory organizes the facts and is in turn confirmed by them. A theory that turns against the facts, or that is contradicted by the facts, accordingly is a wrong theory. Traditional social science, empirical or not, quantitative or qualitative, would find it impossible to take seriously a theory that demands better facts, or reprimands the facts for not living up to the theory. As will become clear later, the critical conception of theory, by contrast, allows itself occasionally to do such outrageous things.

Horkheimer concludes this first section of the essay with a remark on Max Weber's conception of historical causality. Historical explanation is, for Weber, not about 'the fullest possible enumeration of all pertinent circumstances' but the establishment of connections between the most significant aspects of an event and the processes that have determined them (193). Weber asserted the importance of demonstrating causality in history against a more old-fashioned historiography that would simply depict *how* things happened: *this happened, then that happened*. What really matters is the question, *why* whatever happened, happened. Weber subscribed to the modern (i.e. nineteenth-century) conception of science that Horkheimer calls 'traditional': Weber and those he leaned on were not content with the 'pre-scientific' notion that history consists of random unpredictable stuff that just happens, but aimed at learning proper lessons from history. Horkheimer does not object to the wish to learn lessons but rather to *the form* these lessons take: he scolds Weber for having aimed at sets of statements on causality in the form 'if *a* and *b* happen then *c* will happen but if *a* and *d* happen then *e* will happen'. Only when historiography is able to formulate history's 'inner laws' in the form of statements of this kind will it be useful for actively influencing the present according to its own inner laws. This is, of course, the conception of social science initially proposed by Comte under the name of 'positivism' – not identical to, but rather close to what Horkheimer called, almost exactly a century later, 'traditional theory'. It is for this reason that Horkheimer puts Weber into the category of positivism, which Weber himself would have rejected (largely because Weber was in fact interested in the uniqueness and individuality of events as much as in their causal determination).

1.2 The immediate role of theory in the context of actual social processes

In the second step of his argument, Horkheimer contextualizes the formation of the traditional concept of theory. In a characteristic move, he starts by pointing out what is the truth content of the traditional concept of theory: it 'corresponds, in fact, to science's immediate task' (194). (The available English translation is here, as elsewhere, imprecise: the translation suggests that the scientists set themselves tasks. Horkheimer clearly means that tasks are set *by society*.) This task is the 'manipulation of physical nature and of specific economic and social mechanisms', and it demands that data are 'given shape' in the form of 'an ordered set of hypotheses', i.e. in the form of 'traditional theory'. Theory, in the form of hypotheses that are to be empirically verified or falsified, is the shape of 'knowledge material' most appropriate for the 'task' of manipulating both nature and society, a process also known as 'production'. The 'technological advances of the bourgeois period' and its specific organization of science are inseparably linked to each other: science was (and remains) a crucial element of the former. Horkheimer emphasizes that 'the concept of theory' must not be 'absolutized, as though it were grounded in the inner nature of knowledge as such' lest it become 'a reified, ideological category'. It can 'be understood only in the context of real social processes'. Neither problems of logical consistency in a theory, nor contradictions between new facts or data and current theory *on their own*, lead to the restructuring of theoretical thinking. Although a scientist *as an individual* may be subjectively motivated only by factors immanent to his or her science, theoretical thinking is shaped by 'concrete historical circumstances'. Horkheimer points to the Copernican revolution as a historical example: Copernicus, who formulated the theory of heliocentrism in a book first published in 1543, *failed* to start a revolution in how humans saw the universe. His idea – for which he had found inspiration in classical literature – became part of such a revolution, though, when several other historical factors combined in the following century, only some of which have to do with science as such:

> In the seventeenth century ... men began to resolve the difficulties into which traditional astronomy had fallen, no longer by supplemental constructions but by adopting the Copernican system ... This change was not due to the logical properties alone of the Copernican theory, for example its greater simplicity. If these properties were seen as advantages, this very fact points beyond itself to the fundamental characteristics of societal practice at that time.

Even the fact that the heliocentric model of the universe subsumed all known data more easily and elegantly than its more complicated competitors, which is considered by theorists of science in the twentieth century a key characteristic of a good theory, only *became* such a characteristic through that same overall process: *society as a whole*, not just scientists, began to think of simplicity as a boon. Horkheimer adds that both sides of the 'traditional' concept of theory, the 'influence of the subject matter on the theory' as well as 'the application of the theory to the subject matter', take place *in society* (196).

1.3 Reflections on the relationship of theory and society in different philosophical traditions

Horkheimer mentions positivism and pragmatism as the philosophical traditions that most explicitly reflected on 'the connections between theoretical work and the social life-process' (196): they 'consider the prediction and usefulness of results to be a scientific task'. ('Pragmatism' is here the name of a philosophical school prevalent in the USA that emphasizes the social origin of knowledge and consciousness: the latter are determined by the *practical* relations that connect me to my fellow human beings.) This does not mean, however, that scientists necessarily or typically subscribe to positivist or pragmatist philosophical beliefs: their individual philosophical convictions rarely affect what they actually do. Horkheimer writes that the scholar

> may just as well believe in an independent, 'suprasocial', detached
> knowledge [like a rationalist or idealist] as in the social importance of
> his expertise [like a positivist or pragmatist]: such opposed interpreta
> tions do not influence his real activity in the slightest. The scholar and
> his science are incorporated into the apparatus of society; his achieve
> ments are a factor in the self-preservation and continuous reproduc
> tion of the existing state of affairs, no matter what fine names he gives
> to what he does. (196)

It is the task of the scholar 'to integrate facts into conceptual frameworks and to keep the latter up-to-date so that he himself and all who use them may be masters of the widest possible range of facts'.

'The dualism of thought and being, understanding and perception' (197) is his daily bread: *I theorist – you data.* The traditional concept of theory derives from scientific practice 'as carried on within the division of labor at a particular stage in the latter's development'. It corresponds to the fact that 'the activity of the scholar ... takes place alongside all the other activities of a society but in no immediately clear connection with them'. Because in the everyday reality of scholarly life 'the real social function of science' remains opaque, the concept of theory – theory's self-understanding – appears as an isolated sphere separate from other societal spheres. In this particular sense, it is true: the production of theory really *is* isolated (when looked at from within the institutional apparatus of science), although it is not, actually (when looked at from the perspective of society as a whole). In fact, the sciences 'are particular instances of the way in which society comes to grips with nature and maintains its own inherited form', which in Marxist terminology is called the 'mode of production'. Horkheimer concludes this step of the argument as follows:

> The seeming self-sufficiency enjoyed by work processes whose course is supposedly determined by the very nature of the object corresponds to the seeming freedom of the economic subjects in bourgeois society. The latter believe they are acting according to personal determinations, whereas in fact even in their most complicated calculations they but exemplify the working of an incalculable social mechanism. (197)

From here Horkheimer moves to a critique of the most influential philosophical tradition of the period, the one that also undergirded most of German and French classical sociological theory: the neo-Kantianism of the Marburg School. (Marburg is a German town in whose university this particular brand of idealist philosophy was developed. It is the exact opposite of pragmatism: neo-Kantians hold that reason exists somehow independent of 'praxis' and 'practical' social relations.) He states that this school expressed most clearly 'the false consciousness of the bourgeois scholar in the liberal era' (198). Horkheimer ridicules this philosophical school as a kind of intellectuals' fetishism of the intellect that brackets out any other aspect of social reality: these philosophers mistake the working patterns of scholarly specialists for the all-determining intrinsic structure of the world itself. Thinking is misapprehended as creating, and all creation appears to these philosophers as a form of thinking. All reality can ultimately be constructed out of the categories of the mind, or even out of mathematics as the latter's crowning achievement. In the minds of the neo-Kantians, science is not an element of the historical practice of humans, but it overcomes and replaces it: theory is superior to practice. Nevertheless, Horkheimer also makes one almost friendly comment on these colleagues of his: he writes that 'such a hypostatization of Logos as reality is also a camouflaged Utopia', because a society directed by 'Logos' – a Greek word that means 'reason' or 'reasonable discourse' – would actually be quite good to live in. A philosophy that gets over-enthusiastic about the idea of reason is surely preferable to one that turns *against* reason and celebrates irrationality, which was the predominant trend at the time Horkheimer was writing, the heyday of fascism. Not even liberal society, however, was a Garden of Eden of reason and humanity: it is still not today. Pretending to oneself and one's peers that existing society is already reasonable and humane does not in fact help the cause of reason. Here Horkheimer for the first time uses the term 'Critical Theory': what we need to develop now 'is not a mathematical science of nature which claims to be the eternal Logos, but a critical theory of the reality of society directed by a concern for reasonable conditions of life' (198–199). This implies that society *as it is now* is not reasonable, but it could *become* so.

1.4 Human practice in society, reason and modern society's irrationality

Horkheimer moves from this first determination of 'Critical Theory' to a reflection on the relationship between facts and theory, or reality and thinking. He begins with the exhortation that analysis of partial processes of the social world must be done with 'concrete awareness of its own limitations' (199): when we look at reality, we look at specific *parts* of it – the whole of reality is too big to look at all at once. The important point is that we must be conscious of the fact that this is what we do, and then try to overcome the one-sided analysis of isolated aspects of reality. The traditional idea that we confront facts with the 'conceptual ordering of facts', aka 'theory', is a starting point for this:

> The whole perceptible world as present to a member of bourgeois society and as interpreted within a traditional world-view ... is seen by the perceiver as a sum-total of facts; it is there and must be accepted. The classificatory thinking ... is one of those social reactions by which [individual] men try to adapt to reality in a way that best meets their needs. (199)

However, the 'traditional' concept of theory as a set of hypotheses that need to be verified by facts grants *things-as-they-are* ultimate authority over their 'conceptual ordering' by thinking humans: *thought has to adapt to facticity*, not the other way round. Horkheimer grants that this perspective has some validity for the individual: as an individual I had better accept the authority of *things-as-they-are* or else I will not survive for long. 'But there is at this point an essential difference between the individual and society': the world as it is, which we inhabit, is also 'a product of the activity of society as a whole' (200):

> The objects we perceive in our surroundings – cities, villages, fields, and woods – bear the mark of having been worked on by man. It is not only in clothing and appearance, in outward form and emotional make-up that men are the product of history. Even the way they see and hear is inseparable from the social life-process as it has evolved over the millennia. The facts which our senses present to us are socially preformed in two ways: through the historical character of the object perceived and through the historical character of the perceiving organ. Both are not simply natural; they are shaped by human activity, and yet the individual perceives himself as receptive and passive in the act of perception.

The world only appears as objective in the very partial perspective taken naively by the individual. It can be overcome by reflection on the individual's authorship of the world, as well as the individual's being part of that world. Traditional theory suggests that sense perceptions are passive and given (the famous 'data', which is Latin for 'givens') whereas theory (i.e. ordering, conceptual thinking) is active. This notion may be true, to an extent, for the individual, but we can recognize it as false when we look at it under the aspect of society: 'The opposition of passivity and activity ... does not hold for society ... in the same measure as for the individual.' The individual experiences him- or herself 'as passive and dependent' and experiences society as 'an active subject' (although a subject that does not have consciousness and is therefore 'a subject only in an improper sense'). It is important to note that Horkheimer, unlike theorists like Weber or Simmel who subscribe to 'methodological individualism', accepts that the individual is in fact passive – *as individual*. The point is, however, that humans do not actually exist as individuals but *as members of society*. As members of society we are active, ever creating our world, albeit not consciously so: we do it unreflectingly, without conscious and explicit deliberation, without planning and critical discourse, behind our own backs, as it were:

> This difference in the existence of man and society is an expression of the cleavage which has up to now affected the historical forms of social life. The existence of society has either been founded directly on oppression or been the blind outcome of conflicting forces, but in any event not the result of conscious spontaneity on the part of free individuals.

(The word 'spontaneity' comes from Latin *spons*, which means 'will' or 'intentionality': I act spontaneously when I act deliberately, on my own will.) When Horkheimer calls existing society 'a subject only in an improper sense' he implies that society could, or perhaps should, become a 'proper' subject that *consciously* and *deliberately* creates a reasonable world. This is in tune with his acknowledgement earlier in the text that the neo-Kantians' notion of a world directed by reason is quite wrong as a description of existing reality but quite right *as a utopian idea*.

In the next paragraph Horkheimer makes yet another qualified nod towards the neo-Kantians: he writes that '[h]uman production also always has an element of planning to it' (200), and insofar as facts or data are products of human action in society, they must contain some (limited) element of reason. Even before being subjected to conceptual ordering, the 'data' are already partially shaped by human concepts: humans *made* the landscape of the Lake District which we somewhat misleadingly refer to as 'nature'. To the extent that this landscape is the product of human, purposeful, deliberate action, it contains elements of human reasoning which it reflects back to us when we look at it. This is what Horkheimer means when he writes that 'facts' are mediated by societal practice, at least to an extent. Secondly, their *perception* is also mediated by human practice: our senses perceive some things but filter out others, they divide and combine data. The way they do so is determined by society as much as by human physiology. Even human physiology itself is worked on and influenced by society: 'the proposition that tools are prolongations of human organs can be inverted to state that the organs are also prolongations of the tools' (201). Our bodies are changed by the machines we use – we adapt our bodies to the machines that we have created. In modern everyday life it is increasingly impossible to distinguish between what is nature and what is civilization, within ourselves, in the things around us and even in the wild and exotic places we visit on gap years and adventure holidays: even when we experience 'natural objects as such', actual nature not already transformed by human civilization, our perception of 'their very naturalness is determined by contrast with the social world and, to that extent, depends upon the latter' (201–202): we would not have a concept of 'wilderness' if we did not first have a concept of civilization; we can think about a (supposed) *outside* of society only from *within* it.

Horkheimer dwells in the following on the point that 'the power of ... common sense', the indeed quite astonishing fact that so many members of society agree on so many things, is 'conditioned by the fact that the world of objects to be judged is in large measure produced by an activity that is itself determined by the very ideas which help the individual to recognize that world and to grasp it conceptually' (202): the same humans *make* the (social) world as *think* about it, and they go about the making and the thinking with the same conceptual tools. It is therefore no miracle that our thinking and the structures of the world – insofar as it has been shaped by humans – correspond quite nicely. Horkheimer argues that the philosopher Immanuel Kant (1724–1804) reflected on this same point in his *Critique of Pure Reason* of 1781, a key text of the Enlightenment. Kant discusses the question of how reason can be confident that it will always be able to subsume the infinity of all kinds of sense data under its own categories and concepts. Kant's is a more abstract, philosophical version of the same problem that sociological theory later came to ask: how can conceptual thinking – theory – be so confident, or perhaps arrogant, as to assume it is always able to order, subsume and make sense of all those facts and data? Kant's answer is: because the reasoning subject has *shaped* the sense data in the first place. At the point when those sense data arrive in the mind ready to be theorized, they are already half-cooked – no really raw data ever arrive in the human mind. The problem that reason might lack the appropriate categories with which to order the data does not arise, as the wrong kind of data, incomprehensible data, never arrive in the first place – we simply do not perceive them. In this sense, we humans *make* the data, and this warrants that we are able to *interpret* them, too. Affinity between reason and facts is guaranteed because we are programmed to ignore sense data that do not fit our reasoning. Horkheimer's quite provocative argument here is that Kant's proposition reflects a state of things – modern society – where most if not all the sense data that any individual will ever perceive are shaped by society: any perception and any experience we individuals make is *already pre-formatted by society*, i.e. by us humans collectively. Horkheimer thus translates Kant's philosophical argument into a sociological one. Either version of the argument, the original philosophical one or the sociological one, *undermines* the 'traditional' distinction between 'passive perceptions' and 'active mind', and indeed between 'facts' and 'theories'. Horkheimer reflects on the difference between Kant's original argument and his own creative reinterpretation when he writes in the following paragraph: 'In accordance with the theoretical vision available in his day, [Kant] does not see reality as a product of society's work' but instead 'imagines the supra-individual activity, of which the individual is unaware, only in the idealist form of a consciousness-in-itself, that is a purely intellectual source' (203). In other words, Horkheimer suggests that whenever the idealist philosopher talks about 'consciousness' (or else, 'spirit'), he *really* talks about *society* and the totality of activities in society, albeit without knowing it. If it is read in this way, idealist 'philosophy of consciousness' was secretly a form of sociology all along. Kant represents 'the activity of society' as 'a transcendental power, that is, the sum-total of spiritual factors'. In spite of his own rationalist outlook and method, Kant used in this context sometimes theological, almost mystical language, emphasizing the obscure, incomprehensible, mysterious aspect of that 'transcendental power', the human mind (or 'spirit'). Again translating 'mind' (or 'spirit') as 'society', Horkheimer suggests that Kant's account of the irrational aspect of human reasoning points to the irrationality of modern society's particular kind of rationality:

> The bourgeois type of economy, despite all the ingenuity of the competing individuals within it, is not governed by any plan; it is not consciously directed to a general goal; the life of society as a whole proceeds from this economy only at the cost of excessive friction, in a stunted form, and almost, as it were, accidentally. (203)

Horkheimer praises at this point 'the depth and honesty' of Kant's thinking. At the time, only the very first beginnings of the theory of modern society existed in the writings of Adam Smith and some others, mostly in Britain – after all, modern society itself was only in its infancy, and Kant was a keen reader of the newest literature coming from overseas. Horkheimer implies here that Kant expressed a crucial aspect of modern society without mentioning society at all. He only wrote very profoundly and honestly about his own subject matter, the philosophy of consciousness, in which he was totally immersed. The idea behind Horkheimer's appreciation of Kant is that a philosopher, or likewise an artist, composer or writer, can *unintentionally* say something important about society simply by doing his or her thing at the highest level attainable: in fact it is as if *society itself* speaks through the work of that philosopher or artist as soon as they work at the highest intensity on whatever it is that they do. *In and through the work of the philosopher or artist, society speaks to itself about itself.* We only need to learn how to read against the grain! This is in fact one of the most important methodological aspects of the tradition of the Critical Theory of the 'Frankfurt School' that Horkheimer, as it were, inaugurated with this essay.

'[B]ehind the discrepancy between fact and theory ... lies a deeper unity, namely, the ... activity of society' as a whole which produces *both* facts and theories at the same time. 'The collaboration of human beings in society is the mode of existence of human reason': this somewhat obscure sentence (which is mistranslated in the available translation, on top of page 204) rejects the idea that reason is some kind of a mystical substance that sits in the brains or souls of *individual* human beings. Instead, Horkheimer suggests in this sentence that society and reason are substantially the same thing, or, to be more precise, that *society is how reason actually exists*, however unreasonable it may in fact be. Horkheimer adapts this idea from Georg Wilhelm Friedrich Hegel (1770–1831), the last of the major philosophers of the Enlightenment and the principal philosophical influence on Karl Marx. (Hegel is briefly name-checked in the next paragraph.) The idea here is that no human being in isolation can have reason: reason emerges in the interaction, communication and collaboration of humans in society. This idea is illustrated by various popular 'Kaspar Hauser'-type stories about feral children, but it is also quite similar, for example, to Durkheim's position on the societal origin of morality.

The problem of this position, both in Hegel and in Durkheim, however, is that it cannot explain the fact that human reason sometimes *objects* to the reality of society (although both were, of course, aware that it does…). This is in fact one of the key questions of Critical Theory: what kind of theory could account for *opposition* to society? The short answer is that neither society nor reason speak with one tongue but are contradictory and fragmented, and this is what Horkheimer hints at in the sentence following the one just quoted. He writes that

> at the same time their work and its results are alienated from [people], and the whole process with all its waste of labour power and human life, and with its wars and all its senseless wretchedness, appears to them as an unchangeable force of nature, a fate beyond man's control. (204)

The societal process that produces reason is not, for that matter, all that reasonable, as it creates the rather messy condition of society as it exists. Horkheimer adds in passing that Hegel failed to fully appreciate the contradictory character of society – although he was aware of it, to an extent – and ended up by simply, undialectically equating reason and society. To sum up this part of the argument: the Critical Theory proposed by Horkheimer aims to take on board the Hegelian translation of Kant's concept of a mysterious, non-empirical something that underlies and connects the minds of individual humans (which Kant called 'transcendental subjectivity') into the concept of reason's grounding in history and society, without, however, jumping to the conclusion that society was therefore all reasonable and hunky dory. This elusive 'thing' that makes possible cognition and communication in society and that goes by the name of 'reason' turns from a 'transcendental' to an ever more *social thing*, and in the process reveals itself to be not so entirely reasonable

2.1 Critical activity and Critical Theory

Horkheimer moves away now from the more philosophical discussion of 'traditional theory' and in the remaining two-thirds of the article develops the concept of 'Critical Theory', mostly out of an analysis of contemporary society. He begins by saying that 'society is divided into groups and classes', and that theories are related to society differently 'according as they belong to one or other social class' (204). It is important here to point out that the English translator changed 'as they belong' to 'as the authors [of the theories] belong' which obscures an important aspect of Horkheimer's approach: the issue is not to which class *the authors* of a theoretical text belong but which social class the theories *themselves* belong: what matters is the content of the *idea*, how the idea itself corresponds to particular characteristics of a class, not who holds it or who came up with it. In other words, it is quite possible that some workers hold some rather bourgeois ideas, and some bourgeois (Marx, Engels, Horkheimer) might well hold some proletarian ideas.

Horkheimer argues that the 'purely scientific theory' that arose with the bourgeoisie in its struggle against feudalism became the prevailing ideology in the age of liberalism, and today – i.e. the 1930s – it has lost its predominance: 'In so far as theoretical thought is not related to highly specialized purposes ... interest in theory has waned. Less energy is being expended on forming and developing the capacity of thought without regard to how it is to be applied' (205). Horkheimer thinks science and theory *also in their traditional forms* are to be defended against their anti-liberal, irrationalist detractors: 'Like a material instrument of production, it represents potentially an element not only of the contemporary cultural totality but of a more just, more differentiated, more harmoniously organized one as well.' Conservative and fascist attacks on the liberal, science-oriented culture that had emerged in the nineteenth century aimed to destroy with the present also the potential seeds of a better future society.

This is the point at which Horkheimer finally turns directly to the development of the concept of Critical Theory: 'We must go on now to add that there is a human activity which has society itself for its object' (206). He explains that 'this activity is called "critical" activity', whereby the word 'critical' refers to 'the dialectical critique of political economy' (206). This is, of course, a code-word for Marxian theory.

> The aim of this activity is not simply to eliminate one or other abuse, for it regards such abuses as necessarily connected with the way in which the social structure is organized. Although it itself emerges from the social structure, its purpose is not ... the better functioning of any element in the structure. On the contrary, it is suspicious of the very categories of 'better', 'useful', 'appropriate', 'productive', and 'valuable', as these are understood in the present order ... [T]he critical attitude of which we are speaking is wholly distrustful of the rules of conduct with which society as presently constituted provides each of its members. The separation between individual and society in virtue of which the individual accepts as natural the limits prescribed for his activity is relativized in Critical Theory. (206–207)

Horkheimer next describes what he calls 'the critical attitude'. (The German word used here by Horkheimer also means 'behaviour' or 'practice'.) The 'critical attitude' translates the 'ambiguous character of the social totality in its present form' into 'a conscious contradiction'. Those adopting the 'critical attitude' recognize that 'the present form of economy and ... culture' is the form of organization 'which mankind ... has provided for itself in the present era' – it has not come from somewhere else. No one else can be blamed for it: 'It is their own world.' At the same time, however, they understand that a society that 'resembles nonhuman natural processes, pure mechanisms ... supported by war and oppression' is not the creation of 'a unified, self-conscious will'. This 'is not their own but the world of capital' (207–208).

The critical actors described by Horkheimer recognize the social world as *their-own-but-not-their-own*. They do not condemn it as if from outside: they know that *they* have constituted this world. They have made it, though, in a way that is not theirs. This is the contradiction central to critical practice and Critical Theory, and it is for this reason that 'the critical acceptance of the categories which rule social life contains simultaneously their condemnation' (208). 'Reason cannot become transparent to itself as long as men act as members of an organism which lacks reason.' Horkheimer adds here that comparing society to an 'organism' is in itself an indictment of society: an organism is something that naturally develops and declines; it cannot *decide to do otherwise*. Society is only 'organic' as long as it 'lacks reason', i.e. self-determination, and thus is not yet a truly *human* society. This critique of the word 'organism' is directed by Horkheimer against the conservative tendencies of writers at the time, who liked to speak of society as an organism, i.e. something natural and not subject to reasoned and deliberate change. Horkheimer writes that 'society must emancipate itself' from being an organism, not celebrate the fact that it is one.

2.2 Beyond the dichotomy of facts and thoughts

Unlike 'sociology of knowledge', Critical Theory does not reduce theory's reflection on itself – the theorizing of theory – to merely describing how intellectual positions are related to their social locations (209). 'Sociology of knowledge' (as conceived by the sociologist Karl Mannheim [1893–1947]) leaves intact the authority of the factual over the intellectual, as it merely maps out how factuality's authority translates into thought: thought is true only if it is in line with facts. Critical Theory, by contrast, looks 'towards a new kind of organization of work': insofar as social facts 'are conceived as products [of human activity] which in principle should be under human control and, in the future at least, are expected in fact to come under it, these realities lose the character of pure factuality'. Horkheimer's argument goes like this:

- in contemporary society, social facts increasingly subsume most non-social facts;
- social facts are constituted by human practice;

- social practice always contains elements of human projection and rationality;
- therefore the dichotomy between fact and thought is diminished,
- so that thinking that is concerned with how to change the facts becomes a fact that is an increasingly central concern of thinking.

In this situation, the attitude of 'traditional theory' that strives to maintain the separation of fact and thought becomes increasingly anachronistic: 'The scholarly specialist "as" scientist regards social reality and its products as extrinsic to him, and "as" citizen exercises his interest in them through political articles, membership in political parties or charity organizations, and participation in elections' (209). Horkheimer rejects this neat separation between scholarship and engagement:

> Critical thinking, on the contrary, is motivated today by the effort really to transcend the tension and to abolish the opposition between the individual's purposefulness, spontaneity, and rationality, and those relationships of the labour-process on which society is built. Critical thinking has a concept of man as in conflict with himself until this opposition is removed. If activity governed by reason is proper to man, then existent social practice, which forms the individual's life down to its least details, is inhuman, and this inhumanity affects everything that goes on in the society. (210)

There will always be nature in the sense of 'something that is extrinsic to man's intellectual and material activity'. No social fact, though, is factual in the sense that non-human nature is, and treating social things as if they were external facts 'is a sign of contemptible weakness. To surrender to such weakness is nonhuman and irrational' (210). Horkheimer also indicates here that those who speak about the 'nature of society' in order to claim that some things never change are doubly wrong, as not even external nature is eternal and unchanging.

2.3 Beyond the dichotomy of bourgeois individualism and nationalist communitarianism

Horkheimer defines 'bourgeois thinking' – a term closely related to 'liberalism' and 'traditional theory' – as individualist: the bourgeois subject is programmed to look at him- or herself by necessity as an autonomous 'I', abstracted from its societal and historical contexts and somewhat arrogantly believing 'itself to be the ground of the world or even to be the world' (210). This last point in particular seems to be an attack on the position of extreme idealism represented by the philosopher Johann Gottlieb Fichte (1762–1814) who doubted whether a world outside our minds exists at all. Fichte's idealism pushed to its extreme limit the Kantian notion that all we know about the world is constructed inside our minds, and that we 'create' it in this sense – albeit, importantly, Kant did not mean to say that there is no outside world at all: in all probability there is one, only we cannot say much about it as our very own human minds format and hammer into shape for consumption all data stemming from (presumed) reality.

Horkheimer continues that 'the direct contrary' of the bourgeois-individualist outlook is 'the attitude which holds the individual to be the un-problematic expression of an already constituted community; an example would be the ideology of the national folk-community' (210). Given that in a class society no such community exists, this thinking is as illusory as the bourgeois hypostatization of the individual. Horkheimer rejects both the individualist and the communitarian-nationalist position:

> Critical thought and its theory are opposed to both the types of thinking just described. Critical thinking is the function neither of the isolated individual nor of a sum-total of individuals. Its subject is rather a definite individual in his [or her] real relations to other individuals and groups, in his [or her] conflict with a particular class, and, finally, in the resultant web of relationships with the social totality and with nature. The subject is no mathematical point like the *ego* of bourgeois philosophy; his [or her] activity is the construction of the social present. (210–211)

Closely following the Marxian conception, Horkheimer proposes here a kind of non-bourgeois, or perhaps a *non-individualist individualism*. The person, or 'subject', conducting 'critical practice' and 'critical theory' applies also a methodology that differs from that of 'traditional theory' where the thinking subject (the '*I think*' of Cartesian rationalism) is sundered from all its objects. In the critical methodology, practice and thought remain connected:

> [I]n genuinely critical thought explanation signifies not only a logical
> process but a concrete historical one as well. In the course of it both
> the social structure as a whole and the relation of the theoretician to
> society are altered, that is both the subject and the role of thought are
> changed. (211)

This conception is radically different from Comtean positivism in
particular, which presupposes a group of *savants* (wise men and top
specialists) who collect all the knowledge, condense it into theory
and then derive from it blueprints for everybody else to set into
practice – still now more or less the practice of most 'administrative'
or policy research.

The practice of the theorist can be represented in a simple formula: '*I – theorize – social relations*' (subject – predicate – object).
From the Critical Theory perspective, we can say two things:

- first, subject and object are not entirely different entities, as the
  'I' is constituted by – albeit not identical to – its presumed object,
  'social relations';
- second, the point of the predicate, 'research', is to *change* both
  subject and object. If they do not change, then the research was
  probably a waste of time.

3.1 The role of the historical experience of exploitation for Critical Theory

Sudden changes in the direction of the argument are characteristic of
the style of presentation of Critical Theory: its authors often explore
one line of argument up to a point, then a contrary one, in order to
exhaust whatever validity can be found in either. Having rejected
in the previous sections the positivist notion of facticity, employing
concepts mainly from the idealist strand of Enlightenment philosophy such as Kant's, Horkheimer changes tack in the following
and expresses what might seem more like an empiricist concern
with the experience of reality. He rejects here self-sufficient, idealist reliance on human subjectivity. Horkheimer begins this section
with a principal objection to one-sided philosophical subjectivism:
were critical thinking to determine its own goals and direction out
of itself, 'it would remain locked up within itself' (211); it would

either be self-referential and, as it were, autistic, or it would need to take refuge in utopianism. As opposed to this, Horkheimer implies that Critical Theory needs to derive its legitimacy from experience, without, however, adopting the empiricist belief in the objectivity of the reality that is being experienced. He develops this conception of the relationship between thought and experience through a historical argument: he writes that 'the power of thought' – the German words used by Horkheimer actually mean 'the activity of the imagination' – throughout human history has always functioned as a 'moment in the work process' (212), whose basic orientation it is to enhance and develop human life. Throughout history, 'however, the full measure of goods produced for man's enjoyment has, at any particular stage, been given directly only to a small group of men'. This fact has influenced and is reflected in the cultural traditions of humanity. But also 'the desire to bring the same enjoyment to the majority' has always 'stirred in the depths of men's hearts' to the extent that '[s]laves, vassals, and citizens have cast off their yokes'. This, too, 'has found expression in cultural creations'. Contradictory historical experiences have produced contradictory cultural resources that are there to be be taken up.

Horkheimer points here to a specific characteristic of modern society that provides him with the basis for the possibility for critical thinking to spread, namely the high degree of integration of modern society: 'every individual in modern times is required to adopt the purposes of the totality as his own and to recognize his own in the former', i.e. we have to identify ourselves as individuals with society. In this process we are forced to reflect on society much more than members of a less integrated form of society would need to. Therefore 'there is the possibility that men would become aware of and concentrate their attention upon what path has been taken by the societal labour process hitherto'. Thought can thus become 'aware of its own function': 'In the course of history men come to understand their own activity and thus to recognize the contradiction that marks their existence' (212). The process of reflection on history and society produces the purposes of the 'critical attitude' – theory and praxis. Horkheimer is saying that goals, purposes, ideas, values develop gradually out of sustained reflection on the historical experience of a very specific 'fact', namely that of the contradictory nature of human action in society: humans have produced through-out history increasing wealth and *potential* happiness, but they have done so in a way that has *actually* produced increasing inequality. Humans become aware of this when they reflect on it, and it is modern society that *forces* them to reflect: whereas in pre-modern forms of society people and groups of people were left more or less alone living over long periods of time according to their particular beliefs and ideologies – as long as they paid their tributes and ser-vices to this or that overlord – in modern, capitalist, bourgeois soci-ety these particular groups have been dissolved and all individuals are forced to adopt uniform, national and supra-national ideologies. Modern society forces us to reflect on who and what we are, which, in an ironic sort of way, is for society's rulers a risky business: in the process of doing the required thinking and educating ourselves, we might well become aware of the contradictions within what we are expected to embrace. Here Horkheimer sees the historical ground-ing of the possibility of critique.

After this relatively optimistic step in the argument, the tone changes again in the next paragraph: the *possibility* of critique comes without guarantee. What Critical Theory 'derives from historical analysis as the goals of human activity, especially the idea of a rea-sonable organization of society that will meet the needs of all, are immanent in human work but are not correctly grasped by indi-viduals or by the common mind' (213). By 'reasonable organization of society' he seems to mean a kind of democratic, inclusive, non-hierarchical form of socialism. It is, as a goal, 'immanent in work': this means that in all human activities that help to reproduce and maintain society – i.e. work – the idea of socialism is already given, as long as other factors – power, exploitation, hierarchy – do not mess around with it. We only need to discover it there, and here's the rub:

> A certain concern is also required if these tendencies are to be per-ceived and expressed. According to Marx and Engels such a concern is necessarily generated in the proletariat. Because of its situation in modern society the proletariat experiences the connection between work which puts ever more powerful instruments into men's hands in their struggle with nature, and the continuous renewal of an outmoded social organization.

Horkheimer introduces here another key concept in Critical Theory's conception of how we produce knowledge: 'a certain concern' is needed (a more literal translation would be 'a certain directedness of interests'). He uses the next half page to sum up what was at the time the conventional Marxist notion of the inevitably revolutionary nature of the proletariat: chiefly, the argument is that proletarians are familiar with the production processes and know that the means of production – science, technology, machinery – allow wealth for all, whereas poverty and misery result from the way society is organized. The obvious conclusion must be to organize society in a reasonable manner so that all have the benefit of humanity's immense wealth and knowledge. So what is the problem? This question is forced upon a non-aligned Marxist like Horkheimer by the experience of the failure of all attempts at proletarian revolution at the end of the First World War, and the subsequent triumph of Stalinism and fascism. Here Horkheimer formulates a critique of contemporary Marxist orthodoxy:

> But it must be added that even the situation of the proletariat is, in this society, no guarantee of correct knowledge. The proletariat may indeed have experience of meaninglessness in the form of continuing and increasing wretchedness and injustice in its own life. Yet this awareness is prevented from becoming a social force by the differentiation of its social structure which is reinforced from above and by the opposition between personal and class interest which is transcended only at very special moments. (213–214)

In other words, 'the proletariat' is not a unified subject in the first place, except in 'very special moments' – Horkheimer means first of all revolutionary moments – when stratification and 'personal interest' are cancelled out. Apart from that, shared experience does not automatically translate into 'social force'.

In the next step of his argument, Horkheimer attacks left-wing intellectuals who fetishize the proletariat, saying that these intellectuals remain stuck in 'traditional theory':

> The intellectual, who proclaims and reveres the creative power of the proletariat and finds satisfaction in adapting himself to it, in celebrating [the proletariat] fails to see that such avoidance of theoretical effort ... and of temporary opposition to the masses – which his own

independent thinking might force upon him – only makes the masses blinder and weaker than they need be. The intellectual's independent thinking is in fact a critical, forward-driving factor in their development. Wholly subordinating himself to the present psychological state of that class which, objectively considered, embodies the power to change society, affords him the happy feeling of being linked with an immense force and a professional optimism. When this optimism is shattered in periods of crushing defeat, many intellectuals risk falling into a pessimism about society and a nihilism which are just as ungrounded as their exaggerated optimism had been. They cannot bear the thought that the most advanced thinking that has the deepest grasp of the historical situation, and is most pregnant with the future, must at certain times isolate its subject and throw him back upon himself. These intellectuals have forgotten the connection between revolution and autonomy. If Critical Theory consisted essentially in formulating the feelings and ideas of one class at any given moment, it would just be another specialized branch of academic scholarship. It would be ... social psychology. (214)

One can hear in these lines the disappointment and anger Horkheimer must have felt about those of his contemporaries who reacted to the double defeat of the labour movement by Stalinism and fascism either with stubborn but uncritical celebration of a demoralized and disoriented movement, or by jumping ship altogether. The Critical Theory that Horkheimer postulates here should not be concerned merely with 'a systematic presentation of the contents of proletarian consciousness' or even its 'more advanced' sections (215). Rather, theory should be 'forming a dynamic unity with the oppressed class, so that [its] presentation of societal contradictions is not merely an expression of the concrete historical situation but also a force within it to stimulate change'. This 'dynamic unity' needs its conflicts and debates because only in 'a process of interactions' can consciousness develop 'its liberating along with its stirring, disciplining and aggressive forces'. This sentence in particular shows quite clearly that for Horkheimer a good theoretical debate was – at this point in time – not so much a polite affair in a lecture room but rather a moment in a historical process that ought to lead to enthusiastic, determined and indeed 'aggressive' proletarian revolution. This process is not served by telling people what they want to hear or what they already believe – it needs uncompromising commitment to critical historical analysis:

> The sharpness of the conflict shows itself in the ever present possibil-
> ity of tension between the theoretician and the class which his [or her]
> thinking is to serve. The unity of the social forces which promise lib-
> eration is at the same time their distinction (in Hegel's sense); it exists
> only as a conflict which continually threatens the subjects caught up
> in it. (215–216)

Horkheimer plays here on the Hegelian idea that the concept
of 'unity' only makes sense when it contains 'distinctions' and
differences – a unity that is made up of identical things is not a
unity but simply an identity. Powerful political or social unity must
accordingly be based on robust differences, i.e. *conflicts within the
unity*. Without honest and fierce conflicts, there can be no honest
and powerful unity. The required fierceness means that conflict
'continually threatens the subjects': the subjects will change in the
conflict that creates unity, their initial identities will be challenged,
and they will come out of it as renewed, reinvigorated, differently
different subjects. For the proletariat to become revolutionary, it
needs input from theorists who formulate unflinching critique, not
ideological yes-men who try to flatter it. Critical theorists are not,
though, conceived – as in Comtean positivism – as the wise men or
high priests of science who direct and educate the masses, but as a
non-identical element in a dynamic unity that changes the theorists –
of whatever class background – as much as their interlocutors.

3.2 Critical Theory lacks incremental, observable successes in the existing society

Whereas 'traditional theory' takes for granted its own 'positive
role in a functioning society' (216), Critical Theory 'does not labor
in the service of an existing reality but only spells out its secret'
(217). Therefore, its goals 'are not sanctioned by common sense or
custom'. 'Common sense' – which is also the starting point of most
scholarly analysis – relates to the visible patterns, structures and
logic of society, whereas the point of critique is to 'spell out' the not
so obvious ones. This means, of course, that it is likely to be rejected
by those who remain wedded to 'common sense'.

Horkheimer pays an unusual compliment here, though: he writes
that all 'traditional theory' somehow, however indirectly, contrib-

utes to some form of future consumption, even when, as in the case of theoretical physics, this consumption 'consists only in a joyous and virtuous playing with mathematical symbols'; and he adds that in allowing such joyous research to take place by funding it, 'high society shows a trace of its humaneness' (217). More, better and more egalitarian consumption (in the sense of material wealth) is also part of the programme of Critical Theory, but it is interesting to note that Horkheimer includes here the 'consumption' of theoretical physics as some kind of art form – and doffs his cap in the direction of the educated bourgeoisie who cultivate such exquisite pleasures as theoretical mathematics on behalf of the rest of us. The implication is, of course, that one day we should all have some of that.

Critical Theory aims to produce the future as 'a community of free human beings' of which the present does not provide any examples. There are, however, actual tendencies in social reality that drive towards this future form of society – as discussed above. Whereas traditional theory might well be happy to study these tendencies as an object of research, Critical Theory, so Horkheimer asserts, does not treat these 'tendencies' as a form of 'facticity' that is external to the activity of the theorist; rather, 'the same subject who wants these tendencies, the better state of things, to come to pass, also embodies them' (217). Critical Theory sees itself as part of those 'tendencies'. More generally, 'the community of those engaged in the struggle … experiences something of the freedom and spontaneity which will mark the future' – which is not entirely different from the fun the aforementioned theoretical physicists have with their mathematical formulas. When the movement allows 'its own bureaucracy' to destroy the difficult 'unity of discipline and spontaneity', it stops being a force for that future state of things.

When Horkheimer rejects with these remarks the idea that a revolutionary organization could take the form of the hierarchical, bureaucratic party or trade union, he also rejects any idea of gradualism: 'Above all, however, Critical Theory has no material accomplishments to show for itself. The change which it seeks to bring about is not effected gradually' (218–219): unlike the case of traditional theory and research, it does not produce that slow but steady and measureable progress. Its only success would be the leap into the liberated society. Until then, 'the first consequence of the theory which urges a transformation of society as a whole is only an intensification of the struggle with which the theory is connected' (219). There are groups in society that manage to improve their material condition with the help of the theory, but Horkheimer rejects the idea that the gradual spreading of these groups 'would finally bring the new society to pass'; although it can only be brought about by actual tendencies in present society, it is impossible to know in advance which ones will be decisive. Against the notion that a social science of revolutionary change would be able to make predictions and lead to a scientifically warranted strategy, Horkheimer asserts the necessity of the 'obstinacy of fantasy', or of the imagination (220). The critical theorist who practises the 'obstinacy of fantasy' has to be prepared to be treated at times as 'an enemy and criminal, at times a solitary Utopian', as 'the historical significance of his work is not self-evident': 'If the proof of the pudding is in the eating, the eating here is still in the future' (220–221).

3.3 The role of intellectuals

'Engels was a businessman', observes Horkheimer, who was the son of an industrialist himself (221). Engels's class position, the source of his income, was neither of relevance to the contribution to theory that he made, nor to whether, where or when any workers embraced it. What mattered was 'the concrete content of his theory'. Horkheimer mocks 'professional sociology' for having created a concept of a class that depends on its constituents' level of education: the notion of 'the intelligentsia'. Horkheimer, who as a young man had gained practical work experience in his father's textile factory and did not come from the 'educated bourgeoisie', seems amused by the way academics speak about themselves and their like as if they constituted a special class of their own: 'the intelligentsia' defines itself by its 'possibility of a wider vision'. Horkheimer mocks the fact that sociologists do not mean 'the kind [of vision] possessed by industrial magnates who know the world market and direct whole states from behind the scenes', but rather 'the kind [of vision] possessed by university professors, middle-level civil servants, doctors, lawyers, and so forth' (221). Sociologists elevate the latter – of whom Horkheimer does not seem to think very highly – to being 'a special social or even suprasocial stratum' whose 'essential mark' is 'detachment from all classes', a 'sign of superiority of which it is proud' (222). Horkheimer implies that industrialists tend to be much better informed and have more 'intelligence', if that means understanding the ins and outs of how modern society actually works; the concept of a class of intellectuals is self-serving hyperbole.

Horkheimer writes that the discipline of sociology reflects the way the liberal bourgeois 'consume' knowledge: as an *instrument*, something that is at least potentially useful. He illustrates this point with a quote from Max Weber's famous lecture 'Science as a Vocation', in which Weber suggests that social scientists ought to advise a politician 'to use "such and such a means" when he takes "such and such a stand"' and 'whether the practical position he adopts can be implemented with logical consistency' (222). Horkheimer challenges 'the formalistic concept of mind which underlies such an idea of the intelligentsia' as politically neutral service providers – consultants, as they are known today. Against a purely formal, instrumental concept of truth, he asserts that 'there is only one truth': his point is that the concept of 'truth' points to 'the positive attributes of honesty, internal consistency, reasonableness, and striving for peace, freedom, and happiness' which are not to be found in just any kind of social theory or practice. All social theories 'contain political motivations, and the truth of these must be decided not in supposedly neutral reflection but in personal thought and action, in concrete historical activity'. To be fair to Weber, it should be noted that he would probably not disagree with Horkheimer on this last point: Weber, who was politically a nationalist liberal, also argued that decisions on what is and what is not 'truth' are political decisions that cannot be delegated to academic specialists: they have to be decided in the arena of historical-societal struggles. The difference between their positions would be that Horkheimer places science and theory within this arena, as a conflicting element of those struggles, not outside it.

Against the 'formal concept of the mind', or of 'spirit' (he uses here the notoriously untranslatable German word *Geist*), Horkheimer asserts a substantive, content-filled, full-flavoured concept: 'The mind is liberal. It tolerates no external coercion, no revamping of its results to suit the will of one or other power' (223). On the other hand, 'the mind' is 'not liberal': it is not 'cut loose from the life of society; it does not hang suspended over it'. Only because 'the mind' has an interest in autonomy and emancipation is it able to recognize their traces in history, and only through struggle can what 'the mind' discovers become relevant. The use of the word *Geist*/mind/spirit resonates here with its various meanings in particular in Hegel's philosophy, and in phrases such as 'world spirit' or 'spirit of the time': these are shorthand for some underlying tendency in the collective striving of humanity towards – humanity. Horkheimer concludes: 'Critical theory is neither "deeply rooted" like totalitarian propaganda nor "detached" like the liberalist intelligentsia' (223–224).

3.4 The role of abstractions in Critical Theory

Here follows an eight-page section in which Horkheimer revisits some aspects of the logical structure of 'traditional theory' and 'critical theory', respectively; most of this restates in more technical terminology things already addressed in similar form, and will be summarized here only briefly. Horkheimer asserts that both traditional and Critical Theory begin their respective analyses with general, or universal, concepts (224). In Critical Theory these include commodity, value and money. Unlike traditional theory, though, Critical Theory 'is not satisfied merely to relate concepts to reality by way of hypotheses' (225): 'The relation of the primary concepts to the world of facts is not essentially one of classes to instances', which means that simply subsuming various 'instances' of commodity relationships under the general concept of 'the commodity' would not satisfy Critical Theory. Rather than conceptual deductions, Critical Theory needs to develop rich, concrete determinations to relate concepts and realities (226–227). Furthermore, the critical theorist considers theoretical and practical critique (of society) itself as *integral to* the historical process that constitutes the object of the theory (society): the *diagnosis* of a social fact such as 'the determination of society by an economic mechanism' necessarily involves therefore the *protest against* such a mechanical order because it violates the human drive to self-determination (229).

4.1 The hostility to theory is a hostility to change

This leads Horkheimer to a rather provocative claim: 'The hostility to theory as such which prevails in contemporary public life is really directed against the transformative activity associated with critical thinking' (232). Horkheimer observes that opposition arises 'as soon as theorists fail to limit themselves to verification and classification by means of categories which are as neutral as possible, that is, categories which are indispensable to inherited ways of life'. Horkheimer implies that '[t]hose who profit from the status quo' quite rightly 'entertain a general suspicion of any intellectual independence', and sometimes are hostile to the traditional *as well as* to the critical type of theory. At the same time, 'the vast majority of the ruled' who have an interest in 'the transformative activity' oppose it for psychological reasons: they unconsciously 'fear that theoretical thinking might show their painfully won adaptation to reality to be perverse and unnecessary'. Horkheimer hints in this remark at a crucial aspect of the empirical work that the Frankfurt Institute of Social Research, whose director he was, had begun to undertake since the late 1920s: the integration of psychoanalysis into empirical social research as well as social theory. The basic idea was that the behaviour of the ruling classes most of the time could be explained by their material interests in more or less rational terms, but the behaviour of the working class could *not*: the latter often supported the order that exploited and oppressed them. Psychoanalysis suggests that people can get enjoyment out of an objectively bad situation: one may 'love' a dictator or demagogue because of the expectation that he might reward subordination and sacrifice with some kind of love (or, in a more general term, recognition) in return. The hope of being loved (recognized, acknowledged, rewarded) by the exploiter might often seem a safer bet than the alternative hope of the benefits of something as risky as insurrection. We all work hard for our 'adaptation to reality', in the family, at school, university and elsewhere, and we hesitate to give up the entitlements that we believe we have earned thereby – until it becomes too painfully clear that no such entitlement in fact exists. To this revelation, many then react either with resentment or with critique.

In the manner of presentation characteristic of many in the Critical Theory tradition, Horkheimer takes up the opposite argument in the subsequent passage: he grants that the 'positivist attitude need not be simply hostile to progress'. It contains 'even today' elements of the motivation that drove Enlightenment empiricism: 'the determination to look at facts alone and to surrender every kind of illusion' was 'a reaction against the alliance of metaphysics and oppression' which is still, to an extent, in place today (232). Horkheimer insists, though, that the anti-feudal 'bourgeois revolution' to which eighteenth-century empiricism had been allied cannot be a model for a future overcoming of the capitalist order:

> In the eighteenth century a new society had already been developed within the framework of the old. The task was then to free an already existent bourgeois economy from its feudal limitations and to let it 'break free'. Bourgeois scientific thought, too, needed, fundamentally, only to shake off the old dogmatic chains in order to progress along a path it had already mapped out. (233)

In a sense, Horkheimer seems to be saying: *that was the easy part* – destroy feudalism, let some heads roll, and bourgeois modernity would steam ahead. As Comte and others described in great detail, modern bourgeois society was already growing to maturity in some pockets of feudal society. The task of the present, or future, is much more difficult, and cannot rely on such crude methods. In the eighteenth century, the future bourgeois society already existed in the enfranchised towns, operated according to capitalist market principles and began producing on the basis of modern science. *Today is different*: although the elements of the future society exist in the present world, they are not constituted as a somehow coherent force that just needs to be 'liberated'. The future will need to be discovered in thoughtful experimentation, and hostility to theory is a hindrance to that: 'Unless there is continued theoretical effort, in the interest of a rationally organized future society, to shed critical light on present-day society and to interpret it through engagement with the traditional theories ... the ground is taken from under the hope of radically improving human existence' (233). Those who abandon the 'theory of emancipation' in fact also neutralize its practice.

4.2 The theory of contemporary capitalism

In the following section Horkheimer discusses the historicity of Critical Theory: how does theory relate to historical time? How does it change with time? He starts out by rejecting two extremes: Critical Theory is neither indifferent to time (like rationalist, strictly deductive theory) (233) nor does it reinvent itself every so often: the theory changes but '[t]he changes in it do not mean a shift to a wholly new outlook, as long as the epoch itself does not radically change' (234). Critical Theory changes but stays the same as long as modern society changes but, in its basic structures, stays the same. Horkheimer enters at this point a discussion of 'the concept of the social class which disposes of the means of production' to illustrate this point.

Horkheimer bases his argument on the observation that in the course of the nineteenth century, a 'liberalist' period of capitalism in which a 'large class of private property owners exercised leadership in society' (234) was followed by a more monopolistic form of capitalism driven by 'rapidly increasing concentration and centralization of capital' (235). Whereas previously legal owners tended to direct their enterprises more or less personally, they were now 'largely excluded from the management of the huge combines which absorbed their small factories, and management became something quite distinct from ownership'. Horkheimer argues that this economic process brought 'with it a change in the way the political and legal apparatus functions, as well as in ideologies'. Although 'the juridical definition of ownership' is not 'being changed at all', the 'influence of management' increases and ultimately extends even 'to the State and its power apparatus'. The entire culture of capitalist society changes with this process:

> Once the owners of legal property titles are cut off from the actual productive process and lose their influence, their horizon narrows; they become increasingly unfitted for important social positions, and finally the revenue which they still receive from their property to whose increase they have contributed nothing comes to seem socially

useless and morally dubious. These and other changes are accom-
panied by the rise of ideologies centring on the great personality
and the distinction between productive and parasitic capitalists. The
idea of right as independent of wider society and defined by clearly
delineated content loses its importance. The very same sector of
society which brutally maintains private ownership of the means of
production – a centrepiece of the prevailing social order – sponsors
political doctrines which claim that unproductive property and parasitic incomes must disappear. With the narrowing of the circle of
really powerful men increases the possibility of deliberately manufac-
turing ideologies, of establishing two kinds of truth – knowledge for
the insiders, a cooked-up story for the people – while cynicism about
truth and thought generally become widespread. The end result of
the process is a society dominated no longer by independent owners
but by cliques of industrial and political leaders. (235–236)

Horkheimer provides in this paragraph a condensed version of the
'Frankfurt School' theory of fascism as it was in the process of being
developed at the time. Although he argues that the historical process is driven by the concentration and centralization of capital, his
main concern is with the political, ideological and cultural changes
that are part of this process. Key is that at the level of ideology, the
historical shift from 'liberalistic' to a more concentrated, corporatist
and bureaucratic form of capitalism is represented as a duality of
two types of capitalists, good productive capitalists versus greedy
unproductive ones. This ideology reifies a historical *tendency* into
solid, clear-cut *types*. It is at the heart of the ideology of German
National Socialism, where it is graphically expressed in the form of
antisemitism (which equates greedy unproductive capitalists with
Jews).

The post-liberalistic culture of contemporary capitalism also
destroys the idea of truth: no one outside the system's managerial
centres really believes anything at all any more, which opens the
way to acting *as if* one believed the most absurd nonsense, including
any number of racial and conspiracy theories. These are thereby
also immunized against any rational critique: one cannot argue with
racists who don't actually believe in arguing. In a sense, they believe
what they believe *because* it is absurd nonsense – the more irrational
the belief, the more enjoyable it is to believe it. The fascist type of

racism is a way of sticking two fingers up to (what they perceive to be) the establishment of liberal individualism. They fail to notice that *actual* capitalism has already moved on to its bureaucratic, monopolistic form. It has left behind only a *simulation* of its older liberal version, with its love of individualism, rags-to-riches stories and entrepreneurial spirit, for the tabloids. Although fascists at grassroots level might think of themselves as anti-establishment or even 'anti-capitalist', their mind-set is in fact quite well adapted to the actual, more modern form of corporate capitalist rule.

'Such changes', Horkheimer argues, 'do not leave the structure of the critical theory untouched' (236). To be sure, it sticks to its basic Marxian premises: 'It does not indeed fall victim to the illusion that property and profit no longer play a key role.' 'Profit continues to come from the same social sources', the appropriation of surplus value through the exploitation of labour, 'and must in the last analysis be increased by the same means as before'. In spite of this continuity, however, there is a fundamental change: the disappearance of 'all rights with a determined content'. The fullest expression of this disappearance is 'the authoritarian state'. Horkheimer asserts, against some more vulgar forms of Marxist theory, that right is (or rather, was) not only an ideology: it is (or was) also 'a cultural factor' whose relative independence had its positive side. Horkheimer's thoughts on this matter reflect in the first place the realities of the time in the regimes of fascism and Stalinism, but he seems also to view contemporary 'Western' societies as moving in the same direction, differences notwithstanding: everywhere the modern state was expanding and assuming functions of governance over increasingly many spheres of society, including the economy and the family, over which the state had not had much sway previously.

Horkheimer distinguishes two modes of Critical Theory, as it were: one mode that is more appropriate to the analysis of 'liberalistic' capitalism, recognizing the relative independence of legal and cultural structures in society; and another mode adapted to the 'totalitarian' present that recognizes the disappearance of that independence. In a crude reality where the subtle distinctions of the complicated web of social relations typical of old-fashioned 'liberalist' capitalism have been destroyed, Critical Theory likewise must become more crude: he writes, perhaps a bit tongue in cheek, that it must become more 'vulgar materialist', as if the economy directly governed most cultural, moral and legal dimensions of society, discarding and dissolving intermediate institutions that had been central to modernity such as the family or an independent judiciary:

> The explanation of social phenomena has become simpler yet also more complicated. Simpler, because economic factors more directly and consciously determine men and because the solidity and relative capacity for resistance of the cultural spheres are disappearing. More complicated, because the economic dynamism which has been set in motion and in relation to which most individuals have been reduced to simple means, quickly brings ever new visions and portents. (237)

The mediating institutions of classical modernity are weakened as the state governs 'into' the family, and the rule of law is replaced by rule by decree that in turn is dictated by economic interests. At the same time the relative stability of, for example, family traditions and the liberal idea of right is replaced by a quickly changing multiplicity of more arbitrary, i.e. less predictable, policies; in this sense Horkheimer suggests that things become simpler and more complicated at the same time. Although the object of Critical Theory is 'historically changing' in this sense, it nevertheless 'remains identical amid all the changes' (239). This 'object' that can, with differing emphasis, be addressed as modern, liberal, bourgeois or capitalist society, has so far remained the same object – it is not a series of successive separate objects. Its theory is therefore 'not a storehouse of hypotheses on the course of particular events in society' but 'a developing picture of society as a whole'.

Theorists approach this 'object' – society – with different questions depending on the situation, and therefore produce different accounts of what this 'object' in fact is. Horkheimer's example here is the concept of the character of 'the bourgeois entrepreneur or even the bourgeois man as such'. In the past, observers as different as Marx and Weber had emphasized (and mostly admired) the rationalism of 'bourgeois man' (sometimes also 'bourgeois woman'). Now, in the dystopian present of the 1930s, other observers, like Horkheimer himself, discover that 'bourgeois man' throughout his history had also demonstrated many irrational and violent traits. It was the *bourgeois but irrational present reality* (of Nazi Germany in particular) that dictated such discoveries: the 'object' has, of course, changed, but it has not changed *entirely*. The irrational traits that seemed to dominate the present had been there also in the past, and likewise the rational traits that had been admired in the past were also still evident in the irrational present: even the Nazis were not *completely* irrational, otherwise they would not have been able to govern a modern capitalist state. (In fact many liberals and socialists wrongly expected that the Hitler regime would only be a brief episode because they underestimated the functionality and rationality of Nazi madness.)

This is the dialectical account of society and history that Critical Theory aims at. 'Traditional theory', by contrast, would rather construct several different 'objects' or 'types', such as 'the rational bourgeois man of the past' versus 'the irrational bourgeois man of the present'. It would present them as two different objects, rather than one object with different aspects or dimensions that temporarily predominate at different points in time.

4.3 Conclusion: reason determines its own goals

The last three pages of the text wrap up some key elements of this quite complicated essay, without, unfortunately, providing any convenient take-home points. Horkheimer states that theory only exists in the minds of those who 'have' it: there is no 'object' called theory that somehow exists out there, slowly but steadily growing and evolving (240). That would be nice: as with a psychic plant, we would only need to look at 'the theory' from time to time and check where it was turning. A statement such as 'the theory has changed' is in this sense merely rhetorical: *we and our thinking have changed*, along with the reality that we think about and of which we are a part. There is no such thing as 'the theory'.

A theoretical perspective that is committed to the 'construction of a radically transformed society' can almost by definition 'not have the advantage of widespread acceptance' (241): its acceptance would more or less coincide with the changing of society, which would make it superfluous. Furthermore, Critical Theory is not supported or embodied by any particular class, stratum or institution of society, but relies only on 'the interest in the abolition of class rule' (242). (The English translator here replaced Horkheimer's 'class rule' with the more polite 'social injustice'.) Going back to the discussion of idealist philosophy in the first section of the essay, Horkheimer asserts that 'this negative formulation' – the 'abolition of class rule' – 'is the materialist content of the idealist concept of reason': to put it the other way around, a society in which one class rules over another is unreasonable. The concept of reason is connected to those of freedom and autonomy, and whatever obstructs freedom and autonomy is unreasonable. From this it follows that 'the characteristic mark of the thinker's activity is to determine for itself what it is to accomplish and serve' (242): it is part of the concept of reason that it does not follow given goals but determines *its own goals* – reason is 'autonomous', which, literally translated, means 'something that gives itself its own laws'. Reason, in this understanding, is driven by its own logic towards historical change. Equating 'thought' with 'reason', Horkheimer concludes: 'But conformism in thought and the insistence that thinking is a fixed vocation, a self-enclosed realm within society as a whole, betrays the very essence of thought' (243).

13
What is a woman, and who is asking anyway? Simone de Beauvoir

Simone de Beauvoir (1908–86) was a French philosopher and novelist whose best-known theoretical work, *The Second Sex* (1949), became one of the core texts of twentieth-century feminism. She did not, though, consider herself a feminist at the time of writing it: de Beauvoir *became* a feminist in the process of working through, at a more general level, the philosophical problem of freedom. In many of her philosophical writings as well as her novels – sometimes described as 'metaphysical novels' as they are really philosophical reflections *in the form of* novels, avoiding the abstractly conceptual and often dogmatic character of academic philosophy – she discussed freedom in relation to where one finds oneself, i.e. in what societal and historical situation and also in what kind of body. If as a human being I am essentially a creature meant to be free, then how can I live in accordance with the commandment to be free in an unfree situation? One of the classical problems of the philosophical tradition, this was central in one way or another to her entire life work. This philosophical problem also forced her into the field of social theory.

De Beauvoir, born in Paris, was from a conservative bourgeois family who had lost their fortune in the war economy and high inflation of the First World War. During childhood, her intellectual development benefited from a rich mix of cognitive dissonances: her family were bourgeois in terms of status and education, but had little money in the bank; her mother was religious, as was Simone until the age of 14, while her father was an atheist and rationalist; her father was very proud of her sharp mind and complimented her on thinking 'like a man'. From this confusing input de Beauvoir drew the very sensible conclusion that she should best live her life her own way, and succeeded in this to such an extent that she became for subsequent generations of independent-minded youth an icon for her lifestyle as much as for her writing. She studied mathematics, literature and philosophy, graduating with a thesis on the rationalist philosopher and mathematician Gottfried Leibniz (1646–1716). She was one of the first women to graduate from the Sorbonne (since the Middle Ages and still at the time the central institution of the University of Paris) and went on to take the examination in philosophy at the even more prestigious École Normale Supérieure, a modern institution founded during the French Revolution whose role it is to train and select the meritocratic elite of the French state, including professors, researchers and high-level government officials. De Beauvoir came second in her cohort, narrowly beaten to first place by Jean-Paul Sartre (1905–80), with whom she then began a life-long relationship. De Beauvoir was just 21 at the time, the youngest person ever to pass this examination.

De Beauvoir worked as a philosophy teacher at a number of *lycées* – the principal institution of French secondary education at the time – from 1929 to 1943, moving from place to place as was common in the French system, and thereafter lived as an independent writer and from giving lectures. She was not based at (or confined to, as she might have seen it) any particular academic institution. Philosophically, she came under the influence of the revival of Hegelian philosophy that was the predominant intellectual trend in France in the 1930s, as well as phenomenology and existentialism, of which she was a chief exponent. At bottom, though, she remained a rationalist thinker very much in the French 'Cartesian' (i.e. from Descartes) tradition. Her career as a secondary schoolteacher seems to have been ended because of parents complaining about her seducing a student. She and Sartre defined themselves as 'essential' lovers who would also enjoy 'contingent' love affairs as desire would command, sometimes in complex intersecting constellations that may not always have been equally beneficial to the 'contingent' partners. They did not marry, nor did they ever move in with each other (they often lived in hotels), let alone have children. In this decidedly anti-bourgeois form, the intellectual and romantic partnership between these two very bourgeois individuals lasted until Sartre's death in 1980. De Beauvoir's first novel, in English entitled *She Came to Stay* (1943), explores the ethical problematic of freedom, responsibility, violence and sexual desire in the form of a psychological study of a triangular sexual relationship. The novel was an immediate success.

De Beauvoir and Sartre lived in Paris when it was occupied by Nazi Germany in 1940. The experience of the occupation and of being forced to take sides politicized her thinking and opened her previously more individualist and ahistorical existentialist philosophy to more historical and societal modes of inquiry. In 1945 she published another novel, *The Blood of Others*, dealing with the moral dilemma of a resistance leader who is forced to send his lover to her death (hence the title), and founded with Sartre and others a left-wing, non-party-aligned journal, *Les temps modernes* (the title being a nod to Charlie Chaplin's film *Modern Times*). She remained an editor of this journal until her death.

Her existentialism was about responding to the modern, post-rationalist truth that God is dead – i.e. that humans are 'thrown into the world' without a mission and a divine plan – with the alternative truth of human freedom, which implied a moral command not to deny or betray this freedom. Existentialist ethics is an exhortation to live 'authentically' in spite of all the obstacles that other people and society throw at us. This can mean not denying one's sexual desire, and it can mean resisting Nazi occupation. It can also mean fighting for equality in society without ignoring the fact that humans are embodied, not just spiritual beings, and as such striving to be equal *as different and particular individuals*: equals but not the same. This is the philosophical perspective from which she wrote her two major works of social theory, *The Second Sex* (1949) and *Old Age* (1970), an analysis of old age as a category of 'otherness' in society. *The Second Sex* analyses how a variety of societal discourses add up to the construction of the myth of 'the eternal feminine', the alleged 'essence' of woman that traps individual, actual women in 'inauthentic' lives in which they are complicit in their own subjugation. *The Second Sex* was included on the Vatican's (for some, highly prestigious) special reading list of the most diabolical of works, the 'Index of Prohibited Books'. De Beauvoir was engaged in opposition to the wars in Vietnam and Algeria and became a declared feminist in the mid-1960s. In 1977 she was involved in founding the Marxist-feminist journal *Questions Féministes*, which developed the notion that women constitute a class in society. De Beauvoir remained involved in the journal when it was refounded as *Nouvelles Questions Féministes* in 1980 following a dispute about the relationship between lesbianism and feminism. De Beauvoir and the editors of the refounded journal came down on the side of those who rejected the argument that the liberation struggle of women-as-a-class required radically breaking off all reproductive relationships with men.

The following discussion of the 'Introduction' to *The Second Sex* is based on the most widely available, condensed translation of the book by H. M. Parshley that originally appeared in 1953. Whoever wishes to study the complete text of *The Second Sex* should work with the unabridged new translation of 2010 by Constance Borde and Sheila Malovany-Chevallier.

Structure of the chosen text

1 Not all female human beings count as women (xiii)
2 The Enlightenment critique of essentialism is important but insufficient (xiv-xv)
3 Woman as the other (xv-xvi)
4 The category of 'the other' (xvi-xvii)
5 The non-reciprocal relationship to 'the other' (xvii-xviii)
6 Differences between struggles by women, proletarians and racialized groups (xviii-xx)
7 Mutual dependency does not warrant liberation (xx)
8 Woman's unequal status (xx-xxi)
9 Accounts of the inequality of woman in the philosophical tradition (xxi-xxiv)
10 Men's attitude in the present period (xxiv-xxvi)
11 The arguments of feminists (xxvi-xxviii)
12 The perspective of transcending immanence (xxviii-xxix)

de Beauvoir, Simone. 1957 [1949]. 'Introduction'. In *The Second Sex*. Translated and edited by H. M. Parshley. New York: Knopf, xiii–xxix.

1 Not all female human beings count as women

De Beauvoir begins her exploration of the concept of 'woman' with the observation that contemporary men tend to make two contradictory statements: on the one hand, the adherents of 'the theory of the eternal feminine' will 'whisper in your ear' that 'even in Russia', i.e. in spite of the modernizing gender policies of the Bolshevik state, 'women still are *women*' (xiii); on the other hand, others say that 'woman is losing her way'. Both statements cannot be true at the same time: either the essence of woman is eternal and a positive fact of the natural or perhaps cosmological order, or essential 'woman' has fallen victim to modernity and is falling apart. Although all seem agreed that 'woman' is defined entirely by having a womb, some 'experts' say that there are women who are not really women. Women are 'exhorted to be women, remain women, become women' which means that 'woman' is not simply a concept that describes a positive – i.e. given – reality but a norma-tive one, something to *aspire* to. There is confusion, it seems, and a need to discuss whether 'woman' actually exists or has ever existed: 'It would appear, then, that every female human being is not nec-essarily a woman; to be so considered she must share in that mys-terious and threatened reality known as femininity.' De Beauvoir turns increasingly sarcastic here: is 'femininity' a material 'essence', perhaps 'something secreted by the ovaries'? Or is it 'a Platonic essence', which means a philosophical idea? In the original French, this last question is literally, 'is it glued into a Platonic heaven?', and she continues to ask mockingly whether 'a rustling petticoat [was] enough to bring it down to earth'. Although some women try 'to incarnate this essence', it is unclear what it is. She writes that it was only in the Middle Ages, 'in the times of St Thomas' (Aquinas), that it was considered 'an essence as certainly defined as the somnif-erous virtue of the poppy': only back then did a spiritual 'essence' like 'femininity', the essence of 'woman', seem as straightforwardly definable and factual as the sleep-inducing material essence that is won by pressing poppy seeds (opium, in case you are wondering). However, femininity is no such 'essence'.

2 The Enlightenment critique of essentialism is important but insufficient

'But conceptualism has lost ground' (xiv). 'Conceptualism' is a philosophical term that denotes the classical idea that concepts are not just products of the human mind which we invent to project order on to a chaotic reality, but have a real existence of their own. 'Conceptualism' would, for example, hold that 'virtue' is not just a normative idea or a descriptor of the behaviour of virtuous individuals, but that there is actually an entity called 'virtue' out there which virtuous people 'have', as it were: the virtuous individual 'has', or partakes in, virtue. In the case of 'femininity', a 'conceptualist' thinker would assert that there is something out there called 'femininity', and presumably that women 'have' that thing – a bit like a poppy seed 'has', or contains, opium. In contemporary social theory, we would use the word 'essentialism' rather than 'conceptualism', with similar meaning.

De Beauvoir attacks such thinking: 'The biological and social sciences no longer admit the existence of unchangeably fixed entities that determine given characteristics, such as those ascribed to woman, the Jew, or the Negro. Science regards any characteristic as a reaction dependent in part upon a *situation*' (xiv). De Beauvoir seems to propose thereby that no living being, biological or social, unchangeably *is* what it is due to some inherent essence. Nothing simply is what it is, but everything is constituted by context, situatedness, interaction.

Her position is not that straightforward, though: she rejects the position taken 'by those who hold to the philosophy of the enlightenment, of rationalism, of nominalism' that 'the word *woman*' has therefore 'no specific content'. Women are not 'merely the human beings arbitrarily designated by the word *woman*', which she writes that 'many American women' in particular seem to think. 'Nominalism' is a philosophical term that denotes the opposite of the 'conceptualism' dismissed earlier by de Beauvoir: a 'nominalist' holds that abstract terms and concepts are nothing more than words, created by the human mind for convenience or as tools for thinking, and beyond that do not have any reality to them. 'Woman' would be, for a nominalist, just such a word, and no more than a word. De

Beauvoir interprets a statement from an American writer, Dorothy Parker, that 'all of us, men as well as women, should be regarded as human beings', as 'nominalist' and dismisses it as 'inadequate'. De Beauvoir rejects both 'conceptualism' and 'nominalism': neither is every woman determined in her woman-ness by the supposedly eternal essence of femininity, nor is it true that 'woman' simply does not exist. 'To decline to accept such notions as the eternal feminine, the black soul, the Jewish character, is not to deny that Jews, Negroes, women exist today – this denial does not represent a liberation for those concerned, but rather a flight from reality' (xiv). She argues here for taking account of empirical, observable reality: 'humanity is divided into two classes of individuals whose clothes, faces, bodies, smiles, gaits, interests, and occupations are manifestly different. Perhaps these differences are superficial, perhaps they are destined to disappear. What is certain is that they do most obviously exist' (xiv–xv). Denying this reality and abstractly claiming that we are all just human beings only plays into the hands of 'anti-feminists' – although it is, of course, true that we are all human beings.

If we want to grasp De Beauvoir's position, we need to grant that *a statement can be true while the opposite of that statement is true as well, at the same time*: all human beings are human beings, and in this respect the same, but 'every concrete human being is always a singular, separate individual'. She follows this proposition up with several examples of women whose denial of their own femininity she interprets (and critiques) as being driven by a wish 'to be counted among the men' and to earn their respect. They are basically letting the side down. De Beauvoir's argument is aimed, in the name of facing the facts of 'reality', against disregarding difference and singularity.

3 Woman as the other

De Beauvoir begins the discussion of 'what is a woman' with her own positioning: it is 'in itself significant', she writes, that she as a woman comes to ask this question. 'A man never begins by presenting himself as an individual of a certain sex' (xv). Although the terms male and female are used symmetrically on some legal papers, in fact

> the relation of the two sexes is not quite like that of two electrical
> poles, for man represents both the positive and the neutral, as is indi-
> cated by the common use of *man* to designate human beings in gen-
> eral; whereas woman represents only the negative, defined by limiting
> criteria, without reciprocity. (xv)

Beauvoir argues that 'for the ancients', the masculine was to the
feminine as the vertical was to the oblique. Ovaries and womb are
'peculiarities' that 'imprison [a woman] in her subjectivity' – it is
said that 'she thinks with her glands' – whereas testicles represent
the norm. Not having testicles means lacking something, whereas
not having a uterus is normal. Man 'thinks of his body as a direct
and normal connection with the world' through which he believes
he apprehends the world objectively, whereas 'he regards the body
of woman as a hindrance' to perceiving the world, 'a prison' even.
De Beauvoir complements these observations with several references to the philosophical canon: Aristotle wrote that '[t]he female
is a female by virtue of a certain lack of qualities', and Thomas
Aquinas (*c.* 1225–74) called woman an 'imperfect man' (xvi). Man
'defines woman … relative to him'. A more contemporary male
author suggested that a woman 'cannot think of herself without
man'. She is simply 'the sex', an absolutely sexual being. 'He is the
Subject, he is the Absolute – she is the Other' (xvi). In a footnote
she attributes this view in particular to the philosopher Emmanuel
Levinas (1906–95), whose background was in the 'phenomenolog-
ical' philosophy of Edmund Husserl (1859–1938). She quotes a
remark from Levinas's 1947 essay 'Time and the Other', where he
states that 'the feminine' is not just the opposite, or complementary,
term to a correlative term (such as 'the masculine'), denoting a 'specific difference', but represents 'the contrary in its absolute sense':
whereas contraries that denote 'specific difference' are complementary, for Levinas there is no such relation between the feminine and
the masculine (xvi). The feminine is the opposite of consciousness,
no less. De Beauvoir takes this as the extreme point of a highly
problematic tradition of thinking about 'woman', and the starting
point for her own reconceptualization. (De Beauvoir disregards the
fact that Levinas associated the figure of 'the Other' with God, i.e.
something superior to 'the subject'. For de Beauvoir, this would not
have cleared his argument of being sexist, though.)

4 The category of 'the other'

In the next passage de Beauvoir moves to the more theoretical level of argument indicated by the reference to Levinas just discussed. She begins with a philosophically charged anthropological claim about the concept of 'the other': 'The category of the *Other* is as primordial as consciousness itself ... Otherness is a fundamental category of human thought' (xvi–xvii). Her point is, against the claim by Levinas just referred to, that in the contexts of 'most primitive societies' and 'in the most ancient mythologies', otherness is *not* as such connected to 'femininity': 'male and female' was simply one of many pairs of opposites. 'Otherness' is a fundamental category of all human thinking, but 'the feminine as the other' is not.

She then shifts this argument about the fundamental categories of thought to the more specific level of society (rather than the very generic one of anthropology): she observes that 'no group ever sets itself up as the One without at once setting up the Other over against itself' (xvii). She illustrates this claim with examples from contemporary society:

> If three travellers chance to occupy the same compartment, that is enough to make vaguely hostile 'others' out of all the rest of the passengers on the train. In small-town eyes all persons not belonging to the village are 'strangers' and suspect; to the native of a country all who inhabit other countries are 'foreigners'; Jews are 'different' for the anti-Semite, Negroes are 'inferior' for American racists, aborigines are 'natives' for colonists, proletarians are the 'lower class' for the privileged.

In the next paragraph she moves back again from these observations to the level of philosophical argument. She quotes the observation made by Claude Lévi-Strauss (1908–2009) that human beings perceive 'series of contrasts' – the French text actually says 'systems of oppositions' – such as 'duality, alternation, opposition, and symmetry' not so much as 'phenomena to be explained' but 'as fundamental and immediately given data of social reality': Lévi-Strauss found it puzzling that we are not puzzled by the observation of dualisms of all kinds. He was puzzled by the fact that we take them for granted rather than trying to explain them. De Beauvoir takes

Lévi-Strauss's observation and tries to explain it with the help of a reference to the philosopher Hegel:

> These phenomena would be incomprehensible if in fact human society were simply a *Mitsein* or fellowship based on solidarity and friendliness. Things become clear, on the contrary, if, following Hegel, we find in consciousness itself a fundamental hostility towards every other consciousness; the subject can be posed only in being opposed – he sets himself up as the essential, as opposed to the other, the inessential, the object.

Mitsein is a German word used by the philosopher Martin Heidegger (1899–1976) – quoted here perhaps because he influenced Levinas – that literally means 'being with', or 'togetherness', an ontological rendering of the idea that human beings form a sort of community simply due to the fact that they 'are with' each other. De Beauvoir rejects such a sociologically naïve view of human sociality and points to Hegel's contrasting point – much more in tune with the empirical observation of society – that human beings form a consciousness of themselves as *subjects* necessarily by separating everything else off from themselves as a mass of *objects*: I construct an idea of '*I*' by constructing an idea of everything else as '*not-I*', and this construction comes with an element of hostility – perhaps because, from the perspective of an infant, the surrounding world of objects might well seem rather frightening. De Beauvoir supports the anthropological claim made by Lévi-Strauss – human thinking is always and has always been organized in dualities – with the philosophical claim made by Hegel – a human subject becomes conscious by positing him- or herself in opposition to everything else which is thereby constituted as 'the other' – but rejects the claim by Levinas and others that the 'otherness' of femininity plays any kind of special role in this. As for the argument on 'woman', the crucial concept is that of 'reciprocity' which is introduced in the next paragraph.

5 The non-reciprocal relationship to 'the other'

De Beauvoir develops now an argument that at first sight seems to redeem the claim made by Levinas that femininity is 'absolute' rather than ordinary otherness, but she confirms Levinas's claim only as a description of (bad) reality, not as a philosophical postulate. She observes that in most cases, those conceived as 'others' make a reciprocal claim about the others' otherness: when I travel abroad those whom I consider others regard *me* as an other, in turn. This is, of course, one of the educational benefits of travelling: finding myself a stranger, I learn something about the process of othering. De Beauvoir points out that many real-world events and relationships such as 'wars, festivals, trading, treaties, and contests among tribes, nations, and classes tend to deprive the concept *Other* of its absolute sense and to make manifest its relativity' (xvii): reciprocity wears off the sharp edges of otherness. Not so in the case of woman, De Beauvoir writes:

> How is it, then, that this reciprocity has not been recognized between the sexes, that one of the contrasting terms is set up as the sole essential, denying any relativity in regard to its correlative and defining the latter as pure otherness? Why is it that women do not dispute male sovereignty?

Reading this seventy years after it was written, one may object here that women *have* disputed 'male sovereignty' quite a bit. Indeed, most people in the more liberal societies of the present probably think of the duality of 'man' and 'woman' as indeed reciprocal and *relative*, and not, as the situation seems to have presented itself to De Beauvoir in 1949, as *absolute*. As in other things, though, such advancements are never to be taken for granted, as they are reversible, and certainly in a global perspective the struggle between the view of the gender division as 'relative' or 'absolute' opposition is far from over.

In a 'reciprocal' relationship, neither side is permanently 'the one' (the subject, the sovereign, the powerful one) or 'the other' (the subordinate) – reciprocity means a constantly shifting relationship of now being in the position of being 'the one', now in that of being 'the other'. 'No subject will readily *volunteer* to become the object' (xviii; italics added); reciprocity must therefore be reciprocity of *power*. De Beauvoir asks now, why is there no reciprocity? Why is 'woman' so submissive?

De Beauvoir points out that there are many cases 'in which a certain category has been able to dominate another completely for a time', but '[v]ery often this privilege depends upon inequality of numbers' as when a majority exploits or persecutes a minority. De Beauvoir points to an important difference: 'But women are not a minority, like the American Negroes or the Jews; there are as many women as men on earth.' The cases of black people and Jews can be historically explained, as present racist exploitation and extermination result from historical events and processes that can be examined and – in principle – understood. Furthermore, in both cases 'the oppressed retained at least the memory of former days; they possessed in common a past, a tradition, sometimes a religion or a culture' which could serve as resources of resistance. De Beauvoir implies that the case of 'woman' is different.

6 Differences between struggles by women, proletarians and racialized groups

De Beauvoir gives a nod here to the Marxist writer August Bebel (1840–1913), a key figure of German social democracy in the four decades before his death, who was a famous opponent of racism and colonialism and the author of the book *Woman and Socialism* (1879): she credits him for having pointed out that women and the proletariat have in common 'that neither ever formed a minority or a separate collective unit of mankind', as distinct from colonized or enslaved peoples. 'And instead of a single historical event', such as military defeat or colonial conquest, 'it is in both cases a historical *development* that explains their status as a class' (xviii; italics added). What distinguishes them, however, is that 'proletarians have not always existed, whereas there have always been women', if defined physiologically, and '[t]hroughout history they have always been subordinated to men'. This reflects the fact that the class 'proletariat' is connected to modern capitalism, whereas the class 'woman' – 'class' used here in the meaning of a category that structures society – is connected to patriarchy, which stretches much further back into prehistory. It is important to note that De Beauvoir does not *herself* argue, in fact, that 'woman' is defined by her physiology – she famously contests this idea later on in the book – nor does she rule out that there might have been a time in prehistory when

women were not oppressed: the sentences just quoted paraphrase
the common conception of woman which De Beauvoir sets out to
challenge. She writes that the otherness of 'woman' 'seems to be an
absolute' (xviii) because it is widely believed 'that it lacks the contingent or incidental nature of historical facts. A condition brought
about at a certain time can be abolished at some other time' (xviii–
xix), as the slave-led revolution on Haiti of 1791 proved. What
appears to be a *natural* condition, though, 'might seem … beyond
the possibility of change' (xix). Against such appearances, De
Beauvoir asserts that the weakness of women does not result from
their 'natural condition' but it is rather the other way around: the
semblance of that natural condition results from women's weakness
– and she is quite brutal here in her assessment of 'woman':

> In truth, however, the nature of things is no more immutably given,
> once for all, than is historical reality. If woman seems to be the ines-
> sential which never becomes the essential, it is because she herself
> fails to bring about this change. Proletarians say 'We'; Negroes also.
> Regarding themselves as subjects, they transform the bourgeois, the
> whites, into 'others'. But women do not say 'We', except at some con-
> gress of feminists or similar formal demonstration; men say 'women',
> and women use the same word in referring to themselves. They do
> not authentically assume a subjective attitude. The proletarians have
> accomplished the revolution in Russia, the Negroes in Haiti, the
> Indo-Chinese are battling for it in Indo-China; but the women's effort
> has never been anything more than a symbolic agitation. They have
> gained only what men have been willing to grant; they have taken
> nothing, they have only received. (xix)

The argument here – taken from existentialist philosophy – is that
proletarians, blacks and colonized peoples achieve 'a subjective attitude' and 'authenticity' – i.e. become *subjects* and stop being mere
objects of the historical process – by turning the tables on their
oppressors: rather than allowing *them* to define what 'proletarian' or
'black' means, they take the initiative, say 'we', and thereby define
for *themselves* what they are, turning the oppressors into 'others',
inessential objects of *their own* agency. De Beauvoir implies that
doing so creates the reciprocity that was lacking in the state of
oppression. The examples she gives, however, inadvertently indicate that the existentialist argument on 'authenticity' is not without

its problems: none of the given examples ended very well, and this might well have something to do with the revolutionaries' asserting an identity that creates a group of 'others' in the process. De Beauvoir's comments on the Russian and Haitian Revolutions and the anti-colonial struggles of the time, notably in Vietnam, suffer from being mere *illustrations* of a philosophical argument without having been developed from adequate critical analysis of what actually happened, including, crucially, what went wrong. These revolutions and struggles certainly succeeded in putting new social actors on the historical map – i.e. they created 'subjectivity', or 'empowerment' as this has been called more recently – but the extent to which they brought *humanity* to an emancipated state of things is dubious. These comments represent a rather undeveloped and insufficiently critical aspect of De Beauvoir's argument, whose main tendency in fact contradicts it. Can we not find emancipatory struggles that avoid creating and subjecting 'an other'?

De Beauvoir examines now what prevents women from 'organizing themselves into a unit which can stand face to face with the correlative unit'. Women lack important means for doing so: unlike ethnic or national groups, they 'have no past, no history, no religion of their own'; unlike the proletariat, they lack 'solidarity of work and interest'. Apart from lacking these essentials, they

> are not even promiscuously herded together in the way that creates community feeling among the American Negroes, the ghetto Jews, the workers of [the Parisian working-class neighbourhood of] Saint-Denis, or the factory hands of Renault. They live dispersed among the males, attached through residence, housework, economic condition, and social standing to certain men – fathers or husbands – more firmly than they are to other women. (xix)

The point here is that many different people with a shared interest or problem being 'promiscuously herded together' is often a good starting point for some kind of insurrectionary activity. Women as such, however, are isolated and *individually* allocated to male-dominated families, and this makes collective action difficult and unlikely. Against this argument, two objections could be made: first, there are societal constellations in which women do have considerable power, at least within the family, and are able to create networks of women that help to maintain this power; and secondly, all the examples of 'communities' given by De Beauvoir in the above quote, except perhaps the 'factory hands of Renault', are groups that half consist of women: empirical analysis would need to show whether and to what extent women *within* these groupings hold some form of reciprocal power and organize *as women*. De Beauvoir's book itself, of which the present chapter looks only at the introduction, provides plenty of empirical material for discussing these matters.

The following sentence, though, is particularly perceptive and formulates a critique that was of huge importance in the subsequent developments of feminist social theory: 'If they [women] belong to the bourgeoisie, they feel solidarity with men of that class, not with proletarian women; if they are white, their allegiance is to white men, not to Negro women' (xix). This sums up, in a nutshell, one of the principal difficulties of the women's movement at the time and, arguably, still today. Save for the word itself, de Beauvoir articulates here the very problem that was addressed in the 1990s in the context of discussions on 'intersectionality': women are always also members of other societal categories and structurings, including race and class, and as individuals they need to negotiate where their belonging and solidarity lie.

De Beauvoir goes on to state that 'the bond that unites her to her oppressors is not comparable to any other' (xix). Her comments on this issue need to be carefully unpacked:

> The division of the sexes is a biological fact, not an event in human history. Male and female stand opposed within a primordial *Mitsein*, and woman has not broken it. The couple is a fundamental unity with its two halves riveted together, and the cleavage of society along the line of sex is impossible. Here is to be found the basic trait of woman: she is the Other in a totality of which the two components are necessary to one another. (xix–xx)

De Beauvoir's assertion that the 'division of the sexes is a biological fact' is confusing because it contradicts her own argument against biological essentialism, most famously expressed in the sentence 'One is not born, but rather becomes, a woman' (at the beginning of part four of *The Second Sex*). Her main point here is that there was no single determinate event in history that resulted in the division of the sexes, in the way that historians can, for example, point to 1492 as the date when modern colonialism began and thus when 'indigenous' Americans were 'created'. Although the division of the sexes is perhaps not 'natural' in the sense of being *outside history*, it certainly occurred before *written* and *known* history; this is probably what De Beauvoir meant here. (She wrote this massive and ground-breaking book within only one year, so we should cut her some slack for sometimes being less than perfectly clear.) De Beauvoir claims here that 'woman' in the present still has not broken what she describes as a 'primordial *Mitsein*', a primitive, pre-historical, pre-civilizational community ('being-with') in which man and woman are welded together by necessity and without a chance of getting rid of each other. The clear implication is that 'woman' *should* finally get her act together and break up this 'primordial *Mitsein*': the imposed 'totality' is to be abolished so that the history of society, properly speaking, can begin.

In this context De Beauvoir also makes a rather bizarre and sarcastic remark: she writes that '[t]he proletariat can propose to massacre the ruling class, and a sufficiently fanatical Jew or Negro might dream of getting sole possession of the atomic bomb and making humanity wholly Jewish or black; but woman cannot even dream of exterminating the males' (xix). I would like to note here, against De Beauvoir, that 'the proletariat' never proposed 'to massacre the ruling class', although some of the more deranged Stalinist regimes, typically led by intellectuals claiming to act *on behalf of* the peasantry or the proletariat, did so in some of the darker episodes of the twentieth century, following the example of the French middle classes who in the Revolution of 1789 guillotined a section of the French aristocracy. Likewise, no Jewish or black people have ever proposed a political programme of exterminating the entire non-Jewish or non-black part of humanity. De Beauvoir indulges here in some rather disturbing fantasies of revenge violence. The point she is *actually* trying to make here, however, is that an extreme political imagination could figure a humanity after the destruction of one or several of its 'classes', 'races', 'ethnicities' or 'peoples', but not without either men or women: humanity would die out immediately. We humans have no other option than to try and make the best of our *Mitsein*. (In passing I should add that one famous feminist text did in fact propose that, thanks to modern reproductive technology, men could finally be done away with: the *S.C.U.M Manifesto* by Valerie Solanas (1936–88), first published in 1967. Given that Solanas was a playwright, it seems safe to assume she probably meant to explore a philosophical thought-game rather than to make a policy proposition; on the other hand she later became famous for shooting Andy Warhol. The *S.C.U.M Manifesto* is highly recommended reading in the more extreme theory department.)

7 Mutual dependency does not warrant liberation

De Beauvoir discusses in the following paragraphs the concept of 'reciprocity'. She critiques here, without saying so explicitly, a famous passage by the philosopher Hegel (from his *Phenomenology of Spirit* of 1807). This passage discusses the relationship of 'master and slave', sometimes also translated as 'master and bondsman', as reciprocal. Hegel's text has often been interpreted, in particular by some Marxists, as saying that the master ultimately depends more on the slave than the other way around: the slave actually produces things whereas the master does not know how to produce anything. The master knows, however, how much he needs the slave. The slave is therefore ultimately more powerful than the master. De Beauvoir rejects such optimistic readings of what is known as 'the master–slave dialectic': because of his resources and power, the master needs the slave *less* urgently than the slave *thinks* he needs the master. For the slave, hope and fear play decisive roles here: the slave fears punishment and hopes that obedience will be rewarded. The master–slave relationship is therefore only *apparently* reciprocal; in reality it is skewed to the benefit of the master. De Beauvoir states that the same is true for the man–woman relationship: 'man' needs 'woman' to satisfy his 'sexual desire and the desire for offspring' (xx), but this has not so far 'facilitated the liberation of woman'. 'Even if the need is at bottom equally urgent for both, it always works in favour of the oppressor and against the oppressed.' She adds that this also holds true for the capitalist class relationship. Inequality of power, according to De Beauvoir, overrules reciprocal dependency and the hope for equality that it holds out for Hegelians and Marxists.

8 Woman's unequal status

In the next stage of her argument, De Beauvoir briefly takes stock of gender relations in the present society. She does this in two steps: first, she states that 'the two sexes have never shared the world in equality' (xx), addressing issues concerning the legal and economic spheres. The world still 'belongs to men' (xxi). Secondly, she comments quite mordantly on women's complicity in this state of things:

> To decline to be the Other, to refuse to be a party to the deal – this would be for women to renounce all the advantages conferred upon them by their alliance with the superior caste. Man-the-sovereign will provide woman-the-liege with material protection and will undertake the moral justification of her existence; thus she can evade at once both economic risk and the metaphysical risk of a liberty in which ends and aims must be contrived without assistance. (xxi)

Her argument here is twofold: on the one hand, she simply states that women benefit materially from accepting their subordinate status; on the other hand, she makes a moral argument based on the premises of existentialist philosophy: 'along with the ethical urge of each individual to affirm his subjective existence, there is also the temptation to forgo liberty and become a thing'. She presupposes there to be two tendencies in the human soul, one urging towards subjectivity and self-assertion, the other to the opposite: to be a life-less, lazy object without responsibilities and moral duties towards oneself or others. De Beauvoir implies that women who live happily within the subordinate status have given in to the 'temptation' of the second tendency. They are basically traitors to the cause of 'authentic' subjectivity. Whoever takes this road, 'passive, lost, ruined', becomes 'the creature of another's will, frustrated in his [or her] transcendence and deprived of every value'. (The French text actually says 'passive, alienated, lost', not 'passive, lost, ruined'.) According to existentialist ethics, a human being who stops striving for 'transcendence', i.e. getting beyond the restraining, limiting reality of *being-in-the-world-as-it-is* (the world of 'immanence'), is hardly any longer worth the title of human. De Beauvoir is not exactly flattering her audience:

> When man makes of woman the *Other*, he may, then, expect her to
> manifest deep-seated tendencies towards complicity. Thus, woman
> may fail to lay claim to the status of subject because she lacks definite
> resources, because she feels the necessary bond that ties her to man
> regardless of reciprocity, and because she is often very well pleased
> with her role as the *Other*.

De Beauvoir's account of male domination of women radically
refuses to cast women in the role of victims. Next, she asks how this
situation came about in the first place.

9 Accounts of the inequality of woman in the philosophical tradition

De Beauvoir begins her exploration of the reasons for woman's
dire situation with a roundup of some philosophical and theological
opinions on the matter. She lets herself be guided here by a comment by a theologian and rationalist philosopher from the seventeenth century, François Poulain de la Barre (1647–1723): 'All that
has been written about women by men should be suspect, for the
men are at once judge and party to the lawsuit' (xxi–xxii). Poulain
was a follower of Descartes and a Catholic priest in the 1670s when
he wrote several important proto-feminist books, including the
one from which De Beauvoir is quoting. He later converted to
Calvinism. He had little impact in France, but it is interesting to
note that an English translation of his book on *The Equality of
the Two Sexes*, published anonymously at the time, was repeatedly plagiarized and became in this way an important element of
Enlightenment thinking in the English-speaking world.

There is a good philosophical reason why a follower of Descartes
would have written a proto-feminist book: Descartes – in Latin,
Cartesius – taught that mind and body are entirely separate, which
is nowadays often referred to as the 'Cartesian mind–body dualism'
and is held by some to be one of those bad Enlightenment ideas that
destroy organic-holistic thinking and other romantic favourites.
This 'Cartesian dualism' allowed rationalist philosophy, however,
to relegate the sexual difference to the bodily sphere only and to
argue that the mind is unaffected by it. In all matters of mind and
spirit, therefore, sexual difference is irrelevant in the rationalist

perspective: from this it follows that women can be as able thinkers as men. Rationalism did not, incidentally, prevent Descartes, like his follower Poulain, from being a religious man: God, too, of course, is a matter of spirit, radically separate from the material world.

De Beauvoir states in characteristically sarcastic fashion that '[e]verywhere, at all times, the males have displayed their satisfaction in feeling that they are the lords of creation' (xxii). Her evidence includes the philosopher Plato thanking the Gods 'that he had been created free, not enslaved' as well as 'a man, not a woman'. Similarly, Jewish men thank God in a prayer 'that He did not make me a woman'. (Similar formulations can be found in other religious contexts, too.) De Beauvoir comments, echoing Poulain, that 'the males could not enjoy [their] privilege fully unless they believed it to be founded on the absolute and the eternal; they sought to make the fact of their supremacy into a right'. Women's subordination must be demonstrated to be 'willed in heaven and advantageous on earth' out of 'a desire for self-justification'. Ideological efforts are often redoubled at times when the order of family and gender relations are actually in the process of changing. Men who advocated women's equality remained exceptions, such as Denis Diderot (1713–84), a key figure of the French eighteenth-century Enlightenment, or John Stuart Mill (1806–73), the English nineteenth-century liberal (xxiii). When women entered into wage labour in the course of the industrial revolution, 'the claims of the feminists emerged from the realm of theory and acquired an economic basis', but they were also opposed more aggressively, as women had become competitors for working-class men. More importantly, the bourgeoisie came to salvage, rather than destroy, the 'old morality' of the aristocracy 'that found the guarantee of private property in the solidity of the family': the bourgeoisie became especially conservative in their defence of the institution of the family. 'Woman was ordered back into the home the more harshly as her emancipation became a real menace.' It was only then that difference began to be theorized in terms of science:

> At most [anti-feminists] were willing to grant 'equality in difference' to the *other* sex. That profitable formula is most significant; it is precisely like the 'equal but separate' formula of the Jim Crow laws aimed at the North American Negroes. As is well known, this so-

called equalitarian segregation has resulted only in the most extreme discrimination. The similarity just noted is in no way due to chance, for whether it is a race, a caste, a class, or a sex that is reduced to a position of inferiority, the methods of justification are the same. 'The eternal feminine' corresponds to 'the black soul' and to 'the Jewish character'. (xxiii)

De Beauvoir argues here that the 'methods of justification' for racism and sexism are the same – she does not say that discrimination and exploitation in terms of 'race' and 'sex' are the same. In fact she makes sure to point to a difference between what were then the two principal paradigms in the discussion of racism, anti-Jewish and anti-black racism:

> True, the Jewish problem is on the whole very different from the other two – to the anti-Semite the Jew is not so much an inferior as he is an enemy for whom there is to be granted no place on earth, for whom annihilation is the fate desired. (xxiii)

Her point here is that there is 'exterminatory antisemitism', but there is no 'exterminatory anti-black racism', let alone 'exterminatory misogyny': radical antisemites aim to kill Jews wherever they are, whereas even the most extreme anti-black racists hardly aim to exterminate *all* black people *everywhere*, and misogynists certainly don't want to exterminate all women – they want to keep them 'in their place' and exploit them. On second thoughts one might want to object that there are in fact exterminatory elements to anti-black racism and misogyny, and that, on the other hand, there is also a 'non-exterminatory' variety of antisemitism along the lines of 'ordinary' racism. For De Beauvoir, though, the intentional, state-directed destruction of six million Jews in the Holocaust was obviously the paramount reference point at the time of writing.

De Beauvoir focuses on the similarity of the situations of women and American black people:

> Both are being emancipated today from a like paternalism, and the former master class wishes to 'keep them in their place' – that is, the place chosen for them. In both cases the former masters lavish more or less sincere eulogies, either on the virtues of 'the good Negro' with his dormant, childish, merry soul – the submissive Negro – or on the merits of the woman who is 'truly feminine' – that is, frivolous,

infantile, irresponsible – the submissive woman. In both cases the dominant class bases its argument on a state of affairs that it has itself created. (xxiii–xxiv)

De Beauvoir points to a 'vicious circle' whereby 'an individual (or a group of individuals) is kept in a situation of inferiority', is regarded by the masters to be naturally 'inferior' and thereby in fact, empirically, *becomes* 'inferior'. She makes an important theoretical point on what it means to say that someone 'is' inferior:

> But the significance of the verb *to be* must be rightly understood here; it is in bad faith to give it a static value when it really has the dynamic Hegelian sense of 'to have become'. Yes, women on the whole *are* today inferior to men; that is, their situation affords them fewer possibilities. The question is: should that state of affairs continue? (xxiv)

This 'dynamic' Hegelian argument is common to De Beauvoir's existentialism and the Marxist tradition: there is no *being* that has not *become* first, and that can therefore also *un-become* and *not-be*. Nothing is ever as fixed as it may appear to be, especially not in the realm of social things.

10 Men's attitude in the present period

De Beauvoir moves now back to the present and relates some egregious examples of male arrogance, such as this statement by a student: 'Every woman student who goes into medicine or law robs us of a job' (xxiv). The most important word here is 'us': the student constructs a collective subject of 'we men' that can be opposed to all women, with the effect that 'the most mediocre of males feels himself a demigod as compared with women', as De Beauvoir comments. She points again to the parallel with race discourse that works in the same way. Reflecting on a similar example, she writes, with exquisite sarcasm:

> What is really remarkable is that by using the questionable *we* he identifies himself with St Paul, Hegel, Lenin, and Nietzsche, and from the lofty eminence of their grandeur looks down disdainfully upon the bevy of women who make bold to converse with him on a footing of equality ... Here is a miraculous balm for those afflicted with an inferiority complex, and indeed no one is more arrogant

towards women, more aggressive or scornful, than the man who is anxious about his virility. (xxv)

These obvious cases are, however, only the easy part of the problem. De Beauvoir argues that 'the vast majority of men' do not 'explicitly ... *postulate* woman as inferior, for today they are too thoroughly imbued with the ideal of democracy not to recognize all human beings as equals' (xxv). Their sexism is of a more subtle nature, which is conditioned by the realities of a democratic society. She writes that contemporary men grow up to see women in the family 'clothed in the same social dignity as the adult males' (xxvi); they experience the factual independence and freedom of their girlfriends and wives. These experiences cannot but produce in man the impression 'that social subordination as between the sexes no longer exists'. 'As, however, he observes some points of inferiority – the most important being unfitness for the professions – he attributes these to natural causes': the more that complete democracy and equality *seem* to have been achieved, the greater the temptation to naturalize the remaining inequalities. This ambiguous attitude is well illustrated by an example she provides in a footnote: 'For example, a man will say that he considers his wife in no wise degraded because she has no gainful occupation. The profession of housewife is just as lofty, and so on. But when the first quarrel comes, he will exclaim: "Why, you couldn't make your living without me!"' (xxvi, n. 2).

11 The arguments of feminists

Knowing that *The Second Sex* became, and remains, one of the key documents of feminist theory, it may come as a bit of a surprise that De Beauvoir thinks '[w]e should consider the arguments of the feminists with no less suspicion ... for very often their polemical aim deprives them of all real value' (xxvi). She makes fun of 'polemical' feminism by stating that male claims that woman is a 'secondary being', since she was created after Adam, are countered by feminist claims that Adam must have been merely a 'rough draft' (xxvii). The problem is, who poses the question?

Man is at once judge and party to the case; but so is woman. What we need is an angel – neither man nor woman – but where shall we find one? Still, the angel would be poorly qualified to speak, for an angel is ignorant of all the basic facts involved in the problem. With a hermaphrodite we should be no better off, for here the situation is most peculiar; the hermaphrodite is not really the combination of a whole man and a whole woman, but consists of parts of each and thus is neither. It looks to me as if certain women are still best qualified to elucidate the situation of woman. (xxvii)

In this tongue-in-cheek manner, De Beauvoir moves on to what in contemporary social theory would be called the question of 'positioning', 'situatedness' or 'standpoint': who is best positioned to speak the truth? Angels are too aloof from and ignorant of empirical reality – a bit like 'detached intellectuals' in the Mannheimian 'sociology of knowledge'. They are also very difficult to get hold of. Hermaphrodites, or perhaps similarly, trans-gender people, will not provide objectivity either as they simply constitute another particular subject position. No one speaks from no-position. There is no better source of wisdom then than 'certain women', De Beauvoir writes – but which ones? Not just any women: 'it is not a mysterious essence that compels men and women to act in good or in bad faith, it is their situation that inclines them more or less towards the search for truth'. A valid perspective does not depend on gender but on situatedness, and De Beauvoir takes here a strikingly optimistic and laid-back position: she states that '[m]any of today's women … can afford the luxury of impartiality' because 'by and large we have won the game'. The 'equality of the sexes is now becoming a reality'. Therefore:

Many problems appear to us to be more pressing than those which concern us in particular, and this detachment even allows us to hope that our attitude will be objective. Still, we know the feminine world more intimately than do the men because we have our roots in it … and we are more concerned with such knowledge … It is significant that books by women on women are in general animated in our day less by a wish to demand our rights than by an effort towards clarity and understanding. As we emerge from an era of excessive controversy, this book is offered as one attempt among others to confirm that statement. (xxvii–xxviii)

De Beauvoir demands here that a scholarly form of argument should supersede a more polemical one. It is also noteworthy that she felt the time of polemics was over, as the case was settled. In this she could not have been more wrong.

12 The perspective of transcending immanence

Although De Beauvoir seems in these lines to advocate a certain degree of 'objectivity', she is not proposing that anyone could in fact be 'non-partisan': 'it is doubtless impossible to approach any human problem with a mind free from bias' (xxviii). Even 'the way in which questions are put' is relative to an interest; 'every objective description, so called, implies an ethical background'. Biases, interests and ethical presuppositions are best stated openly rather than concealed. De Beauvoir observes that many writings on women adopt the point of view of 'the public good, the general interest', however this is defined. De Beauvoir argues 'that the only public good is that which assures the private good of the citizens; we shall pass judgement on institutions according to their effectiveness in giving concrete opportunities to individuals'. The concept of 'private interest' is to be distinguished from that of 'happiness', she writes, as the latter is particularly vague: 'There is no possibility of measuring the happiness of others', and there is the risk that one will describe 'as happy the situation in which one wishes to place' others.

De Beauvoir asserts here on the last pages of the introduction to her book that hers is the perspective of 'existentialist ethics'. This ethics is dynamic in the sense that it prioritizes *becoming* over *being*: 'There is no justification for present existence other than its expansion into an indefinitely open future' (xxix). Liberty is achieved 'only through a continual reaching out towards other liberties', which is called 'transcendence' of the existing state – liberty is, in this sense, never in fact reached. 'Every time transcendence falls back into immanence, stagnation, there is a degradation of existence into ... the brutish life of subjection to given conditions – and of liberty into constraint and contingence.' Life that is worth living is committed to the ongoing project of transcendence.

From a Marxist or Critical Theory perspective, one might object that De Beauvoir's existentialist ethics resembles modern capitalism in its imperative of restlessness: capitalism demands of us that we never simply 'are', as it always constructively destroys

itself and forces everyone to move on and on and on. De Beauvoir
writes that falling back into 'immanence', a stable unquestioning
life that accepts given conditions, is an 'evil' that spells frustration
and oppression, or even 'a moral fault if the subject consents to it'.
Don't just stand there! Do something! Emancipate yourself!, yells the
existentialist at the modern individual. On the positive side, existentialist ethics probably helps one to write great, massive books like
The Second Sex. Unlike most modern ethics, existentialism does not
aim at happiness: De Beauvoir states that she writes this book out
of a concern with 'the fortunes of the individual as defined not in
terms of happiness but in terms of liberty' (xxix). The 'situation of
woman', 'a free and autonomous being like all human creatures', is
defined by her 'living in a world where men compel her to assume
the status of the Other' and 'propose to stabilize her as object and
to doom her to immanence'. Staying in this dark place of immanence not only reduces one's chances of pursuing happiness: it is
unethical.

14

Society as mediation: Theodor W. Adorno

The last chapter of this introduction to 'classical' social theory looks at a short, typically dense text that exemplifies the writing style and theoretical perspective of Theodor W. Adorno, another key figure of the 'Frankfurt School' of Critical Theory. The text is entitled 'Society' and was initially published as an entry in a social science handbook. This article creates a kind of dialogue between some of the principal positions within sociological theory on one of its key concepts: *society*. It discusses many of the themes that are constitutive of 'classical social theory', which makes it a good piece to wrap this volume up with. At the same time, it is quite different from all the previously discussed texts due to its style.

Theodor W. Adorno (1903–69) spent – rather unusually among the great theorists – a happy childhood in what sounds like a rather nice family (as happy as childhoods in bourgeois families come, that is). He was baptized a Protestant. His father, a wine wholesaler in the commercial city of Frankfurt on the Main, was a convert to Protestantism from Judaism; his mother, a singer, was Catholic. Cushioned by music and bourgeois education, in a somewhat bohemian family that seems to have valued the arts more than money, Adorno finished school early and entered university at 17, studying philosophy, music, sociology and psychology; he later described his younger self as a 'greenhouse plant', brought up in warm and nurturing conditions. Like school, he despised the formalistic business of academia and received most of his key intellectual influences from a milieu of friends who discussed writers and philosophers who were not academics, including Siegfried Kracauer (1889–

1966), Georg Lukács (1885–1971), Ernst Bloch (1885–1977) and Walter Benjamin (1892–1940). They were independent thinkers steeped in Kant and Hegel, but also strongly influenced by contemporary theorists such as Simmel and Weber, and were all in differing ways moving towards a philosophical reading of Marx. Adorno also became increasingly interested in Freudian psychoanalysis from the mid-1920s, and during frequent visits to Berlin, where his girlfriend Gretel Karplus lived, he hung out in the circles around the playwright and poet Bertolt Brecht. From 1921 to 1932, while studying, Adorno published many pieces of music criticism, and even spent a year in Vienna (1924–25) studying music with Alban Berg, a key figure of the Schönberg school of 'new music' of which Adorno was an important advocate and theorist. His first publication in philosophy came out only in 1933, a year before he went into exile to England and then to the USA, where he became a member of the Institute of Social Research led by Max Horkheimer, whom he had known informally since his student days. Adorno became a professional sociologist and pioneer of empirical research methods more or less by accident when he was in the USA as a refugee from Nazi Germany and needed a job. His best-known contribution from the exile period is the large, multi-disciplinary and multi-author study *The Authoritarian Personality* (1950), which was dedicated to exploring various factors that made people receptive to fascist ideology. With Horkheimer, he co-authored the 'philosophical fragments' of *Dialectic of Enlightenment* (1947), an initially rather obscure publication that gradually became recognized as one of the principal twentieth-century philosophical reflections on modernity. Its core message was that enlightenment, including the emancipatory movements that rely on it, must reflect on its own limitations and contradictions in order to avoid reversing and destroying itself. Adorno left the USA for West Germany in 1949, returned for a year in 1952, and accepted a professorship in Frankfurt in 1953. For the last sixteen years of his life, he used to the full the strange opportunity created by the need of post-fascist West German society to embrace this heterodox follower of Marx and Freud who had managed to make himself a name in America after narrowly escaping Hitler's concentration camps: Adorno became a key figure in German academic life as well as a public intellectual who could regularly be heard on the radio, and as a lecturer he exerted an important influence on the thinking of the post-Second World War generations of students, including those who rebelled in 1968. Apart from several collections of essays, Adorno's main works in the post-war period include *Minima Moralia* (1951) and *Negative Dialectic* (1966).

Adorno was something of an artist as a writer: he had initially hoped to be a concert pianist and was a composer of modern 'classical' music as well as a philosopher. Adorno sometimes wrote essays as if he were composing music: one theme goes through a few variations, then another theme appears, goes through variations, then

---

Structure of the selected text

Adorno, Theodor W. 1989 [1965]. 'Society'. In Stephen Eric Bronner and Douglas MacKay Kellner (eds), *Critical Theory and Society, A Reader*. New York and London: Routledge, 267–275.

the contrasting themes enter into a dialogue of sorts, and then the fun suddenly stops – though without a nice and comforting resolution. It is a form of dialectical argument, but not of the notorious 'thesis–antithesis–synthesis' variety – Adorno practises the much more puzzling, sometimes irritating 'negative dialectics' (the title of his most important theoretical work), which refuses to satisfy or to instruct. The text is designed to be a strange, awkward *thing* that provides food for thought more than 'instruction' (quite like a modern artwork, or perhaps a prose poem). An essay by Adorno would be marked down seriously if it was handed in by a student at a contemporary university: no introduction that sets out clearly what he is about to do, no section headings that make it nice and easy to follow the steps of the argument, no conclusions. In a sense there is not even an argument: the argument emerges in the mind of the reader in the process of repeated reading. It is hard work, though: Adorno's 'handbook entry' is not for quick orientation.

1 Society, process, humans

Adorno uses the first four paragraphs chiefly to disappoint the reader's expectation of being given a definition of the concept of society. In the process he mentions quite a few things that society is *not*, as if he wanted to 'define' society in the negative (which is not possible, of course, because one would need an infinite number of pages to list everything that something is not). 'Society is essentially process' (267): this is as far as Adorno is prepared to go towards a definition. However, one cannot *define* a process because a process is, by definition, not *finite*. One can hope to get at its essence by describing its 'laws of movement', but not any supposed 'invariables'.

Next, Adorno rejects more modest attempts to define the concept of society by describing it as a very large number of people, or even all people: one could define society as *mankind*, the sum of all its subgroups, or 'the totality of all human beings living in a given period'. Such a 'formal definition', though, would miss 'all the subtler implications of the concept', and these are what distinguishes a concept from a mere name: society is not simply 'all, or lots of human beings' because the most interesting aspect of the concept of 'society' is that society does something to the human being. The 'formal definition presupposes that society is already a society of human beings, that society is already human', whereas in reality 'the specifically social' consists precisely in 'the imbalance of institutions over men, the latter coming little by little to be the incapacitated products of the former' (267). If English-speakers find this argument somewhat obscure, they might find consolation in the fact that it works much better in German than in English: the hard-nosed English language distinguishes, for very good reasons, between 'human' and 'humane', acknowledging that a human being is not always and necessarily humane; the Germans, like the old-fashioned idealists and tree-hugging liberals that they are well known to be, use the same word for both concepts: *menschlich*. Adorno demolishes here the nifty little piece of ideology that inhabits the twofold meaning of this word, of which speakers of German would not normally be aware: *human society is not (yet) humane*. And this is what, for Adorno, makes thinking about society relevant in the first place.

In keeping with his professed refusal of definitions, Adorno turns to discussing historical *process* right away in the first lines of the text: humans gradually 'come to be' the 'incapacitated products' of society, which is, of course, itself a product of human agency. Adorno claims to be describing a tendency, not an invariable state of things. Secondly, he brings in some conceptual history: in the past, say, the Stone Age, the concept of society would have had a different meaning from now. Critical social theory is concerned with concepts that belong to the modern period and does not normally claim to make valid statements on human history (or human nature) in general. Adorno then turns to an observation made in the nineteenth century, in the historical context of ascending liberal capitalism, by the legal historian Johann Kaspar Bluntschli (1808–81): society is 'a concept of the third estate'. (The 'third estate' referred then to the estate of the producers, i.e. what we would call the middle and working classes, as opposed to the clerics and aristocracy.) He endorses this observation, explaining that the concept of 'society' as used by the middle classes had an egalitarian connotation in opposition to the feudal use of the word in expressions such as 'fine' or 'high society'; he adds that 'in its very structure' the concept of society 'follows the model of middle-class society', which seems to mean that whenever, in the present, we use the word, we automatically invoke an entire middle-class programme of what 'society' is or ought to be – unless, of course, we *reflect* on these connotations and subject them to theoretical, conceptual critique. Theory can then be an escape route from the conceptual cage that is language.

2 Society as dynamic and functional totality

Next, Adorno rejects an understanding of society as 'a classificatory concept': it is not simply the most abstract category under which all others can be filed in the process of logical subsumption, as is typical of the positive sciences. In social theory 'a continuous and hierarchical ordering of categories' (267) would be misleading: the concepts *individual – family – clan – society* do not stand in the same relationship to each other as do, for example, *brown-throated sloth – sloths – mammals – animals*: mammals have always been and will always be animals, whereas individuals-as-clan-members have not always formed societies, and in fact become different kinds of individuals when they do. This makes 'society' a *dynamic* category, whereas 'animals' is merely a *taxonomic* category.

Beyond that, however, 'society' is also a functional category: everyone in society is dependent on everyone else. 'The whole survives only through the unity of the functions which its members fulfill' (268), and vice versa. In order to live, every individual 'must take some function on himself', and 'is taught to express his gratitude' for being allowed to be functional and, hence, to live. The compulsion to function cannot but change the characteristics of all the more particular units and categories that make up society: the family in (modern) society is different from the family in any other historical context. It has become something new through its subsumption under the functional structures of society.

3 The concrete and the abstract mediate each other

A British politician once very famously said in an interview that 'there is no such thing as society [but only the] living tapestry of men and women and people'. This politician (who was a scientist by training) seems to have suspected that so abstract a concept as 'soci-

ety' would only serve wrongheaded ideological purposes, while reference to the warm-as-life, concrete reality of the 'living tapestry of
men and women', to *Gemeinschaft* rather than *Gesellschaft*, was tes-
tament to sound, evidence-based argument.[1] Adorno deals with this
kind of fetishization of 'the concrete' over 'the abstract' in his third
paragraph: 'such realism is itself unrealistic' (268). Adorno grants
that society cannot be grasped immediately nor verified scientifically, but '[p]ositivistic currents in sociology' are wrong to dismiss
the concept as an empty philosophical abstraction. Society cannot
be 'apprehended as an individual fact' but 'there is nonetheless no
social fact which is not determined by society as a whole', and therefore nothing in society can be comprehended without the concept
of society. Society as a whole appears in every concrete situation.
Adorno names as an example a conflict between a manager and
employees: such conflict does not constitute an 'ultimate reality'
that could be understood from within itself. Only comprehension
of the society that *makes* managers and employees in the first place
can unlock the reality of the conflict. The decisive social fact here is
'the power structure, whether direct or indirect, the control by the
entrepreneurs over the machinery of production' (268).

This does not mean, however, that the concrete should be understood merely as a specific instance or example of the generic: this
would mean falling into the opposite trap of believing that the
generic or the abstract, such as 'the deeper antagonisms', was 'the
reality', and the concrete conflicts mere symptoms. Adorno suggests that neither the concrete nor the abstract, but both together *in
their mutual mediation* are 'the reality'. Either side serves as the other
side's medium: the concrete situation is the medium, or the material, in which the abstract and general (such as society) becomes
manifest, while no concrete social thing can exist without being
mediated, that is, shaped or constituted, by the abstract category
(society). There *is* such a thing as society (although it is a *social*

---

[1] The nominalism (concepts are just words) of Thatcher's position is clearly
expressed in the statement that was issued by her office after the publication of the
interview: 'society as such does not exist except as a concept'. She emphasizes the
reality of individual, family and community versus the abstract, ideological unreality of 'society' [http://www.margaretthatcher.org/document/106689].

thing), but it exists only in and *through* such concrete social things as 'the living tapestry of men and women and people' (to use once more the words of Mrs Thatcher). Society has concrete families, individuals, people as its body, but families, individuals, people would not be families, individuals, people if it was not for the formative power of society. A discussion of 'the individual' or 'the family' in a wider temporal framework, reaching back to a period *before* society came into existence (in the sense in which modern social theory uses the term), would no longer be a discussion of a concrete reality but, on the contrary, a very abstract one. It would not really be a sociological question but rather one for speculative, philosophical anthropology. In the context of modern society and social theory, the concrete only becomes concrete when a historically determinate general category such as society constitutes it.

4 Only theory can tell

Adorno throws in here a very short paragraph in which he hammers home once more that only theory, not a simple definition, 'can tell us what society really is' (269). Theory here means sustained reflection on concepts. The concept of society cannot be fixed by way of definition, warranting 'mental tidiness', but must remain open-ended, untidy and in the process of development. The concept of society is an 'emphatic concept' as opposed to 'a conventional, definitional concept'.

5 Society is mediation

In the fifth paragraph Adorno brings together the argument of the previous four and gives it a new twist. Society cannot be *defined* because only *finite* objects can be defined, and society is clearly not a finite object. Therefore, 'society must be defined through theory'. Saying this, though, merely shifts the problem from 'definition' to 'theory': now it needs to be discussed what 'theory' means in the context of the science of society. In the 'natural', 'exact' sciences, theory typically involves 'well-defined concepts and repeatable experiments' and answers to the demands for 'immediacy and presence': when A happens then B follows, immediately, right here when you do your experiment. If it does not, then your theory goes down the drain – it has been 'falsified'. Adorno argues that 'if society is mediation, then these criteria have no validity for it' (269): society is not a something with an *immediate* presence; it is a *mediated* absence, present only in its mediations with other mediated somethings. Adorno defends now the theoretical perspective most often associated with Max Weber against a wrong form of critique. (He does this, of course, only in order to attack it with his own, more powerful critique, in the next step.) Anti-Weberian positivists argue that the subjectivist position that aims to understand things 'from the inside' – the perspective that English-language textbooks love to denote with the German word *Verstehen*, although this word simply means 'understanding' – was unscientific. Adorno defends the partial truth of subjectivist sociology: 'society is both known and not known from the inside. Inasmuch as society remains a product of human activity, its living subjects are still able to recognize themselves in it, as from across a great distance.' This is entirely different from chemistry and physics: it is hard to put it into words, but there is a sense in which we understand society – which we make, which we are, which is us – which is radically different from how we can know something about trees: we can hug but we cannot understand a tree. One could argue here against Adorno that we also *make* quite a lot of chemical and physical substances, say, fizzy drinks or umbrellas, but we cannot 'understand' these 'from inside', as it were: we can understand why and how we produce fizzy drinks and umbrellas, as their production processes are social facts, but we cannot understand these things *themselves* in the same way that we can 'understand' the feelings and motivations of a fellow human being. The reason probably is that umbrellas don't have feelings and motivations. When we 'make society' we make ourselves *as* society: understanding society therefore means understanding ourselves and our likes. Making umbrellas is both much less complex and much more alien.

Adorno uses in the next step of the argument an equally partial defence of the opposite perspective, that of *objectivist*, Durkheimian sociology, to put the partial merits of *subjectivism* into perspective:

> It is a fact that in middle-class society, rational action is objectively just as 'comprehensible' as it is motivated. This was the great lesson

of the generation of Max Weber and Dilthey. Yet their ideal of comprehension remained one-sided, insofar as it precluded everything
in society that resisted identification by the observer. This was the
sense of Durkheim's rule that one should treat social facts like objects,
should first and foremost renounce any effort to 'understand' them.
He was fully persuaded that society meets each individual primarily
as that which is alien and threatening, as constraint. Insofar as that is
true, genuine reflection on the nature of society would begin precisely
where 'comprehension' ceased. (269)

Adorno credits Weber and Durkheim each with a partial truth about
society: Weber registered a truth to which his class background
made him sensitive: people in society act out of clearly defined
motivations which they articulate nice and clearly so that others
can understand what they are all about. (To be honest, this at least
is how middle-class people in Weber's day *thought* they behaved,
or perhaps thought they *should* behave. If you think middle-class
society is not in fact very rational at all, then this could be because
you were not born into a well-regarded family of liberal notables.
Or perhaps because you have somehow, e.g. through education,
acquired a more critical perspective.) The subjectivist or *Verstehen*
perspective implies that you grow up in society, you learn the ropes
and henceforth society is comprehensible to you 'from the inside'
because that is where you are. You are an insider.

The other truth about society, the one that Durkheim knew,
resulted from a different experience of society: remember that,
although Durkheim quickly rose to be a hugely influential figure
in the establishment of the French Third Republic, he came from
a Jewish family in a provincial town, very much the hard-working
outsider who did well. This truth is considered equally important by Adorno but *equally partial*: society is an alien, threatening,
constraining thing, something that offers resistance to whatever I
want to do or be. Adorno pays Durkheim a big compliment here
by pointing out that his 'thingism' resembles Hegel's concept of
'second nature': this is the idea that the world humans create (society, culture, civilization) comes to form a structure as alien and
hostile as (first) nature. This concept, central to Adorno's own
social philosophy, is deeply ironic, or tragic: humans created soci-
ety/culture/civilization in the effort to defend themselves against,

and to conquer (first) nature, to humanize the non-human world, but instead their own human (but not so humane) world turns out to be just a duplication of (non-human) nature – 'second nature'. Something, somewhere, went seriously wrong.

Although each is partially true, Adorno rejects both the objectivist and the subjectivist approaches to social theory. He reproaches both for failing to 'transcend' the ideas of comprehensibility and incomprehensibility, respectively. Durkheim and Weber both capture something important about society ('society is by and through us' *versus* 'society is opposite to and against us') but both are limited. Social theory needs to go beyond them:

> Yet this resistance of society to rational comprehension should be understood first and foremost as the sign of relationships between men which have grown increasingly independent of them, opaque, now standing off against human beings like some different substance. It ought to be the task of sociology today to comprehend the incomprehensible, the advance of human beings into the inhuman. (270)

Society is a product of human activity. The human subjects and the object they create are alien to each other, but not entirely alien. Insofar as the social facts are alien objects they cannot be 'understood' (an argument that presupposes that one can only 'understand' what is substantially like the subject who aims to understand). Insofar as social facts are constituted by humans, however, we can (try to) understand why society resists our understanding. Society is a thing *and* a process, i.e. not a thing, at the same time. The question remains: why? Does it have to be like this? Can it be otherwise?

6 Intentionality, rationality, incomprehensibility

The (much shorter) sixth paragraph contains two additional perspectives on the Weberian and Durkheimian approaches. Weber is scolded for taking his idea of 'comprehension' or 'understanding' (*Verstehen*, again) from Hegel without fully comprehending its implications: whereas Hegel made it the task of philosophy to comprehend the totality (everything and how it all hangs together), Weber aims to comprehend 'particular acts' which (according to Adorno, who argues here in a Hegelian mode) is not possible because the particular only becomes particular by being shaped by a (specific, determinate) totality. At the other end of the scale, Durkheimian objectivism is critiqued for ending up with 'enthusiasm for the incomprehensible' (270): if expressed in a positivist framework that refrains from critiquing the 'laws' it describes, the recognition that there is something incomprehensible and irrational about modern society turns into its acceptance as fact. This 'positive' attitude leads Durkheim to insist that *society as such* – i.e. any society past, present and future – has quasi-religious (i.e. irrational) traits that are ultimately incomprehensible. This aspect of positivist theory is contrary to what Adorno recognizes as the emancipatory element of Hegelian theory, since Hegel believed in the passage from comprehension via critique to change. Both strands of sociology, the *Verstehen*, 'subjectivist' one and the 'social things', 'objectivist' one, seem bound to lead to the glorification of the existing state of things. To avoid this, Adorno argues, we need to go beyond both.

7 Critique of the concept of roles

Adorno adds here, almost as an aside, a critique of one of the more fashionable concepts of contemporary (i.e. 1960s) sociological theory, the notion of 'roles'. Adorno argues that, just as Weberian sociology trivialized the Hegelian notion of comprehension and removed its critical edge, the sociology of social 'roles' borrows but trivializes a concept first used by Marx, who had written of 'character-masks' with a critical intention. Playing a role means 'being-for-others' (270) rather than being-for-oneself; it refers to social constraint, to self-conservation at the price of giving up the concern with one's self: one has to assume roles, such as being a worker, in order to maintain oneself. Not having to play roles is not an available option. While sociological theory is right to observe that humans in society play roles, it ought to ask why they do so. Adorno argues that role-playing is an 'expression of underlying social antagonism' and concludes: 'The concept of role, lifted without analysis from the social facade, helps perpetuate the monstrosity of role-playing itself' (271).

8 Market society, domination, the general and the particular

In the next paragraph, Adorno derides as 'trivial', 'empty' and 'abstract' another popular notion in contemporary sociology: the idea that 'everything is interrelated' (271). He writes that this notion is empty and banal, but he does not dismiss it as wrong: on the contrary, the banality of the sociological idea that 'everything is interrelated', as in 'network theory' perhaps, correctly but uncritically reflects a rather banal reality. Adorno translates this notion into the language of Critical Theory by pointing out that its 'emptiness and abstractness' are those of 'the market system in modern-day society' itself.

Abstractness is not first of all a characteristic of thinking but one of societal reality: 'The first, objective abstraction takes place, not so much in scientific thought, as in the universal development of the exchange system itself' (271). Adorno points here to the classical conception of commodity exchange as regulated by 'exchange-value': we exchange commodities because they are qualitatively, concretely different things and satisfy different specific needs, but we expect this exchange to be an 'exchange of equivalents' (which makes it 'fair'). The point of reference of this 'equivalence' or abstract equality is a common, abstract, universal substance ('exchange value') to which determinate amounts of the two respective commodities, in spite of their concrete, qualitative difference, can be reduced. The Marxist argument that Adorno alludes to here is that everyday life in modern society is increasingly dominated by myriads of abstracting processes, in particular whenever we use money (the pre-eminent medium of exchange): we equate all kinds of things to each other by reducing them to certain amounts of money – what they 'are worth', their value – and thereby we train our brains to think abstractly all the time, day in, day out. Or to say the same thing differently, *society* trains and conditions us to do so. This is what Adorno refers to here as 'objective abstraction'.

The institution that relates everything to everything else is the market, which has turned humanity into consumers:

> Above and beyond all specific forms of social differentiation, the abstraction implicit in the market system represents the domination of

> the general over the particular, of society over its captive membership
> ... Behind the reduction of men to agents and bearers of exchange
> value lies the domination of men over men ... The form of the total
> system requires everyone to respect the law of exchange if he does not
> wish to be destroyed, irrespective of whether profit is his subjective
> motivation or not. (271)

'Market', like 'network', is not as neutral a concept as it may sound:
it presupposes domination.

9 Pre-capitalistic social structures are functional to the system

Adorno uses the next short paragraph to anticipate and respond to
a possible objection to his notion of society as a totality, namely that
the whole world does not in fact constitute one closed system: there
are 'retrograde areas and archaic social forms in various parts of the
world' (271). These (rather unflattering) terms refer to (what at
the time would have been called) the 'Third World' and the bourgeois family. As for the former, Adorno invokes 'the older theory
of imperialism' that had already demonstrated that the 'advanced'
capitalistic areas and the 'backward', supposedly non-capitalistic
ones 'maintained [each other] in existence', and that this systemic
interrelation did not disappear when 'old-fashioned colonialism was
eliminated': the 'precapitalistic remnants and enclaves ... are vital
necessities for the market system'. This is why they are granted
'developmental aid', too. From the 'Third World', Adorno makes
a surprising leap here to 'precapitalistic remnants and enclaves'
within 'developed' Western societies themselves, for which the same
argument holds: 'Irrational institutions are useful to the stubborn
irrationality of a society which is rational in its means but not in
its ends' (271–272). The institution Adorno mentions here is the
family, which forms a kind of 'enclave' not directly regulated by 'the
equivalency of exchange'. The family 'owes its relative power of
resistance' to the fact that it is needed 'as an irrational component'
– i.e. a societal element that does not obey capitalistic means–end
rationality – to allow 'certain specific modes of existence such as
the small peasantry' and other middle-class 'modes of existence' to
survive (272). Adorno is here quite close to the arguments of World
System Analysis later developed by Immanuel Wallerstein.

10 Antagonism, unity, class struggle

Following this almost structural-functionalist discussion of 'enclaves' within the system, the tenth paragraph reverts to a clearly conflict-orientated argument: society is a totality based on antagonism. 'The process of increasing social rationalization, of universal extension of the market system' works through 'specific social conflicts and antagonisms' which at the same time tear society apart. Antagonism is fundamental to the dynamism of this process, although it could at some point destroy 'organized society'. It is worth noting that Adorno talks about 'organized society' in the singular here, which means he refers to *society as such*, as in the related concept of 'human civilization'. He might have had in mind here a total catastrophe like nuclear war, an extreme point of antagonism that (dialectically) results from the mechanisms that 'hold society together'.

'Society remains class struggle.' Adorno adds that this is also true of what were then the (state-capitalist/state-socialist) 'Eastern bloc' countries, which had never stopped being class societies. He mentions that sociologists at the time based their rejection of the concept of class on a perceived decline in class consciousness in society generally, and retorts that a decline in class *consciousness* does not indicate a decline in the *reality* of class divisions: consciousness of class divisions does not automatically follow from their reality but needs to be created by agents' active work of reflection. Furthermore, he points out that available data then showed that the lower classes generally had 'fewer illusions' on these matters than middle-class members of society (272).

11 Class difference increases

Although 'subjectively' it may be more hidden than in previous periods, the 'difference between the classes' is in fact growing and determines the lives of individuals ever more rather than less. 'The separation of social power from social helplessness has never been greater than it is now' (272–273). Social existence can hardly ever be said now to result from one's own 'personal initiative' (273): rather, one has to search for and react to 'gaps' and 'openings' – vacancies

– in order to make a living in a hostile environment. There is little chance of following one's individual talents or inclinations – let alone a 'calling' – so that many have actually suppressed any awareness of these, as they are unrealistic anyway. 'The profoundly social-Darwinistic notion of adaptation, borrowed from biology and applied to the so-called sciences of man in a normative manner, expresses this and is indeed its ideology.' Linking back to the brief comments on colonialism in the ninth paragraph, Adorno adds that some say that 'the class situation' has also been 'transposed onto the relationship between ... the technically developed and underdeveloped countries', but he somewhat cryptically declines to discuss this here – perhaps he was not quite sure what to make of this (indeed highly problematic) argument.

12 Totalitarian tendencies of the social order

Societies are only prevented from tearing themselves apart through the political control of social antagonisms. The 'totalitarian tendencies of the social order' reflect and complement politically the increasingly total closure of society (273). Adorno emphasizes, however, that this is not 'the fault of technical development or industrialization as such', as was often claimed at the time: 'Technical advancement is ... only a moment in the dialectic between the forces of production and the relations of production, and not some third thing, demonically self-sufficient. In the established order, industrialization functions in a centralistic way', whereas in another order 'it could function differently'. Technology must not be treated as if it were a third factor outside what he calls, in Marxist terminology, the 'forces of production' (humanity's capacities to produce, which include knowledge and experience) and the 'relations of production' (the social arrangements that determine what is being produced and how): technology does not somehow 'evolve' on its own terms but is determined by society, of which it is a part. Adorno's sarcastic use of the term 'demonically self-sufficient' echoes Marx's concept of fetishism, the notion that something that humans have in fact produced, and are continuously reproducing, is seen by them as if it had an existence, power and agency of its own: some critiques of modern industrial society can in this sense be accused of 'fetishizing' technology. This important critique would similarly apply to some contemporary discussions of 'network society' which tend to assume that developments in computing technology determine the development of society – it is the other way around: we, society, make it all happen, although not always consciously and certainly not, all in all, very sensibly.

Technology as it is developed in contemporary society is a force of centralization. Adorno points here to television as a symbol for the social fact that 'nearness is itself mediated through social distance': just as the television set in one's living room seems near although it is in fact operated by distant, greatly concentrated power, so people's lives, even in their most private aspects, 'actually receive their concrete content in large measure from above'. Private life is in fact 'mere re-privatization' – what seems most real is, in fact, most unreal.

13 Administration, bureaucracy, means–end rationality, emancipation

The next paragraph is particularly difficult to understand as it condenses a very complex argument into a few lines, almost like an aphorism. Adorno observes that in modern society 'all over the globe, administrations have tended' towards greater 'independence from their administered subjects' (273) and thereby have tended also to reduce subjects to 'objects of abstractly normed behavior' (274). Adorno's critique is directed at the *independence* of administration, not its existence as such: he emphasizes that in 'a rational and genuinely free society' there would also be some form of administration, just as there would be some degree of division of labour (273). We can presume that he thinks that a sensible form of society will somehow casually integrate the necessary amount of administration into the general flow of activities. Adorno credits Max Weber with the next argument, namely that the existence of an independent and increasingly self-sufficient bureaucracy reflects the 'means–ends rationality of the economy itself' (274). The latter, though, is (by definition) indifferent to its own end: 'means–end rationality' is about how to reach a given goal with the least effort, but brackets out questions about what the goal is. This is after

all what 'the economy' as a *separate* special sphere, imagined as
independent from the 'social', 'political', 'cultural' and 'spiritual'
spheres in society, is all about. In particular, economic and, in its
wake, administrative 'means–end rationality' is indifferent to the
goal of a rational society, and that makes it for its subjects – the
human beings who constitute society – irrational. To make sense of
this – on the face of it – paradoxical statement we need to fill in what
Adorno means by a 'rational society': he seems to presuppose here
the notion taken from idealist philosophy that reason is connected
to freedom – only that which serves human emancipation is in tune
with human reason, i.e. reasonable. It is telling that in contemporary
everyday language, the word is used with almost exactly the opposite meaning: when your parents or some other authority admonish
you to 'be reasonable', they want you to be realistic, modest and to
obediently follow instructions which they imply are *of course* there
for a reason. It is 'reasonable' in this particular usage of the word
that you do not question the reasonableness of the instruction. In
Critical Theory, as in idealist philosophy before it, the opposite is
the case: it is reasonable to question everything.

The notion that 'means–end rationality' becomes problematic
when it is disconnected from the overriding concern with 'substantive rationality', i.e. the concern with a reasonable society that
serves human emancipation, is central to Critical Theory (although
it can similarly be found in Max Weber). Such irrational rationality
manifests itself in the form of modern bureaucracy and in particular
the figure of 'the expert', who is now, under the rule of an autono-
mized bureaucracy, a specialist in issues of process *as such*, unlike
the formerly dominant specialists in concrete work processes. This
should sound frighteningly familiar to many contemporary readers
– we have all met some of those experts and 'consultants' who know
in the abstract how to manage processes of *any kind* and are given the
power to oversee those who have practical and *specific* knowledge
of a *specific* work process. From experience it seems fair to say that
specific experts are in fact often directed by a 'substantively rational'
societal goal: in the case of, for example, a university lecturer, such a
goal could be the promotion of enlightenment and the formation of
strong personalities capable of independent thinking. In the *specific*
expert, specific expertise and a specific but general substantive con-

cern seem to nurture each other. It is sobering to see that Adorno was able to hint at these developments more than half a century ago: the *experts in being experts* have been a long time coming.

14 No outside of society

The 'massive social forces and institutions' of modern bureaucratic rule 'are essentially the reified work of living human beings' (274). The word 'reified' (from *res*, Latin for 'thing') means 'thingy-fied': societal processes and relations have become *things*, not unlike in Durkheim's concept of the 'social fact'. If 'essentially' these mighty apparatuses are the effects of what multitudes of humans actually do on a day-to-day basis, then surely one would assume that humans could easily break through them as mere ideology, a 'socially necessary mirage', a set of illusions? Well, not so, as painful experience shows. Adorno writes that 'the force of gravity of social relationships' strengthens them to the extent that the power of 'reified' human doing, thing-like apparatuses and machineries, is 'the most real of [social] facts', our ultimate reality. Adorno uses here the Latin phrase *ens realissimum*, 'the most real being', a term that is common in modern philosophy but stems from medieval scholastic philosophy, where it refers to God; Adorno surely intended here a theological undertone, somewhat tongue in cheek: *modern bureaucracy is God*.

Next Adorno points to a historical shift: in the middle of the nineteenth century, the proletariat could still be seen as a class half outside society, half inside, fighting off the process by which the middle classes gained overall domination. Modern society, then still recognizably the project of the middle classes fighting the aristocracy, has since integrated all groups that were still half outside society, to the effect that now there is no 'outside society'. Adorno tips his hat to Herbert Spencer here for having noted the centrality of 'integration' to the concept of society. Integration has since 'seize[d] on the very minds of those who are to be integrated into society'. Societal integration does not, though, constitute human beings as subjects, i.e. persons who are conscious of and can command their own fate: 'Both automatically and deliberately, subjects are hindered from coming to consciousness of themselves as subjects.' Factors that lead to this result are the inundation with consumer goods in conjunction with intellectual control by the culture industry, which tends to praise the existing state of things for no other reason than that it exists: whatever is on offer will be celebrated. (For example, no weekly magazine will ever write: 'All the new films this week are rubbish – stay at home and save your money!') Capitalists must try and adapt consumers to the commodities they need to sell, and in turn will produce commodities – including cultural and intellectual ones – that they can expect to sell well. This feedback loop is inherently conservative. Without these forms of control, Adorno states, people would 'do away with this state of things in impatience'.

15 Things could be entirely different; no one knows how

In the final paragraph Adorno recaps the argument that integration of society has gone far beyond the level that is necessary for humanity to survive, and then cautiously attempts to gauge the possibilities of escape, of transcendence: what needs to be done, and what is to be avoided, to leave behind this sorry state of things.

Integration has triumphed: human beings 'owe their lives to what is being done to them' to the effect that they are 'little better than cogs to their own machines' (275). They perpetuate voluntarily what is 'obviously a perversion of real life'. Rather than full-blown ideologies – which are coherent systems of ideas, however spurious they may be – it is a set of innocuous everyday *practices* that warrant the integration of social institutions and individual psychologies. As examples of practices that have taken the place of ideologies, Adorno mentions '[t]he affective rearrangement of industries, the mass appeal of sports, the fetishization of consumer goods' as examples. These practices are more powerful, and more difficult to overcome, than ideologies, as they change not only what we think but how we *are* (somewhat in the way that horses follow almost imperceptible signals in dressage):

> So we come full circle. Men must act in order to change the present petrified conditions of existence, but the latter have left their mark so deeply on people, have deprived them of so much of their life and individuation, that they scarcely seem capable of the spontaneity nec-

essary to do so. From this, apologists for the existing order draw new
power for their argument that humanity is not yet ripe. (275)

Proportionately with the *necessity* of radical change grows its *difficulty*. Against the 'apologists for the existing order', however,
Adorno asserts that this need not be the end of the story: although
it is not possible to outline the route to radical change, it certainly
must begin with a faithful description of how difficult it will be. The
powers that be consider negativity a taboo and encourage their critics always to look for the silver lining on the horizon: Adorno holds
against this that the optimism of plucky piecemeal reform is just
another brick in the wall (not his words), along with mass spectacle
and brand fetishism. Integrated society

> keeps an eye out to make sure that anything which is thought or
> said serves some specific change or has, as they put it, something
> positive to offer. Thought is subjected to the subtlest censorship of
> ... [having] to indicate the positive steps desired ... That is the point
> at which society can be recognized as a universal block, both within
> men and outside them at the same time. Concrete and positive suggestions for change merely strengthen this hindrance, either as ways
> of administrating the unadministrable, or by calling down repression
> from the monstrous totality itself.

It is pointless to try and be positive, as proposals for reform will
either be integrated into the administration of antagonistic society
(which can only ever result in the reactive limitation of the worst
damage), or it will be crushed. Adorno rejects in these words (the
wrong kind of) reformism as well as (the wrong kind of) radicalism:
reformism without illusions, however, can be a good thing if making
society more humane whets people's appetite for more. It should
not simply help to pacify and beautify the existing state of things,
though. At the same time, his warning against 'calling down repression from the monstrous totality' may have reflected the strategy
discussed by some at the time, and adopted a few years later by parts
of the student movement and the radical left, of provoking the state
into brutal acts of repression that would destroy its liberal image.
These provocations worked extremely well – the repression proved
to be as brutal as expected – but while the state survived the (temporary) loss of its liberal image just fine, the radicals who provoked

it did not. Their radicalism was not radical enough, in Adorno's sense: it was still too positive in being fixated on a negative reality.

Only in the very last sentence of the text does Adorno reveal the trump card that he has kept up his sleeve. Here, finally, he reveals after all what presumably made him get out of bed in the mornings and sit down at his desk:

> The concept and the theory of society are legitimate only ... when they merely hold in negative fashion to the basic possibility inherent in them: that of expressing the fact that such possibility is threatened with suffocation. Such awareness, without any preconceptions as to where it might lead, would be the first condition for an ultimate break in society's omnipotence. (275)

Adorno asserts here that social theory ought to point to the possibility of emancipation *negatively*, rather than *positively*: not by identifying it, writing positivistic blueprints for the future ideal society or detailed party programmes for revolutionary action, but by pointing out obstinately that the *possibility of emancipation* is being suffocated by the very society that created it in the first place, and even by some of the activities intended to make it better. This is what legitimizes the 'concept and the theory of society'.

Not much perhaps, but better than nothing.

Recommendations for further reading

Beginning must be followed by continuing. I hope this book has whetted your appetite for reading more of the primary sources of classical social theory. This was my main goal with this book. No one can read everything by everybody, though, which is why you will also need to read some competent surveys that fill in the inevitable gaps in your reading, and secondary literature that gives you a variety of ideas on how to think about it all, and how to think *beyond* what you read. Here are some recommendations – I have listed first textbooks that are explicitly on classical social theory, then books that cover both classical and contemporary.

Books on classical social theory, its emergence and background

Adams, Bert N., and Rosalind A. Sydie. 2002. *Classical Sociological Theory*. Thousand Oaks, CA: Pine Forge Press. [This textbook has a very good balance between detailed enough overviews and breadth; includes the usual suspects plus Saint-Simon, Martineau, Spencer, Sumner, Lenin, Luxemburg, Marianne Weber, Pareto, Michels, Veblen, Schumpeter, Gilman, Webb, Du Bois, Cooley, Mead, Freud.]

Adorno, Theodor W. 2002. *Introduction to Sociology*. Cambridge: Polity Press. [This book consists of transcripts of lectures that Adorno gave to first-year students. Adorno used to speak off the cuff, with just minimal notes, which makes this a rather different reading experience. Theorists covered include Comte, Durkheim, Hegel, Horkheimer, Marx, Spencer and Max Weber.]

Aron, Raymond. 1969. *Main Currents in Sociological Thought Vol. 1: Montesquieu, Comte, Marx, de Tocqueville. The Sociologists and the Revolution of 1848*. Harmondsworth: Penguin. [A classic of philosophically informed intellectual history.]

Aron, Raymond. 1970. *Main Currents in Sociological Thought Vol. 2: Durkheim, Pareto, Weber*. Harmondsworth: Penguin.

Calhoun, Craig, Joseph Gerteis, James Moody, Steven Pfaff, Kathryn Schmidt and Indermohan Virk (eds). 2002. *Classical Sociological Theory*. Malden, MA, and Oxford: Blackwell. [This contains large chunks from Marx, Engels, Durkheim, Max Weber, Mead, Simmel, Freud, Du Bois, Mannheim, Horkheimer, Adorno, Marcuse, Parsons and Merton, plus very useful introductions and commentary.]

Camic, Charles (ed.). 1997. *Reclaiming the Sociological Classics. The State of the Scholarship*. Malden, MA, and Oxford: Blackwell. [This is an edited volume consisting of survey essays by leading scholars on Comte, Marx, Spencer, 'the Women Founders' (!), Durkheim, Simmel, Weber, Thomas, Park and Mead.]

Chambliss, Rollin. 1954. *Social Thought from Hammurabi to Comte*. New York: Holt, Rinehart and Winston. [Some of the things you will probably never hear about in your sociology degree course: this ranges from ancient Babylon via Confucius, Aristotle, Thomas Aquinas, Ibn Khaldun, Vico and Locke to Comte.]

Coser, Lewis A. 1972. *Sociology through Literature*, 2nd edn. Englewood Cliffs, NJ: Prentice Hall. [A personal favourite. Coser goes through a large list of sociological keywords and provides extracts from literature – Diderot, Tolstoy, Kafka, etc. – that illustrate what the keywords are all about.]

Craib, Ian. 1997, *Classical Social Theory*. Oxford: Oxford University Press. [Marx, Durkheim, Simmel, Weber. Very readable, one of the best.]

Edling, Christopher, and Jens Rydgren (eds). 2011. *Sociological Insights of Great Thinkers. Sociology through Literature, Philosophy, and Science*. Santa Barbara, CA: Praeger. [Short chapters on sort-of sociological thinking by all kinds of non-sociologists: philosophers, writers, scientists. Good to put things into perspective.]

Hawthorn, Geoffrey. 1976. *Enlightenment and Despair. A History of Social Theory*. New York: Cambridge University Press. [This is written in the mode of richly contextualizing intellectual history, starting from the Enlightenment and covering a very wide range of theorists in France, Britain, Germany and the USA, connecting social theorists to their philosophical reference points. Essential background reading.]

Kandal, Terry R. 1988. *The Woman Question in Classical Sociological Theory*. Miami, FL: Florida International University Press. [A comprehensive exploration of the male canon concerning what they say about women, plus a sketch of the women's movement as its context.]

Lengermann, Patricia Madoo, and Jill Niebrugge-Brantley. 1998. *The Women Founders. Sociology and Social Theory 1830–1930. A Text/ Reader*. Boston: McGraw Hill. [Martineau, Addams, Gilman, Cooper, Wells-Barnett, Marianne Weber, the Chicago Women, Webb. I am not aware of any other similar book.]

Lengermann, Patricia Madoo, and Jill Niebrugge-Brantley. 2001. 'Classical Feminist Social Theory'. In Smart Ritzer, *The Sage Handbook of Social Theory*. Thousand Oaks, CA: Sage, 125–37.

Lepenies, Wolf. 1992. *Between Literature and Science. The Rise of Sociology*. Cambridge: Cambridge University Press. [This is another work of intellectual history, describing the rise of sociology as an effort by nineteenth-century thinkers to find a space between literature and 'hard' science. Covers many theorists, including Comte, J. S. Mill, Beatrice Webb, Simmel, Weber.]

Liebersohn, Harry. 1988. *Fate and Utopia in German Sociology, 1870–1923*. Cambridge, MA: MIT Press. [Tönnies, Troeltsch, Weber, Simmel, Lukács.]

Marcuse, Herbert. 1970. *Reason and Revolution*. Boston: Beacon Press. [Hegel, Marx, Comte.]

McDonald, Lynn (ed.). 1998. *Women Theorists on Society and Politics*. Waterloo, Ont.: Wilfrid Laurier University Press. [Text extracts with helpful introductions. Beginning in the fifteenth century, all the way through to the early twentieth. Wide-ranging, an indispensable resource.]

Morrison, Ken. 2006, *Marx, Durkheim, Weber, Formations of Modern Social Thought*, 2nd edn. Thousand Oaks, CA: Sage.

Offe, Claus. 2005. *Reflections on America. Tocqueville, Weber & Adorno in the United States*. Cambridge: Polity Press.

Ray, Larry. 1999. *Theorizing Classical Sociology*. Maidenhead: Open University Press. [In spite of the misleading title, this is perhaps the best-presented, most readable short survey textbook on the Enlightenment, Comte, Marx, Durkheim, Tönnies, Simmel and Weber. The chapter on Dilthey's hermeneutics is very good as background reading to Tönnies, Simmel and Weber.]

Royce, Edward. 2015. *Classical Social Theory and Modern Society. Marx, Durkheim, Weber*. Lanham, MD: Rowman & Littlefield.

Sayer, Derek. 1991. *Capitalism & Modernity. An Excursus on Marx and Weber*. London and New York: Routledge.

Seidman, Steven. 1983. *Liberalism and the Origins of European Social Theory*. Berkeley, CA: University of California Press. [The Enlightenment, Marx, Durkheim, Weber].

Therborn, Göran. 1976. *Science, Class and Society, On the Formation of*

Sociology and Historical Materialism. London: New Left Books. [A very wide-ranging account from a structuralist-Marxist perspective.]

Tucker, Jr, Kenneth H. 2002. *Classical Social Theory, A Contemporary Approach*. Malden, MA: Blackwell. [The Enlightenment and historical context; Marx, Durkheim, Weber, Freud, Simmel, Mead, Du Bois, Perkins Gilman.]

Books on classical and contemporary social theory

Appelrouth, Scott, and Laura Desfor Edles. 2008. *Classical and Contemporary Sociological Theory, Text and Readings*. Los Angeles: Pine Forge Press. [Text extracts with useful introductions. The 'classical' section includes Marx, Durkheim, Weber, Perkins Gilman, Simmel, Du Bois and Mead.]

Coser, Lewis A. 2003. *Masters of Sociological Thought, Ideas in Historical and Social Context*, 2nd edn. Long Grove, IL: Waveland Press. [This is a comprehensive, albeit exclusively male and white canon. It provides detailed descriptions and contextualization.]

Crow, Graham. 2005. *The Art of Sociological Argument*. Basingstoke: Palgrave. [Marx, Durkheim, Weber, Parsons, C.W. Mills, Goffman, Foucault, Ann Oakley.]

Dinerstein, Ana Cecilia (ed.). 2016. *Social Sciences for an Other Politics. Women Theorizing Without Parachutes*. Cham (Switzerland): Palgrave Macmillan. [A thematically broad collection of critical feminist theory with a strong focus on social movements.]

Elias, Norbert. 1978 [1970]. *What is Sociology?* New York: Columbia University Press. [Thematic introduction that is beyond 'schools'; takes his cues from Comte, Marx, Durkheim and Weber; most interesting on Comte.]

Harrington, Austin (ed.). 2005. *Modern Social Theory, An Introduction*. Oxford: Oxford University Press. [Like the volume edited by Camic above, every chapter is written by another expert, which makes this a very solid book. Only the first quarter of the book is on 'classical' social theory, the rest is mostly on the twentieth century.]

Inglis, David, with C. Thorpe. 2012. *An Invitation to Social Theory*. Cambridge: Polity Press. [Only the first chapter of this book is explicitly on classical social theory, but it makes nineteenth-century references throughout its discussions of twentieth-century theories.]

Lemert, Charles. 2001. *Social Things, an Introduction to the Sociological Life*, 2nd edn. Lanham, MD: Rowman & Littlefield. [This is a short and very enjoyable book that offers a broad vision of sociology with lots of contextual and biographical background; good to be read on the bus, train or at bedtime.]

Lemert, Charles (ed.). 2017. *Social Theory: The Multicultural and Classic Readings*, 5th edn. Boulder, CO: Westview Press. [Gloriously broad – contains about twenty pages of original text from Marx, Durkheim, Weber and Freud each, and up to five pages each from well over one hundred others. Great to get lost in, productively.]

Marshall, Barbara L., and Anne Witz (eds). 2004. *Engendering the Social, Feminist Encounters with Sociological Theory*. Maidenhead: Open University Press. [This is a collection of essays, most of which interrogate classical social theory in terms of what it has to say on women, and how some classical theorists interacted with some women theorists.]

Nehring, Daniel. 2013. *Sociology. An Introductory Textbook and Reader*. Harlow: Pearson. [This is a sociology textbook, not a theory textbook, but it works at a very theory-driven level.]

Ritzer, George (ed.). 2000. *The Blackwell Companion to Major Social Theorists*. Malden, MA: Blackwell. [Substantial chapters on all the usual suspects plus Martineau, Perkins Gilman, Du Bois and Schütz. Provides just the right level of detail.]

Seidman, Steven. 2013. *Contested Knowledge: Social Theory Today*, 5th edn. Chichester: Wiley-Blackwell. [Only the first of seven parts is on 'classical social theory'. This is the most explicitly social movement-inspired textbook I know of. A good general, very condensed overview textbook.]

Stones, R. (ed.). 2008. *Key Sociological Thinkers*, 2nd edn. Basingstoke: Macmillan. [Short chapters on 23 mostly post-Second World War theorists.]

Swingewood, Alan. 2000. *A Short History of Sociological Thought*, 3rd edn. Basingstoke: Macmillan. [Very thorough, especially the earlier editions. The third edition offers more breadth at the cost of less detail.]

Wallerstein, Immanuel. 2001. *Unthinking Social Science: The Limits of Nineteenth-century Paradigms*, 2nd edn. Philadelphia: Temple University Press. [Marx, Braudel, modernization theory, world system analysis.]

Social theory journals

Constellations
Critical Review of International Social and Political Philosophy
Cultural Critique
Cultural Logic
Culture Theory and Critique

Dialectical Anthropology
Economy and Society
European Journal of Social Theory
European Journal of Women's Studies
Fast Capitalism
Feminist Theory
History of the Human Sciences
Hypatia
International Journal of Philosophical Studies
International Journal of Politics Culture and Society
Journal of Classical Sociology
Journal of the History of the Behavioural Sciences
New Left Review
Philosophy and Public Affairs
Philosophy and Social Criticism
Philosophy of the Social Sciences
Politics and Society
Public Culture
Radical Philosophy
Radical Philosophy Review
Science and Society
Signs
Social Epistemology
Social Forces
Social Science History
Social Theory and Practice
Sociological Inquiry
Sociological Perspectives
Sociological Theory
Theory and Society
Theory, Culture and Society
Thesis Eleven
Triple C
Women Studies International Forum

Social theory websites

http://ajcarchives.org/main.php?GroupingId=1380
http://oyc.yale.edu/political-science/plsc-114
http://oyc.yale.edu/sociology
http://understandingsociety.blogspot.co.uk/

http://www.iep.utm.edu/
http://www.isa-sociology.org/en/research-networks/research-committe
    es/rc16-sociological-theory/
http://www.marcuse.org/herbert/
http://www.sociosite.net/sociologists/
http://www.sociosite.net/topics/theory.php
http://www.socwomen.org/
http://www.uta.edu/huma/illuminations/
http://www.theory.org.uk/lego-theorists.htm
https://archive.org/details/texts
https://persistentenlightenment.com/
https://plato.stanford.edu/index.html
https://thecharnelhouse.org/
https://www.marxists.org/

Index